TRADITION AND INNOVATION

IN LATE ANTIQUITY

Tradition and Innovation in Late Antiquity

Edited by

F. M. CLOVER and
R. S. HUMPHREYS

The University of Wisconsin Press

The University of Wisconsin Press
114 North Murray Street
Madison, Wisconsin 53715

The University of Wisconsin Press, Ltd.
1 Gower Street
London WC1E 6HA, England

The appendix to chapter 13, the letter of ʿUthmān to the inhabitants of Mecca, will
appear in *The History of al-Tabari, Volume XV: The Crisis of the Early Caliphate: The
Reign of ʿUthmān,* A.D. *644–655*/A.H. *24–35,* translated by R. Stephen Humphreys, to
be published in 1990 by the State University of New York Press. Printed by permission
of the State University of New York Press.

Library of Congress Cataloging-in-Publication Data

Tradition and innovation in late antiquity / edited by F.M. Clover,
    and R.S. Humphreys.
        p.   cm. — (Wisconsin studies in classics)
    Rev. versions of papers presented at a seminar held Apr. 25–27,
1984, University of Wisconsin, Madison.
    Bibliography: pp. 293–333.
    Includes index.
    1. Mediterranean Region—Civilization—Congresses. I. Clover,
Frank M., 1940–   . II. Humphreys, R. Stephen. III. Series.
DE59.T7   1989
909'.09822—dc20   88-40427
ISBN 0-299-12000-7

To the memory of George Hourani,
and to the memory of Arnaldo Momigliano

Contents

Maps

Illustrations

Preface

The papers in this volume were originally presented in a seminar entitled "Cultural Change in the Mediterranean World and the Near East in Late Antiquity," held at the University of Wisconsin–Madison on 25–27 April 1984, and at the University of Chicago on 18 October 1984. However, the participants have taken advantage of the vigorous discussions at the two sessions of the seminar not only to make corrections but even to rethink the arguments and conclusions of their contributions.

The Wisconsin and Chicago seminars were made possible by generous grants from the Social Science Research Council, the Kemper H. Knapp Bequest (University of Wisconsin–Madison), the University Lectures Committee (University of Wisconsin–Madison), Queen's College (Oxford University), and the Deutsche Forschungsgemeinschaft. Meeting rooms were provided by the Memorial Union of the University of Wisconsin–Madison and the Center for Middle Eastern Studies of the University of Chicago. Finally, we have been greatly aided in the final stages of publication by subventions from the Kemper H. Knapp Bequest, the Social Science Research Council, and the University of Wisconsin–Madison's Cartographic Laboratory.

Many individuals merit our warm thanks for their advice and support. In particular, we wish to thank Professors Peter Brown and Alexander Kazhdan for their critical and constructive comments on the manuscript, which were very helpful in our final revisions. For any errors of fact or interpretation which remain, we are of course responsible. We are also grateful to Vincent Burns and Ruth Melville for their skillful copyediting of a difficult text, and to Thea Schlumberger for her assistance with the translation of Professor Schlumberger's contribution.

Early in 1985 we realized that we would require additional time to prepare an introduction for the collection. We therefore invited participants in the seminar to seek prior publication elsewhere, while keeping their contributions in this collection. Two contributors accepted our offer; accordingly, chapters 7 and 8 have appeared in *Jahrbuch für Antike und Christentum* 29 (1986), and *Dumbarton Oaks Papers* 40 (1986), respectively. We wish to thank these journals for their permission to reprint (with some changes) the two contributions.

A book of this kind requires maps and a consistent scheme of transliteration. The two maps in this volume, in which we try to include important place names and topographical features referred to in the text, will not be cited in the notes to individual chapters; the reader should simply consult them as necessary. As to transliteration, Latin, Greek, and Germanic names are handled in the usual way. For Arabic names, we have followed the system used in the *International Journal of Middle East Studies*. A transliteration table follows this preface.

Finally, we have dedicated the book to the memories of two scholars who made fundamental contributions to the topics discussed here, and who were colleagues, mentors, guides, or critics of the contributors to this volume.

Madison, Wisconsin
July 1988

Arabic Transliteration

CONSONANTS			VOWELS		
ء	'		*Long* ا or ى		ā
ب	b		و		ū
ت	t		ي		ī
ث	th		*Doubled* ي ّ		iyy (final
ج	j				form ī)
ح	ḥ		و ّ		uww (final
خ	kh				form ū), etc.
د	d		*Diphthongs* و َ		au *or* aw
ذ	dh		ى َ		ai *or* ay
ر	r		*Short* ‑		‑a
ز	z		ُ		‑u
س	s				
ش	sh		ِ		‑i
ص	ṣ				
ض	ḍ				
ط	ṭ				
ظ	ẓ				
ع	'				
غ	gh				
ف	f				
ق	q				
ك	k				
ل	l				
م	m				
ن	n				
ه	h				
و	w				
ى	y				
ة	-a[1]				
ال	[2]				

xvii

---

[1] (-at in construct state)
[2] (article) al- and 'l-

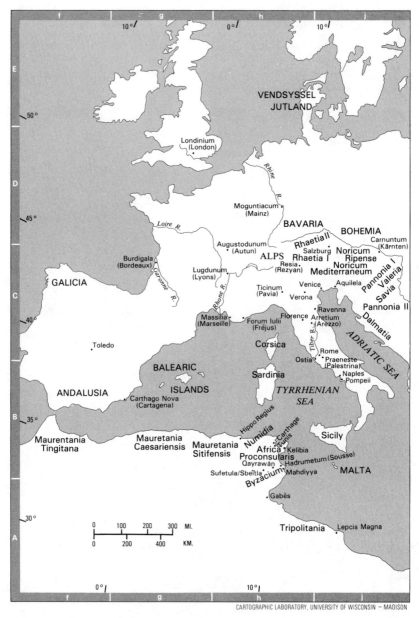

Map 1. The Mediterranean Basin. The provinces of the late Roman Empire, according to the Notitia Dignitatum, are indicated in the upper- and lower-case type.

xviii

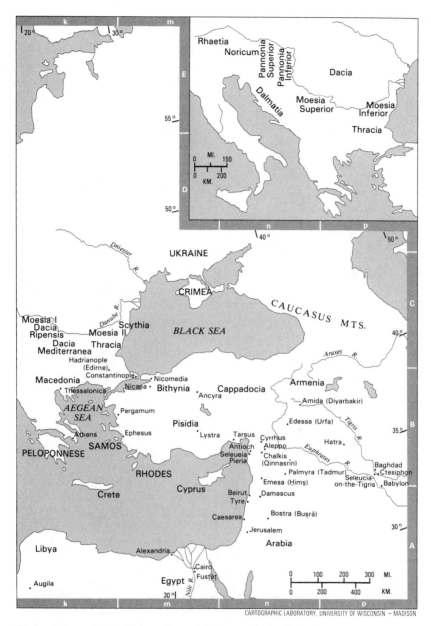

The insert shows the Danubian provinces of the Roman Empire during the developed Principate (ca. A.D. 100–200).

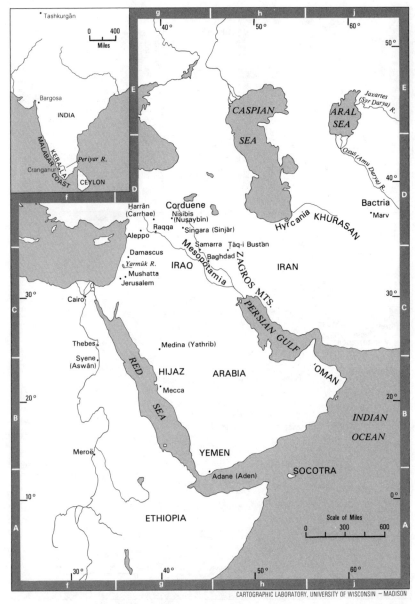

Map 2. The Near and Middle East. The regional names in use during classical antiquity are indicated by the upper- and lower-case type. The insert shows South Asia.

PART I

Introduction

CHAPTER 1

Toward a Definition of Late Antiquity

FRANK M. CLOVER AND R. STEPHEN HUMPHREYS

The search for chronological limits is perplexing. Moved by a desire to understand the past, the historian manufactures ages that had little or no meaning for the societies under investigation. The history of western Eurasia in the first millennium A.D. is a case in point. According to a common interpretation (present since the fifteenth and sixteenth centuries), a *medium aevum* ("Middle Age") of chaos and disruption followed the collapse of classical civilization around mid millennium and preceded the return to order in the modern era. By the nineteenth century, however, some critics began to question this neat division of history. Among those who were dissatisfied with the boundary between the classical Mediterranean and the Middle Age, the Viennese art historian Alois Riegl was most influential. In a study of Egyptian textiles (published in 1889), Riegl introduced the term *Die Späte Antike* ("Late Antiquity") to describe a distinctive style that could be characterized as neither Roman nor medieval. He argued that this "Late Antique" style, influential in other realms of art, endured from the reign of Constantine the Great until that of Charlemagne.[1] During the present century the Belgian historian Henri Pirenne has brought about a useful extension of Riegl's concept. In an important article published in 1922, Pirenne suggested that the Roman version of classical antiquity lasted until Muḥammad and Charlemagne set in motion the removal of two centers of civilization from the Mediterranean coast.[2] Today the idea of a Late Antiquity, generalized to cover many aspects of culture, society, and politics, enjoys a wide currency.

The concept of a transitional phase between cosmopolitan classical antiquity and a localized Middle Age seems useful. Yet an age of transition ought to be short—no more, let us say, than one or two centuries. From this perspective, the contributors to the present volume make difficult the search for a brief period during which all that was ancient ceased to exist and everything medieval came into being. Particularly—and, in the end, beneficially—

3

troublesome are the Islamicists. Professor Donner observes that all modern aspects of nomadic pastoralism, an important part of early Islam, were present in the Near East as early as the third century B.C. On the other hand, Professor Humphreys gives attention to a historiographical harvest of the *Qurʾān* during the ninth and tenth centuries A.D.[3] Slightly beyond the limits set by Humphreys and Donner stand two major events, the conquests of Alexander the Great (*regn.* 336–23 B.C.) and the Crusades (beginning in A.D. 1096). Should one therefore argue that Late Antiquity began with Alexander's sacrifices to the memory of Achilles at the Hellespont (334 B.C.) and concluded with Pope Urban II's call for a holy war at the Council of Clermont (A.D. 1095)?[4] It is obvious that a period of transition fourteen centuries long has little conceptual value. Is it possible to identify a few generations within this millennium and a half during which the societies of the Mediterranean and the Near East underwent major adjustments that one may associate with the concept of Late Antiquity?

The first step toward a usable definition of Late Antiquity is to identify its foundations—elements that were present in the Near East and the Mediterranean from the time of Alexander until the Crusades. Two such elements require attention: cities and local cultures.

A local culture may be defined as an aggregation of peasants, transhumant pastoralists, and villagers, all practicing a distinctive style of life and speaking a distinctive language. A local culture may include city dwellers when they observe a manner of living that is at variance with the cosmopolitan culture sponsored by a large state. The contributors to the present volume discuss several local cultures present in western Eurasia during the fourteen centuries in question. The Celts remained an integral part of Europe, although the area in which they were predominant changed dramatically. In Alexander's day they were the masters of nearly every village between the Bay of Biscay and the lower Danube, but by the fifth century A.D. they were most active in the British Isles and the Brittany Peninsula. As the Celts retreated to the northwestern tip of Europe, however, the Germanic peoples took their place. Village dwellers like the Celts, they managed (between the first century B.C. and the eighth century A.D.) to cast some of their numbers from the Rhine and Danube valleys to western Europe and the Mediterranean coast. The Balkan Peninsula attracted some of their attention—the Ostrogoth Theodoric the Great, for example, began his career in that quarter—but some of the most influential peoples there belonged to the Thracian and Slavic branches of the Indo-European language family. Centered in the northeastern projection of the Balkans, the Thracians maintained their identity under Macedonian and then Roman rule. The Roman emperor Leo I (A.D. 457–74), for instance, boasted affiliation with the tribe of the Bessi. In the sixth century A.D. the Slavs overran much of the Adriatic and Peloponnesian parts of the peninsula. As they did so, they encountered another enduring presence, the Greek-speaking population.[5]

The successors of Alexander and then the Roman authorities had made Greek an administrative language in the Near East and eastern Mediterranean, but merchants and Christians had done more to assure the penetration of *Koinē* (a standard form of Greek based on the dialect of Attica) at the local level. After the arrival of the Slavs, Greek speech and customs remained strong in the northeastern Mediterranean, but they endured elsewhere as well, most notably in the Levant and the Tyrrhenian basin.[6] In the meantime another cultural nexus was establishing itself in the central and northwestern Mediterranean. The basis of this aggregate was the Latin language—not the polished classical or administrative Latin, but the Latin of the street and countryside. Evident already in Petronius's *Satyricon* and the graffiti of first-century Pompeii, this common form of Latin (again with the encouragement of Christians and merchants) became at least a second language in the western Mediterranean, and from the middle Danube westward within the interior of Europe. From A.D. 400 onward, movements of peoples in Europe and the spread of Islam removed North Africa from the zone of Latin speech and reduced the Danubian component to a few islands. But the common Latin persisted in the central and northwestern Mediterranean, thereby becoming the parent of various Romance dialects which first reached written form around the ninth century.[7]

Between Alexander's expedition and the Crusades, Latin and Greek enjoyed some currency in the southern Mediterranean and Near East. Here, however, populations belonging to the great Hamito-Semitic language family fielded the principal local cultures—Semitic, Egyptian, and Berber.

From the High Atlas to Egypt's Thebaid, various Berber groups circulated or maintained settlements. Some of these aggregates managed, under the leadership of big families, to construct durable hegemonies. The Numidians under Massinissa (*regn.* 203–148 B.C.), the Tripolitanian Luwata, and the Blemmyes of the Thebaid were perhaps the most successful. In the Nile basin the native Egyptian population managed to keep some of its ancient traditions under Macedonian, Roman, and Islamic rule. The persistence of local dialects—first Demotic and then (with strong encouragement from the Christian community) Coptic—is the best indication of this substratum's survival.[8] East of Egypt lay the heart of the Fertile Crescent (Palestine, Syria, and Mesopotamia) and the Arabian Peninsula. Here speakers of various Semitic dialects held sway. In the Fertile Crescent or the coastal regions of Arabia they held fast to the urban way of life for which the entire region had long been famous. The desert dwellers were perforce nomadic pastoralists. Before A.D. 600 the most visible natives of this region were the Jews, who repeatedly exported some of their numbers to cities from Mesopotamia to Spain; the Aramaeans, whose language and literature continued to flourish in Syria during the first millennium; and the great Arabian coalitions such as the Nabataeans, Ghassānids, and Lakhmids, all of whom proved adept at blending urban and nomadic manners.[9]

To a modern observer, the entire preserve of the Hamito-Semitic language groups is a cultural continuum. There are ancient precursors of this phenomenon. One thinks especially of the old Persian Empire's ability to dominate the eastern Mediterranean from Egypt to Asia Minor, and of the continuing allegiance of Carthage in North Africa to the Phoenician motherland.[10] But during the millennium and a half under review only the Islamic conquerors brought the lands from Gibraltar to the Persian Gulf under one aegis.

It has already been noted that local and cosmopolitan cultures may exist side by side in cities. From Alexander to the Crusades, the major cities of the Mediterranean and Near East were so sophisticated and heterogeneous that they could not be preserves of single cultures. Because they were centers of trade and ideas, they were essential elements in the society and culture of Late Antiquity, howsoever one defines that concept. During the fourteen centuries in question, many new urban centers came into being and then disappeared, sharing the fates of the state systems that sponsored them. The modern observer who wishes to identify the nature and limits of Late Antiquity must look not for periodic urbanization—one thinks especially of Roman expansion in the European and North African interiors—but for areas in which cities flourished with little or no interruption. Between the death of Alexander and the dawn of the Crusades, the urban way of life persisted in five such areas. First, the Tunisian Promontory, the Gulf of Tunis and vicinity: Phoenician and then Roman Carthage was the focus of life there until the arrival of Islam, whereupon nearby Qayrawān, Mahdiyya, and then Tunis took her place.[11] The coast of western Italy between the Bay of Naples and the lower Tiber River was another region. Here Rome—at first a city-state, then an imperial capital, and finally a center of ecclesiastical administration—was easily the leader.[12] In the northeastern corner of Italy stood a third durable cluster. Aquileia, founded at the head of the Adriatic Sea in the second century B.C., remained a major focus of contacts between the Mediterranean and central Europe until Attila the Hun destroyed it in A.D. 452. Venice did not begin to take its place until the seventh century, but during the interim nearby Ravenna (under a variety of administrations) continued to flourish.[13] East of the Adriatic lay the area in which cities had long endured and therefore had the best chance of weathering political and economic changes. In the Aegean basin the most enduring urban nexus hugged the straits separating the Aegean and Black seas. Byzantium on the Bosporus, refounded in A.D. 330 by the Roman emperor Constantine I, was the focus of life in this quarter.[14] Finally, there was the megalopolis of the greater Fertile Crescent. In Lower Egypt Alexandria was predominant until the coming of Islam, and then Fusṭāṭ and Cairo took the lead.[15] Among the innumerable towns of Syria and Palestine, Damascus and Jerusalem (Aelia Capitolina) were most influential, while the lower reaches of the Tigris and Euphrates rivers maintained major centers of life from Babylon to Baghdad.[16]

The cities and local cultures of the Near East and Mediterranean, then, were the durable foundations beneath the patterns of change that Alois Riegl's heirs have called Late Antiquity. It is futile, however, to define a transitional phase at the end of antiquity solely in terms of its foundations. One might argue, for instance, that classical civilization entered its final phase when northern European villagers established kingdoms on or near the Mediterranean, when Greek culture was predominant in the Aegean basin, and when native peoples of the Near East revolted against rulers who originated from southern Europe. The Germanic kingdoms, the Eastern Roman Empire, and Islam generated such events between A.D. 400 and 700, but so did the Celts of Galatia, Athens, and Pergamum, and Egypt's fellahin (who rebelled against and severely weakened the Ptolemies) during the third century B.C.[17] The modern critic has a better chance of defining and setting temporal limits to Late Antiquity by bringing to view two attempts—both occurring between the reign of Alexander and the Crusades—to set the cities and local cultures of western Eurasia under one standard.

The first attempt was embodied in the Roman Empire, and the second in the creation of the Islamic caliphate. The origins of the Roman Empire, whose center always stood on or near the Mediterranean littoral, were complex. Since the beginning of the first millennium B.C., Phoenicians and Greeks had extended their urban ways to Spain and the lower Rhone basin. From that time onward, normal sea traffic made coastal inhabitants from the Balearic Islands to the Bosporus members of a single, loosely knit community. The philosopher Plato best described this situation when he had Socrates state that people living between Gibraltar and the Caucasus Mountains were "like ants or frogs dwelling around a pond."[18] Soon after Plato penned these words, Alexander and his Successors brought some of these pond dwellers closer together by constructing a network of Mediterranean and Near Eastern states amid a sophisticated cultural continuum. Today the term *Hellenism,* denoting a major extension of the Greek way of life into the Near East, is the common characterization of this political and cultural nexus.[19] The Successors, however, abandoned precedents set by Alexander as they attempted to maintain the legacy of a Macedonian empire. In the last months of his life Alexander had organized his conquests from Babylon, one of the capitals of the old Persian Empire. Competition among the Successors forced a shift of the center of Hellenism to the eastern Mediterranean, and the eventual loss of Mesopotamia and Iran to non-Hellenic powers.[20] While Hellenistic civilization retracted to the coast, Rome came to dominate the Mediterranean. The empire of the Roman Republic, achieved between the outbreak of the Hannibalic War and the beginning of Julius Caesar's Gallic campaign, was a true heir of Alexander's Successors: it stayed close to the Mediterranean shore, and it embraced Hellenism.[21]

Once it was formed, the *Imperium romanum* proved to be an amazingly plastic organization. Between the ages of Julius Caesar and Septimius Severus it brought urban civilization into the European and North African interiors, so that not only the seacoast of the Mediterranean but also the lands from Britain to the second cataract of the Nile came under a single administration. Then in the third century the empire splintered, only to reassert its authority (under the Constantinian and early Theodosian emperors) at limits that were nearly identical to those of the Julio-Claudian era.[22] During this period of growth, fission, and reformation, the Roman Empire remained true to its Hellenistic and Republican heritage in three important respects. Senatorial magnates of the late Republic had relied in part on client kings to maintain Rome's overseas hegemony, they had tried without success to conquer the Parthians (the first successful heirs of Alexander's eastern realms), and they had regarded with both fascination and repulsion the various religious enthusiasms of the Hellenistic East.[23] Between the first and the fourth century A.D. the Roman emperors made clients of the distant peoples whom they could not or did not choose to conquer. They occasionally tried to bring down the Parthian and (beginning in the third century A.D.) Sassanian empires. In this endeavor a Trajan made no more progress than a Crassus or indeed one of the later successors of Alexander. The Roman continuation of Hellenistic civilization remained fixed in the Mediterranean basin. Finally, the Roman emperors echoed the republican ambivalence toward eastern religions by intermittently encouraging and persecuting the so-called oriental cults, the Judaic community, and one of its offshoots, the Christians.[24]

The destiny of the Roman Empire has a central place in any definition of Late Antiquity. Since modern critics regard Late Antiquity as an age of transition, one ought to locate its chronological limits at or near the time when the Roman Empire underwent dramatic transformation. The present editors believe that the changes that this plastic organization experienced between the outbreak of the Hannibalic War and the death of Theodosius the Great (A.D. 395) are less significant than those that occurred between Theodosius' demise and the end of the Heraclian dynasty (A.D. 395–695). An extension of a Mediterranean-based state to the North Sea and the High Atlas is a spectacular feat, but during the empire's first six centuries Rome was an effective center of administration, and thus the Latin ways of Italy contributed to the Roman version of Hellenistic civilization. Modern observers use the term "Graeco-Roman" to describe the imperial way of life, a veneer covering the

Mediterranean basin's disparate local cultures.[25] After the death of Theodosius the Great, the Roman Empire retained and indeed recovered much of its ancient heritage, but it also underwent an extraordinary shift of its cultural, religious, and geographical center.

Some traditional aspects of the late Roman Empire may be considered first. Ancient observers—most notably Augustine of Hippo and Eunapius of Sardes, both of whom wrote influential tracts in the early fifth century—adopted the common notion that the lands from Britain to Egypt were the natural limits of the Roman Empire. They therefore regarded the loss of western provincial lands to Germanic and Berber coalitions as an indication that the Roman Empire was at or near its end.[26] Modern readers of these compositions or their derivatives have shared this opinion. Today many histories place the fall of the Roman Empire in the fifth century A.D.[27] This interpretation does not take sufficient account of the real nature of the *Imperium romanum*. In its republican form the Roman hegemony had been an effort to dominate the Mediterranean littoral by direct or indirect means. Client princes had done Rome's bidding in regions that the Senate had not chosen (or had not been able) to annex as overseas provinces. Beginning in the fifth century, the Roman Empire returned to the seashore of the Mediterranean after a few centuries' sojourn in the European and North African interiors. The Germanic kingdoms and the equally successful (but less noticed) southern coalitions such as the Ghassānids, Blemmyes, and Luwata were the functional equivalent of late Republican clients such as Herod of Judaea.[28] The Roman Empire did not collapse after A.D. 400. Instead, it began to recover its original character.

During the process of recovery, however, the empire experienced not so much a break with tradition as an intensification of part of its inheritance. Since the days of the Republic the Roman state had embraced Hellenism, the sophisticated way of life developed by Alexander's Successors. The losses of territory that began in the fifth century made Constantinople the new center of the Roman Empire. Under the emperor Justinian I (A.D. 527–65) the New Rome was able to regain some of the empire's Balkan and western Mediterranean holdings, but subsequent vicissitudes (most notably the onset of the Slavs and the rise of Islam) reduced the imperial sway to Asia Minor, the Aegean basin, and parts of Italy and Sicily. The Roman Empire stabilized these diminished limits by the end of the Heraclian dynasty, when the emperors Constans II and Constantine IV Pogonatus (*regn.* A.D. 641–85) tried briefly to transfer the court to Italy.[29] After Constantine IV returned to Constantinople, the empire of the *Rhomaioi* ("Romans") retained its new configuration amid later fluctuations until the end of the eleventh century.[30] The modern observer will notice that the frontiers of the new Roman state encompass the region in which the Greek language was predominant or at least common.[31] The coincidence made it inevitable that the New Rome would accentuate the Hellenic component of the Hellenistic tradition. Under Constantinople's aegis, the imperial Hellenism, decidedly Greek in form and outlook, replaced the old Graeco-Roman culture as the dominant way of life in the Roman Empire.[32]

At the same time, the religious outlook of the imperial elite underwent a major change. Two generations before the death of Theodosius the Great, a portion of the Christian community—the well-organized branch that maintained a monarchic administration and a rigid canon of sacred writings (the so-called New Testament) appended to the Bible—had reached the top of Roman society in such numbers that the emperors had abandoned the traditional ambivalence in favor of toleration of or even conversion to the new faith.[33] Theodosius ratified the new attitude by proscribing the traditional Roman pantheon and ordering all Roman subjects to embrace the form of Christianity approved by a universal assembly of the faithful at Nicaea in A.D. 325.[34] Theodosius' orders altered forever the religious aspect of the Roman government. Under the Theodosian, Justinianic, and Heraclian emperors, the Roman government became both Hellenic and Christian in orientation.

The contrast between the Roman Empire of Theodosius I (A.D. 379–95) and Heraclius I (A.D. 610–41) is considerable, and therefore it is understandable that an Augustine or Eunapius would speak of the collapse of the Roman Empire. However erroneous this perception, it was still the view of many literate observers who lived through the great transformation of the Roman Empire.[35] Another ancient characterization of the empire's destiny is equally interesting—and more accurate. Between the late fourth and the sixth century Christian witnesses in particular began to speak of *Romania*, a term that denoted Roman civilization both within and beyond the reach of the imperial administration. The limits of *Romania* were nebulous. It ceased to prevail only in *Barbaria* or the *Barbaricum*, the lands where correct (i.e., Christian) belief and Roman urbanity were absent.[36] The concept of *Romania* is most helpful for the modern critic who wishes to characterize the destinies of Roman civilization between A.D. 400 and 700. Some of the contributors to the present volume consider phenomena that fit within this ancient framework: the Roman landowning aristocracy, a durable presence in the northwestern Mediterranean (beyond the reach of the New Rome's administration) and a reluctant but ultimately resolute supporter of Christianity; the New Rome of the East, whose army remained attentive to the Old Rome's military usage; late imperial Africa, a Romano-Berber mélange that absorbed one group of intruders, the Vandals, and then so resisted Constantinople's brand of Roman civilization that it paved the way for Islam; and Islam itself, which drew on the traditions of both *Romania* and its millennial competitor Iran to generate a distinctive cultural tradition of its own.[37]

The present editors believe that the Roman Empire underwent its most dramatic transformation between A.D. 400 and 700. These three centuries may be identified as the span of Late Antiquity, but only from the standpoint of the Roman destiny. The next step in a proper definition of this epoch is to determine when Islam's efforts to organize the Near East and the Mediterranean under one aegis met with similarly profound changes.

The rise of Islam represents a second attempt to bring political and cultural unity to western Eurasia. Here we seem in certain respects to find an inverse image of the Roman experience between A.D. 400 and 700. First, we are dealing not with an organization that had existed more than half a millennium before its amazing transformation, but with a new entity that arose from obscurity and marginality to immense territorial scope in an astonishingly short time, absorbing not only the southern and eastern littoral of the Mediterranean but in addition all the domains of Rome's ancient rival Sassanian Iran. Moreover, in contrast to Constantinople's growing emphasis on Hellenism, a single dimension of its cultural heritage, the newly emergent Islamic empire synthesized a distinctive tradition of its own out of the most disparate possible elements: ancient Arabia, Christian Rome, Iran, and Rabbinic Judaism. The formative age of Islam—from around A.D. 570 (the traditional birth year of Muḥammad) to 900—is similar but not identical to the period during which the Roman Empire experienced its most dramatic changes. But although they were roughly contemporary, the Roman and Islamic adjustments were fundamentally different. Far from defending and redefining an ancient heritage, Islam embarked on a path of exploration and innovation.[38]

It is true that the very rapidity of Islam's rise provoked a series of conflicts within the Community of Believers, played out simultaneously on the political, religious, social, and cultural levels. These conflicts proved extremely obdurate, and in many cases (e.g., the Sunni-Shiʿite schism stemming from the struggle for power between ʿAlī and Muʿāwiya) remained beyond any broadly satisfying resolution. Around the middle of the ninth century, the very moment when a distinctly Islamic culture was clearly emerging, Muslims were no longer sure that they could achieve the goals they had defined for themselves over the preceding two hundred years. Their aim had been to institute the will of God through the establishment of a universal political community. Although they had attained immense political power, they were not certain that this power reflected the divinely ordained order of things. In this sense early Islam, like the late Roman Empire, was in crisis. As with the Romans, the awareness of crisis compelled a process of self-definition, a making of difficult choices among a dazzling array of possibilities.[39]

What guidance could the Believers of Islam call upon as they made their choices? Romans of the fifth, sixth, and seventh centuries could call upon two sources: the imperial tradition, supported in particular by slowly evolving legal and administrative habits; and the Bible, especially as interpreted by the Christians of the Nicene Creed. In regard to both scripture and government, Muslims stood on less secure foundations.

The political tradition to which Muslims could appeal was far more circumscribed in time and space. Only the two decades that spanned the career of the Prophet in Medina (A.D. 622–32) and (for most but not all Muslims) the reigns of his first two successors (632–44) could unquestionably provide guidance for later generations, especially because schism, heresy, and dissension became so widespread thereafter. Some Muslims—those whom we call Shiʿites—profoundly admired ʿAlī b. Abī Ṭālib and his descendants, but they had to admit that his purposes had been totally frustrated during his lifetime, and that he and all his heirs had fallen martyr in the effort to achieve them. Others, especially bureaucrats and courtiers, exalted the political wisdom and the conceptions of kingship inherited from Sassanian Iran, but the religiously sensitive felt that the Iranian tradition at best represented an idea of rational government and had no organic connection with the political imperatives of Islam.[40]

In the matter of scripture, Muslims seemed to be on an equal footing with the Romans, if not superior to them. The Qurʾān was a new revelation, but it was of precisely the same kind as the Torah and the Gospels. Indeed, it was explicitly meant to supplant them. It addressed the same concerns as did the older scriptures and provided a critical commentary on the theology and anthropology that they taught. Moreover, just as the Torah had generated an oral law ascribed to Moses, so the Qurʾān was accompanied by the example and teaching of Muḥammad—the *Sunna* of the Prophet, embodied in countless discrete narratives (*ḥadīth*) of his sayings and doings. On the other hand, the issue of who had the right to explicate and interpret God's word remained a vexing one.

By the early eighth century three contrasting positions on this matter were beginning to emerge. An egalitarian and populist stance—that every pious and virtuous Believer had the right to expound the sacred text—was espoused by those more or less aligned with the Kharijites. The Shiʿites, those loyal to the person and teaching of ʿAlī, held that authoritative doctrine could be set forth only by a divinely authorized and infallible *Imām* of the Prophet's own lineage. (It is true that Shiʿites often differed about the identity of this *Imām*, just as Kharijites had conflicting standards of piety and virtue.) The Sunnis slowly emerged out of the welter of schisms and sects as the party of consensus and compromise, and their doctrine reflects this orientation: the right to interpret scripture belonged to the Community as a whole, but the authoritative spokesmen of the Community were a small, essentially self-selecting body of scholars (*ʿulamāʾ*), men whose role was not to conduct liturgy and sacrament, but to study and teach. In the end the Sunnis would create no church, no formally constituted institution with the power to define faith and morals. Nevertheless, their demand that everyone propound doctrines publicly and demonstrate that they were congruent with the religious and ethical consensus of the Community was a powerful deterrent to aberrant or idiosyncratic notions.[41]

In spite of its evident connections with the past, Islam brought a new scripture, a new people, a new language, and a new political system to the fore. Is it appropriate then to regard early Islam as a final phase of Late Antiquity? After all, the majority of commentators have preferred to take the Arab conquests of the seventh century as a terminus, an event after which the cultural and political institutions and values of the fifth to seventh centuries were definitively superseded. To this issue, our contributors have developed a complex response.

In the realm of state formation Islam clearly did establish a new entity. Not since Alexander had so many lands and peoples been brought within a single political and administrative framework, and never before or since was such a vast construct effectively maintained for so long—two hundred years by any reasonable calculation. (The entire region between the Nile and Amū Daryā rivers stood in at least a tributary relationship to the Islamic government by the time Muʿāwiya seized power in 660, while caliphal control over this area was not seriously challenged until the assassination of al-Mutawakkil in 861.) Moreover, the new empire was created and managed largely by frontiersmen, the oasis settlers and Bedouin of Arabia, who had never before played any serious part in world politics. Of course they used the materials left to them by their Roman and Iranian predecessors, especially as regards fiscal and administrative practices, but no edifice can be built *ex nihilo*. There is one important qualification to this characterization: by the late seventh century the caliphs were taking on more and more the attributes of emperors and kings, in ideology, in court ceremonial, and in the concrete powers that they asserted over their subjects. They became more, not less, like the rulers of the fifth to seventh centuries. By the tenth century the caliphal and regional courts appealed explicitly and routinely to the precedents of Sassanian Iran to legitimize their manner of government.[42]

In the realm of religion, the situation is more ambivalent. We have already suggested that the Qurʾān belongs to the scriptural tradition established earlier within Judaism and Christianity. It both elaborates certain themes stated in the Bible and rejects crucial points in the Jewish and Christian interpretation of these themes. From either perspective, however, Muslims were drawing on concepts—those of the Chosen People, the New Israel, the Covenant, and the Sacred Community—which Jews and Roman Christians had long maintained.

We find, then, a real continuity between the scriptural tradition of the late Roman Empire and that of early Islam.

The parallel can be carried further. At first glance, the Bible and the Qur'ān appear to have had different meanings for the Christian Roman Empire and the early Community of Believers. For the former the Christian interpretation of Holy Writ was one guide to life. Other guides such as the Roman legal tradition and the heritage of classical literature were becoming imbued with Christian values, but not so effectively that they lost their ancient identities. Islam's scripture, in contrast, was the foundation document of the polity. Without the Qur'ān there could be no Community of Believers, and without the Community there was no caliphate. Even the earliest Muslims, however, could and indeed did appeal to an autonomous tradition predating the new scripture: the tribal values and *mores* of ancient Arabia. Here too, old attitudes and ways of life had to undergo a slow and never entirely completed transformation.[43]

The coming of the Arabs brought no more disruption of the Mediterranean and Near Eastern populations than did the appearance of Germanic kingdoms in Italy, Gaul, Spain, and Africa. Relative to the numbers of their subjects, there were not many immigrants from the Arabian Peninsula. The Arab conquests brought about a demographic revolution in only a few isolated pockets of western Eurasia. In contrast, the rise of the Arabic language caused a sharper and more decisive cultural break. The Germanic peoples who reached the Mediterranean littoral had quickly taken up the local varieties of Latin in the Roman lands they occupied. Why then did the Arabs not lose the use of Arabic? Even more, why did the great majority of the peoples west of the Tigris River ultimately give up their native tongues for the strange language of a few barbarians? So far no persuasive solution to this problem has been proposed. Two possible lines of argument, however, suggest that the linguistic change was a matter of form more than substance—that it did not in itself create a decisive break with the past.

First, the religious and political identity of the conquerors was tightly bound up with their Arabic scripture. The Qur'ān had been vouchsafed to them in "pure Arabic," so that to abandon their language would be to abandon their religion, the very thing that marked them as a people apart. The incentive to avoid the indigenous languages of the conquered lands was thus very strong. But since the Qur'ān was scripture in the Judaeo-Christian mold, adherence to the language in which it had been revealed did not seal the Arabs off from the established religious traditions of the region—though doubtless the linguistic difference did shape the way in which these traditions would be brought into the Islamic consciousness.

Second, Arabic initially displaced two tongues, Greek and Persian, which had been used chiefly among small sociopolitical elites in Africa, Egypt, and the Fertile Crescent. When the conquerors killed or exiled these elites, Arabic had the field more or less to itself at the top levels of society. The supplanting of the languages of the masses (for example, Berber, Coptic, or Aramaic) was a far slower process, one which probably emerged in connection with conversion to Islam. But again, the new language was receptive to the living aspects of the displaced elite cultures—for instance, to the political wisdom literature of Sassanian Iran, and to Greek science, medicine, and even theological disputation. In regard to the rise of Arabic, the metaphor to keep in mind is that of a filter, not a barrier.[44]

Finally, we may glance at the visual arts. One may argue at length whether there ever was such a thing as "Islamic art." Whatever this entity may have been, however, it is hard to discern it before the ninth century. Until that time, what we see is a fascinating amalgam of late Roman and Sassanian themes, images, and techniques. These are often found in new settings (e.g., the mosque) or combined in heretofore unexampled ways (e.g., the Roman mosaics and Sassanian stucco carvings in the bath of Hishām's palace at Khirbat al-Mafjar), but they all belong to the repertory established in late Roman and Sassanian times. In architecture, decor, and objects produced in (rather than by) early Islam, we have unmistakable evidence of the enduring cultural tradition that emerged in the latter half of the first millennium.[45]

All this suggests that the newness of Islam lay not in a radical break with the past, but in the specific emphases and interpretations that Muslims gave to the ideas, institutions, and forms to which they had fallen heir. They were knowledgeable and respectful of this heritage, sufficiently so that they did not wish either to discard it or to imitate it blindly, but meant instead to use it selectively and critically in the definition and pursuit of their own goals and values. By the end of the ninth century, most of what *Romania* had to offer them had been internalized. After that time, a distinct and integrated Islamic culture began to develop, one which would generate its principal problems and solutions from within itself. Within the perspective provided by the evolution of the Islamic world, then, the year 900 is perhaps the most satisfactory point at which to set the end of antiquity.

The search for a brief age of transition at the end of classical antiquity has yielded two creative epochs that overlap but do not coincide. The Roman Empire, it has been argued, underwent dramatic change between A.D. 400 and 700, whereas the foundations of Islamic civilization were laid between about 600 and 900. Five hundred years of noncoincident three-century periods is hardly the ideal limit of an epoch—a few generations between Alexander and the Crusades, during which the societies of the Mediterranean and Near East experienced dramatic transformation.[46] The editors of the present volume have therefore taken a step toward a definition of Late Antiquity, but a full delineation of this elusive concept remains for other critics to achieve.

NOTES

1   A. Riegl, *Die ägyptischen Textilfunde im K. K. oesterreichischen Museum* (Vienna, 1889), esp. xv–xxiv. Cf. K. F. Stroheker, *Germanentum und Spätantike* (Zurich, 1965), 275–308.

2   H. Pirenne, "Mahomet et Charlemagne," *Revue belge de philologie et d'histoire* 1 (1922): 77–86.

3   See chapters 4 and 12 of the present collection.

4   For these events, see H. U. Instinsky, *Alexander der Grosse am Hellespont* (Godesberg, 1949), passim; and K. M. Setton et al., eds., *A History of the Crusades,* 5 vols. to date (Philadelphia and Madison, Wis., 1955–85), vol. 1, 2d ed., pp. 220–52.

5   See B. Cunliffe, *The Celtic World* (New York, 1979); L. Musset, *Les invasions,* 2 vols. (2d ed., Paris, 1969–71); R. F. Hoddinott, *Bulgaria in Antiquity: An Archaeological Introduction* (London, 1975); and R. Browning, *Byzantium and Bulgaria: A Comparative Study across the Early Medieval Frontier* (Berkeley and Los Angeles, 1975). On the early career of Theodoric and Emperor Leo's Thracian background, see A. H. M. Jones et al., eds., *The Prosopography of the Later Roman Empire,* 2 vols. (Cambridge, 1971–80), 2:663–65 (Leo 6) and 1077–84 (Theodericus 7). In the present volume, Thomas Markey (Chapter 4) examines the evanescent presence of the Germanic peoples in the western Mediterranean.

6   For *Koinē* and Byzantine Greek, see F. W. Blass and A. Debrunner, *A Greek Grammar of the New Testament and Other Early Christian Literature,* trans. R. Funk (9th–10th ed., Chicago, 1961); and N. H. Baynes and H. St. L. B. Moss, *Byzantium: An Introduction to East Roman Civilization* (Oxford: Clarendon Press, 1948), 252–67. The *Chronographia* of the sixth-century Antiochene John Malalas is a measure of Greek spoken in the Levant at mid millennium. Cf. K. Wolf, *Studien zur Sprache des Malalas,* 2 vols. (Munich, 1911–12). On Greek culture in the Tyrrhenian basin, see A. Guillou, *Culture et société en Italie byzantine (VIᵉ–XIᵉ s.)* [London, 1978].

7   See L. R. Palmer, *The Latin Language* (London, 1966), esp. 148–205; and I. Iordan et al., *An Introduction to Romance Linguistics* (2d ed., Oxford, 1970), passim.

8   See J. Ki-Zerbo et al., eds., *UNESCO General History of Africa,* 8 vols. (London and Berkeley and Los Angeles, 1981–85), 2:184–225, 423–512.

9   See R. Hamerton-Kelly and Robin Scroggs, eds., *Jews, Greeks and Christians: Religious Cultures in Late Antiquity* (Leiden, 1976); A. Sharf, *Byzantine Jewry from Justinian to the Fourth Crusade* (New York and London, 1971); N. Garsoïan et al., eds., *East of Byzantium: Syria and Armenia in the Formative Period* (Washington, D.C., 1982), 3–134; G. W. Bowersock, *Roman Arabia* (Cambridge, Mass., 1983); I. Shahid, *Rome and the Arabs* (Washington, D.C., 1984); Shahid, *Byzantium and the Arabs in the Fourth Century* (Washington, D.C., 1984); and F. E. Peters, "Byzantium and the Arabs of Syria," *Annales archéologiques de Syria* 27–28 (1977–78): 97–107.

10 When Alexander captured Tyre (332 B.C.), for instance, he found Carthaginian envoys among those who had taken refuge in the Temple of Melqart. See Arrian

Anabasis 2.24.5; and W. Huss, *Geschichte der Karthager* (Munich, 1985), 169–75, 511–46. On the organization of the Persian Empire under the Achaemenids, see R. N. Frye, *The History of Ancient Iran* (Munich, 1984), 88–135.

11 See A. Audollent, *Carthage romaine, 146 avant Jésus-Christ–698 apres Jésus-Christ* (Paris, 1901); J. G. Pedley, ed., *New Light on Ancient Carthage* (Ann Arbor, Mich., 1980); and J. D. Fage and R. Oliver, eds., *The Cambridge History of Africa*, 8 vols. (Cambridge, 1975–86), 2:490–555.

12 See M. Hammond and L. J. Bartson, *The City in the Ancient World* (Cambridge, Mass., 1972), 237–302; and R. Krautheimer, *Rome: Profile of a City, 312–1308* (Princeton, N.J., 1980), 3–160.

13 Cf. A. Calderini, *Aquileia romana* (Milan, 1930); F. W. Deichmann, *Ravenna: Hauptstadt des spätantiken Abendlandes*, 3 vols. (2d ed. of vol. 3, Wiesbaden, 1969–76), vol. 1, esp. pp. 1–38; and W. H. McNeill, *Venice, the Hinge of Europe, 1081–1797* (Chicago, 1974), 1–45. The Annals of Ravenna place the destruction of Aquileia on 18 July 452. See B. Bischoff and W. Koehler, "Un'edizione illustrata degli Annali ravennati del Basso Impero," *Studi romagnoli* 3 (1952): 1–17.

14 See A. H. M. Jones, M. Avi-Yonah, et al., *The Cities of the Eastern Roman Provinces* (2d ed., Oxford, 1971), 1–27, 147–73; G. Dagron, *Naissance d'une capitale: Constantinople et ses institutions de 330 à 451* (Paris, 1974); and R. Krautheimer, *Three Christian Capitals: Topography and Politics* (Berkeley and Los Angeles, 1983), 41–67.

15 Cf. P. M. Fraser, *Ptolemaic Alexandria*, 3 vols. (2 ed., Oxford, 1984); Jones, *Eastern Roman Provinces*, 295–348; and J. L. Abu-Lughod, *Cairo: 1001 Years of the City Victorious* (Princeton, N.J., 1971), 3–36.

16 See K. Wulzinger and C. Watzinger, *Damaskus*, 2 vols. (Berlin: de Gruyter, 1921–24); and J. Gray, *A History of Jerusalem* (London, 1969), 123–227; J. G. MacQueen, *Babylon* (London, 1964), 155–233; M. Streck, *Seleucia und Ktesiphon*, Der Alte Orient, vol. 16, pts. 3–4 (Leipzig, 1917); and G. Le Strange, *Baghdad during the Abbasid Caliphate* (2d ed., Oxford, 1924).

17 For these antecedents, see C. Préaux, *Le monde hellénistique: La Grèce et l'Orient (323–146 av. J.-C.),* [2 vols. (Paris, 1978)], 1:136–52, 295–357 passim, 389–98; 2:602–21, 661–79.

18 Plato *Phaedo* 109b.

19 On the origins and influence of this concept, see H. Bengtson, *Griechische Geschichte von den Anfängen bis in die römische Kaiserzeit* (4th ed., Munich, 1969), 295–300.

20 See H. Braunert, *Politik, Recht und Gesellschaft in der griechisch-römischen Antike* (Stuttgart, 1980), 129–52.

21 On the limits of Roman conquests before the age of Julius Caesar, see C. Nicolet, *Rome et la conquête du monde méditerranéen*, 2 vols. (Paris, 1977–78), 2:545–718, 729–829. On the Roman elite's acceptance of or surrender to Hellenism, see E. Rawson, *Intellectual Life in the Late Roman Republic* (Baltimore, 1985).

22 The *Notitia dignitatum*, an illustrated list of high offices and military units edited between the early 390s and the first quarter of the fifth century, demonstrates (with corroborating evidence) that the empire once again extended from the lower Danube to the Sahara, and from England to the second cataract of the Nile. See

A. H. M. Jones, *The Later Roman Empire, 284–602: A Social, Economic and Administrative Survey,* 3 vols. (Oxford, 1964), 3:347–80, with Map II. J. Carcopino, *Le Maroc antique* (13th ed., Paris, 1948), 231–304, expressed noteworthy doubts that the emperors of the late third and fourth centuries restored Roman authority to the lands between Tangier and Sétif, but investigations of the past generation have revealed a restoration of the Mauretanian provinces at that time. See, e.g., P. Salama, "Bornes milliaires et problèmes stratégiques du Bas-Empire en Maurétanie," *Comptes rendus des séances de l'Académie des inscriptions et belles-lettres,* 1959, pp. 346–54.

23   See P. C. Sands, *The Client Princes of the Roman Empire under the Republic* (Cambridge, 1908); K.-H. Ziegler, *Die Beziehungen zwischen Rom und dem Partherreich* (Wiesbaden, 1964), 1–44; and J. H. W. G. Liebeschuetz, *Continuity and Change in Roman Religion* (Oxford, 1979), 1–54.

24   See E. Kornemann, *Gestalten und Reiche: Essays zur alten Geschichte* (Leipzig, 1943), 323–38; Ziegler, *Beziehungen,* 45–153; and Liebeschuetz, *Continuity and Change,* 55–308. In the present volume, John Matthews (chapter 3) considers the nature of communications between the Roman Empire and its eastern neighbors.

25   See F. Millar et al., *The Roman Empire and Its Neighbours* (2d ed., London, 1981).

26   Eunapius *Chronikē historia,* passim (with the celebrated epitome of Zosimus *Historia nova,* esp. 2.1–5.26 (cf. Photius *Bibliotheca* Cod. 98); and Augustinus *De civitate Dei,* passim.

27   Edward Gibbon's views are still influential. Gibbon extended his narrative to the end of the Roman Empire in A.D. 1453, but he honored the interpretations of fifth-century observers (such as Augustine and Eunapius) by inserting a section entitled "General Observations on the Fall of the Roman Empire in the West" soon after his narration of the events of A.D. 476. See *The History of the Decline and Fall of the Roman Empire,* ed. J. B. Bury, 7 vols. (London, 1896–1913), vol. 4, chap. 38 ad fin.

28   See above, nn. 5, 8, 9, 23.

29   See G. Ostrogorsky, *Geschichte des byzantinischen Staates* (3d ed., Munich, 1963), 19–122.

30   Romilly Jenkins places the end of the Roman Empire as an effective imperial power around the beginning of the Crusades. See *Byzantium: The Imperial Centuries, A.D. 610–1071* (London, 1966).

31   See A. Philippson, "Das byzantinische Reich als geographische Erscheinung," *Geographische Zeitschrift* 40 (1934): 441–55; and above, n. 6.

32   See N. H. Baynes, *Byzantine Studies and Other Essays* (London, 1955), 1–23; and J. Herrin, "Aspects of the Process of Hellenization in the Early Middle Ages," *Annual of the British School of Athens* 68 (1973): 113–26.

33   See T. D. Barnes, *Constantine and Eusebius* (Cambridge, Mass., 1981), 3–77, 191–275.

34   See *Codex Theodosianus* 16.1.2, 5.6, 10.10, and 10.12.

35   See P. Courcelle, *Histoire littéraire des grandes invasions germaniques* (3d ed., Paris, 1964).

36   On the early expressions of the idea of *Romania,* see F. M. Clover, "The Pseudo-Boniface and the *Historia Augusta," Bonner Historia-Augusta-Colloquium 1977/78* (Bonn, 1980), 73–95, at 80–81.

37   See the contributions of Schlumberger, Shelton, Clover, Cameron, Kaegi, and Allen (Chapters 6 through 11) in the present volume.

38   M. G. S. Hodgson, *The Venture of Islam,* vol. 1, *The Classical Age of Islam* (Chicago, 1974) remains the most comprehensive and best-integrated account of the cultural synthesis achieved in early Islam. See esp. 103–45, 233–40. An alternative perspective is developed in the eccentric but challenging essay of Patricia Crone and Michael Cook, *Hagarism: The Making of the Islamic World* (Cambridge, 1977).

39   The pessimism—or perhaps simply the cultural anxiety—of the late ninth century is often referred to in the literature. A starting point would be H. A. R. Gibb, "Government and Islam under the Early Abbasids: The Political Collapse of Islam," in *L'élaboration de l'Islam* (Paris, 1961), 115–27.

40   An important recent analysis of the development of political thought in early Islam is Tilman Nagel, *Rechtleitung und Kalifat: Versuch über eine Grundfrage der islamischen Geschichte* (Bonn, 1975). A. K. S. Lambton, *State and Government in Medieval Islam* (Oxford, 1981), presents a good overview of juristic doctrine but focuses on the eleventh and later centuries.

41   The most nuanced treatment of these issues is that of Hodgson, *Venture of Islam,* 1:252–67, 315–35. W. M. Watt, *The Formative Period of Islamic Thought* (Edinburgh, 1973), provides a competent overview of the theological and ideological debate, but he has little to say about the specific question of religious authority.

42   The "imperialization" of Islamic political culture began early. See Oleg Grabar, *The Formation of Islamic Art* (New Haven, Conn., 1973) on the six-kings fresco at Quṣayr ʿAmra, pp. 45–58; W. M. Watt, "God's Caliph," in *Iran and Islam,* ed. C. E. Bosworth (Edinburgh, 1971), 565–71. The integration of Sassanian themes and values within Islamic political thought is reflected in many texts from the late ninth and early tenth century: Ibn Qutayba, "The Book of Government," trans. J. Horovitz, *Islamic Culture* 4 (1930): 171–98, 331–62, 487–530; 5 (1931): 1–27; *Livre de la couronne,* trans. C. Pellat (Paris, 1954); Hilāl al-Ṣābiʾ, *Rusūm Dār al- Khilāfa: The Rules and Regulations of the ʿAbbasid Court,* trans. E. A. Salem (Beirut, 1977). In the present volume, Jacob Lassner (Chapter 11) examines the connection between the ʿAbbasid caliphate and early Iranian statehood.

43   The most richly documented and suggestive discussion of the tension between Arabian tribal mores and Islam remains a century-old monograph of Ignaz Goldziher, "Muruwwa and Din," in *Muslim Studies,* trans. C. R. Barber and S. M. Stern, 2 vols. (London, 1967–71), 1:11–136.

44   The process of Arabization (ethnic and linguistic) is much alluded to in the literature but is not satisfactorily analyzed anywhere.

45   These issues are developed in Grabar, *Formation,* throughout; see esp. 206–13.

46   See the expectations expressed above, at nn. 3–4.

CHAPTER 2

Teleology and the Significance of Change

MICHAEL G. MORONY

Teleology in the modern interpretation of the past is the identification of a consequence as a cause. Aristotle is to be thanked for this problem because he defined the "final" cause as the purpose or end (*telos*) for which something was done.[1] But, although the reason one has for doing something may be expected to contribute to the outcome, it is teleological to say that a result necessarily, and without supporting evidence, was intended.

Aristotle also said that purpose operated as the "final" cause both in intelligent beings and in nature.[2] Since, in nature, like produces like, the parent is the active agent or "efficient" cause of that into which the offspring will grow,[3] while the "final" cause, the potential form which the offspring realizes, is inactive.[4] Nevertheless, even in nature, living things have a drive to realize their potential; according to John Randall, "acorns 'strive' to become oak trees, eggs 'strive' to become chickens."[5] In modern biology the concept of a drive or striving in living things for the actualization (*entelecheia*) of their natural potential (*dynamis*) has been used to explain self-preservation and growth.[6] As a result teleology is built into biological models of history and lurks behind references to organic growth and natural development, which are inconceivable without having to proceed in some direction toward some end.

One aspect of teleology, then, lies in determining the significance of historical change in terms of its outcome. In particular, the differences between classical and Late Antiquity may be examined with regard to what died out or disappeared and with regard to what appeared that was new. The former procedure sometimes treats the fate of classical urban traditions or polytheistic religion in a nostalgic way. The latter tends to focus attention on those new elements that seem to be protomedieval in a teleological way. *Coloni* (proto-serfs), a Christian emperor, a pope, a state-supported church, Benedictine monasticism, and Germanic kingdoms are represented as important new developments mainly because they appear to be precedents for or contributed to

21

conditions in medieval western Europe. The same may be said of proto-
Islamic features of Late Antiquity, such as the expansion of pastoralism, when
they are selected for emphasis.

Although changes during Late Antiquity tend to be considered as more significant, teleology may also be found in the treatment of early Islamic history.
It is contained in assumptions that when Muḥammad began preaching he intended to accomplish what he had by the time he died, or that because Muslims created a universal empire by the early eighth century, they had been
motivated from the beginning by the belief that Islam was a universal religion.[7] It is equally teleological to overrate the importance of Shiʿism in the
first/seventh century, especially in comparison with Kharijism, to allow the
tragic death of Ḥusayn at Karbalāʾ to overshadow the battle of al-Ḥarra,[8] to
focus attention to the Banū Marwān during the second *fitna* at the expense of
the Banū al-Zubayr,[9] or to see the fall of the Banū Marwān during the third
fitna only in terms of the ultimately victorious ʿAbbasid propaganda while ignoring the internal problems of the Marwānī regime.[10] In other words, the
only important acorns are those that become oaks.

One problem with such a teleological determination of significance is that it
minimizes differences over time since Late Antiquity and emphasizes continuities from Late Antiquity to medieval Europe, Byzantium, and the Islamic
world. The most important changes are considered to be those between classical and Late Antiquity. Examples are easily found. For Peter Brown, a fore-
most interpreter of this period, Late Antiquity "littered the future with
so many irremoveable institutions" such as Roman law codes, the Catholic
church, the Christian empire, and the monastery.[11] Jacob Neusner argues that
the Yerushalmi Talmud deserves attention because (1) it indicates the start of
the "modern" period in the history of Judaism, (2) conditions described in it
are recognizable today, and (3) it survived.[12] With support from Brown,
Neusner describes how, once the old order had crumbled in the third century,
"the rubble of the classical age was reshaped into the foundations of the medieval world" during the fourth century, which then "looked forward to a long
and continuous future, with institutions stretching towards Europe and the
Middle Ages."[13] Among these enduring, normative, protomedieval institutions was the social order of Talmudic Judaism under the authority of rabbis.[14]

Late Antiquity is thus turned into a transition zone between classical antiquity and the medieval world without having any distinctive characteristics of
its own. Neusner, consistent with his own view, makes Late Antiquity disap-
pear between the end of antiquity and the beginning of the Middle Ages in the
period from A.D. 200 to 400.[15] Brown's view is more problematic because he
sees Late Antiquity as lasting for six hundred years (A.D. 150 to 750), which
is rather long for a mere transition period. Still, his emphasis is on change.
Although it is customary to illustrate the impact of ascetic piety in fifth-

century Gaul by the difference between Ausonius and Paulinus of Nola, Brown also finds "the silent turning of an age" in the controversy over sexuality between Augustine and his younger contemporary Julian of Eclanum. The view in ancient medicine, represented by Galen and others, that sexuality is an uncomplicated physiological drive for the purpose of reproduction, subject to social control and individual choice, is contrasted with the Christian view of reproduction as compensation for the loss of immortality after the Fall of Adam. But Augustine, in fact, went further and regarded *concupiscentia carnis* as a lifelong psychological drive, beyond conscious control by the will, imposed on humans as punishment since the Fall. It could be restrained through marriage but could never be entirely tamed and remained a mark of permanent human weakness.[16] Brown, however, warns his readers to be "careful not to exaggerate the immediate consequences for the Latin Church of the triumph of Augustine's opinions. The moral texture of late Roman Christian society did not change dramatically," but it took centuries of "steady drizzle for many of Augustine's ideas to work their way deep into the soil of Latin Christianity." Nevertheless, Augustine laid down "the outlines of the momentous choices that would slowly separate" Latin Christians from Eastern Christians, Jews, and Muslims.[17] It is the eventuality of this statement that amounts to a teleological determination of significance. Augustine was not typical of his time in many ways, and understanding him does not necessarily mean that we have understood the fifth century. Similarly, Neusner concedes that the fourth-century rabbis' view of themselves as being in God's image may not have been very popular, "but in the time to come, the rabbis would become Israel's model for sanctification."[18] Since the ideas of Augustine on sexuality or the rabbis' self-image were of little significance at the time, their significance is judged in terms of later consequences or legacies. Why not? Surely consequences are important.

The reason is that the teleological determination of what constitutes significant change selects features that were only alternatives when they first appeared, merely because they survived. It begs the question why certain alternatives succeeded while others failed. Who preferred or opposed them? Whose interests did they serve? Who preserved the ideas of Augustine and the rabbis, and why? Our own view of what the important changes were during Late Antiquity is very likely to be affected by the loss of information from that period, and by the selective transmission of information by the winners. The rabbis who preserved their own views in the Talmud cannot reasonably be expected to have transmitted much objective information about Samaritans or apostates (*minnim*) any more than representatives of the Roman church would have preserved unbiased information about Arians, Pelagians, or Donatists.

In addition, a teleological determination of significance is made with the advantage of hindsight and in terms of what is important to people today. The teleological significance of Late Antiquity, in particular, appears to be semi-apologetic in tone and intended to justify paying attention to this period by appealing to recognition by a modern audience. Contemporaries living during Late Antiquity had no way of knowing how things would turn out, as Neusner notes,[19] and may have considered other things to be more important. Julian of Eclanum was probably more typical of the fifth century than was Augustine. Neusner, in fact, identifies the contemporary significance of the Yerushalmi Talmud in the fourth century as the triumph of "certainty over doubt, authority over disintegration, salvation over chaos, above all, hope and confidence in an age of despair."[20] This would certainly be significant even if there had never been a future for rabbis. The fact that there turned out to be a future is evidence of successful adaptation.

There is also a tendency in practice to emphasize specifically those features of life in the Mediterranean world and western Asia that spread to northwestern Europe and survived there. Not only does this rest on unjustified assumptions about the monolithic nature of the late Roman world, but it assumes that what existed in Syria or Egypt (such as monasticism) was more important for Britain than it was for Syria or Egypt.

But acorns do not always become oak trees; sometimes they are eaten by squirrels.[21] These other acorns, distinctive circumstances that existed only during Late Antiquity, are at least equally significant. The historical "dead ends" or alternatives that failed during this period include the sectarian gnosticism of Marcionites and Manichaeans; the political dominance of Christians in Syria, Egypt, North Africa, and Spain that lasted for only three hundred years; the political dominance of Arian and Semi-Arian Christianity in the fourth century; state-supported Magianism in Iran from the third to the seventh century; Vandalic North Africa; Visigothic Spain; the brief Jewish dominance in the Yemen in the early sixth century; the degree of social stratification; and the degree of centralized, bureaucratic, hierarchic government. From early Islamic history the most notable alternatives that failed include the rival "prophets" in Arabia at the time of Muḥammad's death,[22] the Zubayrī movement during the second *fitna*,[23] the Khārijī movements during the second and third *fitnas* in the east (except for ʿUmān), and the Qadarī program of Yazīd b. al-Walīd.[24] There are other examples, but these will serve to illustrate the point.

Why are such distinguishing aspects significant? First, an understanding of this period would be incomplete without including them. Second, some of them were considered more important by contemporaries than were those that ultimately contributed to future developments. Third, some of these circumstances were important because of the reactions they provoked. How likely is Augustine to have said what he did if he had not been exposed to

Manichaeans? Fourth, the reasons for the failure or disappearance of such distinctive conditions may help to put the significance of those conditions that survived into perspective and to explain why the latter were more successful or adaptable. Fifth, such circumstances alone enable us to appreciate the contrasts and to identify the changes from one period to another.

It would be trite to point out that all periods are transition periods in some way. Not only does Late Antiquity deserve to be understood in its own terms, as any period does, but we need to ask what makes change significant and to whom. We should also realise that historical significance is one of the most difficult concepts to treat or to measure, because ultimately it involves subjective judgments.

NOTES

1 Aristotle *Physica* 2.3. See also Charlie Dunbar Broad, "Mechanical and Teleological Causation," in his *Induction, Probability, and Causation* (Dordrecht, 1968), 159–83, and Richard Sorabji, *Necessity, Cause, and Blame: Perspectives on Aristotle's Theory* (Ithaca, N.Y., 1980), 152–81.
2 Aristotle *Physica* 2.5 (196b), 8 (198b–199a).
3 Aristotle *De partibus animalium*, 1 (641b.23–31, 33–642a.1). See also H. Weiss, *Kausalität und Zufall in der Philosophie des Aristotles* (Basel, 1942), 64–65.
4 Aristotle *De generatione et corruptione* 2.9 (324b, 335b.7–8).
5 John Randall, *Aristotle* (New York, 1960), 127.
6 H. Dreisch, *The Science and Philosophy of the Organism*, 2 vols. (London, 1908), 2:135–51; E. S. Russell, *The Directiveness of Organic Activities* (Cambridge, 1945), 91. Russell defends teleology.
7 The universality of Islam as a motive for conquest is discussed critically by F. Gabrieli, *Muhammad and the Conquests of Islam* (New York, 1968), 103–4, 107.
8 M. J. Kister, "The Battle of the Harra: Some Socio-Economic Aspects," in *Studies in Memory of Gaston Wiet*, ed. M. Rosen-Ayalon (Jerusalem, 1977), 33–49.
9 This appears to be the case in the way the subject is defined by A. A. ʿAbd Dixon, *The Umayyad Caliphate, 65–86/684–705* (London, 1971); G. Rotter, *Die Umayyaden und der zweite Bürgerkrieg 680–692* (Wiesbaden, 1982); and R. Sellheim, "Der zweite Bürgerkrieg im Islam (680–692)," *Sitzungsberichte der Wissenschaftliche Gesellschaft an der Johann Wolfgang Goethe-Universität Frankfurt/Main*, vol. 8, no. 4 (1969): 87–111.
10 Hodgson, *Venture of Islam*, 1:272–75.
11 Peter Brown, *Religion and Society in the Age of Saint Augustine* (New York, 1972), 13.
12 Jacob Neusner, *Judaism in Society: The Evidence of the Yerushalmi: Toward the*

Natural History of a Religion (Chicago, 1983), xi. The second subtitle is significant: Neusner employs an extended biological metaphor of comparing specimens to each other (x, xiv–xvi).

13 Ibid., 3.

14 Ibid., x–xi, 248–49.

15 Ibid., xii, 246–47.

16 Peter Brown, "Sexuality and Society in the Fifth Century A.D.: Augustine and Julian of Eclanum," in *Tria Corda: Scritti in onore di Arnaldo Momigliano*, ed. E. Gabba (Como, 1983), 55–57, 60, 63–67.

17 Ibid., 69–70.

18 Neusner, *Judaism in Society*, 252.

19 Ibid., 3, 19.

20 Ibid., 17, 26, 247, 253. Neusner (xx, 198) is also concerned with the teleology of the Yerushalmi Talmud itself. It is intended to accomplish the salvation of individual Jews in the world to come and the salvation of Jews as a group by their return to Jerusalem and the restoration of the Temple. But he eschews teleology in the historical formation of the Yerushalmi Talmud and opposes the idea that at the beginning "the decision was made to do the work precisely in the way in which, two hundred years later, the work turns out to have been done" (70). Its formation was rather the work of the final redactors.

21 Randall, *Aristotle*, 233.

22 E. Shoufani, *Al-Riddah and the Muslim Conquest of Arabia* (Toronto, 1973), 75, 83–84, 91–94.

23 ʿAbd Dixon, *Umayyad Caliphate,* discusses the miserliness of ʿAbdullah b. al-Zubayr (p. 16), his relationship to al-Mukhtār (30ff., 55ff.), the nature of support for him (140–41), and the reasons for his failure, but gives little indication of what, if anything, he stood for. Rotter (*Die Umayyaden*, 1, 54–58) is much the same.

24 J. van Ess, "Les Qadarites et la Gailānīya de Yazīd III," *Studia Islamica* 31 (1970): 269–86. For another example from the third *fitna* see W. F. Tucker, "ʿAbd Allāh ibn Muʿāwiya and the Janāhiyya: Rebels and Ideologues of the Late Umayyad Period," *Studia Islamica* 51 (1980): 39–57.

PART II

The Interactions of Cosmopolitan
and Local Cultures

Hostages, Philosophers, Pilgrims, and the Diffusion of Ideas in the Late Roman Mediterranean and Near East

JOHN F. MATTHEWS

My theme in this paper, the diffusion of cultural understanding within the Mediterranean world and in its relations with its neighbors, is a large one, which I have tried to "scale down" to more manageable proportions by selecting certain categories of travelers to whom a cultural role attaches, more or less directly, because of the purpose and outcome of their travel. The size and complexity of the issues involved need no emphasis; they include, among other matters, the role of late Roman government and the formation of its diplomatic policy; the knowledge of alien, especially eastern, cultures, and their significance in the development of a classical "world view"; and trade relations with India and the East and the moral preoccupation with luxury and decline generated by these relations. I am aware that my choice of travelers may seem arbitrary in relation to the magnitude of such issues, but I propose to make light of this objection by presenting immediately yet a further category of "involuntary traveler," that of the castaway.

   It is hardly surprising that the theme of the castaway has been one of great, and sometimes of profoundly serious, appeal in literature, for these travelers present in a particularly colorful form the question of the confrontation of strange cultures and their mutual understanding. To find oneself bewitched by a sorceress and one's companions turned into farmyard animals, in a landscape that had appeared familiar and welcoming, is nothing if not a culture shock of major dimensions, and the theme of the unexpected cultural consequences of unplanned travel recurs constantly in literature after the *Odyssey*. It is not fortuitous that Medea the sorceress comes from outside the Greek world, from the regions beyond the Hellespont explored, with varying degrees

29

of intention, by the Argonauts; I think too of Sinbad the Sailor and Gulliver, not to mention those science fiction stories of modern times that plant space travelers in distant worlds (or alien beings on ours) and then explore the communications that take place between visitors and residents. (I say this while noting the reluctance of the writers of popular science fiction to envisage the social structures, as opposed to the magical technologies, of times far in the future and societies very unlike our own: how often does one see such societies equipped with devices for time travel and instant universal destruction, but apparently governed by the political structures of the distant past, with councils of elders, praetorian guards and consuls, and names and costumes reminiscent of classical Greece and Rome, Mycenae, or ancient Assyria?).

Above all, the theme of the castaway generates curious stories, and I want to begin with one of these, as told by the elder Pliny in the first century. It is the tale, widely enjoyed by classical historians, of a freedman of the tax collector Annius Plocamus who, while assessing the taxes payable at ports of the Red Sea in the time of Claudius, was blown off course and found himself cast up on the shores of Ceylon.[1] It was from this event and its sequel, noted Pliny, that the Romans first acquired a "fuller knowledge" of that island. In six months the freedman had learned the language of the Ceylonese and could communicate with his hosts, to whom he gave an account (one would love to have heard it) of the Roman emperors. For their part, the Ceylonese were very taken by the honesty of the emperors, judging this by their visitor's carrying with him denarii bearing the portraits of different emperors, all of the same weight!

To discover more, the Ceylonese sent an embassy to Rome under one Rachias (i.e., Rajah), and it was from this embassy, according to Pliny, that the Romans first learned details of the topography and customs of Ceylon. Pliny's account is particularly interesting in that it takes up first those customs and practices best explained by direct and deliberate comparison between the two cultures. There was greater wealth in Ceylon (so it seemed to the visitors) but that in Rome was put "to greater use" (*in maiorem usum*), a comment that should surprise those historians who suppose the ancient world to have been totally devoid of any economic theory. In Ceylon, no one has a slave, people get up at sunrise, and there is no midday siesta. The buildings there are of only moderate height, the price of corn is never inflated, and there are no law courts or litigation. As for the king, he is chosen for gentleness and lack of children; if he has a child he is deposed to avert the risk of hereditary monarchy. The King is advised by a panel of thirty "governors," who may by a majority impose sentence of capital punishment, appeals against which, if upheld by a further panel of seventy, lead to the disgrace of the thirty, and so on. . . . These points, which I have mentioned in the order in which they are set out by Pliny, seem to reflect systematic comparison between Ceylonese and Roman modes of life and government, it being natural that the first stage in mutual understanding should relate to the comparison and exploration of common features and intelligible points of contrast between them.

Pliny's account also yields the remark that Ceylon is "placed by nature beyond the bounds of the civilized world" (*extra orbem a natura relegata*), especially in relation to the luxury of living standards there—a frequent preoccupation of the moralizing Roman. The remark is rather anomalous, given that Pliny has also described, on the authority of Rachias, whose father had been personally involved, how the Ceylonese traded with the still more distant Chinese, across a river on whose banks were stacked goods for exchange, to be accepted or rejected in a sort of "silent trade," as the Chinese thought fit.[2] What is beyond the civilized world for one observer may be the center of it for another, and Pliny appears not fully to realize that the Ceylonese found the Romans as exotic as the Romans found them.

The Ceylonese were for the Romans a new contact, made possible in unexpected circumstances by the accident that had befallen the freedman of Annius Plocamus, and in this respect not an extension of existing contacts. Equally interesting, though with a longer and more complicated history, is the Indian embassy that came to see Augustus in 20 B.C.; it was seen at Syrian Antioch by Nicolaus of Damascus, whose account was incorporated by the geographer Strabo (15.1.73). Three ambassadors had got as far as Antioch, though the Greek letter they carried indicated that there had been more, the others having died on the journey; the letter was written by one Poros, a ruler of "600 other kings" who wished nevertheless to become Augustus' friend. (It is hard to know whether his expression indicates recognition of, or is meant diplomatically to conceal, Poros' real conception of the true extent of Augustus' power.) The ambassadors brought with them gifts, which were presented to Augustus on Samos by eight servants clad in loincloths: namely, a man (whom Strabo himself had seen) born without arms, callously called by his Greco-Roman observers a "Herm," who could stretch a bow and aim arrows, and hold a trumpet to his lips, all with his feet; huge vipers and a serpent ten cubits long; a river tortoise of three cubits; and a "partridge larger than a vulture." And last, there came with the embassy an Indian philosopher who, going on to Athens, was initiated into the Eleusinian mysteries and then, "in order to preserve at its height the happiness of his life," anointed himself and, wearing only a loincloth, leapt laughing onto a funeral pyre and burned himself to death. The Athenians inscribed on his tomb that this was "Zarmanochegas the Indian from Bargosa, who immortalized himself according to the native customs of his country" (*kata ta patria Indōn ethē*).[3]

One is prevented from seeing in this a culture shock of immense dimensions by understanding that, as both Strabo and Plutarch realized, the philosopher, in immolating himself, was following the example of a predecessor who had done just the same thing before Alexander the Great.[4] The scene is transposed from India to Athens, the audience is Roman princeps rather than oriental conqueror; yet it was precisely because of the campaigns of Alexander, and all that went with them, that the philosopher could know that his act would be understood as *kata ta patria,* in a tradition of Indian philosophy with which the Athenians would be familiar. Eccentric behavior it might be, but it could be comprehended and treated with the respect due to recognized ancestral custom. It has been well emphasized by Albrecht Dihle just how dependent is Strabo's entire account of India on the descriptions of that land brought back three and a half centuries before by men who had accompanied the campaigns of Alexander the Great.[5] It was these campaigns—and little had been learned since—that provided the cultural context within which the customs of an alien people could be understood.

On the other side, something can be said of the Indian view of the classical world, for people known as "Yavanas"—that is, "Ionians" or Greeks—are seen from time to time in early Tamil poetry as residents in or visitors to southern India and its cities.[6] Some appear as merchants "whose fine ships, the marvellous works of the Yavanas, stirring the white foam of the Periyar, river of Kerala, come with gold and depart with pepper" from the rich city of Muziris,[7] or who "bring in their fine ships sweet-smelling wine to be served to the king in vessels of chased gold, by girls with jeweled wrists" in palaces lit by oil lamps in the form of statuettes made, again, by Yavanas; some as skilled craftsmen employed in the building of palaces, or as flourishing inhabitants of a wealthy quarter of the city of Puhar (to be identified with Ptolemy's Chaberis),[8] or, in a very different image, as fierce bodyguards of Tamil princes on hunting expeditions, or as Yavanas of barbarian speech living in mountainous regions to the north. It is an intriguing variety of roles. There is no need to doubt that the merchants coming to Muziris were actually Greeks (that is, Greco-Romans) sailing from the Red Sea to southern India and back by using the monsoons. Periyar is still the name of the chief river of the region, coming to the sea through lagoons at Cranganur; the city of Muziris, which stood here, is shown on the Peutinger Map as possessing a temple of Augustus, a monument no more incredible than the temple of the imperial cult known to have stood in the early second century at Vologesias in Parthia.[9] "Ionian" craftsmen cause no surprise either, when one thinks of the apocryphal Acts of St. Thomas, whose hero is brought to northwest India by King Gundaphoros (an authentic king of the period) for his skill as a builder of "pillars, temples and royal palaces."[10] The fearsome royal bodyguards can readily be taken as mercenaries from the partly Hellenized Afghan and Bactrian communities in the far north. Although the word *Yavanas,* handed on from Sanskrit to Tamil, comes later to denote Arabia and Muslim countries, the Muslim inhabitants of the Malabar Coast, and even Turks, the circumstantial evidence supports its interpretation in these early Tamil poems as denoting Greek-speaking "foreigners" from the north, or from the eastern provinces of the Roman Empire.[11]

Against this, partially successful, understanding by the one world of the other achieved by Rome and India, we can set the uncomprehending nature, already hinted at by Pliny, of the mutual contacts between Rome and China. In the late first century A.D. it appears that a Chinese man turned up at T'iao-tche or Mesene (Maishan) at the head of the the Persian Gulf as an envoy of the Han governor Pan Tch'ao, asking how he could "cross the sea" to the Roman Empire.[12] The men of Mesene, who told him nothing of the land route through Parthia, with equal cunning warned him off the sea journey. So long was it, and so unpredictable the winds, they told him, that though in favorable circumstances the journey could take as little as three months, in unfavorable circumstances it could take as long as two years. Travelers took provisions for three years, and some even died on the journey, from sheer homesickness! So deterred, the envoy decided not to go—and the "wily merchants" of Maishan kept their monopoly of the trade; they had no wish to surrender their lucrative role as middlemen to direct contact between the two great empires of Rome and China.[13]

The Chinese annals that record this story also preserve a description of the eastern Roman Empire, with its four hundred cities and their walls built of stone; its agriculture, trees (especially pine and cypress), and vegetation; its public relay system and paved roads leading to the "royal capital"; its gold and silver coinage; its administration with written records; and its people, regular in features and of middle height, with barbered hair and embroidered clothing, honest in trade and expert in the making of perfume.[14] This is recognizably, once one is given the hint, the Levantine Roman Empire. The limits of the Chinese understanding of the empire, however, appear with equal vividness in their description of the "king," or emperor, who is alleged to go about on a white carriage with a black canopy, accompanied by drums and banners and followed by a man carrying a bag into which his subjects throw their letters and petitions, to be read and judged by the king when he returns to his palace. And what are we to make of the description of the Roman emperor as not appointed in perpetuity but chosen for his wisdom, on the understanding that he may be deposed in case of disaster, ill omen, or unseasonable wind or rain, and in such circumstance will accept his deposition equably and without protest?[15]

The oddity of this description of the Roman emperor surely reduces to a perfectly intelligible interpretation, once we recognize the Chinese word for the Roman empire, Ta-Ts'in, as denoting the province of Syria, and realize that the potentate I have described is actually not the emperor at all but Roman provincial governors as they are sent out and receive successors according to

Roman decisions and conventions. Governors no doubt were replaced if they were the victims or perpetrators of misfortune or disaster, and the *legati pro praetore Syriae* of course held office and left it at the emperor's pleasure; this aside, what we have in the Han accounts is simply a Chinese interpretation, distorted but not unintelligible, of the operation of Roman senatorial careers in the emperor's service. If a man left office, he must naturally have been deposed; what other reason could there be? One is led to wonder what the provincial populations of the Near East itself, used to the rise and fall of Hellenistic dynasts, made of the replacement of their provincial governors by orders emanating, in circumstances entirely hidden from them, from Rome.

A similar failure of understanding arises in the case of the celebrated embassy sent to the Chinese in A.D. 166 under the emperor Ngan-touen (or An-tun: that is, Marcus Aurelius Antoninus); it was the first time, so it was said, that contacts between Rome and China had been made after many years of obstruction by the Parthians, whose policy it was to prevent direct communications between the two empires.[16] The emissary passed by the province of Je-nan, modern Tonkin (the district of Hanoi), to China and there offered as his gifts elephant tusks, rhinoceros horns, and tortoise shell. The Chinese concluded from these gifts that the rumors they had heard of the wealth of the Roman Empire were greatly exaggerated—quite misguidedly, if only because the gifts mentioned were products, not of the Roman Empire at all, but of the lands to its east, notably India.[17] The "envoy" assumes the more manageable proportions of an individual, no doubt again from Syria, claiming imperial support for his venture and offering to his Chinese hosts gifts he had picked up on his journey to the east.

So far I have tried to keep together the two facets of my subject: the actual process, whether random or deliberate (or a combination of the two), by which contacts were made between one society and another and, equally important, the cultural framework within which mutual understanding was attempted. Now, Strabo noted that knowledge of India had been opened up by those who had traveled there with the army of Alexander the Great, and that the private individuals who subsequently made the journey were neither perceptive nor interested enough in what they saw to be of any use to a serious geographer (15.1.4). A similar remark is made by Ptolemy (1.11.6) in describing the knowledge transmitted to his predecessor the geographer Marinus of Tyre by a "Macedonian"—that is, a Greek Syrian—merchant named Maes Titianus of the route from Lithinos Pyrgos ("Stone Tower," identified as Tashkurghān) to the metropolis of the Seres. Maes Titianus, remarked Ptolemy, had recorded the distance, not having gone himself but sending agents, but Marinus "appeared not to believe the stories told by the traders with those parts." Marinus had commented that men intent on trade cared little about truthful observation and were apt to inflate their self-esteem by exaggerating distances. Yet someone, merchant or not, had reported that the Chinese metropolis of Thinae did not, as was apparently supposed, have walls of bronze or anything else worthy of note (7.3.6).

Historians of the Roman Empire have often been struck by the lack of consistently organized attempts by the government itself to undertake or sponsor foreign exploration on any sort of official basis.[18] This is an aspect of a much broader issue, the failure of ancient governments in general to establish relations with foreign powers on a permanent footing—if by this one means, for example, the foundation of foreign legations supported by an organized diplomatic service, and institutions for the exchange of information and the conduct of espionage. This failure is not really so surprising when one reflects on the conditions suggested by Garrett Mattingly as necessary for the development of diplomatic institutions in early Renaissance Italy: numerous cities in a restricted area, possessing superabundant social energies and similar and therefore conflicting aims; the absence of any single dominant power that had no need to fear others; and a common language and culture that made communications a matter of great facility.[19] It takes no great insight to see that these are in general conditions opposite to those applying in the Roman Empire, with its immense geographical area and wide divergences of language and culture, not only beyond but also within its frontiers. Mattingly's criteria come closest to being satisfied, say, in Asia Minor of the Antonine Age, had other essential conditions, like political freedom, been present; apart from this, one would imagine, the cultural and economic divergences within the empire, and between it and its neighbors, would have tended to inhibit, rather than to encourage, the formation of permanent institutions for the discovery and exchange of information, even when the conduct of successful political relations in the narrow sense would seem overwhelmingly to have required them.

We must not underestimate the extent of the officially sanctioned exploration and discovery that was conducted in Roman times. Both Strabo and, particularly, Pliny the Elder provide repeated examples of missions undertaken to prepare for military campaigns, and of the geographical and cultural information gained as a result. These examples range, in the case of Pliny, from Armenia, Arabia, and Ethiopia through the Libyan desert and Mauretania to Gaul, Britain, and the North Sea.[20] Strabo gives a particularly full description of the Nabataeans, who later formed the province of Arabia;[21] and we must add to such information the constant flow of reports sent in by provincial legates and governors, and accounts given by them to emperors after their departure from office. The extent of this flow of information has been doubted, but I would assume, to take only one example, that reports made by the Neronian governor of Moesia, Plautius Silvanus, whose exploits in negotiating with barbarian tribes, settling them on the Roman side of the Danube, receiving hostages for their good behavior, and so on, are recorded in his funerary inscription from Tibur, played an important part in determining both the general shape and the specific detail of Flavian policy on the Rhine and Danube frontiers.[22] Then we have the account of the Black Sea regions given to Hadrian by his governor of Cappadocia, Arrian, combining literary allusions to Xenophon, accounts of diplomatic relations with client kings, and descriptions of the quality and condition of imperial and other statues in cities of the region;[23] not to mention the meticulous work of exploration and annotation implied by the reliefs of Trajan's Column at Rome. For all their qualities of accuracy and observed detail, the sculptures can give only a most incomplete impression of the fieldwork, documentation, and applied draftsmanship that went into their design.[24]

The extent of information acquired in this way about foreign lands and peoples was considerable and can easily be documented. Yet it tends by definition to concern those peoples and areas over which war was conducted or contemplated, *at those times when this was so:* Strabo's information about India, as we saw, had essentially not been updated since the campaigns of Alexander, the last time that war had been made in those regions. Now, Strabo also remarked that the expansion of the Roman and Parthian empires had made available new information about regions hitherto imperfectly known, mentioning in the case of the latter Hyrcania, Bactria, and the regions to the north of them.[25] Yet when Strabo wrote, war against the Parthians was not seriously contemplated, and to explain how this information had come to the West we have to look to those more informal means by which communication was maintained between Rome and its neighbors—namely, to that "traffic in embassies, fugitive princes, hostages, letters [and] gifts" acknowledged by Fergus Millar without (it seems to me) sufficient indication of the importance of these forms of traffic as, in effect, the replacement for organized exploration and diplomacy.[26] It was to these more personal, social, as well as political relationships that were "displaced" those diplomatic functions that would have been conducted by permanent legations and other such institutions, had they existed. To put this the other way round: the absence of such *institutions* in no way implies the absence of diplomatic *functions,* or of the forms of imperial policy-making that these made possible.

The contribution of the merchant, as always in these circumstances, is pervasive and of central importance. One of the fascinating stories told of the Sassanian monarchs in the so-called Book of the Crown, a ninth-century Arabic handbook attributed (incorrectly) to al-Jāḥiẓ, is intended to illustrate the patience of Chosroes I in exacting vengeance.[27] A slave, believed but not proved guilty of criminal conduct in respect of the royal harem, is set up by Chosroes as a merchant in Byzantium with instructions to keep his ears to the ground and report useful information back to the king. This he does, and after a first, apparently successful, tour of duty is sent back to Byzantium to do the same for a further six years, during which he becomes well known there. At this point Chosroes commissions the making of a silver cup bearing the slave's image as if in intimate conversation with the king, and he gives the cup to another merchant with instructions to trade with Byzantium in such a way that it will fall into the emperor's possession. The cup is duly sold to the emperor, who recognizes on it the portrait of the slave, known to him as a merchant. The emperor realizes, and has the "merchant" agree, that no man of low birth has his portrait engraved on royal cups, and also (to meet pedantic objections from the listeners to the story, at some cost to the logic of his own position) that no slave and nobleman in Persia look identical. He invites him to a feast, ignoring his protestations to be a man of low birth and unworthy of the honor, and then has him arrested and executed in the highest place possible, the top of a high tower—his head being displayed on high and his body cast down to earth. The end of the story, though not strictly relevant here, is worth telling for its disconcerting air of surrealism. Chosroes, on hearing of the execution, had a proclamation made in his own city by a herald to the effect that "anyone meriting death is executed on earth, but he who assaults the honor of the king's wives is executed in the sky." But no one, ends the story, knew what the proclamation meant!

Fairy tales aside, the significance of the role of the merchant, as of modern trade missions, in East-West relations is obvious. An excellent example on the Roman side is the merchant and former bureaucrat Antoninus, who contrived his desertion to the Persians just before the great invasion of Sapor II in 359. Forced to this desperate remedy by debt to the imperial *fiscus,* Antoninus, who knew Greek and Latin from his service in the bureaucracy, devoted himself to collecting all the information he could about Roman military dispositions in Mesopotamia.[28] He was able to do so freely, since as a former merchant he was "very well known in those parts" and could move about without giving cause for suspicion. He finally covered his departure from the Roman Empire by purchasing a farm at its very edge near the river Tigris, which he visited frequently to allay suspicion, before having himself ferried over the river at dead of night. The Persian satrap with whom he arranged this was, as Ammianus Marcellinus specifically says, "known to him already."[29]

I mention the case of Antoninus chiefly because of his counterpart on the Persian side, who also played a prominent role in the events of 359. This was the satrap of Corduene (Kurdistan), Jovinianus—at least, as Ammianus explains, this was his Roman name, since Jovinianus was a foreigner who had adopted his name when he had been "detained as a hostage" in Syria and educated there.[30] It was during his time in Syria that he had come to know Ammianus Marcellinus, who was sent to him on an espionage mission to try to discover the exact scale and intentions of the Persian forces being massed

against the eastern Roman Empire. Ammianus found his way to Jovinianus
across the difficult country and was provided by him with a guide, who went
with Ammianus to a vantage point from which they could see the Persian
army; then, on his return, he rested and was entertained by his old school-
friend. Jovinianus professed nostalgia for the Roman Empire, to which, he
said, he would dearly love to return.[31] As it was, he stayed in his satrapy,
which, as Ammianus clearly implies, he had carried over into the Persian
sphere of influence. To be given as a hostage at all, Jovinianus was obviously
a young man of a noble oriental family, whose stay in Greco-Roman Syria
was a striking extension of his cultural range. In fact, an eastern source shows
him in the explicit role of local dynast, in describing how he settled transhumant Arabs on land in the territory east of Nisibis and Singara, where sedentary occupation and cultivation were possible in the conditions provided by
stable government.[32]

An analogous case from the West is that of a German prince who appears in
Ammianus with the incongruous name "Serapio." His father, Mederichus
(brother of the fierce Alamannic king Chonodomarius), had been "long detained as a hostage in Gaul" and, having become interested in Greek mystery
cults, had his son named Serapio after one of them. Serapio's German name
was Agenarichus.[33]

The exchange of hostages was of course standard practice in the diplomatic
relationships between ancient peoples. The conventions involved, both political and social, were refined and highly complex (there has not to my knowledge been a general study since André Aymard noted the lack of one in an
article published in 1961).[34] The interplay of interests that might be involved
is well illustrated by the views expressed by Augustus in the *Res gestae* and
by Parthian envoys to the Senate in the time of Claudius. For Augustus, Parthian kings and princes sought refuge with him from their own people, offered
their sons as pledges of peace, and sent embassies to request that kings be
provided for them.[35] For the envoys in the time of Claudius, the whole point of
providing princes as hostages was in order that, if they ever grew tired of their
government, they could apply to Senate and emperor for a change.[36] The envoys referred before the Senate to the educational and social advantages of a
sojourn in the Roman Empire, a repeated theme in references to the institution
of hostage exchange. It did not always work out to the advantage of the nomi-
nee, for a regular pattern, at least in Tacitus' accounts of these exchanges, is
of an initial period of popularity followed by dissension and expulsion—the
motive for this often being precisely that the new king was too well versed in
Roman ways for the taste of his compatriots. One king, and there are other
examples like him,[37] had so far forgotten ancestral customs that he not only
rarely went hunting and was indifferent to the practice of horse riding, went
around in a litter, disliked native banquets, and was attended by Greek com-

panions, but also, to cap all this, locked away even the cheapest of his dinner plates! I take this at first sight eccentric ground for complaint to refer to that careless ostentation of wealth that was in itself an expression of an oriental monarchy and a demonstration of its confidence, and so of its power.[38]

Through the exchange of hostages, many cities of the Roman Empire (Rome, Ravenna, and Fréjus are just three of those attested) possessed enclaves of foreign nobles and their sons, which, with the personal attendants allowed the hostages, might form quite considerable communities (they have been well compared with the colonies of English at Florence in the late nineteenth and early twentieth centuries, the setting of E. M. Forster's novel *A Room with a View,* a beautiful celebration of the superiority of insight over ignorance and the awakening effect, for some, of foreign travel). On one occasion the emperor Caligula faked an attack on Germans by taking prisoners from his own German bodyguard; he then rounded up a number of German hostages who were having their lessons at a school of literature and took them to his headquarters as if he had captured them in war.[39] In rather similar circumstances, though not strictly involving hostages, when the Gallic notables Julius Florus and Julius Sacrovir initiated a rebellion against Tiberius in A.D. 21, their first move was to seize sons of the Gallic nobility who were devoting themselves to liberal studies at Augustodunum (Autun).[40]

The cultural implications of the extensive and regular exchange of hostages were considerable, best documented from an earlier period of Roman history. In the late Hellenistic period Rome and Italian cities contained many Greeks interned there, or detained as hostages. There are many examples, for instance, the one thousand Achaeans, including the historian Polybius, deported to Italy in 167 B.C.; when they were repatriated in 150, only three hundred survivors remained of an evidently elderly original contingent.[41] The successors of one hundred hostages taken from Carthage in 202 B.C. were still in Rome, by the usual exchange arrangements, in 168; they would remain there, in a curious but not inconsequential reversal of the principle of Overseas Scholarships for Higher Education, until the tribute agreed to after the end of the Second Punic War was fully paid off.[42] The opulence in which a hostage could live, and the style of life and freedom of movement he could enjoy, are splendidly illustrated by the account in Polybius of the escape from Italy of King Demetrius in 162 B.C. In a plot hatched with the help and advice of his friends—including Polybius, whom he had first met at a boar hunt—Demetrius contrived his escape by getting himself invited out to dinner and then leaving the party as if he felt ill. He had meanwhile covered his tracks by sending slaves to Circeii with nets and dogs to arrange a hunting party, but instead of joining them he slipped away to Ostia and took ship there. He was well out to sea before his departure was realized, and nothing could be done about it.[43] Polybius himself, though a political internee, through his friendship with Scipio Aemilianus ac-

quired the use of a fleet with which he explored the eastern Mediterranean and reached the Atlantic coast of Mauretania;[44] and F. W. Walbank has made it very clear how Polybius' contact with Greek exiles in Italy enabled him to write a history broader in scope and sympathy, and certainly more critical of Rome, than the Romans could ever have written for themselves: it was, too, a view of events in Greece that he could not have acquired had he stayed there.[45] This is more than the obvious practical advantage of foreign travel for the aspiring historian who must seek out his sources; it is a genuine cultural enlargement on the part both of Romans and of Greeks, which was absolutely fundamental to the development of both parties. At a later date, Pliny the Elder remarked similarly (*Hist. Nat.* 6.23) on the great increase of knowledge of inner Asia Minor made possible by the campaigns of Corbulo, by the kings sent from there as suppliants to Rome, and by their children as hostages. There is no reason that such increase in knowledge should be confined to the facts of geography and economic life, even if this happens, by reason of his own interests, to be the emphasis adopted by Pliny.

The relative deficiency of the Roman imperial government in sponsoring foreign exploration and in organizing the collection of information about foreign peoples should not then be taken to imply that this information was not collected, or that it was not available for the use of the government. The presence in Rome of one thousand Achaeans, one hundred Carthaginians, forty Aetolians, as later of the Bohemian king Maroboduus at Ravenna,[46] of Jovinianus at Antioch, or of Agenarichus, alias Serapio, in Gaul should clearly be allowed for in any assessment of Roman intelligence operations regarding their foreign neighbors, for the hostages moved in high social circles, attended schools with leading Romans and members of the official classes, and learned their languages. The nature of the institution of hostage exchange can best be documented from earlier Roman history, but it continued undiminished and must at all times be taken into account, even if the sources bear no sort of witness to its importance. It is clearly relevant to fifth-century relations between the Romans, the Goths, and the Huns, for example, that the patrician Aetius served three years as a hostage with Alaric and a later period as a hostage with the Huns;[47] or that Fl. Orestes, the father of Romulus Augustulus, was what is described as a "secretary" (*hypographeus*, or *notarius*) to Attila the Hun.[48] This was an appointment, if ever there was one, to stagger the imagination, though as it happens another *notarius* of Attila's is mentioned, one Rusticius, a Latin-speaking prisoner of war from Moesia; he also knew Hunnish and composed Attila's letters.[49] In the other direction, the Ostrogothic king Theodoric spent ten years, between the ages of eight and eighteen, as a hostage at Constantinople. There he received what his panegyrists described as the best Greek education available and was sent back to his people with great gifts by the emperor Leo.[50] The implications of hostage

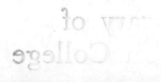

exchange for the mutual understanding between Romans and barbarians about language, national culture, and political aim seem to me not to have been fully realized or studied with sufficient interest. The topic throws floods of light on the conduct of Roman foreign policy and its gathering of intelligence, and on the broader questions of mutual understanding with which I began: and it is in this perspective that I want now to move on, much more briefly, to other categories of travelers.

The role of philosophers in the conduct of political and cultural relations between cities and governments is well recognized. They were among those classes of men whose persuasive gifts werre essential to societies in which public policies were defined and mobilized (and also limited) as much by the spoken as by the written word.[51] Even in this relatively well-defined area anomalies could arise, which may be of great interest in defining the limits of understanding between one side and the other. The Neoplatonist philosopher Eustathius was sent to Persia to try to negotiate peace with Sapor II in 358. He was, wrote Ammianus Marcellinus, "a philosopher and good at persuading" (*philosophus, ut opifex suadendi;* 17.5.15). Some, according to Eunapius' unconsciously revealing account of the embassy, accompanied it in order to see whether Eustathius would retain his persuasive powers before the tyrannical Sapor.[52] So impressed, indeed, was the Persian king that (we are asked to believe) he was within an ace of laying down his tiara and jeweled robe in favor of the philosopher's cloak! But something went wrong, for Sapor's actual reply to the embassy, prompted, it is alleged, by magi in the king's entourage, was rather different. It was to ask why, when the Roman emperor could have sent any number of distinguished men as envoys, he had chosen men "no better than slaves who had enriched themselves?" The emperor had made an error of judgment. He himself had intellectual ambitions, had a soft spot for philosophical (and theological) discourse, and tried, without much success, to write poetry;[53] what impressed Sapor, as Constantius should have realized, was solid social rank and distinction by which he might feel himself to be honored. Nor does Eunapius' narrative give any hint of the procedures of control that had to be undergone by envoys to the Persian king; they had, for example, to report their purpose to successive regional commanders and receive escorts as they advanced on their journey, and, for envoys who came from Syria, to wait at Hit until the king's permission was received for them to proceed further.[54] Their reception at the king's court itself was naturally a matter involving great formality, and even a Neoplatonist philosopher could expect no exception to be made in his favor.

Persia had of course a well-defined role in the "cultural landscape" of the late Roman philosopher, not merely as the origin of "Chaldean" magic and astrology, but also as the royal road, if it lay open, to the wisdom of India.[55]

The philosopher Plotinus is said to have accompanied the Persian campaign of Gordian III in the hope, incredible as it may seem, of making his way to India. In the event, the defeat and death of Gordian left him in some difficulty about how to get back to Antioch.[56] It was alleged by Ammianus Marcellinus that a philosopher's lies were the cause of the outbreak of war between Constantine the Great and Persia, though the details have to be recovered from a much later source, the Byzantine writer Cedrenus.[57] Metrodorus had gone to India to visit the Brahmin wise men and had been greatly honored by them and enriched with gifts from their shrines. In a striking though presumably unhistorical reminiscence of the works of the "Yavanas" in India mentioned earlier, Metrodorus is said also to have taught the Indians how to construct water mills and baths! Returning with his gifts through Persia, in an episode reminiscent of the surveillance of the trade route through Iran exercised earlier by the Parthians, he was stopped by Sapor's agents and much of his wealth confiscated. So at least he told Constantine, who was provoked to write to Sapor demanding the return of the confiscated property unless he wanted war with Persia.

Metrodorus' journey was emulated, with equally interesting, though largely unintentional, consequences, by a successor, Meropius of Tyre.[58] Meropius, returning from India by the sea route around Arabia, was killed by Ethiopians hostile, as they sometimes were, to Rome; but his two young companions, taken to the Ethiopian court, became influential there and initiated the conversion of the people to Christianity, building churches, in the first instance for the benefit of Roman merchants who came by. Eventually one of the young men, Aedesius, returned to Tyre and told his story, many years later, to the church historian Rufinus; the other, Frumentius, was at his own request sent back to Ethiopia as its first bishop, consecrated by Athanasius of Alexandria.[59]

Frumentius' role in Roman diplomatic relations with the Ethiopians of the kingdom of Axum was closely paralleled by the almost contemporaneous activities of the "Indian" Theophilus (he came in fact from the island of Dibous, or Socotra).[60] Theophilus, earlier sent as a "hostage" from his homeland to the Roman Empire and baptized and ordained there by Eusebius of Nicomedia, was dispatched by Constantius II to the kingdom of the Sabaioi, otherwise known as the Homeritae or Himyarites, the ancient kingdom of Sheba in the Yemen; his purpose was to secure the building of a church for the Romans who traveled to the country, and he took with him to aid his petition valuable gifts, including two hundred horses from the imperial studs in Cappadocia; it was evidently quite a fleet that accompanied him. In the event, he was able to found no less than three churches; one at the Himyarite capital, one at the "Roman" emporium of Adane (Aden), and the third at a Persian emporium at the mouth of the Persian Gulf, no doubt in the territory of 'Oman.[61] Theophilus later went further afield in Constantius' interest, on a theological-cum-diplomatic mission to south India (there were Christian communities in those parts also) and, finally, to the kingdom of Axum in which Frumentius resided. It is possible, though not certain, that Theophilus was responsible for the summons (ignored by its recipient) of Constantius to Frumentius to present himself at Alexandria to be "straightened out" theologically by the Arian bishop George—Frumentius' patron Athanasius being now exiled by Constantius.

As in the case of Frumentius, the evangelizing role of Theophilus among the Sabaioi converges with the political and diplomatic connections otherwise attested between them and the Romans; a law of 357 refers to Roman envoys to the Axumites or Homeritae passing through (or rather delaying at) Alexandria on their way there.[62] As in other contexts, the "diplomatic" function in foreign relations is displaced in favor of a cultural, in this case a religious, one, and the emphasis in its performance is shifted from the domain of public policy to that of private interest, without any loss of purpose and possibly with a considerable gain in flexibility and subtlety. The role of Christianity as an instrument of diplomatic policy in this sense clearly has wide implications. One wonders at once about the presbyter of the village of the Gothic martyr Saba, absent as a fugitive in "Romania" from the persecution of Gothic Christians initiated by Athanaric;[63] about the Christian priest sent by the Goths with his followers to make representations to the Romans before the battle of Hadrianople in 378;[64] and indeed about the entire role of the Gothic evangelist Ulfila in Romano-Gothic relations in the mid fourth century, in the sense at least that he will surely through his religious mission have been able to make the views of each party on other issues also more intelligible to the other. The transmission of the Passion of Saint Saba, in the form of a Greek letter to the Cappadocian church, is in itself a document of cultural relations between the occupants, Roman and barbarian, of the lower Danubian basin and Asia Minor in the years preceding the great crossing of the river in 376.[65]

Philosophers and missionaries express an already defined cultural preoccupation rather than create a new one. Yet they were men whose profession made them mobile, and they were from this general point of view, as well as from the more precise one of their intellectual interests, a significant aspect of the maintenance of cultural unity within the Mediterranean world, and in certain respects outside it. They also provide a link with the last category of traveler I wish to discuss, that of the pilgrim.

Philosophers provide this link because they too, as we have seen, had established and followed a tradition of traveling to see personally the "holy places" of their belief, not only in India. Under Constantine the Great an Athenian sophist, Nicagoras, went to the Valley of the Kings in Egypt to view the "syringes" or funeral galleries there. Traveling by means of the public transport system with warrants provided (a point of some interest) by Constantine, Nicagoras added his name to the many others engraved there over centuries to commemorate such journeys of sentiment and cultural allegiance.[66] Almost a century later a Greek poet, rhetorician, and historian, Olympiodorus of Thebes, went to Upper Egypt "in order to see it" and visited the Blemmyes.[67] Reappearing on an embassy to the Huns and on visits to Athens and Rome, Olympiodorus can well be seen as one of the first in a notable tradition of Byzantine diplomat-historians. In a more eccentric vein, Olympiodorus is notable also for his faithful companion of many years, a parrot that could "sing, call its owner's name, dance, and do many other tricks."[68] And it was the campaign of C. Petronius under Nero—to resume a theme mentioned earlier—that had brought back to Rome many details of Ethiopian geography not precisely known before, among them the exact point, beyond the island of Gaugade between Syene and Meroe, at which dog-faced baboons and parrots were seen.[69]

The cultural importance of Christian pilgrimage in the late Roman Empire is great and profound and discussed in a manner that fully meets the claims of its subject in the recent book by David Hunt.[70] For the pilgrim of Bordeaux of the year 333, as Hunt remarks, his journey was from a land in which Christianity had hardly yet begun to make inroads into an "exclusively Biblical world." In the West, without knowledge of the geographical locations, the Bible was "disembodied" from its physical context.[71] Eusebius of Caesarea composed his *Onomasticon,* a gazetteer giving as many contemporary locations as he could for the sites mentioned in the Bible, for the benefit of an eastern Christian audience that wished to put its religion into its historical setting: the work had already been once translated into Latin by the time Jerome set himself to produce a scholarly translation in the late fourth century to meet the needs of a by then rapidly increasing, and ever more exacting, western audience.[72] In the early 380s, too, the pilgrim Egeria was able from personal experience to inform her "sisters" living in Spain of the many holy sites she had seen, each with its specific biblical setting. She could compare the river Euphrates with the familiar Rhone, describe the Christian cults of the city of Edessa and the paganism of nearby Carrhae, and, in the second part of her work, give a long account of the distinctive liturgy of the church of Jerusalem.[73] Beyond Carrhae she could not go, for since the surrender of northeastern Mesopotamia to the Persians in 363, the border was closed and further travel prevented. It is rare but decisive documentation of the effect upon contacts between East and West (at least by the main roads, an important reservation in a region of such open communications for those who enjoyed the mobility) of hostile relations between Rome and Persia.[74]

For the pagan pilgrim, to visit the Tombs of the Kings and the wise men of India or Egypt was naturally an experience satisfying to the emotions and improving of the intellect. For the Christian pilgrim, what was at stake was more definite, it being the explicit claim of Christianity to be a historical religion, the precise point of which was that certain particular events had happened at certain places and at certain times. The broader significance of pilgrimage, and the personal testimony it made available to distant communities of Christians who lacked the opportunity to undertake it themselves, was thus as a direct expression of a feature fundamental to their religion. The "disembodied" Bible in the early fourth-century West therefore acquired theological in addition to merely antiquarian substance through the reports of pilgrims—a development soon extended, on an ever-increasing scale, by the traffic in saints' relics in the late Roman and early medieval periods. From the True Cross on, the Christian ideology of the Roman Empire was strengthened, in distant places, by the transport of relics, a process in which pilgrimage played a central, creative, and significant role.

Further, through the connection of Helena the mother of Constantine with the discovery of the Cross (a connection that as a matter of authentic history first appears only in the late fourth century), through attempts like that of Eusebius of Caesarea to set the Christian Roman emperor in a historic succession deriving from Abraham and the Patriarchs,[75] and through the adherence of the emperors themselves and their supporters to the "physical ideology," as I have outlined it, of the Holy Land and the cult of martyrs—through all these aspects, the developing ideology of a Christian empire was linked with and gained strength from the privately inspired initiatives with which it was in harmony. From Roman relations with India and China, to Abraham and the Patriarchs as facets of the ideology of the Christian empire, all are products of the "displacement" of effort from a centrally organized enterprise in diplomacy, intelligence, and exploration, to private initiatives with a direct or indirect bearing on the needs, policies, and ideologies of government. It is with this, it seems to me all-important theme, that I began, and with this too I shall end.

NOTES

1 *Hist. Nat.* 6.84–91. The historicity of the story (not strictly necessary to my argument) is viewed with possibly undue rigor by A. Dihle, *Umstrittene Daten* (1965), 27 n. 24. The "firm" of Annius Plocamus is attested by inscriptions of A.D. 6 from the Red Sea area; David Meredith, "Annius Plocamus: Two Inscriptions from the Berenice Road," *JRS* 43 (1953): 38–40.

2 *Hist. Nat.* 6.89. "Silent trade" is the expression of E. H. Warmington, *The Commerce between the Roman Empire and India* (2d ed., 1974), at 58, 64, 88, etc.

3 Dio 54.9.8ff. gives a characteristically hostile view of the Indian's action (Dio did not like philosophers). Bargosa is the port of Baryazga (Broach), often mentioned in reference to trading contacts between the Roman Empire and India.

4 Strabo 15.1.4; Plutarch *Alexander* 69.

5   A. Dihle, "The Conception of India in Hellenistic and Roman Literature," *Proceedings of the Cambridge Philological Society,* n.s., 10 (1964): 15–23.

6   See on these poems the fascinating article of Pierre Meile, "Les Yavanas dans l'Inde tamoule," *Journal asiatique* 232 (published under the title *Mélanges Asiatiques*) (1940–41): 85–123. The relevant passages are often quoted, e.g., by Mortimer Wheeler, *Rome beyond the Imperial Frontiers* (1954), at 132f. The key to the journeys to India is the seasonal monsoon named after the legendary (late Hellenistic?) navigator Hippalos, on which see Wheeler at 126 and esp. Lionel Casson, "Rome's Trade with the East: The Sea Voyage to Africa and India," *TAPA* 110 (1980): 21–36, esp. 31–35 (with a chart of the winds at 26).

7   Meile, "Les Yavanas," 89–95, gives the evidence on Muziris.

8   Ibid., 97f. locates Chaberis = Kaviripattinam at lat. 11°9'N, to the north of Tranquebar (on the eastern coast). For the emporium at Pondicherry (Arikamedu) see Wheeler, *Rome,* 145–50.

9   *SEG* 7:135; see John F. Matthews, "The Tax Law of Palmyra," *JRS* 74 (1984): 157–80.

10 *Acts of Thomas* 3 (trans. R. McL. Wilson, *New Testament Apocrypha* [1965], 444); "In wood I can make ploughs and yokes and balances . . . and ships and oars for ships and masts and pulleys; and in stone, pillars and temples and royal palaces." And Abban the merchant said to him: "It is good, for of such a craftsman are we in need." On King Gundaphoros (Guduvhara), see George Huxley, "Geography in the Acts of Thomas," *Greek, Roman and Byzantine Studies* 24 (1983): 71–80, at 74f. A north Indian inscription gives the equivalent of A.D. 45 as year 26 of his reign.

11 Meile, "Les Yavanas," 99–102.

12 Chavannes, ed., "Les pays d'occident d'après les Heou Han Chou," in *Archives de l'Asie orientale* 8 (1907): at 177–78. The chapter of the Han annals reporting this episode dates to the fifth century but repeats the contents of a report of A.D. 125.

13 S. A. Nodelman, "A Preliminary History of Characene," *Berytus* 13 (1960): 106f. "Wily merchants" is Nodelman's phrase (107).

14 Chavannes, "Pays d'occident," 179–84.

15 Ibid., 180–81.

16 Ibid., 185.

17 As noted by ibid., 185 n. 2.

18 See esp. Fergus Millar, "Emperors, Frontiers and Foreign Relations, 31 B.C. to A.D. 378," *Britannia* 13 (1982): 1–23.

19 Garrett Mattingly, *Renaissance Diplomacy* (1955), esp. chap. 5, "The Renaissance Environment."

20 Robert K. Sherk, "Roman Geographical Exploration and Military Maps," *Aufstieg und Niedergang der römischen Welt* 2, no. 1 (1974): 534–62, at 537–43.

21 Strabo 16.4.21–26, cf. 2.5.12; G. W. Bowersock, *Roman Arabia* (1983), 47ff.

22 Dessau, 986. The inscription is discussed by Millar, "Emperors, Frontiers," 8—without noting the (surely significant) inference that Plautius Silvanus reported his experiences to the emperor. The inscription quotes from a speech in Silvanus' honor by the emperor Vespasian.

23 Arrian, *Periplus Ponti Euxini,* ed. G. Marenghi (Naples 1958). At 11, Arrian refers to distant kings who take to brigandage or refuse to pay tax and reminds Hadrian that certain clients had received their kingdoms from him or from Trajan. For statues and inscriptions at Trapezus, 1. At 6.10, Arrian refers to "Latin letters" sent, or to be sent, to Hadrian, presumably in the form of the regular reports of a provincial governor.

24 Lino Rossi, *Trajan's Column and the Dacian Wars* (1971).

25 Strabo 1.2.1; cf. 7.1.4, where he remarks that certain tribes beyond the Elbe "would have been better known if Augustus had allowed his generals to cross the Albis in pursuit of those who had emigrated there."

26 Millar, "Emperors, Frontiers," 11.

27 *Le livre de la couronne: Kitāb al-tāj,* trans. Charles Pellat (Budé ed., 1954), 89–93.

28 Ammianus Marcellinus 18.5.1–3.

29 Ibid., 18.5.3, "et antea cognitus."

30 Ibid., 18.6.20–7.1, cf. 6.20, "obsidatus sorte in Syriis detentus."

31 Ibid. 18.6.20, ". . . et dulcedine liberalium studiorum inlectus remeare ad nostra ardenti desiderio gestiebat."

32 G. Hoffmann, *Auszüge aus syrischen Akten persischer Märtyrer* (Leipzig, 1880), 22–24; cf. L. Dillemann, *Haute Mésopotamie orientale et pays adjacents,* Institut français d'archéologie de Beyrouth, no. 72 (1962), 110.

33 Amm. Marc. 16.12.25; E. A. Thompson, "Barbarian Collaborators and Christians," in *Romans and Barbarians: The Decline of the Western Empire* (1982), 230–48, at 233.

34 H. Aymard, "Les ôtages barbares au début de l'empire," *JRS* 51 (1961): 136–42; also in Aymard, *Études d'histoire ancienne* (1967), 451–60.

35 *Res gestae* 32–33, "Ad me rex Parthorum Phraates Orodis filius filios suos nepotesque omnes misit in Italiam non bello superatus, sed amicitiam nostram per liberorum suorum pignora petens," and "a me gentes Parthorum et Medorum per legatos principes earum gentium reges petitos acceperunt: Parthi Vononem," etc.; cf. Strabo 16.1.28, "Now all his [Phraates'] surviving children are cared for in royal style at public expense in Rome, and his successors have also continued to send ambassadors."

36 Tacitus *Annals* 12.10 (requesting Meherdates to replace Gotarzes).

37 *Annals* 2.2.5f. (the Vonones mentioned above, n. 35); cf. 6.32.4, 14.26,1f., etc. *Annals* 2.2.3 alludes to "petitum ex alio orbe regem."

38 J.-M. Dentzer, *Le motif du banquet couché dans le proche-orient et le monde grec du VIIᵉ au IVᵉ siècle avant J.-C.,* Bibliotheque des écoles françaises d'Athènes et de Rome, no. 246 (1982), 68–69: "Il est certain qu'en Orient le concept que recouvre la *tryphe* [luxury] est politique et non moral."

39 Suetonius *Caligula* 45, discussed in this sense by Aymard, "Les ôtages barbares," 141.

40 Tacitus *Annals* 3.43.1: "nobilissimam Galliarum subolem liberalibus studiis ibi operatam," etc.

41 Pausanius 7.10.11f.; see F. W. Walbank, *Polybius,* Sather Lectures, vol. 42 (1972), 7f., 75f.

42 Polybius 15.18.8, cf. A. Aymard, "Les ôtages carthaginois à la fin de la deux-
    ième guerre punique," *Pallas* 1 (1953): 44–66 (*Études d'histoire ancienne*,
    436–50); and F. W. Walbank, *A Historical Commentary on Polybius*, vol. 2
    (1967), 470f.

43 Polybius 31.11–15 (Loeb ed., vol. 6, pp. 186–93) with Walbank's *Historical
    Commentary*, vol. 3 (1979), 478–83; see also his introduction to vol. 1 (1957) of
    the *Historical Commentary*, 3f., and his *Polybius*, 9.

44 Pliny *Hist. Nat.* 5.9 (= Polybius 34.15.7; Loeb ed., 6:338); cf. F. W. Walbank,
    "The Geography of Polybius," *Classica et Medievalia* 9 (1948): 155–82, at
    159–62. It is not clear how much of Pliny's account comes from Polybius and
    how much from Agrippa, whom he also cites. Strabo 4.2.1 cites Polybius (=
    34.10.7; Loeb ed., 6:322) on the geography of the Loire region.

45 Walbank, *Polybius*, 7–10 and esp. 10f.

46 Aetolians: Polybius 21.32 (Livy 38.11), with Walbank's *Commentary*, 2:135ff.,
    cf. 2:470f. (on 15.18.8); F. E. Adcock and D. J. Mosley, *Diplomacy in Ancient
    Greece* (1975), 264. Maroboduus: Strabo 7.1.3; Tacitus *Annals* 2.62f., with
    E. A. Thompson, *The Early Germans* (1965), 95–106, esp. 99ff.

47 Gregory of Tours *Historia Francorum* 2.8 (citing "Frigeridus"); Merobaudes
    Carmen 4.42–46, etc. In 408 Alaric asked for Aetius to be sent to him as a hos-
    tage, but was refused; Zosimus 5.36.1. See *PLRE* 2, Aetius 7, at pp. 21–22.

48 Priscus, frag. 8 (C. Müller, *FHG* 4:78; R. C. Blockley, *The Fragmentary Classi-
    cising Historians of the Later Roman Empire*, vol. 2 (1983), 248–49); *Anon. Val.*
    2.8 (38).

49 Priscus, frag. 8 (*FHG* 4:80, 93; = Blockley, 2:252ff. and 288f.)—surely the
    same man, despite *PLRE* 2, Rusticius 2, pp. 961f. Aetius' son Carpilio was also a
    hostage with Attila; *FHG* 4:81, Blockley, 2:256f.

50 Jordanes *Getica* 271, 281; cf. Ennodius *Panegyricus* 11; Theophanes *Chrono-
    graphia* 5977.

51 Fergus Millar, *The Emperor in the Roman World, 31 B.C.–A.D. 337* (1977),
    e.g., at 203ff. (and passim; it is a central theme of Millar's book); and John F.
    Matthews, "Gesandtschaft," in *RAC* 10 (1977): 654–87, esp. 669–72.

52 *Vitae sophistarum*, 465–66 (Loeb ed., 394–99).

53 Amm. Marc. 20.16.4, cf. 18.

54 A. Christensen, *L'Iran sous les Sassanides* (2d ed., 1944), 414f.

55 Dihle, "Conception of India," and his "Indische Philosophen bei Clemens Alex-
    andrinus," in *Mullus: Festschrift für Theodor Klauser* (1964), 60–70; Walter
    Schmitthenner, "Rome and India: Aspects of Universal History during the Princi-
    pate," *JRS* 69 (1979): 90–106, at 97f.

56 Porphyry, *Life of Plotinus* 3 (Loeb ed. of Plotinus, vol. 1, p. 9).

57 Amm. Marc. 25.4.23; Cedrenus 1, p. 516 (Bonn). Cf. Jerome, *Chronicon*, s.a.
    330 (ed. R. Helm, *GCS* [1956], 232): "Metrodorus philosophus agnoscitur."

58 Rufinus *Hist. eccl.* 10.9f.; cf. Socrates 1.19, Sozomen 2.24; and A. Dihle, "Fru-
    mentius und Ezana," chap. 2 of *Umstrittene Daten*, 36–64.

59 Athanasius, *Apologia ad Constantium* 29, 31 (ed. J.-M. Szymusiak, Sources
    chrétiennes, no. 56 [1958], 121, 124–26).

60 Philostorgius *Hist. eccl.* 3.4–6, 4.1 (ed. Bidez and Winkelmann, *GCS* [2d ed.,

1972], 32ff., 57). See again A. Dihle, "Die Sending des Inders Theophilus," *Politeia und Res Publica: Palingenesia* 4 (1969), 330–36; Dihle, *Umstrittene Daten,* 50f.

61 See for Ommana/Oman, *Periplus Maris Erythraei* 36 (trans. and commentary by W. H. Schoff [1912], 36, 150f.), "market town [emporion] of Persia."

62 *Cod. Theod.* 12.2.2, with (for the date) O. Seeck, *Regesten der Kaiser und Päpste* (1919), 21.4–8.

63 *Passio Sancti Sabae* 4.2, in H. Delehaye, ed., "Saints de Thrace et de Mésie," *Analecta Bollandiana* 31 (1912): 216–21; cf. E. A. Thompson, *The Visigoths in the Time of Ulfila* (1966), esp. 65, 77, and 84f. on the racial composition of Christians among the Goths—Phrygians, Cappadocians, Syrians, Dacians—deriving, no doubt, from Roman prisoners and their descendants.

64 Amm. Marc. 31.12.8f., "cum aliis humilibus"—presumably meaning other Gothic Christians.

65 *Passio Sancti Sabae;* R. Knopf and G. Krüger, *Augsewählte Martyrakten* (4th ed., 1965), no. 33, pp. 119–24.

66 W. Dittenberger, ed., *OGIS* 720–71; with J. Baillet, "Constantin et le dadouque d'Eleusis," *CRAI,* 1922, pp. 282–96; P. Graindor, "Constantin et le dadouque Nicagoras," *Byzantion* 3 (1926): 209–14; and Fergus Millar, "P. Herennius Dexippus: The Greek World and the Third Century Invasions," *JRS* 59 (1969): 17.

67 Olympiodorus, in *FHG* 4:58–68, frag. 37 (= Blockley, frag. 35).

68 Huns, frag. 18; Athens, frag. 28; Rome, frags. 43, 44; parrot, frag. 36 (= Blockley, frags. 19, 28, 41.1.2, 35, respectively). See John F. Matthews, "Olympiodorus of Thebes and the History of the West," *JRS* 60 (1970): 79f.

69 Pliny, *Hist. Nat.* 6.184—together with the resolution by the campaign of divergent opinions about distances.

70 E. D. Hunt, *Holy Land Pilgrimage in the Later Roman Empire, A.D. 312–460* (1982), 83.

71 Ibid., 88 (writing of Egeria).

72 Eusebius of Caesarea, *Onomasticon,* ed. E. Klostermann, *GCS* (1904), repr. 1966, with Jerome's translation.

73 Hunt, *Holy Land Pilgrimmage,* 86ff.; John Wilkinson, *Egeria's Travels* (1971). Note esp. 18.2 (Euphrates), 19.1ff. (Edessa), 20.8 (Carrhae), 24–end (liturgy; cf. Hunt, chap. 5, Wilkinson, 54–88).

74 *Itin. Eg.* 20.12. On the interplay of political and cultural factors in this frontier zone see Fergus Millar, "Paul of Samosata, Zenobia and Aurelian: The Church, Local Cultures and Political Allegiances in Third-Century Syria," *JRS* 61 (1971): 1–17, at 1 (though not mentioning this item).

75 D. S. Wallace-Hadrill, *Eusebius of Caesarea* (1961), at 168ff.

CHAPTER 4

Germanic in the Mediterranean: Lombards, Vandals, and Visigoths

THOMAS L. MARKEY

The linguistic presence of Germanic peoples in the Mediterranean and the Near East in Late Antiquity and the cultural changes supposedly triggered by that presence have, until recently, been poorly understood. Traditionally, this presence is not a detailed part of the conventional wisdom presented in our handbooks.

In his *Comparative Germanic Grammar,* a posthumous publication from 1939, Eduard Prokosch, for example, dismisses the Goths, both Visi- and Ostro-, in some three pages and summarily concludes that "the Gothic kingdoms were destroyed by the Huns, and later the Goths disappeared in the Roman Empire. But some Gothic settlements in the Crimea survived the Hunnish invasion and existed as late as the sixteenth century" (1939, 30). Thus it is that Prokosch merely alludes to Crimean Gothic, which, as every Germanic philologist knows, was scantily recorded from the mouth of a nonnative speaker by the Flemish merchant and diplomat Ogier Ghiselin Busbecq (1522–92) in Constantinople sometime during the years 1560–62 and published in 1589.[1]

Whereas the Gothic presence in Scandinavia, along the Danube, and elsewhere in the Balkans generally has been studied in great detail on the basis of references to the Goths and accounts about them by classical authors (e.g., Pliny, Ptolemy, Tacitus, and Jordanes, particularly in Jordanes' *Getica*), by a careful sifting of the relevant onomastic material, and by exacting comparative attention to the Bible translations by the Visigothic bishop Ulfila (b. 311–d. 383), copied by Ostrogothic scribes, primarily in northern Italy (c. 500), as well as to other fragments of East and West Gothic that have come down to us, this has not, until recently, been the situation for the other Germanic Mediterraneans, namely, the Vandals, the Iberian Visigoths, and the

Langobardians.[2] In what amounts to the usual "guidebook" statement for the time, no less a scholar than Holger Pedersen summarized the then-current state of the art with respect to Langobardian in but one paragraph in his *Sprogvidenskaben i det Nittende Aarhundrede: Metoder og Resultater* from 1924:

> It was the destiny of the Gothic peoples to disappear, linguistically speaking, as one consequence of the vast expenditure of energy attendant upon the migrations. A West Germanic tribe who shared their fate were the Langobards. Originally they dwelt far to the north, near Lüneburg, but they migrated thence and after many vicissitudes, having dwelt in northwestern Hungary and in Pannonia, south of the Danube, they finally reached Italy in 568. Here they preserved their own language for a surprisingly long time, even after Charlemagne in 774 ended the empire of the Langobards; and it finally died out about the year 1000. We know this language through names and through scattered words in Latin writings such as the laws of the Langobards. Through these we can determine that Langobardian participated in the consonant shift which is one of the principal characteristics of High German.[3]

Before we proceed to the linguistic evidence proper for the Germanic Mediterraneans, here with primary emphasis on the Langobardians (i.e., Lombards), Vandals, and Iberian Visigoths, and a necessary prefatory statement on procedures for evaluating that evidence, let us sketch in the historical facts concerning these groups. These facts are but the merest framework, the boldest highlights, while the specifics are left to the historians, archaeologists, and social historians.[4] However, these facts are an obligatory prerequisite for a meaningful linguistic presentation, for they demonstrate that the Germanic Mediterraneans were always and everywhere a transitory, minority superstrate, only thinly plastered over a broadly based and long-indigenous substrate. Moreover, the historical evidence suggests that enclavement, which, as the anthropologists tell us, normally promotes linguistic and cultural persistence if not continuity, was rarely, if ever, a viable alternative for the Germanic Mediterraneans in Late Antiquity.[5]

Traditionally, the Goths, said to have come from Scandinavia, are thought to have divided into western (between the Danube and the Dniester) and eastern (in the Ukraine, the predecessors of Crimean Gothic) branches ca. A.D. 200. The Visigoths pressed into Dacia shortly thereafter and caused the Roman evacuation of that province (270–75). For a century, from about 275 to 376, the Visigoths held sway over Dacia (primarily, it seems, around the modern-day Romanian province of Buzău) until they were driven across the Danube and into the Roman Empire by the Huns. They apparently remained mainly pagan until about 395, when, under the leadership of Alaric (ca. 370–410), they left Moesia and wandered to Greece and Italy, eventually sacking Rome in 410, the year in which Alaric died, just before his contemplated invasion of Roman North Africa. Alaric was succeeded by Ataulphus, who led the Goths to southern Gaul. They then wandered around the northern rim of the Mediterranean, besieging the Vandals (409), and reached southern Spain (Cartagena) in 415. Three years later they were called to Gaul and settled between the lower reaches of the Garonne and Loire rivers. After the collapse of the Hun empire (455), those Ostrogoths left in Dacia began to move once again, first to Moesia (ca. 475–88) into the vacuum left by Alaric and then to northern Italy, specifically Verona, where Theodoric became king in 493 and died in 526. The emperor Justinian I, whose plan it was to see the Mediterranean basin "Roman" once more, declared war on Theodahat, the Ostrogothic king of Italy, in 533, that is, just one year after his general Belisarius had completed the defeat of the Vandals in North Africa. The ensuing war, a disastrous affair for all of Italy, lasted for some eighteen years until the last Gothic leader in Italy, Teias (Teja), fell in the two-day Battle of Mons Lactarius (Sant'Angelo, near Naples) in 553 at the hands of Narses, an event that spelled the end of Gothic power in Italy. Just where the remaining Italian Goths ended up remains a mystery.

When the Langobardians entered Italy in April of 568 under Alboin, they found the country virtually stripped of soldiers and provisions, a result of the disastrous Gothic wars, and they quickly established themselves in the north just three years after the death of Justinian I (d. 565). The Langobardians remained a disunited lot throughout their precarious history in Italy, and even their most capable leader, Rothari (636–52), who succeeded in conquering all of the north and in establishing the Langobardian Law (*Edictum Rothari*, 643), was never able to establish political harmony. After the last king, Desiderius, the kingdom fell to Charlemagne, who had taken Pavia, and the Lombard territory was to remain attached to the empire of Charlemagne and his successors until 843, when an independent kingdom arose, though before its end (961) it had splintered into a number of independent duchies and civil republics.

In our earliest records of them, the Vandals (Pliny's *Vandili*) are said to inhabit the eastern ramparts of the Carpathians. Earlier, they had been joined by the Iranian Alans, said to be the ancestors of today's Ossetians, a barbaric group whom Ammianus Marcellinus described as nomadic herdsmen without temples who worship a naked sword thrust into the ground. The Vandals, too, apparently originated in Scandinavia, presumably Jutland (Vendsyssel). They were divided into two groups: Hasdingi and Silingi, and their early neighbors were the Visigoths and Sarmatians. About A.D. 370, they were overwhelmed by the Huns and fled into Gaul (406) with the support of the Suevi (or Suebi, Swabians, etymologically "we ourselves"). In 409–10 they entered the Iberian Peninsula and divided it among their various groups (411); Galicia for the Hasdingi and Suevi, Andalusia ('Land of the Vandals') for the Silingi, and the Southwest for the Alans. Under the pressure of the encroaching Visigoths, they were led to North Africa by their leader Geiseric in 428, who took Carthage in 439 and who was recognized as the first independent German lord on Roman soil (442). Carthage saw six Vandalic kings from 439 to 534, from Geiseric to Gelimer, who was defeated by Belisarius at Decimum. Little more than a century and a half later (697), Carthage was to be taken by al-Ḥasan b. al-Nuʿmān al-Ghassānī, the Arab governor of Egypt, to be destroyed and to vanish from history. For details of Vandalic Carthage, see the comprehensive account by Christian Courtois ([1955] 1964) and the recent, excellent survey by Frank M. Clover (1982).

While the Suevi followers of the Vandals settled in northern Portugal and sowed the seeds of a new nationhood under Recharius (445–456), the Visigothic kingdom of Spain (475–711) may be said to begin with Euric (466–484) and his son and successor, Alaric II (484–507), who was defeated and killed by Clovis. Under Reccared (586–601), the Visigoths rejected Arianism in favor of Catholicism (part of the Arian clergy followed him in this decision at the Third Council of Toledo in 589), and Catholic culture and Gothic power rose to its height in Visigothic Spain under Saint Isidore, whose influence reached its zenith at the Fourth Council of Toledo (633). The Gothic nobility was readily and easily Romanized, even to the extent that Reccared ordered the burning of all Gothic "books," not one of which has survived. After a lengthy period of internal dissension, a hideous persecution of the Spanish Jews, and interminable religious squabbles, Visigothic Spain became an easy prey for the Muslim invasion from North Africa in 711, when Visigothic power evaporated forever.

This caption history of the Germanic Mediterraneans may be summarized as follows:

Visi- and Ostrogothic power in northern Italy (ca. 450–550)	ca. 100 years
Langobardian power in northern Italy (ca. 568–774)	ca. 206 years
Vandals in North Africa (428–534)	106 years
Visigothic power in Spain (ca. 475–711)	ca. 236 years

There remains yet another group of Germanic peoples who, though certainly Romanized, may, to some extent at least, also be considered Mediterranean. These are the Bavarians (traditionally, the *Bawarii, Boiarii, Bajuwarii,* a Germanic group thought to have come from what is now Bohemia = *Bojihaim* 'home of the Bavarians'). Perhaps as early as the sixth century, they came to what had been the Roman provinces of Noricum and Vindelicia (later incorporated into Rhaetia), which had been governed from Aquileia, a city whose fortunes reflect the shifting allegiances of the time. This city, founded in 181 B.C., was besieged by the Marcomanni and Quadi in A.D. 169, destroyed by Alaric in 410, burned by Attila in 452, and finally destroyed forever by the Langobardians in 568. Noricum, one of the richest northern provinces of the empire and one with large and flourishing cities (Juvavum = Salzburg was its administrative center), may be said to date from about 50 B.C. to about A.D. 500. The Slavs entered Carnuntum (= Kärnten) about 600, and the Germanic peoples—in force and to stay—nearly a century later. Whether or not these Germanic peoples were, in fact, the legendary Bavarians as recounted by our handbooks remains to be seen and is a topic that will be discussed in some detail below. However, the significant fact of note here is that Greater Rhaetia remained a Roman area for over half a millennium, more than twice as long as any of the areas in Mediterranean Germania remained Germanic (see table 1). The area was only partially Slavic for but a century, though today Val Resia is the only perch in Europe where Romance (Friulan), Slavic (Slovene dialect), and Germanic (Bavarian) meet. Since the eighth century, Carnuntum, formerly Roman and before that Celtic, fell under Germanic domination and has remained so ever since. However, if considered part of Mediterranean Germania, Bavarian did not suffer the same fate as did the other parts of Mediterranean Germania: it persisted as Germanic, while the others did not. Of course, to underscore the matter, Roman Noricum was founded on an earlier Celtic substrate, cultural parts of which persisted, albeit in new guises: for example, Celtic *Noreia* = Roman *Isis,* an effective translation of the inscription on the Roman building stone inserted, however surreptitiously, above the main entrance to the church at Michelsberg outside present-day Klagenfurt.

Now, other than the Gothic Bible translation, the *Skeirreins* (a commentary on the Gospel of St. John), a calendar, the Arezzo Deeds, and other fragmentary bits and pieces scattered here and there (with Ostrogothic scribal coloring in all cases?), the linguistic evidence for Mediterranean Germanic is shockingly scanty. We know virtually nothing about Mediterranean Germanic before the onomastics of its predecessor dialects emerge from the pens of classical historians and geographers. We can glean precious little from these records, and there are, to repeat, virtually no, with the exception of Gothic, native texts. Then, too, we know next to nothing about Mediterranean Germanic once Germanic power had eroded in the Mediterranean basin. With the loss of power, we witness the loss of language and even, at the hands of Reccared, distinct embarrassment about one's linguistic roots. Mediterranean Germanic (here: Langobardian, Visigothic, and Vandalic) is very definitely a *Rest-* or *Trümmersprache:* it has a shadowy existence at best and then vanishes altogether. Of course, *Restsprachen* have always held a certain fascination for the historical linguist, for there is always the hope that just a little more sleuthing, just one more find, will unlock a multiplicity of secrets.

Nevertheless, tantalizing as, say, Langobardian may have been for nineteenth-century scholars such as C. Meyer (1877) and Wilhelm Bruckner (1895), who provided the most detailed accounts we have yet today, Langobardian remained but an enticing enigma until the dawn of modern methodology and its insights taken from a variety of disciplines.

We can now discuss, as a sort of prolegomenon, the procedures for evaluating linguistic relics, here specifically the *Restsprachen* of Mediterranean Germania. Today, we know infinitely more about the following areas of inquiry than the nineteenth-century neogrammarians, or even such eclectic rebels as Hugo Schuchardt, could ever hope to know: (1) language death, (2) the chronographics of language death/genesis, (3) the evaluation of evidence, (4) the sociolinguistics of contact stratification, and (5) language change, variation, and contact in general.

1. *Language death.* Language acquisition is the inverse of language loss (or death). In the former, rules become more general, whereas in the latter, rules become less general. Much recent work has suggested that the order of acquisition for inflectional morphology is precisely the reverse of the order of loss (or death). In loss/death it is first nominal, then pronominal, and finally verbal. That is, conversely, verbal morphology is acquired first, nominal morphology last. However, what is preserved in texts is a very different matter from the observation, in the field, of language death (or acquisition). For Langobardian, we have only the pronoun *ih* 'I', and three verb forms (*līd* 2nd pers. sg. imper. 'go'; *fulboran* [1×] 'fullborn, honorable' p. part.; and *Armand,* a personal name that preserves the pres. part. of an otherwise unattested **arman,* cf. Goth. *arman* 'to embarrass one's self').[6]

2. *Chronographics of language genesis/death.* Here creolistics has taught us a lot. Creoles, true, stratified creoles, apparently develop with lightning speed, and, as recent research has shown us, thirty years in the life of a creole may well be roughly equivalent to three centuries in the life of a stable non-creole.[7] For example, Sranan was developed as an English-based creole in Suriname during the seventeen years (1650–67) of British occupation, but the space of three centuries failed to produce a *virulent* Dutch-based creole in this Dutch colony, though we have noted the recent identification of Berbice and Essequibo Dutch. It is difficult to compose an adequate definition of *creole,* but I propose that it is an amalgamation language distinguished from its superstrate primarily by recursive morphosyntactic restructuring of fundamental subsystems, for example, certainly tense/aspect, passivization (and diathesis generally), nominalization, deixis, and *Aux* (= the auxiliary system). Indeed, much significant work on creoles has concentrated on precisely these aspects of the grammar.[8] From this it follows that, conversely, a language can probably die very quickly. Langobardian may well have been a mere cultural artifact, largely restricted to onomastic usage, after but one generation. Reccared, if lit-

erate, probably could not have read the "Gothic" books he ordered burned. Vandalic may have enjoyed the same status as Etruscan apparently did in the first century B.C., that is, as a purely cultural (cultivated) register reserved for formulaic inscriptions. Then, too, given the diverse ethnic and linguistic composition of the Germanic Mediterraneans (Vandalic = Ostrogothic [?] + an Iranian subdialect + Swabian + Celtic + various Romance argots), there is every reason to suspect that Mediterranean Germanic was highly creolized and certainly without any fixed standards; it was more than likely a welter of tongues, little more than a lingua franca akin to that Mediterranean jargon recorded in Molière's *Le bourgeois gentilhomme* (1671) as sabir, and employed only in select contexts (military, judicial, courtly, and ritualistic).

3. *The evaluation of evidence.* The usual sources of evidence for historical *Restsprachen* are: (*a*) glosses; (*b*) inscriptions, typically brief, and often fragmentary, formulaic, and repetitive; and (*c*) onomastic data, the personal and place names of a linguistic landscape no longer a linguistic reality. The evidence we have for synchronic *Restsprachen* are the data of language death, the imperfect memories of informants, often enough highly colored by interference, of a language that may well not have been the informant's native language. The historical evidence of *Restsprachen* may not even be readable (e.g., Minoan Linear A, which has yet to be deciphered), or, if readable, it may lack the comparative support necessary for credible interpretation (e.g., Etruscan, which, though written in a well-understood Western Greek derivative alphabet, is a non-Indo-European language without a known etymological pedigree), or so brief and so unique as to lead us nowhere (e.g., the Lemnos stele from the sixth century B.C., which contains 198 letters, forming 33 words written in an alphabet from Western Greek, that is Chalcidian, really Euboean). Clearly, in the case of Mediterranean Germanic, our evidence is that of a historical *Restsprache* and falls into categories (*a–c*) above.

Recently, there has been increased awareness of and insight into such evidence, and some of the Indo-European *Restsprachen* (the pre-Romance dialects of northern Italy, Continental Celtic, Umbrian, Phrygian, Lycean, and Venetic) were the subject of an international conference.[9]

In evaluating glosses, one must be cognizant of the language of the glossator, the degree of correspondence between lemma and gloss, and possible variant readings (*facilior* vs. *difficilior*), and one must make allowances for the possibility of wholesale corruption. The glosses in the later redactions of the *Lex Salica,* for example, are so corrupt as to bear practically no resemblance to their probable spoken ancestors, and most of the onomastic and glossarial evidence for Langobardian has been heavily Romanized.

The same words of caution also apply to inscriptions, which may (1) later turn out to be forgeries (e.g., as in the case of the Praenestine [Palestrina] Fibula with its exquisitely reduplicated *Fhe:Fhaked* = *fēcit* dated to 600 B.C.;

see the literature cited in Bonfante and Bonfante 1983, 97–98), or which may (2) be restored to uncover new information and yield a better reading (e.g., as in the case of the Ibero-Celtic bronze tablet from Botorrita, see Beltrán and Tovar 1982), or which may (3) later be lost or destroyed with only imperfect copies remaining (e.g., as in the case of the runic Gold Horns of Gallehus).

Onomastic evidence, although it has the advantage of being frequently recorded at well-placed intervals, also has distinct disadvantages. It is well known that onomastic material is not a part of normal linguistic communication: it is not subject to the same sorts of change as are other parts of the grammar and frequently presents *Entgleisungen*. As onomastic elements, *Dayton, Bakersfield, Springfield,* and so on, are seldom open to literal or etymological interpretations on the part of native-speaker intuitions, nor are they perceived as normal elements of English grammar. Then, too, there are well-known ethnographically determined repartitions in onomastic data. For example, although toponyms are frequently replaced by an intruder population, river names rarely are. These are but a few of the intriguing problems associated with the evaluation of onomastic data, but I cannot provide a full account here.

A major problem in evaluating the evidence (*a–c*) typically available for *Restsprachen* is that of probable or possible continuity versus discontinuity. Consider the case of the Iberian *Restsprache,* which Wilhelm von Humboldt viewed as being continued in Basque, a thesis upheld by no less a scholar than Hugo Schuchardt and which has found opposition only in this century (see Schmoll 1959).

If there is any possibility at all, it is highly tempting to see an otherwise totally lost *Restsprache* continued in some remote dialectical enclave, for there is always the temptation to project the present onto the past. In fact, this sort of inferential projection is a primary motivation in the scrutiny of onomastic evidence and the survival of loans in the successor languages of *Restsprachen.* Note the perennial citation of Langobardian loans in Italian: *strale* m. 'arrow' (cf. OE *stræl,* OHG *strāla*), *aggueffare* 'to enclose, weave into' (cf. *OE wefan* vs. OHG *weban*), *romire* 'to roar, make noise' (cf. OE *hréam,* Lang. *[h]raumjan*). Just as Jan Baudouin de Courtenay wanted to see the Rezijan (It. Resia) enclave in northeastern Friuli as a mixture of archaic Slavic and an otherwise unknown Turanic (Avaric) element, so too some Germanic philologists wanted to see the so-called Cimbrian enclave, the Tredici Comuni northeast of Verona, as the last linguistic stronghold of the Langobardians or the Goths in northern Italy (see Lencek [1977] and the references to Cimbrian in n. 5 above). Despite such romantic attempts, the truth of the matter is that there was no continuation of Mediterranean Germanic anywhere. It was never preserved by enclavement, and only a handful of loans and a thin and well-disguised onomastic substratum have survived in Italian and Ibero-Romance.

All of the evidence we have for Mediterranean Germanic may be subsumed by categories $(a-c)$ above.[10]

4. *The sociolinguistics of contact stratification.* During the past two decades there has been enormous progress and increasingly sophisticated methodological insight into what has been termed sociolinguistics, an avenue of inquiry that attempts to pinpoint the sociological motivations that promote or even curtail linguistic change and variation. By and large, this has been a statistically based search for causal explanations, a quest that frequently omits processual reasoning and that tends to favor consideration of what is normal over what is natural/unnatural in change and variation. The two are not to be confused: while death is "normal," it is not "natural." Here, we simply cannot go into the vast body of literature that has appeared during the past twenty years or so but must content ourselves with some of the results that are particularly relevant to the topic at hand.

An adequate knowledge of (1) the demography of a contact/isolation situation, (2) the relative prestige/stigma attached to a minority/majority superstrate/substrate, and (3) the typologies of the languages involved in and that emerge from a sociolinguistic situation is a prerequisite for sociolinguistic analysis.[11] Linguistic isolates (e.g., some of the minor languages of the Caucasus, some Amerindian languages) tend to have complex linguistic structures, whereas massive contact usually leads to simplification (e.g., given massive contact, highly divergent word orders typically simplify to Subject-Verb-Object [SVO] order, an ordering found in all true creoles). Although massive contact "naturally" leads to simplification, language does not become simpler (borrowing and reanalysis continue to complicate). Irrespective of the demographics of language contact, there are certain constants with respect to linguistic levels, for example, the prosodic features of an indigenous language prevail over those of an intruding language. Isolation of a "dialect" does not always yield a new "language." The speech of prestigious speakers is not always imitated. Changes may proceed in directions opposite to those of migrations. Although change may spread somewhat uniformly through social spaces (upper/lower classes, etc.), this may not always hold for geographical spaces: seas unite, mountains divide, yet there are even exceptions to this generality. An exhaustive and accurate detailing of sociolinguistic facts (history, demography, relative prestige, social stratification, etc.) provides no ironclad basis for predicting how a linguistic variable will pattern: some loans vanish, while others persist, irrespective of discernible "social" correlates. Sociological features should not be attached to rules of linguistic variation, as this obviates the difference between linguistic form and linguistic function: an onomastic shape may have the form of the prestige lect but be employed (function) solely by the lesser lect (as a token of class aspiration). Linguistic strategies foreign to those present in related systems in a contact situation are more often due to mixture than to natural internal change. Finally, then, in the interpretation of contact variation—language death as well as genesis—the mere deduction of causality, real or probable, from an analysis of statistical norms and a historical reconstruction of degrees of social prestige/stigmatization is, in effect, a denial of processual reasoning, is epistemologically insufficient, and neglects what is actually at stake in all contact situations, whether massive or not. What is at stake is that constellations of variables ordered in implicational hierarchies (preferably ranked along continua) constrain both the numbers and kinds of combinations of variables that are possible.

5. *Language change, variation, and contact in general.* Both the linguist, particularly the historical linguist, and the historian are obviously concerned with all of these facets of evolution, but the two disciplines are seemingly separated by fundamental differences, or what appear to me to be fundamental differences, in the divergent epistemological assumptions they have individually embraced.[12] The historian is profoundly concerned with the teleological determination of significance, so that, for him, teleology is a definition of cause, consequence is defined as cause (the Aristotelian result as final case argument), and results are correlated with intentions. These may also have been the presuppositions of structural linguists some three decades ago (both the historian and the structural linguist attempt to assign cause to taxonomy), but—without going into detail—I dare say these are not the cardinal evaluative metrics for the general linguist of today. For the historian, continuity is not, as it is for the linguist, a manifestation of change. The historical linguist necessarily views both continuity and discontinuity as change: the former is implicationally contextualized as a sort of Hegelian *Aufhebung,* and the latter is a nongradualistic shift, sometimes akin to a catastrophe (a change without discernible intermediary stages), that presents far more interpretive difficulties and that requires far more analytic insight than the former.

To understand better the convergence of Germanic and Romance in the Mediterranean in Late Antiquity, let us now design a typological matrix of what are quite possibly the three most significant kinds of (massive) linguistic contact, the three most salient kinds of linguistic mixing and their results. First, however, let us provide a plausible visual analogue of what that Germanic-Romance (basically) contact situation must have entailed geographically. With the southern Alps as a convenient and even somewhat accurate line of intermediary division, Germanic was more dominant in the north, tapering, as it were, to a point of intrusion of a triangle in the south from its northern base. The Romance situation would have been precisely the converse of that of Germanic: Romance had its base south of the Alps and tapered to some point of intrusion in the north, the last outpost of a declining Roman Empire (see Diagram 1). By imposing the Germanic triangle on that of Romance, we get a visual impression of Mediterranean Germanic: firmly based in the north, the triangle of Germanic gradually shaded to oblivion in the south (see Diagram 2).

DIAGRAM 1

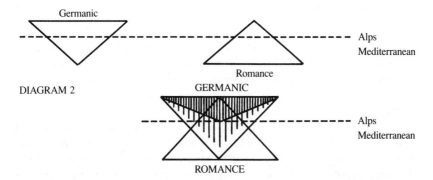

Romance

DIAGRAM 2

ROMANCE

What we have, then, in Alpine Europe is a fusion of two of the major languages in western Europe, Germanic and Romance, into a speech community (as opposed to a "language" community per se, a community with two separate languages).

We now establish the following typological matrix.[13]

Typological Matrix

Type		Continuity	Compart-mentalization	Fulg.	Comp. Rel.
Diffusion/dialect	1 L	+	−	−	−
Fusion creole	2 L	α	+	−	+
True creole	3+ L	−	α	+	+

Where Fulg. = Fulguration, Comp. Rel. = Complex Relexification, + = presence, − = absence, α = facultative presence/absence, L = language(s)

Compartmentalization is a reserved paradigmatic relationship in which the morphological markers from one input (L_2) are *generally* reserved for the lexicon from that input (L_2) in the construction of composite paradigms. Compartmentalization is an unstable state or stage in development, and its instability is characterized by the spread of L_2 morphology to the lexicon of L_1. A case in point is the general reservation of the (Norman French) *age*-suffix, originally a collective marker, for lexicon that is Romance in origin in English. Compare *leav-es* plural and *foli-age* collective, that is, Anglo-Saxon versus Romance, respectively, and note *leaf-age* versus *plumm-age,* but not **featherage.* The *age*-suffix is part of a mass-based enumerative system, a strategy that had been all but lost in Germanic at an early stage that became part of a composite paradigm when conflated with the indigenous, Anglo-Saxon count-based (singular:plural) system:

	L_1 count based		L_2 mass based
Anglo-Saxon	singular ($-\emptyset$)	Norman-French	collective ($-age$)
	plural ($-s$, etc.)		distributive ($-?$)

Fulguration is a term borrowed from the noted biologist Konrad Lorenz to describe a fusion of two or more input systems in such a way that no part of that resulting fusion may be traced back to an original input source: the result is qualitatively different from the ingredients. Etymological opacity in creolization is thus a sign of fulguration.

Complex relexification is signaled by the substitution of the lexicon and markers from one (or another or several) inputs to express some one semantactic strategy derived from yet another input source. Use of 'surpass' to form the comparative is a strategy commonly found in West African languages and is frequently relexified in numerous, particularly English-based, creoles of the greater Caribbean basin, e.g., Gullah *i tal pas mi* 'he/she/it is taller than I', lit. 'he/she/it is tall surpasses me'.

Fulguration is a function of input multiplicity, a key definitional factor in contact typologies, and [− continuity] and [+ complex relexification] are coordinate variables dependent on input multiplicity.

Given this typological matrix and a relatively full discussion of areas 1−5 above, we have now been afforded a basis for more-penetrating than hitherto insights into the fate of Mediterranean Germanic in Late Antiquity. Before proceeding further, I should stress that the Germanic that confronted Romance both south of the Alps and in North Africa, as well as the Germanic that plunged headlong into a variety of divergent Indo-European and quite possibly non-Indo-European tongues in the Balkans (Dacian, Thracian, Illyrian) was probably never identifiable as one "fixed" language, but was instead—in every instance of contact—a conglomerate of dialects with varying degrees of mutual intelligibility. Mediterranean Germanic (ethnographically labeled Ostrogothic, Visigothic, Vandalic, and Langobardian) had probably already been well mixed and stirred before or immediately after confrontation with the non-Germanic languages of the Mediterranean basin. Langobardian, for example, though it shares certain hallmark features with Alemannic of the time, is known to have included Franks, Saxons, settlers from Noricum (Proto-Ladin?), Swabians, Gepidians (from the Rhineland), Sarmatians, Pannonians, the remnants of Goths and Burgundians left over after the Ostrogothic wars, the last of the Rugians defeated by Odovacer, and even a sprinkling of south Slavs (Bulgarians?) in its ranks.[14]

A fusion creole is clearly more than the simple result of lexical borrowing, or the acceptance/rejection of some rather low-level phonological innovations (i.e., a partial definition of diffusion/dialect); it involves tapping the bases of convergent and divergent derivational strategies (e.g., count-based vs. mass-based enumerative systems), the constitution of composite paradigms, and a merger of systems that approaches the threshold of fulguration. Nevertheless, true fusion creoles are relatively rare; English, Yiddish, and quite possibly Swahili, to name but a few well-known examples, are clearly fusion creoles. Langobardian in its contact with the Romance dialects of northern Italy did not, on the basis of the available evidence, yield a fusion creole: here a Germanic mixture merely ebbed away to the point of absorption by Romance. Conversely, at the northern end of the Romance-Germanic teeter-totter with its Alpine fulcrum, Romance ebbed away to the point of absorption by Germanic. Probably, there was some, as yet undetermined, turning point (forty percent, say, of the lexicon and derivational morphology), which led to a state of critical mass, whereupon Germanic plunged into Romance, or, conversely, Romance plunged into Germanic.

The most opportune way to reconstruct a scenario for the shifting linguistic allegiances in Late Antiquity—here, specifically the evaporation of Mediterranean Germanic—would be to project the present onto the past, preferably in some highly principled way, as per areas 1–5 and the typological matrix above.

Recently, in a distinct and highly controversial break with tradition, Willi Mayerthaler has convincingly argued that Bavarian is a fusion creole (Alemannian + Proto-Ladin), a fusion creole that is, in fact, located along the fulcrum between Romance and Germanic.[15]

The traditional Bavarian hypothesis accepts (at least) the following:

(i) Bavarian and the Bavarians stem from Bohemia as a distinct, separate Germanic ethnic entity.

(ii) Bavarians "take over" (= *Landnahme*) Bavaria in the seventh century.

(iii) Bavarian is an independent Germanic dialectical entity, independent of Alemannian and Frankish.

(iv) Bavarians, eastern in origin, had early and prolonged contact with the Goths and other east Germanic groups.

(v) Bavarian qua "dialect" emerged totally independently, completely without connection with Roman Noricum or Ladinian culture of linguistic affinities.

Point (v) simply defies derision: to accept it one would have to document the wholesale evacuation of one of Rome's richest (and closest) provinces north of the Alps. As for (iv), every shred of Gothic evidence, and there are only shreds, adduced by the traditionalists can be better and more cogently explained in other ways. Moreover, shreds are hardly a basis for positing long and intimate contact with another linguistic entity. Point (iii) is peculiarly and particularly chauvinistic: the fact of the matter is that more careful philological scrutiny shows that Bavarian texts are in reality Alemannian redactions (in Bavarian *territory,* and they are not distinctly Bavarian. There is simply no archaeological evidence to support a Bavarian *Landnahme,* so *pereat* point (ii). Point (i) is based on an erroneous, however deeply embedded it may be in the traditional handbooks, interpretation of *Bavarian* as a derivation from *Bohemian* (see above). More plausibly, as Mayerthaler (forthcoming [b]) has shown, Bavarian stems from *Pago Ivaro* (*pagus I[u]varus, pago Juvave[n]se,* etc.), that is, Salzburg as an administrative center, whose name was later extended as a *nomen gentile* after having been used as territorial/regional classifier.

Linguistically, Bavarian shows every sign of being a fusion creole generated by reciprocal interpenetration (Alemannian and Proto-Ladin). A full marshaling of the relevant evidence would go far beyond what is required here, but some of the more salient features are:

(*a*) SVO word order;
(*b*) divergent reanalysis of directionals; *auf* + *i* < *hin* vs. *hinauf;*
(*c*) future with *kommen;*
(*d*) position of clitics: *Gib ma's!,* cf. It. *Damelo!* vs. Germ. *Gib es mir!;*
(*e*) partitives with quantities;
(*f*) reciprocal (Romance/Germanic) influence in the establishment of paradigms: e.g., the personal pronouns:

  ih < *ego/ih   mir* < *-me/-mus*
  du < *pu/tu   es/ös* < *vester/voster*

and anaphorics:

   use of definite article (*de, di*) instead of the anaphoric proper (*er, sie, es*), cf. Italian.

We may conclude this cursory synopsis by pointing to the Bavarian (and Alemannian) use of diminutive *-l-* with verbs (also with nouns). Nowhere else in Germanic are diminutive formants regularly invoked to mark iteratives that also connote graduality. Note, for example, *herbsteln* (to *Herbst* 'fall, autumn') 'gradually become fall/autumn'. This southern innovation spread northward and became marginally productive in Modern High German. We find derivational sets in High German that are not usually related as sets by the native speaker, for example, *streicheln* (to *streichen*), 'stroke, caress' (to 'strike'), *nieseln* (to *nass*), 'drizzle' (to 'wet, moist'). The verbative use of diminutive *-l-* is also a characteristic of Italian (and its dialects). Even more arresting, however, is the Bavarian use of *-ez-* (*-iz-*), particularly in Salzburgerland, the Bavarian *Urheimat,* as an alternative to *-l-,* compare *tröpfeln* 'drizzle' and *tropfezen* idem. This formant can only derive from Italic (Ladin) **-it-* (currently *-ut-*), compare Lat. *cantitare* 'to sing regularly' and Bav. dial.

noffetsn 'to doze', OHG *(h)naffezen* idem, related to OE *hnappian* 'to nap, doze'. The important points here are as follows. Although employed as a diminutive suffix for nouns throughout Germanic from its earliest attested history onward, *-l-* is not a Germanic verbative suffix. In this role, it is first attested and subsequently most productive in the one area most heavily influenced by a Romance speech community, a community in which *-l-* is a common verbative suffix and, as such, has the same function as its dialectical Germanic congener, namely, Alemannia-Bavaria. The obvious conclusion is that Germanic-Romance contact prompted categorical transfer: *l*-nouns → *l*-verbs. This transfer then opened the door for the introduction of the diminutive *Vt*-suffix from Romance areas which employed this suffix for both nouns and verbs, compare It. V *parlare : parlottare* and N *casa : casetta*.

We may conclude by noting that, in both its persistence as a fusion creole and in its absorption (by Romance) as a limited (chronologically and numerically) superstrate, the fate of Mediterranean Germanic is a function of graduality, of gradation, of the more or the less. Neither its persistence nor its absorption is a vanishingly brief or cataclysmic sea change, and both its persistence and its loss are conditioned by a subtle interplay of highly complex factors that lie well below the surface of the historical record. When Langobardian finally (ca. 1000—after almost half a millennium) gave way to Italian, a new ethnic identity was achieved, and, just so, another kind of new identity was achieved when Ladin and Alemannian combined as a fusion creole. The Ladin-speaking peasant of what had been Noricum throughout a lengthy heritage was probably just as unaware of the shift to a fusion creole as was his Langobardian cousin to the south that Germanic in northern Italy had all but evaporated. In fact, it is altogether probable that the graduality and subtlety that attended the shifts in linguistic allegiances we have observed here are more characteristic of the dramatic cultural changes in the Mediterranean and the Near East in Late Antiquity than the cataclysmic breaks so often attributed to those changes by the historian. However, as linguists we do have certain advantages over the historian, for not only do we have data, albeit inadequate in many instances, and criteria for proper evidence, we also have evaluative typological matrices for the calibration of change and variation.

NOTES

The author-date system of citation has been adopted in this article. Full information can be found in the Works Cited section at the end of the volume.

1   For the most recent account of Crimean Gothic and a rich bibliography of current research in this area, see Grønvik (1983), who concludes (p. 105) that the pho-

nemic system of the Busbecq gloss material (80 words, 5 sentence fragments with Latin translations) agrees with that of the *cantilena* (three lines recorded, but not glossed, by Busbecq) and that Crimean Gothic was originally West Germanic in its dialectical garb. Crimean Gothic was completely extinct by the beginning of the nineteenth century.

2   Certainly one of the most diligent investigators of the Gothic presence in Scandinavia has been the Uppsala scholar Josef Svennung (e.g., 1963, 1967, 1974), but his onomastic and philological interpretations must be accepted with caution, see the review of Svennung (1963) by Hoffmann (1965) for an example of the sort of criticism leveled at this line of inquiry and Svennung's results generally.

3   Here I quote from the English translation by John Webster Spargo, originally published by Harvard Univ. Press in 1931, and subsequently reissued many times, most recently as a paperback by Indiana Univ. Press (1962). This is not to denigrate Pedersen's "The Discovery of Language," the rather commercial Indiana Univ. Press title, for this is one of the more, practically in fact the only, readily available and comprehensive survey of historical linguistic research and the flowering of Indo-European studies in the previous century. The quotation here is from Pedersen (1962, 31).

4   During the past half century or so, an enormous amount of very credible work has been done to ferret out details of the social reality of the Germanic Mediterraneans in Italy, the Iberian Peninsula, and North Africa, specifically in Carthage. The following is a working bibliography of studies in these areas, while source materials for the linguistic evidence proper are provided in n. 10.

Ludwig Schmidt's ([1941] 1969) classic studies of the East Germanic peoples and the Vandals ([1942] 1969) have been superseded by Wolfram ([1979] 1980). Note, too, the corrective account of the Goths and Vandals by Helbling (1954). The tortured history of the Balkans from the end of the Roman Empire through the eighth century has been admirably outlined by Lemerle (1954). For a general history, from the Roman through the Byzantine empires, see Stein ([1959], 1968); for material on the Germanic Mediterraneans, see esp. vol. 1, chaps. 7, 9–11; vol. 2, chaps. 1, 5–6. On the adoption of Christianity by the Germanic peoples in the West, see Boissier (1891). For a general history of the Goths in Italy, see Kohlrausch (1928), and for details about Stilicho and Alaric, Mommsen (1903) is still a valuable source. For a general account of the Visigoths in Spain, see Thompson (1969). On the label "Visigothic," see Mastrelli (1966). For archaeological evidence of the Visigothic presence in Spain, see Zeiss (1934), and in southern France, see Baye (1887). For a history from Fritigern to Euric, see Thompson (1963). The most exhaustive account to date of the Vandals in North Africa is still that by Courtois ([1955] 1964), cf. Clover (1982), Gautier (1932), and Dennis (1925). The Halle social historian Diesner (1966) has written a convenient and convincing survey of the rise and fall of the Vandalic empire. On the Vandalic eponymy, see Vasmer (1942). Finally, then, for a general history of the Goths and Langobardians in Italy, see Åberg (1923), cf. Mor (1957). The most recent survey of historical research and studies of the social history of the Langbardians, together with a rich bibliography, is that by Diesner (1978) in the series Stand und Aufgaben der Langobardenforschung, ably assembled and edited by

Piergiuseppe Scardigli (1978–1979), Florence, to whom I am grateful for providing this material, as well as many other helpful references over the years.

5   On the anthropology of enclavement, see the important collection of papers edited by Castile and Kushner (1981). Enclavement offers no certain assurance of linguistic survival, as is shown by the loss of so many Amerindian languages "enclaved" by "reservations," but the picture is a varied one, ranging from total loss to astounding degrees of preservation. Some enclaves resist language loss better than others, and the isolation of effective causes for preservation is a delicate matter. E.g., Fox, an Algonquian language actively spoken by some 300 of the ca. 700 inhabitants of the Sauk and Fox of the Mississippi Settlement near Tama, Iowa, is much better preserved than Winnebago Sioux (only a handful of the oldest generation, over 65 years old, speak the language) at the Winnebago Reservation in Nebraska. One remarkable instance of preservation in the Germanic sphere is that of so-called Cimbrian, the last of the Tredici Comuni northeast of Verona to speak a Germanic dialect in the isolated village of Giazza (Ljetzan), just north of Selva di Progno (Brunghe). This eleventh century, primarily Alemannian-based *Sprachinsel* has against all odds preserved its dialect to the present day. Cimbrian has, however, been distinctly influenced by the Italian that surrounds it. For details, see Hornung (1977), Kranzmayer (1981), Mayer (1971), Meid and Heller (1979), Rapelli (1980, 1981, 1983*a*, 1983*b*, 1983*c*, 1983*d*). I am grateful to Giovanni Rapelli, Verona, for instructive correspondence and for sending me literature that would otherwise have been difficult to obtain on this side of the Atlantic. Here it should be pointed out that I conducted fieldwork in Giazza in October 1980, and among the Fox at Tama, Iowa, during the summers of 1981–83. Finally, then, the sociolinguistics of intransigent enclavement, the preferred isolation that resists external linguistic interference, seems to be an unnatural state, is exceedingly rare, and tends to present an insoluble—insoluble in the epistemological sense of this term as employed by Peter Brian Medawar (*The Art of the Soluble*, 1967).

6   The Langobardian data are from Bruckner ([1895] 1969). This synopsis of the grammatical stages of language death represents an abstraction resulting from numerous conversations with Charles-James N. Bailey at Technische Universität Berlin while I was an Alexander von Humboldt Fellow there during the academic year 1980–81. For fascinating data on language death, a record in print and in live recordings, here for Rhaeto-Romance in Hinterrhein, see Solèr and Ebneter (1983). For the effects of language death on derivational morphology, see Dressler (n.d.). For a case study of language death (the Wind River, Wyoming, Shoshoni), see Miller (1971). The well-researched and well-documented studies of language death by Nancy C. Dorian (e.g., 1973, 1976*a*, 1976*b*, 1977) are models of clarity and instructive guides to further research. Here, too, a note of gratitude is in order: this time to Theodor Ebneter, Zurich, for conversations about language death and enclavement and the provision of many useful references over the years. For a survey of lexical replacement patterns in language death, see Hill and Hill (1977). The "dynamics" of language death have yet to be worked out in any detail, but some aspects of general tendencies are by now fairly clear. There is, e.g., the general phenomenon of markedness reversal/assimila-

tion: loans (= highly marked) are generally assigned to moribund (= dying and highly marked) inflectional categories, that is, what is highly or more marked in an unmarked environment becomes unmarked or less marked in a marked environment: marked loan becomes unmarked in a marked environment. Witness the case of the *u*-stems, a dying noun class in Gothic that is composed primarily of loanwords. Jane Hill reports to me in a letter that this form of markedness reversal is a frequent event in Nahuatl threatened by Spanish.

7   I once had the opportunity to compare work on Palenquero done in the late 1940s and early 1950s by the Giessen Romanist Jean Caudmont with the data presented by Bickerton and Escalante (1970) on this creole. (I am grateful to Caudmont for making these data available to me in Giessen in the fall of 1980.) The differences between this early Palenquero vs. its later records were roughly of the same magnitude as, say, the differences between Middle High German of ca. 1350 and Early New High German of ca. 1650. Palenquero (from Spanish *palenque* 'palisade, enclosure') is a Spanish-based creole spoken by ca. 2,300 Negroes in San Basilio de Palenque, Bolivar, Colombia, who are descended from bush Negroes who escaped slavery in the early seventeenth century. For further references, see the literature inventoried in Reinecke et al. (1975, 132–33).

In summary, pidgins tend to remain pidgins, while creoles either emerge quickly or not at all. The Caribbean is a basin of creoles, whereas the Pacific is a sea of pidgins, a distinction that is probably due in large measure to the prevailing differences in labor employment in these two areas: indentured, term-contract labor in the Pacific vs. slave labor in the Caribbean. For a case study, see Mühlhäusler's (1983) account of the emergence of Samoan Plantation Pidgin English.

8   Broadly speaking, there are basically two, diametrically opposed, theses about creole origins: (1) monogenesis/relexification, a view that contends that some one (Portuguese is the usual choice) pidgin become a creole was successively relexified by European colonial acrolects (French, Spanish, English, Dutch, etc.) to yield French-based, etc., creoles; and (2) the universalist view, which contends that, given the vast variety of highly divergent inputs (African, European, etc.) and the wide geographical distribution (without dialectal contact) of the various creoles around the globe, as well as marked discrepancies in their chronological emergence (sometimes centuries apart), and—and this is the clincher—the fact that all creoles display certain identical grammatical structures (irrespective of area, inputs, or time or origin), e.g., all creoles have three and only three tense/aspect markers (anterior, irrealis, and non-punctual), creoles, true, stratified creoles, are evidence of the recursive creation of human language itself and provide firm evidence to support the nativist, prewired, and preprogrammed theory of language origins, so in an extreme statement by Derek Bickerton (1981), a leading creolist, in a book that includes a rich reference bibliography covering recent work in the field and one that has attracted mass-media coverage exceptional for such a technical study.

9   Le lingue indoeuropee di frammentaria attestazione/Die indogermanischen Restsprachen, Udine, 22–24 September 1981, the proceedings of which have been edited by Edoardo Vineis (1983). I am grateful to Roberto Gusmani, Udine, for inviting me to participate in this conference, the papers and discussions at which I

found most fruitful. Here, too, I would like to thank Antonio Tovar, Madrid, for sending me the report on the Botorrita inscription and for providing helpful references and encouragement over the years.

10   The evidence from coins is by nature almost exclusively onomastic, see Wroth (1911). The bulk of the evidence for Mediterranean Germanic is contained in the impressive series, *Germanische Denkmäler der Völkerwanderungszeit,* 7 vols. (1931–62), cf. Fiebiger (1939), and Fuchs (1943). Courcelle (1964) provides an indispensable presentation and evaluation of the literary evidence. For the Vandals, Wrede's (1886) linguistic analysis, however dated, is practically the only thing available. For Visigothic there are the *Leges Visigothorum,* the personal and place names, see Kremer (1972) and Gamillscheg (1935), and Gamillscheg (1932) has sketched a linguistic history on the basis of this evidence.

Langobardian is the best documented, if one can call it that, but certainly the most well researched of the Germanic Mediterranean dialects, but here, too, the evidence is restricted to that covered by categories (*a–c*) above. As for texts, there is Paul the Deacon's *Historia Langobardorum;* the ethnography, *Origo gentis Langobardorum;* the laws (*Edictum Rothari; Leges Grimauldi, Liutprandi, Ratchis, Aistulfi, Sicardi principis pactum cum Neapolitanis, Radelgisi et Siginulfi divisio ducatis Beneventani*); and various civil and monastic records (e.g., *Il regesto di Farfa, Codex diplomaticus cavensis*). Inventories of forms and grammatical descriptions in the typical handbook format by Meyer (1877) and Bruckner ([1895] 1969), as well as more recently by van der Rhee (1970), provide the best sources for tracing the linguistic history of this dialect that we have to date. The fullest account of the onomastic data is still that by Gamillscheg (1935), cf. Scardigli (1976). Massmann (1841*a*) composed a dictionary, albeit prematurely, for he failed to avail himself of all the evidence. The language of the laws, specifically the Latin of the laws, has been thoroughly studied by Löfstedt (1961). Mitzka (1951) attempted to relate Langobardian dialectically to Old High German, and Ganz (1957) has treated a number of minor philological problems. The most recent and instructive survey of research and problems to date is that edited by Scardigli (1978–79).

Finally, then, Höfler (1957) attempted to show that the High German consonant shift was also carried out, though only to varying degrees, in Mediterranean Germanic, but this is a work that must be used with caution and accorded the usual skepticism for works by this Viennese Germanist. Wrede (1891) has provided the most complete survey of Ostrogothic in Italy; Schröder (1891) traced the development of the adjective formant *-ahs* in Gothic and Mediterranean Germanic; and Massmann (1841*b,* 1842) included bits and pieces of evidence from Mediterranean Germanic in his *Gothica minora.*

Here, it should be pointed out that in 1964 the Centro per lo Studio delle Civiltà Barbariche in Italia, with "barbariche" signifying non-Roman and non-Greek, was established in Florence for the direction and coordination of research into the linguistic, archaeological, and social history of Italy. Of course, Langobardian falls under this heading.

11   For a recent study that fulfills these conditions very admirably, see Baker and Corne (1982). This study is an areal investigation of creolization (the Indian

Ocean French-based creoles, particularly that of Mauritius). Here, in a detailed examination of the historical records, Baker shows that, in the establishment of the plantation economies of the area, whites first outnumbered blacks with subsequent reversal of these demographics; knowledge of the acrolect (French) became increasingly diffuse, quite possibly the very situation that obtained in northern Italy with respect to the Langobardians—initially a majority and later a minority as the indigenous population moved in to fill the gap left by the Ostrogothic wars.

12 I was made aware of these differences via Michael Morony's presentation, "Teleology and the Significance of Change" (see the Introduction to this volume), and a subsequent discussion with that scholar at the Madison conference. Such exchanges are, after all, the presumed virtues of interdisciplinary gatherings.

13 For a fuller exposition of the notions introduced here, see Markey (1981), which was an early attempt to define contact typologies and the specific features that define those typologies, especially fusion as an intermediary linked in this developmental chain.

14 Scardigli (1976) has attempted to demonstrate that there were three periods in the evolution of Langobardian, namely, Gothic (*anagrift* 'arbitrary marital or extra-marital union'), Langobardian (*anagrip*), and German or Germanized (*deutsch oder verdeutscht*) (*anagrif*), see Florus van der Rhee in Scardigli (1978–79, 10.2.77–86). Various elements of the lexicon appear archaic and point to a variety of associations, e.g., *arga* 'cowardly', the very characteristic that forms the core of the accusations charged in the Nordic *níðstöng* 'scorn pole': *argr/ragr*. The umlaut of *a* ($>$ *e* before *i, j*) is feebly attested and then only in later (eighth century onward) sources, and this is a change not recorded for Gothic. Lgb. *e* $>$ *i* before *i, j* (e.g., *wirigild* = OHG *wirigelt*), a change that is only exceptionally attested in Gothic (e.g., *hiri, hirjats*). Lgb. has *a*-umlaut of *u*, e.g., *fulboran* (instead of **fulburan*). This is not attested in Gothic, nor is it typical for the eastern, so-called Gothic, portions of Sweden, i.e., the *holt/hult*-isogloss. Gmc. *ē*[1] $>$ Lgb. *ā* vs. Goth *ē*, a change that must have been initiated in Alemannian in the fifth/sixth centuries (*Suevi* $>$ *Suabi* in the fifth century). Gmc. *ē*[2] is retained in Lgb. as *ē* and is not diphthongized to *ea, ia, ie* as it is in later OHG, e.g., Lgb. *mēta* = OHG *mēta/miata, mieta*. Cognate Goth. *mizdō*- is a Slavic loan, one of many in Gothic, e.g., *plinsjan* 'to dance' = OBul. *plęšǫ* $<$ **plensy-ō*, otherwise unknown in Germanic. Gmc. *ai* is retained and not reshaped as *ei* or monophthongized, e.g., Lgb. *gair*- = OHG *gēr*-. Similarly, Lgb. *au* = Gmc. *au* vs. OHG *ou*. Gmc. *eu* (before *e, a, o*) $>$ Lgb. *eu/eo*, later *e/o* (ca. 1100), while Gmc. *eu* (before *i, j, u*) $>$ Lgb. *iu*, later (ca. 1000) *i* as a result of Italian influence. All of the above remarks apply to vocalism in stressed syllables, for the evidence for weakly stressed finals, largely inflectionals, is severely complicated by virtue of rampant Italian/Latin influence. Finally, Lgb. participated in the High German Consonant Shift, though not to the extent or in the same manner as did Alemannian. Provision of a detailed account of these discrepancies, also of the simplification of consonant clusters (e.g., *ht* = *ct* $>$ *tt*), as well as an inventory of probable Romance influence on scribal practices, would lead us into an even more involved philological excursus and is not warranted here.

15 Mayerthaler, currently professor of linguistics, University of Klagenfurt, Austria,

first formally announced this hypothesis at the conference Das Romanische in den Ostalpen/Il Romanzo nelle Alpi orientali, Salzburg, Austria, 6–10 October 1982, a conference that I was fortunate enough to attend. At first highly skeptical, I gradually became convinced that Mayerthaler's thesis was essentially correct. Invited to Klagenfurt as a guest professor for the fall semester (1983) by Mayerthaler, I gladly accepted and soon began to see pieces of the kaleidoscopic variation of lects in the eastern Alps fit together into a coherent pattern suitably explained by means of the fusion creole hypothesis. The traditional view (that Bavarian is a separate, entirely Germanic, ethnolinguistic entity) must now be abandoned (see Mayerthaler, forthcoming *a*, *b*). It was while I was in Klagenfurt that I became convinced that the *ez-* and *l*-verbative diminutives, otherwise troublesome in lieu of an etymological or processual pedigree, were readily explicable in terms of this hypothesis. The evidence continues to mount in favor of its acceptance, and I hope to catalog this and further, more detailed, linguistic evidence elsewhere.

Noricum, a large and prosperous province with imposing cities (e.g., *Zollfeld* = *Solium* (< **sodium*), *Magdalensberg* = ?) must have remained bilingual well into the Middle Ages. Innsbruck was demonstrably bilingual until the latter half of the thirteenth century. There are numerous Romance loans, e.g., *Brezel/Prezl* 'pretzel' < Lat. *bracchium, Krempel* 'junk' < Ladin *graffe/grappe,* and so on). Onomastic details (e.g., *Tirol/Zirl* < *Teriolis/Teriola* with shifted *t* in the geographically appropriate places at the requisite times) point to the incursion of Alemannians on a Ladin substrate at an early date (ca. fourth century A.D.). Note *gamp*-names (< Lat. *campus*), and, conversely, note the restructuring of Alemannian by Ladin, e.g., *spitze* > *piz*. The fusion of Alemannian and Ladin in Noricum is, in a sense, merely a continuation of fusion in the area, for Celtic + Italic had previously combined to yield Ladin. Note Pre-Celtic **ɔbɔl* 'apple' + Italic *mālum* → Friuli (etc.) *àmoll(o)* 'prune, plum (tree)', a secondary interpretation, cf., similarly, Rhenish *öllich* 'onion' < Lat. *unio* + Saxon *lōk*. I take this opportunity to express my abiding debt of gratitude to Mayerthaler for a pleasant and instructive stay in one of the finest laboratories for language contact study in Europe.

CHAPTER 5

The Role of Nomads in the Near East in Late Antiquity (400–800 C.E.)

FRED M. DONNER

Nomads were an essential feature of life in the Near East in Late Antiquity and have remained so since. They interacted continuously with the settled population of the region and were one of the prime reasons that the history and society of the Near East differed markedly from those of contemporary Europe. Europe, after all, has never (at least in historic times) supported a significant population of nomads—by which I mean indigenous people who undertook regular, cyclical migrations in order to pursue pastoralism. We must distinguish this kind of pattern from massive "folk migrations" (*Völkerwanderungen*). Europe had such folk migrations, to be sure, but these represented either the intrusion of alien peoples onto the European scene (e.g., the Avars or Magyars), or the movement of an essentially settled European people from one part of Europe to another in search of new areas of settlement (e.g., the Visigoths, Vikings, or Normans). In all such instances, however, the migration, though drawn out over years, was fundamentally a single operation and resulted in the definitive settlement of the migrants into a new abode, where they led the settled life of village farmers or townsmen, with fixed habitations.

The Near East also had its share of "intrusive" migrations of alien groups and of internal movements of populations. Among the former, the thirteenth-century invasions of the Mongols, or even more the incursions of the Turks from the eleventh century onward, come most readily to mind. Among the latter, the clearest example is probably the movement of Arabians, many of them townspeople or oasis villagers, from the Yemen, the Hijaz, and other parts of the peninsula, to new settlements in Egypt, Syria, Iraq, and Iran in the course of the Islamic conquest movement of the seventh century.

As important as such mass migrations have been in Near Eastern history, however, they are not the object of my present concern. I wish instead to assess the role of indigenous nomadic pastoralists in settled society in the Near East. Before doing so, however, it is appropriate to describe, in very simplistic terms, some of the main forms of nomadic pastoralism found in the region from about the third century B.C.E. on.

Three main varieties of Near Eastern nomadic pastoralism can be identified. The first, sometimes called "transhumance," is found in mountainous regions such as the Zagros and Anatolia. The pastoralists of these regions, who herd primarily sheep and goats, move between low-lying winter pastures in the plains or foothills and high summer pastures in the mountains. These main pasturing areas are fixed and reserved; that is, a particular pastoral group normally returns to the same summer and winter pastures year after year, and other pastoral groups may use them only with their permission, or by exerting superior force. For one reason or another, these summer and winter pastures are agriculturally marginal—for example, the winter pastures may be too hot and arid in summer, and too difficult to irrigate, to permit cultivation, while the summer pastures may be sufficiently cold that the growing season is shorter than needed for successful cultivation. Both the summer and winter pastures are fairly extensive, and because of their low agricultural utility, they tend to be essentially unpopulated, except when the pastoralists themselves are present. The routes followed by the nomadic pastoralists in moving from summer to winter pastures and back are usually well defined; they are frequently dotted with villages, and the pastoralists, in their predictable passages back and forth, establish customary agreements with the villagers about such matters as grazing privileges, trade, social contacts, and so on.

The second general variety of nomadic life is found where a large river valley or otherwise well-watered district adjoins an extensive tract of arid or otherwise agriculturally marginal land. Pastoralists in such settings can keep sheep and goats, which they graze in the arid tract during the winter and spring, when the seasonal rains "make the desert bloom" with short-lived herbage. As the pasture fails with the coming of summer they drive their livestock closer to, and ultimately into, the better-watered river valley, where water and fodder for their flocks are always available. The arid district is normally unpopulated, and the pastoralists may disperse very widely in it while exploiting its spring grasses; in the riverain district, on the other hand, the ready availability of fodder and water permits the nomads and their flocks to come together in large concentrations. Moreover, the riverain district is likely to be filled with villages, and the pastoralists must keep their flocks well under control during the long summers to prevent them from ruining the villagers' crops. The pastoralists' fairly long stay among the villagers results in very intimate social ties between the two groups. Indeed, the two sometimes become virtually one social group, part of which stays in the village year round and part of which takes the flocks into the steppe in the proper season. Such arrangements are found mainly along the Tigris and Euphrates rivers and their tributaries in parts of northern Syria and Iraq, along the agricultural fringe of the steppe in inland Syria from Aleppo south to the Gulf of Aqaba, and in other areas that are agriculturally marginal but still fairly close to some permanent source of water.

The third variety of nomadism in the Near East is really a further refinement of the second, involving the herding primarily of camels (the dromedary or one-humped variety) rather than sheep and goats. In comparison with sheep and goats, camels are much faster, can go much longer without watering, and can eat much-less-desirable fodder plants; they can also live entirely without water if succulent herbage is available and can carry loads far exceeding that of the donkey, horse, or ox. These qualities of the camel freed camel pastoralists to undertake much longer annual migrations, to penetrate much-more-arid areas in search of pasture, and to stay "in the field" for a much greater part of the year than sheep and goat herders, whose movements are quite narrowly restricted by their animals' needs. In some areas, camel pastoralists may roam from one seasonal pasture to another in a well-established pattern for almost the whole year and may have very little contact with settled communities. Much more frequent, however, is a pattern in which the camel-herding groups spend several of the driest months of summer at an oasis, along a river, or elsewhere where permanent water can be found—usually in the company of other pastoral groups and some villagers. Such nomadic patterns are best attested in the Arabian and Syrian deserts, in the Eastern and Western Deserts of Egypt, and in the Sahara.

The three basic patterns just described are, of course, grossly oversimplified "ideal types," and variations and hybrid forms abound; above all, these simplified models tend to obscure that "nomadic" and "sedentary" ways of life are really but the opposite ends of a spectrum of ways of life, with many groups falling somewhere in between. Nonetheless, these models do, I think, reflect some of the essential characteristics of Near Eastern nomadic life. These include the rhythmic, even predictable nature of the nomads' movement in response to seasonal changes in pasture; their lack of a permanent, fixed habitation, and their having regular contact with settled people, especially villagers, in the course of their annual migratory cycle. Two additional points need to be emphasized, however. The first is that nomads have always been a minority of the population of the Near East; this is not particularly surprising, since their goal of exploiting tracts of land too poor to support any concentrated population requires them to be spread exceedingly thinly, albeit over vast areas, for much of the year. The second is that nomads, despite their relatively small numbers, have exercised a profound influence on the evolution of Near Eastern society. Indeed, it is not going too far to say that the presence of nomads in the Near East was one of the decisive factors that made life and history in the Near East evolve so differently from in Europe—at least in the period from about the third century B.C.E. until recent times.

This paradox of the nomads' limited numbers but disproportionately profound impact can best be appreciated by looking, very quickly, at some of the ways in which nomads have interacted with settled society in the Near East. It will soon become evident that many aspects of this interaction remain poorly known, and as a consequence we shall, in many cases, have to be satisfied for the present with questions raised rather than answers given. My further comments, moreover, are restricted mainly to the interaction of nomads and settled people in the Arabian Peninsula and Fertile Crescent. The rather different ecological conditions facing the nomads in mountainous regions (Iran, Anatolia), or in North Africa have generated patterns of interaction that are different in some ways from those in Arabia and the Fertile Crescent, although some similarities and parallels can doubtless be found as well.

ECONOMIC RELATIONS

The economic interaction of nomads with their settled neighbors has long been acknowledged, but the importance of such interactions has not always been fully appreciated. The older, one-sided view of nomad-sedentary relations as constituting an endless struggle between "the desert and the sown" has more recently given way to one stressing the economic interdependence of nomads and settled people. It is recognized that nomadic and seminomadic pastoralists depend on village communities for most agricultural staples (grain, dates, etc.) as well as for numerous manufactured items essential to their life in the desert—weapons, cooking utensils, clothing, tent material, and other indispensable items. In turn, the nomads provide the villagers with livestock—sheep and goats for food, camels and horses for hauling and riding—as well as with a limited range of products of animal origin, such as hides, wool, hair, and milk products. In some instances, the nomads effectively "own" lands which peasants work as sharecroppers. The nomads may also undertake important transport functions on which depend the survival of peasant communities, and even of larger towns; it was often with the nomads' camels and under the nomads' protection that urban manufactures or imports were borne from one town to another, or that a village's crops were taken to market. The ability of nomads to pass, under appropriate conditions, through inhospitable areas, and the necessity of securing their protection or acquiescence in entering certain tribes' territories, made their cooperation fundamentally important to the opening of certain resources, such as mines, that happened to be located there. Needless to say, the nomads benefited greatly from these transport functions, which brought payment in cash and goods to participating *shaykhs* and their followers. In many areas, it was only with the cooperation of nomadic pastoralists that long-distance and even much local trade could be pursued.

These are some well-known aspects of this symbiosis, which was sufficiently important that neither group—nomad or sedentary—could probably have existed in the absence of the other without a radical transformation in its way of life. What needs greater emphasis, however, is that this interdependence influenced the lives of settled people (particularly villagers) just as greatly as it did the lives of nomads. It has long been clear that the nomad could not survive without the villager and townsman, but the economic impact of nomads on villagers and townspeople may go far beyond the few aspects noted in the preceding paragraph. Unfortunately, these influences must remain for the moment hypothetical, because so little of the essential spadework that might verify them has been done. We can, however, formulate a few of them at least as questions that merit closer examination in future research.

The role of nomads in providing transportation has been noted already, but several aspects of this function seem hardly to have been explored. Did it influence significantly the location or distribution of villages in certain areas and in relation to certain market centers? Did the limitations or advantages of the forms of transport used influence the kinds of products villages produced? Did these influences, if they existed, take regular enough form to permit us to generalize about them?

Similarly, the possible impact of nomadic groups on market structures has not been sufficiently explored. To what extent did the nomad's production of some things (livestock, etc.) but not others (manufactured goods, some agricultural products) shape the economic life of villages? Did the nomads provide a sufficient market for certain types of goods (e.g., tents) to enable some (many?) villages to specialize in the production of those goods? Did the specialization of nomads in stock raising cause villagers to pursue other aspects of agricultural life in a more specialized way by freeing them of the need to tend flocks?

In other respects, too, the presence of nomads may have had profound effects on the agrarian evolution of the region under study. We know that the agricultural evolution of Europe was influenced significantly by fertility of land, and that the latter was greatly affected by the manuring rate (amount and kind of manure per unit area per annum). Was the fertility of agricultural land in the Near East adversely affected, viewed over the long term in comparison with Europe, because nomads herded livestock in areas distant from farm settlements for much of the year? Did this factor or the rather rigid timing of the nomads' migratory cycle, which in many agricultural districts fixed the season when the nomads' flocks would arrive to graze on the stubble left after harvest, hinder technological changes that might have transformed agricultural relationships, such as the shift from two-field to three-field rotation that was undertaken in Europe? In making these comparisons it is not my intent to suggest that the European patterns were "better," of course, but to show that other agricultural arrangements than those that prevailed in the Near East (e.g., a more fully mixed farming regime, or a different annual agricultural cycle) are theoretically conceivable but may have been thwarted in their development by the exigencies of the nomadic cycle.

Finally, we might ask whether the periodic raids launched by nomadic groups on agricultural settlements might not have had repercussions far more serious than the obvious disruption of agriculture on the local level that they caused. For example, might these raids, by periodically ruining marginally productive peasants, have contributed to sharecropping arrangements by furthering the consolidation of agricultural plots in the hands of larger landowners after the raiders had withdrawn? Might the nomads' penchant for taxing certain areas have had a similar effect in a less sensational manner? Did the raiding pattern significantly increase the risk of investing in agricultural land and consequently force more investment into other sectors of the economy (commerce, crafts) than might otherwise have been the case?

In short, there are numerous possible economic relationships between nomads and their settled neighbors that remain to be explored on the basis of a careful study of both historical records and more-recent ethnographic data.

SOCIETY AND CULTURE

In turning our attention to the social and cultural dimensions of the nomads' impact on Near Eastern society, it is perhaps appropriate to begin by reminding ourselves of what seems to be virtually a natural law—or is at least as close to a natural law as one can come in the human sciences: that the social isolation of a group generates social and cultural conservatism, or put the other way round, that continuous contact of one group with others tends to engender social and cultural change as the community comes to terms with "alien" social and cultural practices. What I wish to propose here is that nomadic groups, despite their almost constant movement and their periodic contact with "outsiders," tended to be socially and culturally isolated.

As good settled people, we may find it a bit hard to accept the idea that these "people on the move" could really be called isolated, and it is true that many nomadic groups had social contact with other communities (whether settled people or other nomads) that were, geographically at least, far more wide-ranging than those experienced by many sedentary people, particularly villagers. Villagers, after all, frequently spent their whole lives and died within a few miles of their birthplace, whereas some nomads undertook annual migrations between summer and winter pastures that were hundreds of miles apart. But in this calculus of contact versus isolation, the mere geographical range of these contacts is of less significance than their timing or rhythm; and here a great difference between the social interactions of settled peoples and those of nomads becomes apparent. Villagers in particular, and even townsmen, may be largely limited to contact with outsiders from nearby regions—the next village or town—and only occasionally meet a truly alien traveler from a wholly different region or country; but this kind of contact continues on an almost daily basis among settled communities, and through it, new ideas and customs can trickle into the community almost unnoticed as they are handed on from one neighboring settlement to another. Nomads are subject to the same kind of cultural "infiltration" during the months they spend in close proximity to settled communities or living among them; but unlike their sedentary neighbors, nomads also spend part of the year—maybe the greater part of it, in some cases—in search of pasture, in a setting that for those months not only isolates them from almost all contact with outsiders but also places them in the sole companionship of others like themselves, in small groups among whom long familiarity and the exigencies of life reinforce their time-honored values and customary ways of doing things. Although there is no way to prove it, we can assert that the "desert" phase of the nomads' annual cycle may have had a kind of culturally purifying effect by which the various cultural and social "contaminations" to which individuals had succumbed during their sojourns amid settled society were annually diluted or forgotten or cast off, and the old values reaffirmed.

The implications of this social and cultural isolation are, it seems to me, quite far-reaching. On the one hand, it helped make nomads culturally conservative, that is, slow to change their ways; on the other hand, it gave them a far greater impact on settled society and culture than their numbers would lead us to expect, because their cultural conservatism meant that in their relations with settled communities they were continually reemphasizing the same values and customs. In exploring this proposition, I would like to select two instances in which we may suspect both that nomads showed themselves to be culturally conservative, and that this conservatism translated into a significant influence on social or cultural practices of the Near East as a whole.

The first involves the problem of language diffusion, in particular the diffusion of Arabic at the expense of other vernaculars. The survival of archaic linguistic usages among nomads—at least among Arabic-speaking ones—is quite well known, but we must yet consider the degree to which this linguistic conservatism influenced language usage in the Near East as a whole. Arabic first came to prominence in the aftermath of the Islamic conquests of the seventh century, of course, when it emerged as the official language of the new state, partly because the ruling elite of that state was of Arabian origin and had Arabic as its mother tongue. But Arabic had been quite widely used before the conquests, at least in parts of Iraq and Syria, as well as in the Eastern Desert of Egypt; and concentrating on the apparent relationship between the rise of Islam and the spread of Arabic obscures other strands of evidence that are perhaps just as meaningful in understanding how, and why, Arabic spread.

Many factors, obviously, contributed to the spread of Arabic in some areas and to its failure to spread in others. They included not only the use of Arabic as the language of administration and literary culture, but also the relative weight of immigration in certain regions (usually applicable only to a very small area, e.g., the environs of Merv, where a small island of Arabic speakers survives to this day, surrounded by speakers of various Iranian and Turkish languages). Another very important variable, however, was the presence or absence of Arabic-speaking nomads in a given region. The eventual Arabization of much of the Fertile Crescent—particularly of the settled communities there—was, I think, made possible partly by the presence of Arabic-speaking nomads in this area long before the rise of Islam. An expansion of these Arabic-speaking nomads into Iran, on the other hand, was obstructed both by the terrain, which did not suit the migratory patterns of Arabic-speaking nomads, and by the presence of other nomadic groups, already adjusted to this terrain, who spoke various Iranian languages; not surprisingly, then, Arabic for the most part never supplanted various Iranian languages on the Iranian plateau, despite long centuries of Arab rule and long use of Arabic as an administrative and cultural (especially religious) language.

My second example in the realm of social and cultural phenomena involves that institution called "the tribe"—which, in the Near East, can be described as a unit of social solidarity defined along lines of real or supposed kinship in the male line, and embracing as well some rather distinctive social practices, such as parallel cousin marriage. The "tribal ideal" is most closely followed among isolated social groups, particularly nomadic groups, and tends to be diluted in towns and cities, where many nonkin affiliations assume great social importance and to some extent counterbalance kin-based "tribal" ties.

It is perhaps not particularly surprising that nomads should adhere so closely to the "tribal" approach to social organization; for this basis of social organization satisfies especially well some of the social and other needs of people pursuing nomadic pastoralism. These include (1) the need for effective protection of small, isolated groups against aggression by others in areas outside the effective control of any state, (2) the need to establish more or less predictable social relationships with groups besides one's own (small) tenting group, (3) the need to maintain one's access to specific pastoral resources (grazing grounds, wells, etc.) and other localities visited during the migratory cycle by establishing the claim in the name of a corporate entity, (4) the need to preserve the stability of the pastoral group through different seasons in order to assure proper maintenance of the herds, and (5) the need to maintain the stability of the camping unit from year to year/cycle to cycle, despite periodic changes in membership due to death, birth, marriage in or out, and so on, so that the economic basis of life for the individual continues.

Similar needs are felt by peasants and others, of course, but because of the spatial fixity of the individual peasant and of the people around him, it is possible for him to establish relations with others that meet these needs without recourse to kin-based arrangements, and this doubtless contributes to the breakdown of "tribal" institutions in settled regions. But nomads almost always have "tribal" ties to settled people; that is, nomadic pastoralists will consider themselves to be members of a "tribe" that also includes some settled people, usually in localities with which the nomads of the tribe have periodic contact. This naturally generates considerable cooperation among nomads and sedentary members of a given tribe; there is even considerable movement back and forth from settled to nomadic life by individuals within a tribe in response to pressures affecting the prosperity of the pastoral or agricultural economy—what is usually called "sedentarization" or "desedentarization." Thus part of the settled population is intimately involved in the nomads' social world—which is "tribally" organized. We must ask, I think, whether the "tribal" social order would be nearly as prominent in the Near East without the presence of nomads, who maintain this "tribal" order in a relatively pure form and reinforce it in the course of their continuing interactions with settled communities.

POLITICAL STRUCTURE

The kinds of nomadic influence on Near Eastern society that we have examined so far have tended to operate toward the base of the social pyramid, even though they sometimes had far-reaching repercussions. It is clear, however, that nomadic groups sometimes exercised a powerful influence also on the organization of political power in the Near East in a more direct way, and it is to this theme that I would now like to turn our attention.

I will begin by drawing a distinction between what can be called *zones of state power* and *zones of nomadic power.* The Fertile Crescent and South Arabia are regions whose ecological conditions have historically permitted the rise of highly centralized, hierarchical, and bureaucratized political structures ("states") based on an agricultural tax base. Northern and central Arabia, on the one hand, because of their vast extent, difficulty of access, and meager resources, have generally lain outside state control, and in them successive confederations of pastoral nomads were, from about the third century B.C.E. onward, able to establish their control over local settlements.

Within the zone of nomadic power, the political life of towns and villages was shaped in its essentials by the vicissitudes of power among the nomadic population. In some cases, towns or villages were simply subjugated by nomads and forced to pay taxes. In others, a town was ruled by a leading family that kept its position by maintaining a network of alliances with local nomadic groups who served as agents of the family's influence in exchange for economic or other benefits. In some cases, a nomadic group might "capture" a town and establish its own leaders as the town's ruling family—a family that ruled partly by utilizing its close ties to its erstwhile nomadic followers. Examples of this process abound from Late Antiquity (Palmyra, Hatra, Edessa) right up to modern times.

In the zone of state power, of course, we might expect that relationships between nomadic groups and local power structures would be somewhat different, because the nomads living in the state zone could not be autonomous foci of power but instead fell under the surveillance and the taxing power of the state. Clearly the state prevented nomads from controlling settled communities directly, or at least seriously limited the character and extent of that control (although it seems that states often allowed nomads to work out among themselves power relationships with other nomadic groups). The states of the region under consideration have generally taken it to be of high priority to prevent nomads from raiding, "capturing," or taxing towns within their territory.

Where the two zones adjoined one another, there arose an intense competition between the neighboring state and the nomadic confederation, each trying to wrest from the other the exclusive power to tax the villages or to exploit the pastures of the border district. A powerful state could hold the nomads at bay by direct military action, or by establishing ties of alliance with other, more manageable nomads in the intermediate zone. It could thus push its control and influence into the desert and so secure in the intermediate zone the stable political conditions needed for fruitful agriculture and effective tax collection. When a state's power deteriorated, on the other hand, nomadic confederations could extend their influence or power from the desert into the intermediate zone. Sometimes this took the form of quick raids to carry off booty; at other times, the nomads might seize towns and reduce them to tributary status or coax settled people and other pastoral groups away from their support for the faltering state and into alliance with them. (We can note in passing that the fullest historical extension of the "state zone" at the expense of autonomous nomadic tribes occurred during the early Islamic period. This was no accident, for the leadership of the Islamic state, which sprang up unexpectedly in Medina, in the middle of an area frequently dominated by nomads, realized most acutely the challenge that independent nomads posed to their power and made concerted efforts to keep the Arabian tribesmen who formed the bulk of their armies firmly under the state's control.)

Even within the zone of state power, however, nomadic groups have been able to shape many aspects of the local power structure of towns and villages. In some cases, this influence was direct, a result of the instability of the border dividing the zone of state power from the zone of nomadic power—that is, the zone of state power shrank and expanded over time, so that a particular town could fall under state control for a certain period and fall within the zone of nomadic power at other times. Depending on the degree of "shrinkage" of the state zone, the relative strength of the nomadic groups and of the town, and other factors, the nomads might raid the town or extort short-term payments from it, or they might enter into longer-term relations with it—whether by "capturing" it and establishing a dynasty of their own there, or by entering into alliances with the town's leading families. In the latter cases in particular, it is clear that the nomads could come to exercise considerable political influence, if not direct control, over the political life of the settlement, and that this influence could remain operative even after the settlement had once again been absorbed into a revitalized and newly expanding state zone.

In indirect ways, too, the presence of nomads often had a decisive impact on the power structure of towns and villages in the state zone. The continuous processes of sedentarization of nomads and desedentarization of settled people meant that most settlements had residents who belonged to tribes the majorities of which were nomadic, and such settled tribesmen kept in close touch with their nomadic kinsmen, who could lend important support in personal or political conflicts, regardless of the position of the settled tribesmen in the town. Furthermore, even urban families with no direct kinship links to one of the nomadic groups in the vicinity might nevertheless establish ties of alliance or mutual support with certain nomads.

An examination of examples of these kinds of interactions between nomadic and settled people—mostly from the early Islamic period, the sources for which provide us with considerable information on this theme—makes it clear that we cannot hope to understand the politics of many towns or cities without reference to the tribes in the vicinity of the city, their alliances, relative strength, and relations to urban factions. Whether such relationships applied in all places must remain open to question—it is, for example, hard to imagine that they had much direct impact in a place like ʿAbbasid Baghdad. We would expect, of course, that such relationships would be more important in smaller towns and villages rather than in larger ones, where presumably the organs of state control (e.g., garrisons) would be stronger and the nomads' influence over local urban politics correspondingly less. Unfortunately, it is only the politics of the larger towns that our sources tend to describe, and then only in summary fashion. The smaller towns, where nomads may in fact have been overwhelmingly the dominant factor in the local power structure, are seldom described by our sources at all.

In conclusion, there is reason to believe that the role of nomads in the social, cultural, economic, and political life of the Near East during the period under examination was more far-reaching than commonly supposed. This observation applies, I think, to the centuries preceding the Islamic conquest as much as it does to those following it. We should perhaps add here a word of reservation, if not of caution, however: nomads cannot be expected to have influenced *every* aspect of life in the Near East. Architecture, for example, is a realm in which there is little to be anticipated by way of direct nomadic influence, since nomads have no true architectural tradition—after all, nothing could be more useless to a nomad, who must keep his culture portable, than a fixed habitation! Nevertheless, their influence was of profound importance to many aspects of life, as I have tried to show. If our picture of these influences is still in many ways incomplete or uncertain, this is partly because our sources for this subject, having been written by settled people with little understanding of and less sympathy for nomads, seldom provide us with the kind of detailed information we need to delineate more clearly the history of these relationships; instead, our sources are content to note, on occasion, the unwelcome incursion of the "Sarakēnoi," "Ṭayyāyē," "Aʿrāb," and so on, giving us no sense of who exactly they were, whence they had come, why they had been set in motion, or whither they vanished after withdrawing from the pages of our chronicles. Viewed in the broad context of social relations in the Near East, however, the importance of these evasive figures—intruders in our sources, perhaps, but nonetheless an integral part of the societies that produced those sources—can hardly be doubted.

BIBLIOGRAPHICAL NOTE

The present essay provides only a rough outline of a vast topic. In view of its general nature, I have made no effort to provide detailed references for specific points; but for those readers who wish to explore the subject further I have here included a bibliographical orientation to guide them to a few selected references that may be of assistance.

From the vast bibliography on nomads and nomadism in the Near East, the following selections can serve as an introduction and cover some of the points raised in the foregoing essay, which determines the order in which the items are listed below. On the Mongols, see Bertold Spuler, *The Mongols in History* (New York: Praeger, 1971), which provides a brief, clear overview of the expansion of Mongol power and their intrusion into many areas, including the Near East. On the Turks, see Claude Cahen, "The Turkish Invasions: The Selchükids," in *A History of the Crusades,* ed. Kenneth M. Setton, vol. 1 (Madison: Univ. of Wisconsin Press, 1969), 135–76. On the Islamic conquests, for a general survey of their overall scope, see C. H. Becker, "The Expansion of the Saracens," *Cambridge Medieval History,* ed. H. M. Gwatkin et al., vol. 2 (Cambridge: Cambridge Univ. Press, 1913), chaps. 11–12; a much more detailed examination of the first stages of the conquest, with special attention to the role of nomads in the process, is Fred M. Donner, *The Early Islamic Conquests* (Princeton, N.J.: Princeton Univ. Press, 1981). On nomadic pastoralism in the Near East, see by way of introduction Emanuel Marx, "The Ecology and Politics of Nomadic Pastoralists in the Middle East," in *The Nomadic Alternative*, ed. Wolfgang Weissleder (The Hague: Mouton, 1978), 41–74. On transhumance, see Xavier de Planhol, "Caractères généraux de la vie montagnarde dans le Proche-Orient et dans l'Afrique du Nord," *Annales de géographie* 71 (1962): 113–30; and Frederik Barth, *Nomads of South Persia* (New York: Humanities Press, 1961). On sheep and goat nomads, see Henri C. Charles, *Tribus moutonnières du Moyen-Euphrate* (Damascus: Institut Français d'Etudes Arabes, n.d. [ca. 1937]), as well as the next entry. On camel (dromedary) nomadism, see Robert Montagne, *La civilisation du désert* (Paris: Hachette, 1947); and Alois Musil, *The Manners and Customs of the Rwala Bedouins* (New York: American Geographical Society, 1928)—both classic studies, though the latter tends to romanticize a bit. On economic symbiosis of nomads and settled people, see the references in Donner, *Early Islamic Conquests,* 26ff. On the general evolution of European agriculture, see B. H. Slicher van Bath, *Agrarian History of Western Europe, 500–1850* (London: E. Arnold, 1963). On the diffusion of the Arabic language, see A. N. Poliak, "L'arabisation de l'Orient sémitique," *Révue des études islamiques* 12 (1938): 35–63, and several chapters in Speros Vryonis, ed., *Islam and Cultural Change in the Middle Ages* (Wiesbaden: Otto Harrassowitz, 1975). On the "tribe" and political relationships, see discussion and references in Donner, *Early Islamic Conquests,* 20ff., as well as the essay by E. Marx noted above. On the distorted view of nomads prevailing in literary sources written by settled peoples, from the ancient Near East to recent times and including the writers of the Late Antique Near East, see Brent D. Shaw, "'Eaters of Flesh, Drinkers of Milk': The Ancient Mediterranean Ideology of the Pastoral Nomad," *Ancient Society* 13/14 (1982–83): 5–31. Although this essay focuses mainly on nomads in the Near East, readers of this volume with a special interest in North Africa will find the following article of interest: Brent D. Shaw, "Fear and Loathing: The Nomad Menace and Roman Africa," in *L'Afrique romaine/Roman Africa,* ed. C. M. Wells (Ottawa: University of Ottawa Press, 1982), 29–50.

PART III

Models for a New Present: *Romania*

CHAPTER 6

Potentes *and* Potentia *in the Social Thought of Late Antiquity*

JÖRG A. SCHLUMBERGER

In every human society there is *potentia* (Lat. "power"), together with the opposition between the powerful and the weak. Yet in the late Roman Empire *potentes* ("men of power") and *potentia*—*dynatoi* and *dynamis* in Greek—played an especially noticeable role. Who were the holders of *potentia* at that time? What changes caused *potentes* to be more prominent in Late Antiquity than in earlier periods of ancient history? How was *potentia* evaluated in the social thought of the age?[1]

In poetry and prose *potentia* quite commonly has an additional meaning: the ability of religious elements, or even of a god, to cause something to happen.[2] I restrict myself to *potentia* in its political and social context. In this instance *potentia* is to be separated from *potestas,* which ordinarily denotes a legal authority whose duration and competence is clearly outlined.[3] The only definition of *potentia* to reach us from antiquity comes from Cicero (*De inventione* 2.56.168): "potentia est ad sua conservanda et alterius attenuenda idonearum rerum facultas" ("*Potentia* is the control of resources suitable for the preservation of one's own interests and the weakening of another's").

In the following pages I look first at *potentes* before the age of Late Antiquity. Then I study the meaning of *potentes, potentia,* and related concepts in the laws of the late Roman emperors. As a counterweight to this I next consider the same concepts in both pagan and Christian literature of Late Antiquity. A résumé will conclude the investigation.

In Cicero's speeches *potentes* often play an evil role; they are the unscrupulous supports of legal and political decisions.[4] The historian Sallust brands as *potentes* certain leading figures of the late republic—for instance,

Crassus and Pompey. With this condemnation comes a reproach: by their ego-centric efforts to gain absolute power, they are destroying the *res publica*.[5]

In the Roman Empire one finds the *summa potentia* or the *potentia Caesaris.* It is a generally recognized power that transcends all else.[6] It can be delegated. That is the way *potentes* appear in Tacitus, Suetonius, and other authors of their age. The *potentes* are individuals made powerful by the *princeps:* trusted advisers of the emperor, freedmen, wives or mistresses, *praefecti praetorio,* or senators with considerable influence at court.[7] In contrast to the *potentia Caesaris* itself, the derivative *potentia* had in most instances the stigma of abuse attached to it.

It is noteworthy in general that the evaluator decides who is powerful, and whether *potentia* exhibits positive, neutral, or negative overtones. In the realm of political, legal, and social affairs, however, the concept is beset, for the most part, with a critical (i.e., negative) undercurrent.

For a long time critics have assumed that in the history of Roman civiliza-tion the *potentes* became a problem for the first time either during the crisis of the third century A.D. or under the influence of Christianity.[8] The difficult be-havior of *potentes* is taken to be a special characteristic of Late Antiquity. We have just seen that the *potentes* make their appearance already in the sources of the republic and early empire. For the field of Roman law in the principate, the Digest attests to same thing. More than a dozen passages therein are con-cerned with the balance between the more powerful and the more humble.[9] The defense of *humiliores* against *potentiores* was recognized as an important legal problem even before the time of the first Augustus.[10] The management of the problem led without interruption to the legal enactments (concerning private possessions, penalties, and judicial procedure) of the late Roman emperors.

Therefore the *potentes* were not a new phenomenon in Late Antiquity. There is no doubt, however, that from the third century onward they attained a power and range of activity that were without precedent in ancient history. The phenomenon must be considered—the critics are right on this point— a special characteristic of Late Antiquity. The principal proof of this is approximately fifty laws of the late Roman emperors from Diocletian to Justinian. These laws survive for the most part in the great codifications—the *Theodosian Code* with its related *Novels,* as well as the *Code* and *Novels* of the Justinianic *Corpus of Civil Law.* In their constitutions the all-powerful em-perors, possessors of the *summa potentia,* designate other individuals as *po-tentes.* Who are the *potentes* of the late Roman imperial edicts?

In 293 Diocletian issued a comprehensive law in which he forbade the mis-use of *patrocinia potentiorum* in the judicial system. Lawsuits were to be de-cided in accordance with stipulated regulations, not by the influence of power-ful estates or by their legal advocates or foremen (*actores seu procuratores*).

In the interests of all citizens, above all the more humble (the *tenuiores*), the magistrates were to keep an eye especially on these *potentiores*. At the beginning of the text Diocletian stipulated that with his edict he was merely renewing a law of Claudius II Gothicus (*regn.* 268–70). At the height of the imperial crisis, the complaints of provincial subjects about the behavior of the *potentes* had moved that emperor to proclaim such an edict. In this instance the *clarissimi*, members of the senatorial order, constituted the nucleus of the *potentes*. Another law of Diocletian forbade coercion with the help of a *potens patrocinium*.[11]

It appears that the *potentes* first posed a serious problem during the crisis of the third century. The imperial edicts directed against them were already in full operation when the empire itself became Christian. Nevertheless, Constantine in particular issued many laws against the *potentes*—specifically, eight out of the fifty. Among these, three echo Diocletian's concern for judicial procedure. In an edict of 325, the emperor noted that *potentiores* had pressured magistrates while they were exercising their duties as judges. He ordered the appropriate procedures to move to the higher court of the *vicarius*. A short time later Constantine found it necessary to become more strict: conflicts with the *potentiores* were to be brought to the attention of the *praefectus praetorio* or to the emperor himself. In Constantine's last years, widows, orphans, and the chronically ill had the special protection of the imperial tribunal itself, in case they were oppressed by the *potentes*.[12]

In 364 Valentinian and Valens installed *defensores plebis* in all *civitates* of the empire. By imperial mandate the *defensores* were to protect—particularly in the realm of judicial affairs—the free poor against the arbitrary action of the *potentes*.[13] In some other constitutions these same emperors struggled against "potentiae terror" in trials involving private citizens.[14] In the same fashion a series of edicts from the reigns of Theodosius I, Honorius, and Theodosius II all the way to Justinian expands on this theme. Apparently the *potentes* and their representatives used ever more innovative means to break the law and in particular to seize the property of others. The *potentes* reached beyond legality, and many new domains of the private judiciary had to be used to check their influence, to the advantage of an individual holding or individual clients.[15]

Seventeen of the fifty laws on the *potentes* concern the matters already mentioned: private possessions, penalties, and judicial procedure. About thirty of the total, however, deal with a domain that never made its appearance, in this connection, in the legal sources of the earlier empire: taxes and duties, the liturgies that citizens and subjects paid to the Roman state.

By means of edicts issued in 313, 325, and 328, Constantine found it necessary to prohibit *potentiores*, in collaboration with municipal financial officials, from shifting the tax burden to the *inferiores*.[16] Since the *curiales* had to use their own wealth to meet the tax payments of their individual cities, they especially suffered from the manipulations and the *oppressio* of the *potentes*. Under such circumstances there is little wonder that from Constantine's time onward the *curiales* made a steady flight from their municipal duties to the protection of the estates and landholdings of the *potentes*. Their escape put the system of public administration and taxation in jeopardy. Constantine was the first emperor to oppose this behavior with a detailed ordinance: *decuriones* were not to escape into the "gremia potentissimarum domorum." Interestingly enough, there is in the decree a full description of the means by which such an evasion could succeed: impoverished decurions in search of wives attached themselves to the slave women of powerful estate owners; they entered into unions with these women, and finally entrusted their *patrimonium* to the *potentes* themselves. By this action a decurion's holdings were withdrawn from their important public—especially fiscal—functions. Tough penalties were threatened, depending on whether the affair occurred in the municipal households of the *potentes* or on one of their landholdings; whether the *actores* and *procuratores* of the *potentes* concealed the ruse; and finally whether the *potentes* themselves were aware of it.[17] The abundance of *curiales'* flights to the private protection of powerful estates increasingly disturbed the imperial administration. In 362 Julian made the penalties more strict, and so did Honorius in 395.[18] In the Western Roman Empire of the fifth century the situation reached the crisis point. In 458 Majorian, one of the West's last emperors, revealed through one of his laws that the *curiales* (the *nervi ac viscera rei publicae,* the empire's vital organs) were escaping to the possessions and *patrocinia* of the *potentes,* where they lost their citizens' freedom and accordingly were taken away from the clutches of the state. Their escapes were so numerous that in the cities the *ordines curialium*, the principal carriers of municipal administration, were perishing.[19] The end of the Western Roman Empire, an event based on inner structural weaknesses, was already being announced.

From 360 onward the Eastern Empire saw also a complete series of imperial constitutions prohibiting the *potentes* from taking free peasants and entire peasant villages into their *patrocinium;*[20] in so doing, they considerably disturbed the levying of taxes. In general, the small freeholders were better taxpayers than the *potentes,* who attempted as much as possible not only to manipulate the tax rates but also to embezzle tax funds.[21]

Some imperial laws reveal that the *potentes* and their foremen simply refused to pay taxes by such stratagems as self-assignment of privileges without any legal basis.[22] Under the protection of private *potentia,* even clients discontinued the payments they owed to the state.[23] The despairing efforts of the emperors Valentinian III and then Majorian mark the culmination of this development in the last decades of the Western Roman Empire. Both emperors sought to legislate an end to this fundamental evil. In a Novel of 441 Valentinian lamented that the Roman West stood on the threshold of its financial ruin, since an increasingly smaller number of exhausted *infirmiores* had to bear the tax burden, while the *potiores,* the *validiores,* and the *locupletiores* refused to pay taxes. The emperor therefore ordered a general suspension of tax privileges.[24]

In his Novel 2 of 458 Majorian once again remitted all tax liabilities in order to assure at least the current tax revenues. The magistrates were asked to pay special attention to the *potentes.* The *actores seu procuratores* of these men were thwarting the payment of taxes in the provinces in such a way that they stubbornly remained on their estates, and therefore scarcely made an appearance in the cities. As a result, the state's bureaucracy and the emperor's edicts did not reach them at all.[25] Despite the financial constraints threatening its existence, the Roman Empire's central administration no longer ventured to impose its claim on the holdings of the *potentes;* such a strategem was an illegal anticipation of what in the Middle Ages became an immunity whose hallmark was the prohibition of *introitus* and *exactio.* Eighteen years later the West Roman Empire came to an end. The *potentes* bear a full measure of the blame for its collapse.

Let us look back at the legal sources. In the laws of the late Roman emperors the attitudes toward *potentia* and *potentes* were mostly negative. *Potentia,* when it was mentioned, had the stigma of abuse attached to it. The portrait of a wealthy estate owner and a highly influential patron stood behind any *potens* who appeared in the edicts. In general, the *potens* belonged to the senatorial order, but he could also be a rich curial.[26] His holdings were widely scattered, and for this reason the *actores* and *procuratores,* his caretakers, played an important role in their unstinting attention to his interests.[27] The *potentes* fit the sense of Cicero's definition of *potentia:* they and their foremen set their own and their clients' private interests above imperial law and the common good. They therefore came into conflict with the more humble subjects, with the Roman state's legal system, and with the imperial fiscal organization. In the edicts, imperial officials (with whom the emperor presumably had good relations) are not even once referred to as *potentes.* The latter were instead rich and powerful individuals, acting in their own interests as owners of great estates. They took free peasants into their *patrocinium,* withheld taxes, and went outside the law to influence the state tribunals. Such actions made them appear (according to the assertions of the emperors themselves) as enemies from within, opponents of the centralized monarchy of the late Roman Empire. They took more and more resources from the central administration and thereby made a decisive contribution to the inner weakness of the empire (especially the western half) in the fifth century. The conflict with the *potentes* became ever more intense, right up to the end of the Western Empire in 476. The most stringent—and indeed the majority—of the laws directed against the *potentes* were issued especially for the imperial West. The problem appears to have burdened the East only after an appreciable delay. The Novels of Justinian show that the conflict was still durable and lively there in the sixth century.[28]

Modern critics have cast an eye on the legal sources of the late Roman Empire and have reached astonishingly different conclusions about the social dynamics of the *potentes*. The ruling elite of Late Antiquity is sometimes divided into two groups: on the one hand there were owners of large estates (a landed aristocracy), and on the other there were high magistrates and generals (a service aristocracy).[29] Some investigators, however, identify the *potentes* with the economically powerful, the estate owners, while others assign the term to the politically influential, the empire's high functionaries.[30] Was the late Roman aristocracy really divided in such a way? Or can the two groups be joined (as often happens elsewhere) to make up the *potentes?*[31] In order to clarify who the *potentes* were, we must bear these questions in mind.

In general, one finds a change of wording in the legal sources: until around 400 the constitutions use the comparative form for the most part—*potentiores* or *potiores;* after that time the positive form *potentes* is almost exclusively in use. Therefore, until the end of the fourth century it is possible to define clearly the group that can be called the *potentes.*

The legal sources are the most informative witnesses of social change in the late Roman Empire. They reflect the imperial bureaucracy's sophisticated information about social developments and demonstrate which of the empire's social problems had become so pervasive and intense that they required a general regulation. Nevertheless, the viewpoint of the men who issued the edicts is one-sided. As we have seen, it represents exclusively the perspective of the empire's central administration. What portrait of Late Antiquity's *potentes* can one obtain from other sources—that is, from the empire's inhabitants and subjects?

Pagan sources such as Ammianus Marcellinus, the *Anonymus De rebus bellicis*, Libanius, and the *Historia Augusta* set forth for the most part the point of view of early imperial authors:[32] *potentia* is principally power delegated by the emperor; *potentiores* and *potentes* are, in general, imperial functionaries.[33] They are, however, now quite different from how Tacitus and Suetonius portrayed them: instead of being restricted to a Romano-Italian nucleus, they are now an empire-wide phenonemon. Ammianus and the *Anonymus De rebus bellicis* gave special credit to Constantine, Constantius II, and then Valentinian I for having spread the coterie of *potentes* throughout the empire, and for having generously tolerated their pernicious greed.[34] Behind this reproach stands a fact of importance to the social historian: just these three emperors were significantly involved in the formation of the aristocracy of the late Roman Empire. Constantine opened the senatorial order to a broad spectrum of magistrates who until then had been equestrians. Constantius II constructed a second senatorial order in the empire's Greek East. And Valentinian placed the military high command in this expanded senatorial elite.[35] When pagan authors mentioned the *potentes*, censure was predominant: their implied goal of personal enrichment was enough to bring forth the charge of power abuse. As always, the recourse to negative attitudes was a matter of individual taste. Libanius, for instance, never reckoned his own social equals, the *curiales*, among the *dynatoi*. On the other hand, Julian (in his *Misopogon*) reviled the *curialies* of Antioch as extremely egoistical *dynatoi*.[36] In the circle of pagan authors, however, one work, the *Historia Augusta*, contains exceptional views.

On the one hand, the author of the *Historia Augusta* designates as *potentes* influential members of the emperor's entourage. Here he uses sources from the principate, and he is critical of such men.[37] On the other hand, the *Historia Augusta* calls rich and powerful estate owners—of the senatorial and even curial orders—*potentes*, but in a completely positive manner.[38] In certain passages of the *Life of Gordian I*, the extent to which the author departs from his model Herodian is noteworthy; his goal, achieved by free invention, is to make what he perceives to be the elder Gordian's excellent character shine forth more brilliantly.[39] Thus, the Gordiani were fashioned after one of Rome's oldest clans. They boasted patrilineal descent—no other source verifies this, and therefore it is presumably a pure invention[40]—from the Gracchi, and matrilineal descent from Trajan. As far as one can see into the past, all their male forebears held the consulate. Then the author speaks of Gordian I himself: "Ipse consul ditissimus ac potentissimus, Romae Pompeianam domum possidens, in provinciis tantum terrarum habens quantum nemo privatus."

In this and certain other passages of the *Historia Augusta*, a *potens*—here even a *potentissimus*—receives an unequivocally positive assessment. Most such evaluations pertain to Roman senators. In the present passage Gordian is a "most wealthy and powerful consul," and the author means *potentia*, not *potestas*. Why so? Gordian's power stems not from his office, the consulate, but from his immense private wealth. He could maintain the House of Pompeius in Rome and an unparalleled amount of privately owned land in the provinces. And this richest and most influential of Rome's senators became emperor. Evidently this was the goal of senatorial conservatives at the end of the fourth century. In all instances the *Historia Augusta* looks at *potentia* with the eyes of a tradition-minded Roman aristocrat: *potentia* is without question an ideal. This positive attitude toward *potentia* is unqualified: nothing is said either about the behavior of the *potentissimus* in relation to the state and the emperor,[41] or about the social element set opposite the *potentes*, the *tenuiores*. The author of the *Historia Augusta* is not interested in the relations between *potentes* and *inferiores*. The fact of exceedingly great power is reason enough for *potentia* to receive a positive evaluation. The richest and most influential senator, the scion of one of Rome's oldest families, is the ideal candidate for the emperorship. Such a point of view reflects the ideology of aristocrats, and indeed only non-Christian aristocrats. The Christian community judged *potentia* in a different manner, as we will see.

The church fathers of Late Antiquity were sometimes prolific authors. In their works one can find much about the *omnipotentia Dei*, the *potentia Christi*, and the like.[42] In contrast, human *potentia*, in the political and social sense, receives only occasional and peripheral attention. According to 1 Corinthians 1:26f., men of power belonged not to the Chosen People and to the world of belief, but to the earthly world of the flesh. Christianity's teachers debated often and heatedly the struggles and divisions of human society. Still, the ambiguities of relations between the highborn and the humble or the powerful and the weak were measured almost exclusively in terms of strict antitheses—the rich (Gk. *plousioi*, Lat. *divites*) as opposed to the poor (Gk. *penētes*, Lat. *pauperes*). Here the church fathers were following in the tradition of biblical thought and giving voice to the Christian precept of mutual love. Seldom did they hint that great wealth attracts great power in worldly affairs.[43] In so speaking, the Fathers depicted wealth and power not as intrinsically bad, but as fundamentally laden with a negative aspect—just as they are in real life. After all, the onset, increase, or even the preservation of wealth and power are hard to connect with God's Commandments and above all with the Christian challenge to love one's neighbors.[44] In Christian literature worldly power and its practitioners bear a negative stamp. The Magnificat of Mary (Luke 1:52) gives early expression to this idea: "Deposuit potentes de sede et exaltavit humiles."

Let us allow Basil the Great of Cappadocia (fl. late fourth century) to speak for the other church fathers. In his *Homily against the Rich* he paints an extremely graphic picture of the *plousios kai dynatos*, the *dives et potens*. His portrait probably derives from his own experience—from his own social surroundings.[45] Here is the pertinent part of the homily in paraphrase:

At first, streams hurry along as insignificant brooks; then tributaries make them bigger and more irresistible, so that finally their forceful current carries off everything that stands in their path. This is the way men of influence co-opt more and more people and force them to be a party to their wrongdoing. As a result, their wickedness knows no bounds, and their power grows unchecked. Nothing can withstand the force of their wealth. Everything falls subject to their tyranny. Everything cringes before their might. The *dynatos* allows his team of oxen to wander into fields which do not belong to him. He lets his laborers plow, sow, and harvest on lands which are not his own. If you oppose him, he beats you back. If you complain, he cries injury and summons you to court. You get arrested and thrown into prison. Sycophants stand ready to threaten your life. You reach the point where you are happy to be freed from this situation, although you have to offer up something else for this.[46]

But Basil did not stop with this description. The typical *potens* was a large estate owner who used illegal means and terror to enlarge his holdings and his circle of dependent clients and *coloni*. The Christian prelate made this man see the terrible circumstances he would live through during the Last Judgment. At that time he would stand before an incorruptible judge who would not allow himself to be duped by paid witnesses and glib defenders. The seigneur would have to plead his case alone, before a crowd of plaintiffs—without money, without the glitter of worldly distinction, without friends, and without assistants.[47]

The Christian authors of Late Antiquity are more explicit than their pagan counterparts: wealth, in the form of extensive landholdings, is the origin and foundation of all worldly *dynamis, potentia*. Public office and social rank come second and play a rather cosmetic role. Yet here also no administrative authority or court appears willing and able to check the inclination of the *potens* and his family to bend or break the law.

Other church fathers offered similar complaints—especially Gregory Nazianzen, John Chrysostom, and (among the Western Fathers) Ambrose and Augustine.[48] But in Late Antiquity Christian social thought found its most comprehensive and colorful representative in Salvian, the cleric of Marseilles who composed (around 440) the *De gubernatione Dei*. Salvian attempted to discover why the Roman Empire of his own day had been so severely afflicted with God's punishment in the form of the barbarian invasions. He placed most of the blame on late Roman aristocrats, to whom he gave various names indiscriminately—*divites, nobiles,* or *potentes* (Salv. *De gub.* 3.10.53, 4.4.20, 6.4.25, 7.3.16). Out of sheer greed, stated Salvian, do these men disregard God's commandments, especially the command to love one's neighbors.[49] In Book 5 of his work the cleric of Marseilles described the social and political consequences of the avaricious behavior of the *divites et potentes:* they were shifting the taxes to the few surviving free peasants—the *infirmiores, humiles,* or *pauperes* (Salv. *De gub.* 5.7.28–33). From the ranks of the elite came the provincial governors, who, together with the *curiales,* were responsible for the brutal tax collections by which they personally enriched themselves (5.4.17f.). For the *humiles* and *pauperes* tax deadlines meant fear of torture and loss of one's last small holding. It was no wonder that in the face of such villainous treatment by the *potentes,* the humble and poor fled to the barbarians (5.5f., 5.21–26). In case this was not possible, the ruined peasants had to hand themselves over to the *patrocinium* of a *potens* who demanded that they give him their landholdings in return for the promise of protection (5.8.38f.). They were clients of the *potens,* but sooner or later they became instead his *coloni*—his bondsmen. After all, everyone who lived on the estates of the *divites* was transformed from being free to being unfree—as if he were touched by the magic of a powerful curse (5.9.45). Salvian thereby condemned the lack of charity in late Roman society. The Roman Empire was on the verge of collapse, and Salvian made the unjust *nobiles, divites,* and *potentes* bear the blame (4.6.30, 4.40.20f.; cf. 1.2.11, 7.1.6).

Salvian portrayed the *potentes* principally from the viewpoint of the *inferiores, humiles,* and *pauperes.* In this respect he resembled other Christian authors and differed from pagan writers. For him, as for Basil, *potentes* were primarily wealthy owners of large estates. But Salvian pointed out more explicitly than Basil that high magistrates like the provincial governors came from the circles of the rich, and used their office to pursue their private interests. Salvian bore witness to the fiscal conduct of the *potentes* and its social consequences, the growth of the colonate and serfdom. His testimony coincides with what we learn from the Novels of Valentinian III and Majorian regarding the decades before the end of the Western Roman Empire.[50]

Let us begin to summarize: In Roman history the difficulties surrounding *potentiores* and *potentia* are evident already before Late Antiquity. Nevertheless, the legal and literary sources show that from the third-century crisis onward these troubles became conspicuously more intense.

In general, the term *potentes* does not describe a tangible and easily delineated social group. Subjective opinion governs the components and the evaluation of the *potentes.* Libanius did not designate the *curiales* of Antioch as *dynatoi,* because they were his peers. On the other hand, the emperor Julian apparently did so (in the *Misopogon*), after he experienced their disobedient opposition. The pagan *Historia Augusta* saw a social ideal in the *potentia,* as great as possible, of Roman aristocrats. In the remaining literature, the application of the idea of *potentia* is for the most part linked to the charge of abuse of power. The assessment of *potentia* in the imperial laws and in the Christian church fathers is fundamentally critical and negative. Here the confluence of imperial and Christian views is plain to see. The origins of the convergence, however, are not the same. Christianity censured the *potentes* for violating the commandment to love. When the late Roman emperors used the terms *potentia* or *potentes,* on the other hand, they blamed the private owners of large estates for putting the judicial and fiscal administration—and hence the state itself—in jeopardy.

On the subject of the *potentes,* the ancient literature is predominantly disapproving and negative. Thus it makes no sense to equate Late Antiquity's elite (as an entirety) with the *potentes.*[51] Is the elite to be divided into a landed aristocracy (the *potentes*) and a service aristocracy? The legal sources do not permit this conclusion.[52] Indeed, two considerations speak against it. First, certain pagan sources of Late Antiquity set forth high magistrates as typical *potentes.* Second, Christian authors regard magistral office and title as an important attribute of *potentia.*[53] In reality, we are dealing with two aspects of the same elite: *potentes* were rich landowners who could also hold high office in the service of the state. It is easy to see how vehement conflicts of interests would occur during their term of office. And how might such conflicts between public affairs and strictly private interests be resolved?

I think that Ammianus Marcellinus provides the best answer to this question in his celebrated portrait of the prominent Roman senator Sextus Petronius Probus. After Vulcacius Rufinus died (in 368), the emperor Valentinian I appointed Probus, who came from Rome, to the praetorian prefecture of Italy, Africa, and Illyricum. Probus was (in Ammianus' own words) "known to the Roman world for the renown of his clan, for his power [*potentia*], and for his great wealth. Throughout nearly the entirety of this world he owned widely scattered estates, whether justly or not"—here Ammianus speaks pointedly—"I, an insignificant judge, cannot say." On the one hand (continues Ammianus), Probus appeared to be a great benefactor who obtained high positions for his friends. On the other hand, he was an evil conspirator who caused cruel injury. During his life he possessed enormous power, partly through the gifts he gave, and partly by holding one magistracy after another. Yet he felt compelled to keep himself in state service without cease in order to cover up the illegal behavior of his family, the relations of his house. "One must nevertheless acknowledge"—here again is Ammianus—"never did that man, so richly endowed with greatness of heart, order either a client or a servant to do something illegal. But if he learned that one of them had committed some wrong, he would (even if Lady Justice objected) refrain from investigating the matter, and defend the man without regard for goodness and virtue."[54]

For our purposes, Ammianus' portrayal is sufficiently clear that it does not require detail-by-detail interpretation. The *potens* is senator and *dominus* of an enormous nexus of landholdings. When he holds high office, he remains loyal to emperor and state as long as his own interests and those of his social order are not affected. As soon as his *amici* and his *familiae*—his *domus*—come into play, he puts their betterment first. The private household of the *potens* is a fascinating phenomenon. It is exceedingly elastic—indeed, it is scattered throughout the Roman world.[55] It appears to be primarily an alliance for the protection of private interests. The rules governing a powerful private estate are placed above those governing empire and state. This facet of life will also be of great importance in medieval society.

In our investigation into the meaning of *potentes* and *potentia* in the social thought of Late Antiquity, we have observed several stages where tradition gave way to innovation:

(1) The change in the ancient sources from the comparative form of the word (*potentiores*) to the positive form (*potentes*) signals, by the end

of the fourth century, a new formation of the late Roman elite. The growth of its landholdings gave it greater influence in social and political affairs than it had possessed in the late principate.

(2) The growth and concentration of large landholdings contributed to the remarkable progress of the *potentes*. So too did a change in the political system: the bureaucratization of the empire, the late Roman system of taxation, and an imperial administration weakened by external and internal developments (especially in the West)—all these were contributory factors.

(3) The differing views of the *Historia Augusta* and the church fathers enable us to observe the change from pre-Christian to Christian social thought. The former made it possible to adopt an aristocratic perspective and set forth *potentia* as an ideal, while the latter gave *potentia* and the *potentes* a negative aspect by bringing to view the *humiles* and *pauperes*. Christianity thereby strengthened and unified tendencies already afoot in the ancient sources, especially in the imperial edicts. In the Middle Ages we encounter the idea of *potentes et pauperes* only in the Christian sense.[56]

Let us set aside the *Historia Augusta,* whose point of view is traditional and aristocratic. When the other Late Antique sources speak of *potentes* and *potentia,* they are referring principally to the owners of large landholdings at their worst. These men upset the social and political order, and they weakened the late Roman state from within by promoting feudalism. They were a centrifugal force. Already influential in Late Antiquity, they prefigured the considerable political importance of the powerful landed aristocracy in Western Europe's Middle Ages.

Translated by Frank M. Clover and Thea Schlumberger

NOTES

1 My *Habilitationsschrift* will deal with this subject more extensively: see J. A. Schlumberger, *Die Potentes in der Spätantike,* Historia Einzelschriften (Wiesbaden, forthcoming).

2 On the significance of spiritual or divine power in ancient religions, see K. Latte, *Römische Religionsgeschichte,* Handbuch der Altertumswissenschaft, Abteilung 5, Teil 4 (2d ed., Munich, 1967), 50ff.; R. M. Ogilvie, *The Romans and Their Gods in the Age of Augustus* (London, 1969), 9ff.; M. P. Nilsson, *Geschichte der griechischen Religion,* Handbuch der Altertumswissenschaft, Abteilung 5, Teil 2, Band 1 (3d ed., Munich, 1967), 68ff.; and W. Grundmann, s.v. *"dynamai,"* etc., *Theologisches Wörterbuch zum Neuen Testament,* ed. G. Kittel, vol. 2 (Stuttgart, 1935), 288ff.

3 Cf. C. Meier, s.v. "Macht, Gewalt," *Geschichtliche Grundbegriffe*, ed. O. Brunner et al., vol. 3, (Stuttgart, 1982), 830f.

4 See, e.g., Cicero *Pro Quinctio* 72; and *In Verrem* 1.25.40; 2.1.2f.; 2.4.7, 22, 133; 2.5.180, 183. On this see also J. Hellegouarc'h, *Le vocabulaire latin des relations et des parties politiques sous la république* (Paris, 1963), 240ff., 308f., 442f.

5 Crassus: Sallust *Catilina* 48.5; Pompey: Sallust *Epistulae ad Caesarem senem de re publica* 1.2.2. See also Sallust *Catilina* 20.7, 39.1; *Iugurtha* 3.4, 27.2, 30.3, 31.19 and 41; *Historiae* 1.12; and *Epistulae* 1.1.5, 2.5.3, 2.11.2. On this see C. Meier, *Res Publica Amissa* (repr. Frankfurt am Main, 1980), 180ff.; Meier in Brunner, *Geschichtliche Grundbegriffe*, 3:833f.; K.-E. Petzold, "Der politische Standort Sallusts," *Chiron* 1 (1971): 219–38; U. Paananen, *Sallust's Politico-Social Terminology* (Helsinki, 1972), 48ff.

6 See, e.g., Tacitus *Historiae* 1.1.1, 1.13.1; Tacitus *Dialogus de oratoribus* 13.4; Suetonius *Augustus* 94.2.

7 See, e.g., Tacitus *Dialogus* 13.4; *Historiae* 1.12.3, 1.13.1, 2.92.1 and 3; 4.2.1; *Annales* 6.8.4, 6.48.1, 11.28.1, 11.29.3, 12.3.1, 13.2.1, and 16.19.3. Cf. also Suetonius *Augustus* 66.3, 69.1; *Tiberius* 50.2; *Caligula* 56; *Nero* 6.4; *Otho* 2.2; *Vitellius* 7.1.

8 Cf. L. Mitteis, "Ueber dem Ausdruck 'Potentiores' in den Digesten," in *Mélanges Paul Frédéric Girard*, 2 vols. (Paris, 1912), 2:225ff., esp. 226f.; J. Gaudemet, "Les abus des 'potentes' au Bas-Empire," *Irish Jurist* 1 (1966): 128ff.; J. Gagé, *Les classes sociales dans l'Empire romain* (2d ed., Paris, 1971), 283f., 294, 335ff., and esp. 401ff., 417ff; and B. Biondi, *Il diritto romano cristiano*, 3 vols. (Milan, 1952–54), 2:174ff.

9 On this see A. Wacke, "Die 'potentiores' in den Rechtsquellen: Einfluß und Abwehr gesellschaftlicher Übermacht in der Rechtspflege der Römer," *Aufstieg und Niedergang der römischen Welt*, no. 2, pt. 13 (1980): 562–607, esp. 569ff., 589ff.

10 See, e.g., *CIC/Dig.* 39.3.14 *pr.*, with Wacke, "Potentiores in den Rechtsquellen," 598ff.

11 *CIC/CI* 2.13.1 (A.D. 293); *CIC/CI* 9.9.23.1 (290).

12 *CTh* 1.15.1 (325); *CTh* 1.16.4 = *CIC/CI* 1.40.2 (328?); *CTh* 1.22.2 = *CIC/CI* 3.14.1 (334).

13 *CTh* 1.29.1 (364). On this see also the other constitutions of both emperors on the same subject: *CTh* 1.29.2–5.

14 *Consultatio* 9.5 (365): "Lites trahi et sub quodam potentiae terrore infimos fatigari iudiciorum expectat invidia."

15 See *CIC/CI* 8.36.3 (380); *CTh.* 9.1.17 = *CIC/CI* 9.2.15 (390); *CTh* 2.14.1 = *CIC/CI* 2.14.1 (400); *CTh* 2.13.1 = *CIC/CI* 2.13.2 (422); *CTh* 3.1.9 = *CIC/CI* 2.19.12 (415); *CTh* 4.4.5 = *CIC/CI* 6.23.20 (416); *NTh* 7.1.1 = *CIC/CI* 3.25.1 (439); *CIC/CI* 1.12.8.2 (after 466); *CIC/CI* 7.39.9 (529); *CIC/CI* 7.40.2 (531).

16 *CTh* 13.10.1 = *CIC/CI* 11.58.1 (313); *CTh* 11.16.3 (325); *CTh* 11.16.4 = (in part) *CIC/CI* 11.48.1 (328).

17 *CTh* 12.1.6 = *CIC/CI* 5.5.3 (319).

18 *CTh* 12.1.50.2 (362); *CTh* 12.1.146 (395).

19 *NMaj* 7 *pr.* (458).

20 *CTh* 11.24 (*De patrociniis vicorum*). The catchword *potentia* appears in no. 3 (issued in 395) of this series.

21 Cf. M. Rostovtzeff, *The Social and Economic History of the Roman Empire*, 2 vols. (2d ed., Oxford, 1957), 1:295, J. Karayannopulos, *Das Finanzwesen des frühbyzantinischen Staates* (Munich, 1958), 8ff.

22 So *CTh* 13.1.5 = *CIC/CI* 4.63.1 with 1.4.1 (364); *CTh* 13.6.4 (367); *CIC/CI* 11.60.1.1 (385).

23 See *CTh* 13.1.15 (386), and also 13.7.1 (399); and *CIC/CI* 11.18.1.2f. (439).

24 *NVal* 10 *pr.* (441).

25 *NMaj* 2.4 (458).

26 E.g., *CIC/CI* 2.13.1.2 (see above, n. 11) and *NMaj* 2.4 (above, n. 25) speak of "clarissimis viris" and "clarissimarum domorum," respectively. *CTh* 12.1.173 (410) speaks of "inpressionem potentium," but *CIC/CI* 10.22.1 elucidates this expression: "impressionem potentium . . . curialium."

27 See, e.g., *CIC/CI* 2.13.1.1 (cited above, n. 11); *CTh* 12.1.6.1 and 2 (above, n. 17) and, most explicitly, *NMaj* 2.4 (above, n. 25).

28 On this see, in addition to the Justinianic edicts of 529 and 531 cited above (n. 15), *CIC/NI* 17.13 (535), 29.4 (535), 30 (536), 102.1 (536), and 69 (538).

29 Thus, e.g., F. G. Maier, *Die Verwandlung der Mittelmeerwelt* Fischer Weltgeschichte, vol. 9 (Frankfurt am Main, 1968), 88ff.; and similarly J. Bleicken, *Verfassungs- und Sozialgeschichte des römischen Kaiserreiches*, 2 vols. (Paderborn, 1978), 1:305ff. Bleicken nevertheless sees the highest senatorial echelons, principally the *illustres*, as a third group, set apart and above the other two groups.

30 For the first point of view, see, e.g., Karayannopulos, *Finanzwesen*, 8ff.; F. Tinnefeld, *Die frühbyzantinische Gesellschaft: Struktur-Gegensätze-Spannungen* (Munich, 1977), 29ff.; and Bleicken, *Verfassungs- und Sozialgeschichte*, 1:308ff. For the second, see, e.g., I. Gothofredus, *Codex Theodosianus cum perpetuis commentariis*, 6 vols. (repr. Hildesheim, 1975), 1:25; and 3:175.

31 Thus S. Dill, *Roman Society in the Last Century of the Western Empire* (2d ed., London, 1933), 267; Gaudemet, "Abus des potentes," 130f.; Maier, *Verwandlung*, 88f.; and Gagé, *Classes sociales*, 421.

32 Ammianus Marcellinus is accessible in M. Chaibò, *Index verborum Ammiani Marcellini*, 2 vols. (Hildesheim, 1983), 2:595–97, s.vv. "potentia," "potis." Libanius' speech *De patrociniis* (*Or.* 47) is full of examples. Cf. L. Harmand, *Libanius: Discours sur les patronages* (Paris, 1955); *Libanius: Selected Works*, ed. and trans. A. F. Norman, 3 vols., Loeb Classical Library (London, 1977), 2:491ff. For *Historia Augusta* see C. Lessing, *Scriptorum Historiae Augustae Lexicon* (repr. Hildesheim, 1964), 461f., s.vv. "potens," "potentia," "potior."

33 E.g., Caesar Gallus (Amm. Marc. 14.1.3), a *magister militum* (15.2.4), and several "potentes in regia"—among them a *praefectus praetorio*, a *magister equitum*, a *praepositus cubiculi*, a *quaestor sacri palatii*, and the great senatorial family of the Anicii (16.8.11–13). In his *De patrociniis* Libanius considers high imperial magistrates to be *dynatoi* or *ischyroi* (*Or.* 47.2, 7, 11, 16f., 22–24). Cf. Harmand, *Libanius*, 148ff.; and *Selected Works*, Loeb, 2:493ff. In the *Historia Augusta* one finds, for instance, the *potentia* of the praetorian prefects Attianus (HA 1.9.3) and Perennis (7.5.2 and 7.6.3), a *cubicularius* (7.4.5), and even the emperor Lucius Verus' sister Fabia (5.10.3).

34 Amm. Marc. 16.8.12f. (Constantine and Constantius II); *AnonRB* 2.2 (Constantine), Amm. Marc. 27.9.1ff. (esp. par. 4). See also Amm. Marc. 30.5.3 and 30.9.1 (Valentinian I).

35 The best authority on this is A. Chastagnol, "L'évolution de l'ordre sénatorial aux IIIᵉ et IVᵉ siècles de notre ère," *Revue historique* 244 (1970): 308–14. On Valentinian I, see E. Stein, *Geschichte des spätrömischen Reiches*, vol. 1, *Vom römischen zum byzantinischen Staate, 284–476 n. Chr.* (Vienna, 1928), 274; A. Nagl, "Valentinianus I," in *RE* 7, A 2 (1948): 2190ff.; A. H. M. Jones, *The Later Roman Empire, 284–602: A Social, Economic and Administrative Survey*, 3 vols. (Oxford, 1964), 1:142ff.

36 Julian *Mis.* 368 C and following, 370 C.

37 See above, n. 33.

38 E.g., "senatores . . . nobiles ac potentes" (*HA* 9.2.1); "Missae sunt et ad amicos nobiles litterae, ut homines potentes et rem probarent et amiciores fierent ex amicis" (*HA* 20.9.8); "Tunc quidam Mauricius nomine, potens apud Afrox decurio" (*HA* 10.7.4).

39 *HA* 20.2.2f.

40 On this see *PIR*, 1:833; J. Burian, "Zur historischen Glaubwürdigkeit der Gordiani tres in der Historia Augusta," in *Atti del colloquio patavino sulla Historia Augusta* (Rome, 1963), 45f., 53f.; R. Syme, *Emperors and Biography: Studies in the Historia Augusta* (Oxford, 1971), 166ff.

41 Gordian was strictly speaking a usurper, but a usurper who had rebelled against Maximinus Thrax, a typical soldier-emperor who was hated by the senatorial aristocracy.

42 On the biblical testimony, see, e.g., H. Haag, ed., *Bibellexikon* (2d ed., Zurich and Cologne, 1968), 49 (s.v. "Allmacht Gottes") 985ff. (s.v. "Kraft oder Macht"). For the Greek usage in the New Testament, see the citation of Grundmann *Theologisches Wörterbuch* above, n. 2.

43 See, e.g., August, *E. Psalm.* 51.14ff.

44 In this connection one recalls Matthew 19:23–24 (cf. Luke 18:24f.), where Jesus says to his disciples: "I tell you this: a rich man will find it hard to enter the kingdom of Heaven. I repeat, it is easier for a camel to pass through the eye of a needle than for a rich man to enter the kingdom of God" (New English Bible translation).

45 Basil *Hom. in div.* 5f. (*PG* 31, 293B–297A).

46 Basil *Hom. in div.* 5 (*PG* 31, 293B–296A).

47 Basil *Hom. in div.* 6 (*PG* 31, 296B).

48 Thus, e.g., Greg. Naz. *Or.* 18.35 and 43.26 (*PG* 35, 1032B and 36, 532C, respectively); Joh. Chrys. *In Matt. hom.* 56.4 (*PG* 58, 555); Ambros. *De off. min.* 1.13.47, 1.15.57, 1.16.62f., 1.28.137f., 2.24.124f., 2.29.144.ff.; Aug. *CD* 2.20; Aug. *E. Psalm.* 21.2.31, 138.10; Aug. *Serm.* 107.8f.; Aug. *De Trin.* 13.13.17; Aug. *Ep.* 96.2.

49 In general, see J. Badewien, *Geschichtstheologie und Sozialkritik im Werk Salvians von Marseille* (Göttingen, 1980), 99ff.

50 See, e.g., *NVal.* 10 (441) and *NMaj.* 2 and 3 (both 458). I have discussed these Novels above, nn. 24–25.

51 See above, n. 31.

52   See above, nn. 29–30.
53   See above, nn. 32–36, 48–50, and refs. to Salvian in the text.
54   Amm. Marc. 27.11.1–4.
55   The *Historia Augusta* emphasizes this same aspect in its characterization of the *potentissimus* Gordian I. See *HA* 20.2.3 and above, nn. 39–40. According to Paulinus of Milan (Paul. Med. *V Ambr.* 25), the *potentia* of Probus reached even beyond the boundaries of the empire: "Duo potentissimi et sapientissimi viri Persarum" wanted to meet Ambrose, the celebrated bishop of Milan, but they also traveled to Rome, "illic volentes cognoscere potentiam inlustris viri Probi." (Peter Brown kindly brought this passage to my attention.)
56   On this see K. Bosl, *Frühformen der Gesellschaft im mittelalterlichen Europa: Ausgewählte Beiträge zu einer Strukturanalyse der mittelalterlichen Welt* (Munich and Vienna, 1964), 106ff.

CHAPTER 7

Roman Aristocrats, Christian Commissions: The Carrand Diptych

KATHLEEN J. SHELTON

Late Antiquity is too often studied by scholars of the Germanic tribes, of the later Roman Empire, and of early Islam, who communicate easily and productively within groups of fellow specialists but who remain unaware, if quite innocently so, of the parallel interests and developments taking place in the research of colleagues whose subjects, if you will, lived in close, if seldom easy relation in the Late Antique Near East and Mediterranean. As a student of Late Antique Roman society, I am sensitive to the hazards of such specialization, further elaborated for my home discipline of Art History, where yet another division obtains: namely, the study of Christian antiquities separate from pagan. I am uncomfortable with these labels, but they will do for now. And, however uncomfortable they make me, the simple division of pagan and Christian, employed with a clear sense of necessary opposition, can be seen to be operative in the existing literature.

Although I may quarrel with vocabulary choices, I cannot, unfortunately, claim exemption from the larger observation. For some time I have studied those visual expressions of classical culture—gods and goddesses, epic heroes, Muses, and personifications—which flourished in the late empire, with no parallel research on my part into the Christian figures that are exactly contemporaneous. Recent years mark a shift of focus, the inclusion of Christian subjects, and find me a somewhat cynical observer of and on the other side. It is a mildly complex situation in that, for my earlier research, I have been consciously pursuing gods and goddesses, personifications, and the like that occur on artifacts which, in a great many cases, are attested by inscription to have belonged to owners whom we know to have been Christian. An elaborate example may serve to clarify: a large silver cosmetic case from the fourth-

Fig. 7.1. Esquiline Treasure, cosmetic case, detail of lid. London, British Museum (courtesy of Trustees of the British Museum).

century Esquiline Treasure carries an exhortation to a Christian couple to live (together) in Christ, inscribed in grand capital letters on the horizontal rim of its lid, below a bas-relief of a nude Venus pictured with her attendants (fig. 7.1).[1] Scholars continue to be startled and have not truly come to grips with this combination of Christian patrons and classical subject in the two hundred years since this object was found. It apparently would be much easier on the modern observer if the ancients had been simpler people; if conversion had been marked by an abrupt and complete rejection of all that went before. Conversely, it would be much easier on the ancients if the modern observer could simply master the lesson of the Esquiline Venus, namely, that what is classical is neither by definition nor by practice necessarily anti-Christian or pagan.

Involved is a romantic vision of Late Antique society in which every Christian endures the intellectual struggles of an Augustine and accepts Jerome's challenge to be either Ciceronian or Christian. By such a standard, the owners of the Esquiline Venus appear of two minds and their Christianity is therefore viewed as necessarily qualified. Involved as well is a far more simple disciplinary problem of mistaking the visual evidence, speaking as though the notional value of signs were constant through or perhaps despite changes of historical context: that a Venus in the fourth century A.D., for example, is identical with an Aphrodite of the fourth century B.C. Also involved is an overvaluing of the evidence, as though images on artifacts were preferred vehicles of expression in the ancient world. Debates between proponents of classical philosophy and Christianity indeed occurred in Late Antiquity but the medium of choice was the written and spoken word, not the images carved on the surfaces of cosmetic cases.

In turning to study Christian imagery, encountering the vast scholarship that seeks to explicate the extant Christian artifacts, I find the familiar problem of the exaggerated importance attached to the material evidence. This error has my sympathy, recognizable as the end result of too many long hours of hard work, whatever the subject or discipline. Also familiar to studies of both classical and Christian imagery is a problematic tendency of scholars, often fine scholars, to overinterpret, to find subtle levels of meaning beyond the obvious and general. To be sure, if they cannot be proved, they also cannot be disproved. But being possible is quite different from being probable. So, in the classical realm, scholars considering Christian sponsors of classical subjects have consistently found clever, clandestine pagans behind many features, apparently undetected until modern times. Unsuspected plots against imperial administrations have been thought encoded in the commissions of patrons more easily considered merely boastful and self-important. The fundamental nature of the evidence might serve as a partial check. Carved or painted by someone other than the patron; intended to be viewed by a larger audience when completed; composed, as a result, of images with easy, often rather broad meanings, necessarily accessible to Late Antique beholders, the artifacts possessed by Christian owners can be seen to participate in plots or to promote paganism only with the complementary assistance of verbal glosses, surely whispered, which do not survive if they ever existed, and which obviously move us beyond the expressive capabilities of the visual media per se.

Problems of overinterpretation exist for Christian images as well, but they are quite different in kind. Early Christian patrons of explicitly Christian iconography are consistently represented in the scholarly literature as innocent of plots and conspiracy. This is a rather interesting turn: after all, Christians who sponsor classical imagery are clearly thought a suspect crew, and therefore Christian patrons of Christian subjects might be anticipated to be open, at the least, to accusations of heresy. Very rarely; in fact, quite the contrary. Instead a scholarly literature exists in which representations are thought satisfactorily explained by the close study of creeds and of decisions of church councils. Never confronted or explicitly combined, these two bodies of Christian patrons, as envisioned in the two bodies of secondary literature, describe a church composed of true believers, that is, those represented by the Christian images, and questionable converts from classical culture, the Christian sponsors of the classical, so-called pagan scenes. I now understand in a way not possible before why so many modern scholars have had difficulties with the Esquiline Venus: they have been representing and defending the interests of the true-believer Christians, pictured as dwelling in a separate, sectarian Christian culture, against the classical tastes of their fellow Christians, who are, faith aside, pictured as their opposite number. Much evidence exists to show that, in Late Antiquity, classical and Christian mixed and, perhaps more important, that if there were difficulties—and there were—it would be difficult to find their trace through the visual evidence. I think it more reasonable simply to see all these Christian patrons as Romans. I should note here that in this modest methodology I follow in the path of colleagues who are historians of the later empire and art historians such as André Grabar, who has argued for the recognition of the common language of forms shared by the population of the Late Antique Mediterranean world, in truth, the only language of forms available with which visual messages, whatever their content, could be intelligibly exchanged.[2]

Analysis based on this premise is perhaps better practiced than preached. Such an approach educates a modern audience to see Jonahs reclining under gourd vines as modeled after classical representations of the sleeping Endymion, and the famous Christ figure from the mosaic vault of tomb M under St. Peter's as a variation on the representation of Helios, the solar charioteer. The list of such Christian transformations of classical types is nowadays obvious, lengthy, and continually growing, but there is no mistaking, in studies of this phenomenon of transformation, the sentiment that the classical forms have here met their fated end, captives in service to a victorious church. The classical forms, in fact, had a healthy life ahead of them, but there is an element of truth to this view, which, military metaphors aside, is but a restatement of the principle that there is but one common language of forms employed in the Late Antique Mediterranean.

I should like to extend this line of thought in a case study of a fairly complex Christian object: complex in that the adaptations from classical culture are numerous and drawn from several spheres of imagery which we moderns tend to keep separate; complex as well in the richness of the literary references which inform the representation; also in the nature of the commission itself, an ivory diptych, which can be seen to carry a meaning of its own, informed by its social function. But complex should not be confused with arcane. No theological debates here, rather, an examination of an apparent marriage of images drawn from the Old Testament, the New Testament, scenes of Roman government and philosophic schools, populated by figural types of classical heritage. Although we lack the reassurance of a detailed inscription, the characteristics, combinations, and structures of the images employed provide excellent indications of the nature of the patronage involved in the commission. The piece in question, the so-called Carrand diptych (fig. 7.2), is well known

Fig. 7.2. Carrand Dyptych. Florence, Bargello (courtesy Hirmer Fotoarchiv München).

to students of early Christian art for its remarkable state of preservation, its excellent technique, its good date in the early fifth century (for some scholars, late fourth) provided by comparison with more securely dated works, and its probable Roman provenance.[3] To the student of late Roman imagery, the ivory is further notable for the fine figure of the Roman consul who centers the left panel of this consular diptych. This last, rather casual observation is perhaps the predictable result of working too long with the corpus of Late Antique consular diptychs, in which officeholders identified by gestures, costumes, attributes, and attendants match those of the figure dressed in the chlamys, with his scroll of appointment, found on the left panel of the Carrand ivory. This bald statement bears modification, of course. Indeed we cannot know that the piece was a consular diptych, and caution perhaps compels us to retract the label consular without, however, eliminating it as a possibility. A larger issue, the identification of the piece as an ivory diptych, whether consular or not, a significant instrument of communication among aristocratic officeholders in the late empire, must remain prominent in any attempt to understand the images displayed on its surfaces. Further, those patterns of image making discerned for contemporary diptychs should inform an analysis and understanding of the piece as well.

What may now seem primary to a proper reading, namely, attention to the then-current definition and usage, the social context, and the conventional properties of this genre of commission, has had a strange history in the scholarship on the ivory. In my reading, there are heroes in this scholarly tale, who seem through their presentations to be sensitive to such concerns, although these are seldom stated. Never explicitly ruled out of bounds, this perspective, rarely voiced, is usually simply ignored. A brief review of the scholarly career of the ivory is revealing in this regard, for the historiography of the piece reveals seemingly clear patterns whereby meanings were deduced.

Involved from the outset are questions of scholars and collectors, as knowledge of the ivory reached an ever larger audience, and its interpretation, once fairly fluid, became fixed. Writing in the early nineteenth century, self-consciously following in the tradition of the great French antiquarians the comte de Caylus and Felix François le Roger d'Artezet de La Sauvagère, the author Claude Madeleine Grivaud de La Vincelle introduced to a scholarly public those ancient monuments and artifacts found in the territory of Roman Gaul in the years since the mid-eighteenth-century publications of the two earlier scholars. Among the objects described, discussed, and illustrated in his *Recueil de monumens antiques* is the Late Antique ivory we have come to call the Carrand diptych, with its representations of Adam in Paradise and scenes featuring Saint Paul. The diptych was said to have been found, "découvert," in the neighborhood, the environs, of the city of Mainz, ancient Mogontiacum, on the frontier of the *Galliae,* from the perspective of the French antiquarian the easternmost extent of the Gallic antiquities under review.[4]

The first private owner, the baron Vivant Denon, all his life a knowledgeable and apparently omnivorous collector of art, was in a privileged position to survey the market in such antiquities. Denon had been Napoleon's Directeur-général des Musées Impériaux, who, along with other agents, traveled with the armies to claim and collect paintings and sculptures as trophies, spoils of war. By 1817, the date of the ivory's first published notice in Grivaud, Denon was no longer directeur-général; the restoration government was in power. He was, however, still an active collector. Where and when he purchased the piece is not known; it was numbered in his collection of over two thousand objects when he died in 1825.[5] Most important for our present purposes, as part of Denon's collection the ivory was seen by an audience of scholars and scholarly amateurs, published in a descriptive catalog, and discussed in the lavishly illustrated folios of the *Monuments des arts du dessin*, conceived by Denon and illustrated almost exclusively by objects from his own collection. Written by the critic and fellow antiquarian Amaury Duval, the *Monuments* was published shortly after Denon's death.[6]

When the collection was broken up, auctioned by the heirs, the ivory entered another large private collection, that of Louis Carrand, a wealthy merchant then resident in Lyons. The importance of the ivory having been assured by its appearance in publications since the early 1800s, the piece was one of only a small number held by private collectors visited by delegates from the Arundel Society at the mid century in order to take impressions suitable for the production of plaster casts. The inexpensive casts, distributed out of the Arundel Society's headquarters in London, allowed a far larger, more heterogeneous audience access to the work. Accompanied by a catalog description, free to all purchasers of the casts, the ivory, even though still in the collection of Carrand, became truly well known, an object understood to be one of a class, to occupy a secure position within a fixed historical sequence. One senses here a canon being formed and promulgated. In the Arundel corpus, which included objects understood to be classical and which specifically included ivory diptychs in the subcategory Roman, with dates ranging as late as the sixth century A.D., the Carrand ivory was ordered under the heading not Classical but Early Christian and, despite the fourth century date then given it, placed in the subcategory not Roman but Italian. Subjects found on the diptych are indeed drawn from the New Testament. But the categorization by subject matter functioned as a social, cultural barrier, suggesting that a Late Antique aristocrat, living in the city of Rome, would not be Roman because the person professed the Christian faith. The patron should be understood to be both Roman and Christian. Yet the artifacts that originate from the patronage of such a person, through the mechanisms whereby the inanimate are housed, were not, are not, allowed to reflect the true dimensions of the patron's life as lived. Separated from the artifacts with which it shares workshop and patronage relations, the diptych came to be understood as one of the first Christian ivories, the head of a chain extending far into the Middle Ages. Within ten years of the Arundel Society casts, for example, it appeared as the frontispiece of a book subtitled "The Origin and Development of the Dress of the Holy Ministry in the Christian Church."[7] It entered a scholarly cloister from which it has not yet emerged.

Treated in the early literature to terse discussions, primarily in the context of corpus and catalog entries, the diptych soon came to be understood essentially as it is today. This is perhaps the point, although none is ideal, at which to comment on the original organization of the panels. Now separately mounted in modern wooden frames, in Late Antiquity the panels were hinged to constitute a diptych that, when opened for display, offered the Adam at the viewer's right, Paul at the viewer's left (as shown in our fig. 7.2).[8] From the first, the panel depicting Adam surrounded by animals in Paradise was recognized and briefly commented upon. The other panel proved more difficult to interpret and, seemingly for that reason, was discussed more frequently and at slightly greater length. Grivaud diffidently suggested successive scenes from the life of the church father Jerome for the three registers, with the Adam panel opposite symbolizing Jerome's periods of solitude. Dismissing this theory as weak, Dubois, an author of the 1826 auction catalog of the Denon collection, agreed with the identification of Adam but noted that the two lower registers of the pendant panel represented a saint (who went unnamed), a magistrate, one soldier with another, two ailing figures, and two attendants. The saint was specified to stand before a fire with a small snake on his hand, and, Dubois objected, no episodes from the life of Jerome could be so described. Three years later, writing in the *Monuments des arts du dessin* Duval supplied names and identities for this blandly described scene of saint and magistrate, citing the New Testament passage of Paul's miracles on Malta (Acts 28:3–9) where, having survived the bite of a snake, Paul cured the sick of the island.

At the midcentury, with the Arundel Society's visit to the Carrand collection and the consequent expansion of the ivory's audience, the last scene to be identified came to be understood as Pauline as well, taken to represent Paul speaking to other figures of the early Church. The Anglican minister W. B. Marriott thought Peter the attentive listener behind Paul's elaborate chair as Paul addressed Linus, Peter's successor as bishop of Rome, whom Irenaeus had identified with the Linus of 2 Timothy as a follower of Paul (*Adv. Haer.* 3.3). J. O. Westwood, one of the main actors in the Arundel campaign, alone in seeing the bottom registers as the miracles of Paul and Barnabus at Lystra (Acts 14:7–10), accepted Mariott's identifications of Peter and Linus at the top but ecumenically noted that Linus bore a "considerable resemblance to Martin Luther." Others switched Linus for Peter, putting Linus at the right; some then substituted Luke for Linus. Still others saw Luke as the figure at the left with the large codex, his gospel. This last, revived many years later by R. Delbrueck, as been largely set aside, replaced in recent literature by various proposals of Pauline speech scenes found in Acts. R. Garrucci, the first to take this approach in 1880, suggested Paul's address on the Areopagus in Athens (17.19–34) and nominated Dionysius the Areopagite as one of Paul's audience on the ivory.[9]

It should be noted that the nominations for the identity of this scene were each accompanied by reasonable, if brief, cases: for example, as mentioned, it was argued that Luke was represented, for he was identified by his gospel book; or that the scene was the Areopagus address because all three figures were depicted as learned men. Both these cases deserve attention and will be examined later. For now the analytic pattern should simply be observed wherein identities have been offered as solutions to small, independent puzzles with little if any regard to their fit within a larger structure of meaning.

With, or perhaps despite, the differing proposals for the actors of the top register of the Paul panel, the ivory has been consistently read as the pairing of Paul on Malta and Adam in Paradise, now for nearly a century and half, finding first voice in Duval's *Monuments* of 1829. And for a century and a half, no one has truly understood the nature of this pairing. There do not appear, indeed, to have been many serious tries. The pattern witnessed in the discussions of the representation at the top of the Paul panel is seemingly repeated as the individual panels came to be understood as satisfactorily identified. No puzzles, certainly not since 1829; instead, an apparent acceptance of separate solutions, separate scenes on separate panels, each quite isolated from the other. Commenting on the piece when it entered the Bargello from the Carrand collection, A. Pératé in fact wondered if the leaves should be separated, if they were actually from two different diptychs, now mismatched.[10] Few have been so public in their doubts or their difficulties in interpreting the ivory. More typically, scholars, in the absence of a missing link, have simply treated the images on one leaf quite independently of the images on the other. A graphic, if indirect, reflection of the scholarly problem is the common choice of but one panel from the pair to illustrate published discussions.

Not to make too much of editorial decisions over plates, the Carrand ivory is indeed one of the few extant diptychs in which the halves seem visually, conceptually independent, in which the representations of one leaf do not easily or automatically call up those of its pendant. Behind the problems of interpretation, behind questions like that of the skeptical Pératé, lie, unexplored, observations of patterns witnessed for most Late Antique diptychs. There, when panels do not simply replicate one another, typical for the extant consular diptychs of the sixth century, the two images seem to speak together, if not in unison. Compositions mirror one another or respond in loose symmetry or repeat with distinct variations introduced. And always the subject of one leaf bears close relation to that of the other: thus a poet on one attends his

Fig. 7.3. Aesculapius and Hygieia Diptych. Liverpool Museum (courtesy Liverpool Museum).

muse on the other; a god is matched with his appropriate goddess (fig. 7.3); an officeholder is shown in two different aspects of his office or in two complementary offices, that is, as consul on one, as *patricius* on another. In a Christian setting, an enthroned Christ is paired with an enthroned Mary.[11] Within a corpus of diptychs so designed, the Carrand diptych has always seemed an anomaly.

Observations of the identity of the size of the two leaves of the Carrand, plus a checklist of technical details witnessed for most well-preserved examples, only serve to emphasize the precision of the physical fit in the face of

Fig. 7.4. Diptych of the consul Anastasius. Paris, Bibliothèque Nationale (courtesy Hirmer Fotoarchiv München).

compositional and iconographical difficulties. First, let us consider an example of a compositional question raised by this ivory and one, to be sure, that is not easily answered. Although disparities of scale often occur within single leaves of diptychs, with consuls twice to five times larger than their attendants or the actors in their games (see fig. 7.4), with sizes clearly related to the social or narrative importance of the figures, a shift of scale from one panel of a diptych to its pendant, that is, from the Adam panel to the Paul panel, has no precedent. Most authors pass over this problem without comment; much to H. L. Kessler's credit, he has noted this detail, proposing that the shift marks the retention of stylistic characteristics of two different models.[12] Indeed, aspects of models from Old Testament and New must surely be seen to effect the visual disjunction, but the question then must simply shift: Why such fidelity to models here? A question of style, of composition, becomes a question of meaning, of intention, and the issue of the weighted genre of the commission itself becomes pressing. If we remain puzzled over the import of the shift in scale from one panel to the next, other large issues, some potentially solvable, remain to be addressed. Perhaps most important, the evidence of extant diptychs would indicate that halves are paired to a purpose: the subject of one leaf reinforces and enhances that of the other; the whole, indeed, being greater than the sum of the parts. How does Paul inform Adam or Adam, Paul? And what do they mean together?

Grivaud de La Vincelle, first to comment upon the ivory and one of the heroes of this tale, was sensitive to the necessity of a relation between the two leaves and cobbled together his awkward solution in which Adam represented an aspect of the life of the holy Jerome displayed in three registers opposite. Self-consciously marking an advance on Grivaud's theory, Duval quite correctly identified the major scenes, briefly discussed the content and purpose of consular diptychs, and observed our ivory to be a Christian adaptation of the form. Quite unfortunately, in rejecting Grivaud's specific solution, that is, the pairing of Adam and Jerome, Duval also abandoned Grivaud's tacit premise of the reciprocity of subject matter for the two leaves. And most subsequent scholarship has followed this pattern. Marriott, a bit of a maverick and a second hero, even as he struggled with the representation at the top of the Paul panel, saw a larger scheme for the diptych, encompassing both halves. It was, he said, about snakes. To quote the reverend Marriott: "Paradise lost through the malice of the serpent, and Paradise reopened through Him who crushed the serpent's head." [13] This passes a bit wide of the specific details so carefully displayed in the organization of the piece, in which the serpent in the ivory Eden is simply one of several beasts that salute or reply to Adam. On the Paul panel, the snake is hardly crushed but rather displayed, dangling from Paul's right hand. But, however intuitive and inexact the observation, Marriott came closer to the solution of the iconographic puzzle than any author before or after, until the present day.

The juxtaposition can now be explained as original to the later fourth century, reflected for us in patristic sources, repeated and adapted, though very little altered, through the writings of subsequent generations. These include

Basil in his *Hexaemeron* (*Hom. in hex.* 9.6), Ambrose in his (*Hex.* 6.6), John Chrysostom in his sermons on *Genesis* (*Serm. in Gen.* 5.2), Augustine in his commentary on *Genesis* (*De Gen. ad litt.* 3.15), and Theodoret of Cyrrhus in his *Questions on Genesis* (*Qu. in Gen.* 1.18). The authors of this roster take us up to the mid fifth century, beyond the date of the diptych, and offer testimony of the widespread and consistent linkage of the themes represented on the Carrand ivory. Patristic exegesis of the Creation story calls up the pairing of Adam in Paradise, safe in the midst of the beasts in Eden, with Paul's immunity from the bite of a viper following his shipwreck on the island of Malta, and allows the understanding that a relation between the two was actively posited by Late Antique Christians, preached in sermons and elaborated in learned commentaries. But we are, after all, dealing with an artifact not a text. To be sure, Christians of this period understood that Adam in Paradise was in some ways like Paul, here specifically like Paul on Malta. Such is the hold, the apparent primacy, of the literary sources that we seem to be saying that an ivory diptych is like a sermon. Perhaps it is more complex: that an ivory diptych is like a translation of literary exegesis into visual imagery. It is worth pausing to question what it is that we are saying or, possibly, not saying but assuming. What is the relation of this analysis, however appealing, to the historical process whereby images come to appear on objects? What then do we mean by translation?

I confess that my skepticism shocks even me. I remember the exhilaration of coming upon the passages linking Adam and Paul, first in Basil, then in other authors. At the point of discovery, I had the sure sense that the meaning of the Carrand diptych was finally recovered. I am less sure now or, rather, know that its full understanding goes far beyond the evidence found in patristic sources. Given the innumerable metaphors with which the church fathers bound characters and events from the Old Testament with characters and events from the New, the earlier question returns: Why this pairing here? What was the process whereby this exegetical, analogical statement came to be selected for representation on an ivory diptych? What does it mean here? And how does it mean? Unwilling to hypothesize the existence of hundreds, if not thousands, of diptychs, no longer extant, once illustrating a corpus of patristic analogies, of which this diptych would be the sole survivor, I posit an act of selection on the part of a patron or craftsman to have resulted in these representations and take the next step of inquiring after the purpose served by that act of selection. The representations on this diptych have much to do with Late Antique conceptions of the biblical Creation and with the growing importance of Paul and of Acts in the theology and in the self-conscious Christian historiography of the centuries following the recognition of Christianity as a legal religion. However, equally important to an understanding of the ivory is the recognition of iconographic conventions employed and purposes served by diptychs, materials very familiar to the Late Antique society in which the piece was commissioned.

First the images: Given, and indeed it is a given, that Adam, surrounded by beasts in Paradise, and Paul, immune from the viper's bite on Malta, was a pairing as vivid and as close at hand to the Christians of Late Antiquity as it is distant from us today, the combination must cease to puzzle. The quantity, consistency, and geographical and chronological range of patristic references ensure that certainly Mediterranean Christians would have recognized here a familiar theme. Introduced in commentaries on the creation of the animals, specifically when they argue the purposes served by the creation of noxious, deadly animals, Adam, safe in the state of grace before the Fall, was likened to Paul, protected by his faith. (Hardly surprisingly, Daniel in the lions' den was occasionally added to this company whom faith and grace protected.) Turning to the diptych, we see an emendation of this basic exegetical notion, for our Adam quite clearly gestures in speech, naming the animals, many of whom roar or growl in apparent reply. Not that the Fathers were silent on the subject of Adam naming the animals; far from it. But the diptych leaf, with its little bird, its grasshopper, and a variety of domesticated beasts, is not the collection of solely noxious animals indicated by the patristic texts that refer to Paul on Malta. The deadly beasts certainly are there, with a great serpent calling up the Fall as well as the viper's thwarted role in the adjacent Pauline episode. But the company on the panel is clearly mixed, both deadly and domestic.

Now it seems plausible that, as reflected in extant visual sources, there was but one scene of Adam and animals, namely, the Naming, in the minds and eyes of a Late Antique audience: the patrons, craftsmen, and the recipients of their commissions. The additional exegetical requirement of a representation of Adam safe in the midst of dangerous beasts drew on this established, conventional image. The Naming, of course, carried its own connotations of the God-like power and dominion proper to man formed in God's image, ideas clearly congruent to the theme of Adam safe in the midst of threatening beasts; after all, the very natures of those noxious animals were defined by Adam when he named them. His power established their natures; their natures, however, were checked by his prelapsarian inviolate state of grace. The Fathers understood the Naming to illustrate the intellectual, rational aspect of man's divine nature. To name, to speak, is to reason and thereby to dominate, to rule. And, with that, we are easily returned to a scene of Adam ruling a Paradise populated by creatures, some of whom would prove dangerous after the Fall.

Just how dangerous can be judged from the reactions of the men on Malta, on the leaf opposite, where Paul is depicted, at the left margin in the middle register, with the viper still firmly attached to his right hand. In the Acts narrative, the snake crawled out from a fire built by the natives of the island to warm the survivors of a shipwreck. One of the passengers on that ship was Paul, who was busying himself gathering branches to supplement the fire when the viper struck. The figure at the right margin shrinks back from the snakebite scene, even as we recognize his open palm gesture as one of witness, which he shares with another figure at the center of the panel. There, dressed in the tunic, chlamys, and great bow fibula of a court dignitary, stands Publius, the chief magistrate of the island, the *prōtos tēs nēsou* of the Greek text, the *princeps insulae* of the Old Latin and Vulgate, with his scroll of appointment in his left hand. All the witnesses, in fact, are good examples of the Late Antique visualization of the narrative. Publius, the centrally placed Roman magistrate, a figural type so familiar from countless consular diptychs, is attended by the *barbaroi* of the island, here transformed with the fur capes, tunics, and trousers of the Germanic guard frequently shown attending emperors and officials in scenes at the imperial court. The complete compositional grouping of that middle register is one associated with speech, here modified: not speech perhaps, but demonstration, exhibition, where the official figures, magistrate and attendants, bear witness to the deeds of a philosopher, a teacher, for that is without question how this and nearly all other representations of Paul were read. Shod in sandals and wrapped in a long mantle, Paul is treated as well to a facial type, balding with a long beard, proper to a philosopher, if not the only philosopher type recognized by a Late Antique audience. That audience could, further, see their Christian philosopher in the company of fellow, if lesser, learned men in the register above.

In addition to the solutions mentioned above, many attempts to identify the scene at the top of the Paul panel have proceeded from the innocent assumption that it represents a second episode from the Acts narrative, preferably one earlier than the miracle on Malta, because (although this is nowhere explicitly stated) it is encountered first, reading down the leaf. Nominated have been Paul's trials before the Roman governors Felix and Festus and his defense before the Roman client-king Agrippa. These passages, after all, immediately precede Paul's shipboard passage to Rome as a prisoner of the Roman state to be tried before Caear; the shipwreck on Malta interrupts this journey. However, the Paul of this top scene is clearly represented as a speaker superior to the members of his audience: he who sits when all others stand enjoys the dominant status. And Paul's appearances before Felix, Festus, and Agrippa were scenes of defense, no matter how eloquent, of a prisoner in court before government officials. Further, a glance back at Publius in the middle register, arrayed in his magistrate's robes with his bodyguard, informs us that the patron and craftsman of our ivory were indeed interested in and knowledgeable about the proper representation of officeholders in the Roman Empire.

An identification of the scene as Paul's speech before the Areopagus in Athens is a further mismatch. The text states that Paul stood to make his address in Athens, and the craftsman certainly did not lack for figural types of standing orators for visual reference. In addition, the Areopagus speech lacks, among other things, the presence of honored listener or recipient, for this is indeed the sense of the figure at the left, in philosopher's dress, who stands on a platform like that on which Paul rests his feet, with a gesture of receipt or hearing. As mentioned before, this prominent listener, with codex in hand, has been identified as Luke, believed by Late Antique Christians to have been Paul's companion and the author of the Acts of the Apostles. With little more than the codex to go on, the old theory nevertheless bears consideration. If scholars like H. P. L'Orange have been struck by the similarity of the conventional Paul type to the portraiture of Plotinus,[14] the pairing of notable teacher with notable pupil, such as Plotinus with Porphyry, provides the type that lies behind this scene of Paul with honored disciple, quite possibly, if not necessarily, the evangelist Luke. Both of Paul's listeners in the top register have been given nicely differentiated physiognomies, sufficiently distinct so as to suggest that two individuals are here marked. Luke and Timothy? Luke and Barnabus?[15] Not necessarily portraits, mind you, simply an indication of the craftsman's intent to signal two separate persons. That we need further signs—a winged bull would certainly help—is simply an indication of our distance from the culture that produced the artifact. But from those more general signs whose import is understood, we are surely right to see here the representation of a wise man, a holy wise man, speaking to his pupils.

This theme, certainly not original to the biblical text, finds support in numerous patristic writings that speak of Paul's teaching, perhaps nowhere as resonantly as John Chrysostom's *De laudibus Pauli,* in which the Pauline mission is favorably compared with the works of the pagan philosophers: both literary and visual models are thus seen to be borrowed from and enriched by the same parallel classical tradition. The theme, with its emphasis on speech, recalls the Adam panel of the diptych with its message of the implicit power of the word. And, as in any Pauline enterprise, works, such as the apostle's teaching, call up demonstrations of faith, which return us to the scene of the miracle below.

There we encounter a biblical narrative transformed, with alterations extending beyond, while still including, the figural types we noted earlier. Patristic exegesis of Genesis, which establishes the pair of Adam and Paul, is here emended and greatly enlarged. The text of Acts gives a sequence that begins with the shipwreck, followed by the kindness of the natives, the miracle of the viper, and the natives' reactions. After an apparent shift of scene, Paul and his fellow shipwreck vicims are received by Publius, who provides food and shelter; Paul then heals Publius' bedridden father; and other ailing natives of the island then seek Paul's cure. Patristic commentaries on Genesis excerpt only the miracle of the viper, with a few alluding to the natives' reac-

Fig. 7.5. Paul struck by the snake, Vat. Barb. lat 4406, fol. 125. Vatican City, Biblioteca Apostolica Vaticana (courtesy Biblioteca Vaticana).

tions. No fellow shipwreck victims, no Publius, and little by way of natives being kind or natives being cured. When we turn to Prudentius' retelling of the tale in his *Contra Symmachum* (1.1–44), we see a dramatic shipwreck scene, much about Paul and his fellow passengers, and, of course, the miracle. No natives, no Publius. Analogous to Prudentius is the fifth-century fresco from S. Paolo fuori le mura (fig. 7.5), with its abandoned sails and shipwreck survivors who witness the snake striking Paul. Again, no natives, no Publius.[16] Only in Chrysostom's commentary on Acts, the only one of several patristic commentaries on Acts to survive, do we hear of Publius, who is, however, discussed in a context exactly opposite to that established in our diptych. Chrysostom cites Publius (*Hom. in ac.* 54.7), as Jerome cites him (*Ep.* 77.10), as the virtual personification of hospitality, *philoxenia,* one who is kind to Paul, as they state, solely out of compassion, for the very reason that Publius had been absent from the scene and therefore *knew nothing of the miracle* that had previously taken place.

Our ivory quite clearly departs both from the biblical text and from the patristic commentaries, whether on Genesis or on Acts. And the departure, hardly minor, becomes the organizing principle of the scene. In the bottom registers of the Pauline leaf are displayed story elements contained neither in the commentaries nor in the New Testament narrative. In the diptych, the official Publius is introduced as a witness to the miracle, and not merely any witness, but the primary one whose reaction is literally central and forceful.

Paul, clearly the dominant figure in the uppermost register, here becomes one of a pair of Paul and Publius, and it is the interaction of these two that is the formal focus of the others. There is no shipwreck, no bedridden father, no kind natives who build a bonfire. Rather, in the lowest of the three registers, we see a skillfully edited narrative: those ailing natives who, in the text, seek Paul subsequent to the healing of Publius' father are in the ivory represented as witnesses to the primary miracle of the viper. The Germanic guards from the middle register might be thought to reappear at the bottom, as attendants to the sick Maltese, thus implying a statement of temporal sequence corresponding to the sequence of the biblical tale. Subscribing to the primacy of the written text for the explication of the visual, however, would here involve ignoring details of the carving, where the two young guards have been given capes of two different furs and the two old ones groomed with two different beards, one longer and less well kempt than the other. Further, the pointing gesture of the elderly attendant at the right in the lowest register would have to be read as purely rhetorical, summoning up the story of the miracle for one who was not present. But the cripple's gaze follows the pointing gesture; involved is the eye as well as the mind's eye. Thus a single great scene of witness is constructed, with natives pictured as official bodyguards and attendants and natives shown suffering various ills taking the place, but, in a sense, swelling the ranks, of the natives on the beach who are the sole witnesses specified by the text. They point and gaze, as much if not more at Publius than at Paul.

The miracle is here understood and displayed for its own sake, to be sure, but perhaps more for its effect on a significant beholder, clearly interpreted as an official of the Roman Empire. Quite tellingly, what Publius acknowledges is more than the miracle of the viper, for the figure of Paul has been elaborated by the addition, or, more properly, the substitution, of an attribute not explained by any version of the text or found in another rendering of the scene. Between Paul and Publius, locked together hand to arm, on the axis established by the vertical of Publius' gesture of witness, we find the fire, the viper, and Paul's offering for the fire. The offering, however, is not the many sticks or branches of the texts (*sarmenta* in the Latin, *phrygana* in the Greek), but a rounded object whose mildly modeled surface would allow a reading as a lump of charcoal or a chunk of wood, but which, caught up with folds of drapery, corresponds closely to the orbs of dominion associated with imperial figures or with figures understood to participate in the imagery of empire, such as winged Victories. It is perhaps necessary to specify that indeed Paul's offering is happily read as a lump of charcoal, but it must also be read as something more. The interpretation is forced by the swag of drapery, for no one in either the ancient or modern world is ever pictured gathering wood or charcoal for a fire and cradling it in drapery as Paul does his. The import of

Paul's display is one of analogy: as the object is like an orb, so Paul is like a ruler; his is a kind of dominion, a power that he exercises, lest we forget, in the guise of a philosopher, a wise man.

It seems appropriate here to remind ourselves that a Late Antique Christian did not require the attribute of the orb to know that Paul was indeed safe from the snake: the orb is simply a visual gloss on the figure of Paul, a familiar reference to power. Similarly, the original audience did not pause over the teaching scene at the top or the natives of Malta arrayed as official attendants or the figure of Publius in his magistrate's robes so prominently displayed. Modern viewers gaze at this panel with eyes only or primarily on Paul—Paul is the single character in the story that we are prepared to see. Yet a thoughtful examination of the scene of the miracle reveals that the central, frontal figure of Publius is the key to the compositional arrangement and the key to its meaning.

Figures like Publius, that is, representations of officials within the imperial government, are a commonplace on ivory diptychs. In the context of a diptych, it is Paul who is unexpected. Literary sources link the commission and distribution of ivory diptychs with the celebrations attendant on entry into various civil offices. And even down to details of his costume—the fibula, the chlamys—plus his scroll of appointment and his Germanic retinue, our Publius is a classic type from the repertory of diptych iconography, conforming to the role of officeholder. The compositional prominence of Publius in this role is analogous to that given the consuls and the holders of other offices who dominate the diptychs on which they appear. To be sure, the officeholders on the majority of extant diptychs participate in scenes of minimal activity: they begin circus games; they acknowledge the acclamations of others. Publius, in contrast, is involved in a scene drawn from an ambitious narrative, and while he is indeed the focus of others in the manner of an officeholder, he is represented in a mild inversion of typical practice. Although robed as a magistrate and centrally placed, he plays the part of one who himself bears witness and acclaims the higher authority of another.

This is not to say that the Publius of the miracle scene is, in fact, a fifth-century Christian consul or *patricius,* but that is the nature of the reference embodied in the representation. An inscription referring to a Christian Publius who was, say, *vicarius urbis Romae* in the early fifth century would be a perfect fit. But, more important, and independent of the limitations of such a storybook match, the "official-ness" of this version of the miracle story is critical and tied to the medium, to the genre of the commission in which it occurs. Why then was this particular scene chosen, and, once chosen, why structured in this manner? The patron of the piece is clearly Christian. The patron, the craftsman he employed, and the audience he wished to address were fluent in the terms, the figural types, and compositional conventions of diptych commissions and able to manipulate them to produce a New Testament scene that explicitly highlights the reception of the Christian faith by a government official. The scene at the top of the panel also sustains such a reading, for the imagery of a philosopher at his study or with his pupils is one found on official diptychs in addition to the scenes of individuals as office-holders conventionally associated with this genre of commission.[17] The patron of such a diptych announces his devotion to a philosophic ideal: here obviously Paul as philosopher, Christianity as the true philosophy.

Reconstituting the diptych, returning to consider the now more elaborate pairing of Adam and Paul, we recognize that the fundamental exegetical notion of the divine protection effected by faith and grace remains unchallenged. However, what seemed a secondary emphasis, a subtext, of the Paradise scene, that is, Adam's dominion exercised through his naming of the animals, now finds resonance in Pauline parallels. In the middle register, Paul, protected by his faith, is simultaneously represented as a power in his own right, acknowledged by civil authorities. The dominion established by Adam through speech, that is, through man's rational, intellectual capacities, finds its New Testament parallel in the top register, in a Paul understood as a philosopher with disciples who attend his word. A sequence might be hypothesized in which the patristic commentaries on Genesis came first and fixed the basic pairing of Adam in Eden and Paul on Malta. But the adaptation of the scenes to the genre of an ivory diptych seems to have involved, in addition, visual commentaries in complement. Man in different spheres and epochs of his authority is here celebrated. An Adam exercising dominion over the natural world is joined with a Paul who amazes the *barbaroi* with his miracles, displays his *insigne* of authority before a pagan magistrate, and preaches the Christian faith to fellow philosophers. Themes of speech and power, both civil and divine, have been introduced that were truly secondary in the patristic sources for the Adam and nonexistent for the Paul, but that are the very language, the conventions, of Late Antique diptych commissions.

As to the function served by this piece, I assume it to have been an instrument of personal communication, relying on the evidence of the richly attested ivories that commemorate civil offices. The sectarian nature of previous scholarship has always shunted it off for "liturgical use," although additional details are not volunteered. Such an assignment is dependent on early medieval evidence, seventh century and later, that indicates that the names of the living and the dead were read from diptychs, the exact nature of which is never specified. We do have a handful of Late Antique official diptychs, painted or engraved on their interior surfaces in medieval script centuries after their original commissions, with lists of bishops, names of saints, and the like. But, remaining in the fifth century, no one discusses a Late Antique patron or a patron's purpose for a diptych made *de novo* for a liturgical function. And certainly no one discusses the nature of the intended Late Antique liturgical recipient. Literary and material evidence consistently indicate that Late Antique diptychs were made for patrons who sent them out as announcements of various events and personal achievements to specific categories of recipients. Those extant official diptychs reused in ecclesiastical contexts, to carry the lists our medieval sources indicate, entered church treasuries by various means and were there respectfully treated: some consuls' heads were trimmed for tonsure, their scepters turned into crosses. The Carrand diptych, however, is no medieval adaptation. With the number of official allusions witnessed in its iconography, the diptych seems appropriately understood as the announcement of entry into office of a Christian magistrate, sent out as other contemporary diptychs were sent, to friends, clients, patrons, family members, and fellow officials.

Could not a Christian holder of civil office speak to another with an image of a Roman civil official, namely, Publius, depicted as a primary witness to the Christian faith? Could not Christian bishops, magistrates in a parallel hierarchy, send diptychs as consuls did, celebrating offices held and honors awarded, with themes biblical and exegetical displayed in images which themselves introduce a level of visual commentary?[18] One thinks, for example, of an aristocratic Roman, familiar with the customs embodied in such commissions, announcing his part in the erection of a church or its restoration, such as the fifth-century campaign that saw the parallel scenes of Old and New Testaments, including an Adam in Paradise and a Paul on Malta, displayed at S. Paolo fuori le mura. In 1829, when Amaury Duval discussed the ivory as part of Denon's collection, the bearded Paul speaking from his elaborate chair, in the top register of the left leaf, was enthusiastically described as an elderly consul seated in the *sella curulis* that marks the office, his scroll misread as the cloth *mappa* with which a consul signals the start of the games. Despite this awkward beginning, Adam in Paradise and the scene of the Miracle on Malta were duly reported, Duval noting that the diptych was obviously a work of the late empire, a time when aristocratic officials were proud to be Christians. With emendations and slightly more elaborate reasoning, I agree.

NOTES

Although aspects of this paper were presented in various fora, it gives me pleasure here to acknowledge the sincere interest and diverse contributions of my students and colleagues in Chicago as the research went forward and the arguments were formulated. A grant from the Stern Fund of the University of Chicago made possible the travel necessary to the project. This article first appeared in the *Jahrbuch für Antike und Christentum* 29 (1986). The University of Bonn's Franz Joseph Dölger Institut and the

Aschendorffsche Verlagsbuchhandlung of Münster kindly granted permission to reprint it here.

1　SECVNDE ET PROIECTA VIVATIS IN CHRI[STO], preceded by a Chi-Rho monogram flanked by Alpha and Omega. K. J. Shelton, *The Esquiline Treasure* (London, 1981); more recently, A. Cameron, "The Date and Owners of the Esquiline Treasure," and K. J. Shelton, "The Esquiline Treasure: The Nature of the Evidence," *American Journal of Archaeology* 89 (1985): 135–55.

2　A. Grabar, perhaps best represented by his *Christian Iconography: A Study of Its Origins,* A. W. Mellon Lectures in the Fine Arts, vol. 10 (Princeton, N.J., 1968).

3　The locus classicus is W. F. Volbach, *Elfenbeinarbeiten der Spätantike und des frühen Mittelalters* (Mainz, 1952; rev. ed. 1976), no. 107. To which now add, H. L. Kessler, "Scenes from the Acts of the Apostles on Some Early Christian Ivories," *Gesta* 18 (1979): 109–19; Kessler, in *Age of Spirituality,* ed. K. Weitzmann (New York and Princeton, N.J., 1979), no. 454; E. Konowitz, "The Program of the Carrand Diptych," *Art Bulletin* 66 (1984): 484–88; H. Maguire, "Adam and the Animals," *Dumbarton Oaks Papers* 41 (1987): 363–74. My thanks to Ellen Konowitz and Henry Maguire for sending me typescripts when all our projects were in progress.

4　Grivaud offered no further details of the discovery and, while clearly favoring manufacture in the Western Empire, refrained from sketching successive stages of a provenance that ended in the vicinity of nineteenth-century Mainz. Considering the excellent state of preservation of the piece, it might be hypothesized that, like so many other extant diptychs, the ivory survived above ground in the centuries following its commission, probably in the protection of an ecclesiastical authority. Even summary knowledge of the peregrinations of art works in late eighteenth- and early nineteenth-century Europe would argue caution in these matters. Social, political, and religious disruptions saw the transfer of art works from defeated powers to victorious powers (then back again when fortunes reversed) and, on a more intimate level, resulted in the release for private purchase of artifacts held by institutions, both church and state. Our ivory was, no doubt, "découvert" in the vicinity of Mainz, but probability favors a discovery on the antiquities market. C. M. Grivaud de La Vincelle, *Recueil de monumens antiques, la plupart inédits et découverts dans l'ancienne Gaule,* 2 vols. (Paris, 1817), 2:231–33, pl. 29.

5　Vigorous to the end, Vivant Denon is reported to have bid for paintings at the auction of the Lapeyrière sale the day before he died: J. Nowinski, *Baron Dominique Vivant Denon (1747–1825)* (Rutherford, N.J., 1970), 110–11. Citing no evidence beyond a general sense of Denon's travels, W. B. Marriott thought many years later that Denon had purchased the ivory in Rome, *The Testimony of the Catacombs and of Other Monuments of Christian Art* (London, 1870), 68–69.

6　Sale catalogs of the Denon collection were separately authored by A. N. Pérignon, L. J. J. Dubois, and Duchesne Aîné, *Description des objets d'arts qui composent le cabinet de feu M. le Baron V. Denon* (Paris, 1826); the ivory is discussed in the Dubois volume (vol. 2), titled *Monuments antiques, historiques, modernes; ouvrages orientaux, etc.,* no. 693. A. Duval, *Monuments des arts du dessin chez les peuples tant anciens que modernes, recueillies par le Baron Vivant Denon. . . ,* 4 vols. (Paris, 1829), vol. 1. The Carrand ivory is discussed in the commentary on pl. 38.

7 W. B. Marriott, *Vestiarium Christianum* (London, 1868).

8 The hinge placement is clear, perhaps most easily seen on the Paul panel at the right border where the figures lap the frame. R. Delbrueck, *Die Consular-diptychen und verwandte Denkmäler* (Berlin and Leipzig, 1929), no. 69; also K. J. Shelton, "The Diptych of the Young Office Holder," *Jahrbuch für Antike und Christentum* 25 (1982): 137–39.

9 Mariott, *Testimony*, 71–81; J. O. Westwood, *A Descriptive Catalogue of the Fictile Ivories in the South Kensington Museum* (London, 1876), nos. 112, 113, acquisition nos. 58.63, 58.263. R. Delbrueck, "Zwei christliche Elfenbeine des 5. Jahrhunderts," *Spätantike und Byzanz, Neue Beiträge zur Kunstgeschichte des 1. Jahrtausends,* vol. 1, Forschungen zur Kunstgeshichte und christliche Archäologie, vol. 1 (Baden-Baden, 1952), 180. R. Garrucci, *Storia dell'arte cristiana,* 6 vols. (Prato, 1873–81), 6:76–77. For recent discussions of speech scenes, see Kessler, "Early Christian Ivories, 113, 117.

10 A. Pérate, "La réorganization des musées florentins," Part 3, "Le musée national et la collection Carrand," *Gazette des beaux arts,* 3d ser., 8 (1892): 335. For the entry of the collection into the Bargello, see U. Rossi, "La collezione Carrand nel museo nazionale di Firenze," *L'archivio storico dell'arte* 2 (1889): 10–23, 215–28; 3 (1890): 24–34.

11 E.g., poet and muse, Volbach, *Elfenbeinarbeiten,* no. 68; god and goddess, no. 57 (our fig. 3); officeholder in two aspects, no. 62; Christ and Mary, no. 137. For further consideration of this issue of pairs, specifically of poets and muses, see K. J. Shelton, "The Consular Muse of Flavius Constantius," *Art Bulletin* 65 (1983): 7–23; for principles of diptych design, Shelton, "Young Office Holder," 132–71, esp. 134–48.

12 Kessler, *Spirituality,* no. 454.

13 Mariott, *Testimony,* 70.

14 H. P. L'Orange, "Plotinus-Paul," *Byzantion* 25–27 (1955–57): 473–85.

15 So Delbrueck, "Christliche Elfenbeine," 180.

16 The fresco, part of a larger cycle now lost, is preserved in a seventeenth-century manuscript copy of a thirteenth-century restoration of the Late Antique original. This formidable recension, with types of Christ substituted for several of the main actors, Paul on Malta among them, nevertheless allows the bare bones of the scenes to be identified. Vatican codex Barberini latin 4406, fol. 125; S. Waetzoldt, *Die Kopien des 17. Jahrhunderts nach Mosaiken und Wandmalereien in Rom,* Römische Forschungen der Biblioteca Hertziana, no. 18 (Vienna and Munich, 1964), 55ff.

17 Shelton, "Consular Muse."

18 For the authority, both civil and religious, of bishops in Late Antiquity, see H. Chadwick and respondents, *The Role of the Christian Bishop in Ancient Society,* Protocol of the 35th Colloquy, Center for Hermeneutical Studies (Berkeley, 1980).

CHAPTER 8

Felix Karthago

FRANK M. CLOVER

The Vandal government of Roman Africa was an uneasy coalition. On the one hand the ruling clan of the Hasdingi took the helm of state. A polyglot elite of Vandals, Alans, Goths, Suevi, and Hispano-Romans supported the royal house. The Romano-Christian aristocracy, on the other hand, contributed magistrates (such as the proconsuls of Carthage) whose relation to the Vandal elite is unclear.[1] Ostrogothic Italy affords an analogy. The royal clan of the Amali shared power with Romano-Italian families of prominence, such as the Anicii and Cassiodori.[2]

For Ostrogoths, Vandals, and other Germanic groups perched on the Mediterranean littoral, the danger of disappearing into Roman society was acute. How could these intruders, always a minority, maintain a separate identity in a Roman milieu? The Amali made a contribution toward survival by persuading Flavius Magnus Aurelius Cassiodorus Senator, consul in A.D. 514, to write a history of the Goths. This work, composed in Latin, mixed classical and biblical commonplaces with what appear to be real traditions about the early Goths.[3] The mechanism that produced Cassiodorus' history—patronage of a Roman man of letters by Ostrogothic overlords—also existed in Vandal Africa. The Roman-African aristocrat Blossius Aemilius Dracontius addressed a panegyric to the Vandal king Thrasamund (*regn.* A.D. 496–523). The poets Luxurius, Felix, and Florentinus honored Thrasamund and his successor Hildiric (*regn.* A.D. 523–30).[4] From Vandal sponsorship of African literati might have come a *Historia Wandalorum,* an account that, like Cassiodorus' history, might have dealt with the northern European origins of the Vandals and the rise of the Hasdingi. Such a work never appeared. Instead, Christian diatribes against the intruder, particularly those originating from the Catholic faction, are the staple of the literary record of Vandal Africa. Victor of Vita's *Historia persecutionis africanae provinciae,* written during the reign of King

129

Gunthamund (*regn.* A.D. 484–96), is the only surviving work that resembles a history of the Vandals.[5]

Polemic from the Catholic sector of African Christendom did not deter the Vandals from advertising their venture on the southern shores of the Mediterranean. From A.D. 439 until the arrival of Belisarius, the Vandals controlled Carthage, the metropolis of Africa, and its hinterland. They brought the city's mint into full productivity, they regulated the system by which they or their subjects dated public works, and they managed to communicate some of their tastes to the poets and artists whom they patronized. The surviving fruits of these efforts—coins, dated funerary monuments, acts of sale, ecclesiastical tracts, poems, and mosaics—give the impression that the Vandals and the Romano-African elite stressed the might of the Hasdingi to be sure, but placed equal or greater emphasis on the glory of Carthage. Four kinds of celebration of the metropolis require attention.

1. THE PERSONIFICATION OF CARTHAGE

Before the Vandals seized Africa the early tetrarchs were the principal superintendents of the mint of Carthage. Gold, silver, and bronze issues appeared between the start of Maximian's campaigns against the native Quinquegentiani (ca. A.D. 296) and his son Maxentius' suppression of the revolt of Lucius Domitius Alexander (A.D. 309). All minting authorities stressed in one way or another the greatness of Carthage. Maximian, for instance, produced an *aureus* whose reverse displayed a robed female figure, standing with her head turned to the left and holding fruits in her outstretched hands. The legend FELIX KARTHAGO encircled this figure.[6] A rare gold issue of Lucius Domitius Alexander shows the same figure on the reverse, and a more elaborate motto: IMVICTA ROMA FEL(IX) KARTHAGO ("Fortunate is Carthage, so long as Rome is unconquered").[7] The inscriptions on these two coins contribute to the identity of the standing female figure. She is the personification of Carthage, the metropolis of Africa. (See figs. 8.1 and 8.2.)

A similar depiction evidently adorned a portion of the *Notitia dignitatum,* an illustrated register of Roman imperial offices and military units edited for the last time between the early 390s and the first quarter of the fifth century. The work survives in late medieval copies (the most important of which are in Munich, Paris, and Oxford) of a lost ninth- or tenth-century manuscript of the Cathedral of Speyer, the *Codex spirensis.* In the late medieval manuscripts illustrations accompany the notices of magistracies and military units. A comparison of these pictures with works of art from Late Antiquity reveals discrepancies, but on the whole the depictions in the *Codex spirensis* seem to have been faithful to the originals.[8] The western section of the *Notitia* contained a summary of the proconsul of Africa's administration. Above the

Fig. 8.1. *Aureus* of Maximian. Paris, Bibliothèque Nationale, Cabinet des Médailles, specimen no. 1600 (photo: Bibliothèque Nationale, Paris).

Fig. 8.2. *Aureus* of Lucius Domitius Alexander. Paris, Bibliothèque Nationale, Cabinet des Médailles, specimen no. 1671 (photo: Bibliothèque Nationale, Paris).

record of the proconsul's *officium* appeared a representation in two registers of the magistrate's domain. The upper panel displayed the *codicilli,* the proconsul's document of appointment, on a cloth-covered table. To the left of the table stood a female figure facing frontally and stretching forth her hands. She held something in each hand, and her attire extended at least to her ankles. A nimbus may have encircled her head. It is difficult to be more precise than this regarding her posture, attire, and accoutrements, for the late medieval manuscripts present differing details. In general outline, however, the female figure on the coins of tetrarchic Carthage and in the *Notitia* resemble one another. The *Notitia* itself provides further information about the lady's identity. She was, after all, part of a notice of the proconsul of Africa, who resided in Car-

proconsul Aphrica

Fig. 8.3. Illustration of *Notitia dignitatum* Occ. 18 in Clm. 10291, fol. 210r. Munich, Bayerische Staatsbibliothek (photo: Bayerische Staatsbibliothek München).

thage. In addition, the lower panel of the illustration under discussion displayed two square-rigged transports, each laden with sacks of grain. Africa was one of Rome's chief granaries, and most African grain bound for Rome departed from Carthage. The female figure, therefore, was the personification of the great city. (The Munich and Oxford versions of the illustration of *ND* Occ. 18 appear in figs. 8.3 and 8.4.)[9]

During the dominate the mint of Carthage helped to propagate the image of the city as bountiful patroness. Tetrarchic coins bearing the representation of Lady Carthage have already received attention. After the age of the tetrarchs

Fig. 8.4. Illustration of *Notitia dignitatum* Occ. 18 in MS. Canon. Misc. 378, fol. 147r. Oxford, Bodleian Library (photo: Bodleian Library, Oxford).

Fig. 8.5. Silver coin of Carthage, dated ANNO IIII K(ARTHAGINIS). Paris, Bibliothèque Nationale, Cabinet des Médailles, no. R/1652 (photo: Bibliothèque Nationale, Paris).

Fig. 8.6. Silver coin of Carthage, dated ANNO V K(ARTHAGINIS). Turin, Museo Civico (gift of Antonio Gariazzo) (photo: Medagliere delle Raccolte Numismatiche Torinesi).

Fig. 8.7. Silver coin of King Hildiric. Munich, Staatlich Münzsammlung (photo: Staatliche Münzsammlung, Munich).

the city's mint experienced a brief revival in the early fifth century,[10] and then more extensive productivity under the Vandal and Byzantine authorities. The personification of Carthage appears on three Vandal series. The earliest of these was a briefly lived silver issue whose obverse displayed a diademed figure wearing a military cloak and cuirass and facing right. Western mints depicted emperors in this fashion. The obverse inscription identified the emperor in question as Honorius (A.D. 393–423): HONORIVS P(ERPETV)VS A(V)G(VS)T(VS) or HONORI- + -IVS A(V)G(VS)T(VS). On the reverse stood the now familiar female figure, more stocky than her tetrarchic counterpart. She wore both robe and cloak and held shafts of grain in her outstretched hands. The reverse bore a date: ANNO IIII K(ARTHAGINIS) or ANNO V + K(ARTHAGINIS).[11] (Illustrations of Paris and Turin specimens appear in figs. 8.5 and 8.6.) This peculiar method of dating was an invention of the Vandal kings. The series may date from the early 440s, soon after the Vandals captured Carthage.[12]

Beginning with King Gunthamund (A.D. 484–96), the later Vandal monarchs minted silver with their own name and titles, some of which they borrowed from imperial usage.[13] One of the issues of King Hildiric (A.D. 523–30) is the descendant of the coinage of tetrarchic Carthage (see fig. 8.7). The obverse showed the same type of bust that appeared on the dated coins minted in the name of Honorius. The inscription named the king with a mixture of imperial and royal titulature: D(OMINVS) N(OSTER) HILDIRIX REX. On the reverse stood Lady Carthage, her head perhaps crowned with foliage and her torso rendered as a rectangle. To identify the female figure Hildiric followed the example of Maximian: FELIX KART(HA)G(O).[14]

A third series—this one of bronze—also bore the standard badge of Car-

Fig. 8.8. Bronze coin of Carthage, valued at 42 *nummi*. Copenhagen, National Museum, Royal Collection of Coins and Medals (photo: National Museum).

thage (fig. 8.8). The issue was without imperial or royal inscription. The *curia* of the city, with the approval of the Vandal kings, may have begun production around the turn of the sixth century. The reverse bore the denominations N(VMMI) XLII, XXI, or XII. The facing female figure, normally on the reverse of tetrarchic and Vandalic issues of Carthage, stood here on the obverse. In comparison with Hildiric's silver her figure was more rounded. She wore both robe and cloak and held in her outstretched hands shafts of grain. A wreath fastened by a circular ornament surrounded her.[15]

Lady Carthage, then, adorned some of the currency minted during the Vandal century. The silver issues of Hildiric in particular show that the Vandal elite sanctioned the common representation of the metropolis. With such official encouragement it is not surprising that the motif continued to be popular. Around the turn of the sixth century a Vandal or Roman dignitary included it in a large mosaic which perhaps stood in a private residence near the city's center. In the nineteenth century excavators found the mosaic on the southern flank of the Byrsa, Carthage's citadel. The Byrsa Mosaic, eight meters long by five meters wide, consisted of a large field of interlacings with symmetrically aligned circular knots frequently inset with diamonds, crosses, or other designs. These features enclosed six rows, each containing five circular medallions. Five interstitial rows, made octagonal by the interlacings, separated the medallions. In the interstices and medallions the mosaicist placed a variety of figures and scenes. The top row of medallions displayed a robed woman flanked by two figures to her right and two to her left. The next (interstitial) row contained four charioteers, each named and perhaps representing the four teams: the Reds, Whites, Greens, and Blues. In the remaining interstices and medallions were hunting scenes. Today the entire mosaic is accessible from the design of the nineteenth-century excavators. Three fragments survive in the Louvre.[16]

Fig. 8.9. Fragment of the Byrsa Mosaic: standing female figure. Paris, Musée du Louvre, no. Ma 2999 (photo: M. Chuzeville).

One of the three remaining pieces of the mosaic is the circular medallion that stood in the center of the top row. The robed woman strikes a frontal pose. She stretches forth her arms and holds flowers and foliage in each hand. A crown of flowers decorates her hair, which is curled and drawn back. Behind her head stands a radiate nimbus. To her right and left (and still within the dark-bordered circle) are candles placed on candelabras, each with a tripod base (see fig. 8.9). Who is this woman? In attempting to answer this question, today's critic faces a problem analogous to that presented by the late medieval manuscripts of the *Notitia dignitatum*. A modern mosaicist has retouched the medallion, so that certain details of the original depiction (for instance, the objects the lady held in her outstretched hands) are uncertain. Nevertheless, the general manner in which the artist depicted the woman is clear: she faced the viewer, she reached out her arms, and her attire extended at least to her ankles. Her attitude, then, resembles that of the figures discussed above. She is Lady Carthage. The candles, common accoutrements of other ancient personifications of cities, lend support to this interpretation.[17]

The identity of the woman in the centerpiece does not in itself establish the date of the Byrsa Mosaic. Indeed, the fragmentary condition and the modern alterations hamper the effort to determine when the ancient mosaicist accomplished his work. Nevertheless, the other two fragments help the modern critic to locate an approximate time of composition (figs. 8.10 and 8.11). One of the

Fig. 8.10. Fragment of the Byrsa Mosaic: horseman. Paris, Musée du Louvre, no. Ma 1789 (photo: M. Chuzeville).

remaining parts of the Byrsa Mosaic stood in the first full scene from the left in the third interstitial row from the top. The scene is incomplete, but it and the nineteenth-century design show a horse galloping to the right. Its rider wears a cloak, a short tunic with long sleeves, and long pants. He faces frontally, stretching his right arm over or near the horse's thigh (Fig. 8.10). The distinctive pose of the rider finds a parallel in a hunting mosaic found in the Bordj-Djedid district of Carthage and now preserved in fragments in the British Museum. The fragments, once perhaps the adornment of a seaside villa in or near Carthage, show three horsemen, dogs pursuing a boar and a hare, two gazelles and a bear.[18] One of the three horsemen wears a cloak, tunic, pants, leggings, and boots. He rides his horse to the right, beside a villa. Like the figure in the Byrsa Mosaic, he faces frontally and extends his right arm over

1788

Fig. 8.11. Fragment of the Byrsa Mosaic: the charioteer Quiriacus. Paris, Musée du Louvre, no. Ma 1788 (photo: M. Chuzeville).

Fig. 8.12. Fragment of the Bordj-Djedid Mosaic: horseman. London, British Museum, acc. no. GR 1860. 10-2. 132 (photo: Trustees of the British Museum).

or near the back of his horse. (See fig. 8.12.) The similarity of pose and indeed the general correspondence of hunting scenes in the Bordj-Djedid and Byrsa mosaics raise the possibility of a common date of composition. Modern critics have placed the creation of the Bordj-Djedid Mosaic around the beginning of the sixth century.[19]

The Bordj-Djedid Mosaic celebrates the hunt. So does the Byrsa Mosaic, but this latter work also observes, in the first interstitial row from the top, the pleasures of the chariot races. The third Louvre fragment (fig. 8.11) belongs to this row. The charioteer depicted—the second from the left, according to the nineteenth-century design—wears a helmet and cassock. He faces forward as he drives a quadriga. His horses (each reined, bridled, and bedecked with a palm branch) diverge, two galloping to his left and two to his right. A frontal plate adorns his chariot. His name appears in Latin characters to the right and left of his head: QVIR-IACVS.[20] For this fragment the parallel evidence (both literary and archaeological) is more abundant, and it enables the modern critic to situate the Byrsa Mosaic more securely in the Vandal century. In recent years the University of Michigan's excavations at Carthage have unearthed a mosaic that once adorned a peristyle house located in the city's southeast sector. Among the many features of the mosaic were four charioteers, each named (in Greek rather than Latin characters) and each clearly representing the Blues, Whites, Greens, and Reds. On the basis of similar but not identical depictions of the charioteers, archaeologists have dated the Mosaic of the

House of the Greek Charioteers to the beginning of the fifth century, and the Byrsa Mosaic to the end of the fifth or even the sixth century.[21] Some literary testimony offers support for this chronology. The *Latin Anthology,* a collection of Latin poems evidently gathered at Carthage between A.D. 523 and 535, contains short pieces by classical Latin authors such as Martial and verses by perhaps ten Roman men of letters flourishing at Carthage around the end of the Vandal century. The anthology survives primarily in the *Codex parisinus latinus* no. 10318, an eighth-century manuscript most frequently called the *Codex salmasianus* after its onetime possessor, the seventeenth-century philologist Claude de Saumaise. One of the Latin poets living in Vandal Carthage was Luxurius. Among the several poems attributed to him is a set of five elegiac couplets addressed to an aged charioteer who habitually loses and then taunts the jeering crowd. The obvious setting of this piece is the circus of Carthage. In the first verse Luxurius addresses the charioteer in the vocative case. The *Codex salmasianus,* the lone manuscript for this poem, reads his name as follows: *Quiriace.*[22] Luxurius knew of a charioteer named Quiriacus. One of the drivers on the Byrsa Mosaic bore the same name. A Quiriacus may have been a prominent figure in the circus at Carthage during the last generation of Vandal rule.

The Byrsa Mosaic, a celebration of the circus races and the hunt, stands near in time to the reign of King Hildiric, who placed the personification of Carthage on some of his silver coins. The artisan who made the large town house mosaic also gave prominence to the same figure by placing her in the center of the top row. A modern critic has identified her four companions— once again, two appear on either side of her—as the Four Seasons (see fig. 8.9).[23] If one accepts this interpretation, the message of the Byrsa Mosaic becomes clear: the viewer is invited to contemplate the pleasures and diversions that Carthage and her immediate surroundings offer residents and visitors the year round. During the Vandal century, Lady Carthage, it seems, symbolized the fertile heartland of Africa and the delights of its metropolis.

2. THE REVIVAL OF PHOENICIAN BADGES OF CARTHAGE

Under Vandal supervision the mint of Carthage utilized a coin type, the personification of Carthage, which had originated in the age of the tetrarchs. At the same time the mint employed other motifs of greater antiquity. Before the Romans occupied Africa, the Phoenician masters of Carthage and the southwestern Mediterranean had placed various badges of the great city on their coinage. The two most common symbols were the horse's head and the palm tree. Both emblems were celebrations of the might of Tanit and Baal Hammon, lunar and solar deities prominent in the Phoenician pantheon, and advertisements of legends associating the foundation of Carthage with the excavation of a horse's head, which some ancient versions located at the base of a

Fig. 8.13. Carthaginian gold quarter. New York, American Numismatic Society (photo: American Numismatic Society, New York).

Fig. 8.14. Siculo-Punic silver tetradrachm. New York, American Numismatic Society (photo: American Numismatic Society, New York).

palm tree.[24] Three gold and silver issues (figs. 8.13–8.15) will show some of the ways in which the Carthaginians drew attention to their heritage. A gold quarter displays a head of Tanit on the obverse and a palm tree with fruits on the reverse (fig. 8.13). A Siculo-Punic silver tetradrachm of the fourth century B.C. also bears on its obverse a Tanit head facing left. The accoutrements of the goddess (plaited hair, necklace, and pendant earrings) and the dolphins surrounding her demonstrate that the Carthaginians of Sicily borrowed from Syracuse, which depicted the goddess Arethusa in the same manner. The reverse shows a horse's head facing left and, immediately to the right of the horse's mane, a miniature palm tree (fig. 8.14). A contemporary Siculo-Punic tetradrachm shows a Tanit head facing right. The dolphins are rendered more schematically, and sprigs of wheat appear in the goddess' hair. On the reverse a horse stands facing right, in front of a full-scale palm tree with fruits. To the right of the horse is a caduceus (a standard associated with solar worship) (fig. 8.15).[25]

When the Romans came to Africa, they inherited and developed further the urban civilization of the Phoenicians. It was to be expected that some Phoenician attitudes would persist in altered form under the Roman administration. Tanit, for instance, became Caelestis ("The Heavenly Goddess"), and as her popularity spread beyond Africa the Romans came to regard her as a manifestation of Juno. One can recognize in Juno Caelestis, who fostered the fertility of Africa's crops, the precursor of the Late Antique Lady Carthage.[26] Indeed, the sprigs of wheat in the hair of Phoenician Tanit are the remote ancestor of the shafts of grain in Lady Carthage's outstretched hands. (Cf. figs. 8.7 and 8.15.) Not all Phoenician symbolism, however, came to late Ro-

Fig. 8.15. Siculo-Punic silver tetradrachm. New York, American Numismatic Society (photo: American Numismatic Society, New York).

Fig. 8.16. Roman bronze lamp with a handle in the shape of a horse's head. London, British Museum, acc. no. GR 1814. 7-4.200 (photo: Trustees of the British Museum).

Fig. 8.17. Roman bronze lamp with a handle in the shape of a horse's head. London, British Museum, acc. no. GR 1824. 4-54.10 (photo: Trustees of the British Museum).

man Africa in the same direct fashion. The horse, horse's head, and palm tree also survived the Roman occupation, but their meaning underwent significant alteration. Some Western Roman bronze lamps, for instance, bore handles in the shape of a horse's head. Two examples, in the British Museum are perhaps of Italian origin (figs. 8.16 and 8.17).[27] But excavators have found lamps of this sort on African soil, and local terra-cotta adaptations of this lamp style have turned up especially in the Mauretanian part of Africa.[28] The palm tree was also a common decoration on African lamps, especially during the late stages of the Roman occupation. The Bardo Museum in Tunis and the National Museum of Carthage contain several specimens of local provenance. One example, found in the Damous el Karita district of Carthage, will suffice: a terra-cotta lamp whose top displays a seven-branch palm tree encased in a ring of spirals and cross-shaped knots.[29] (See fig. 8.18.) The presence of the

Fig. 8.18. Terracotta lamp found at Damous el Karita, Carthage. Tunis, Musée de Bardo, inv. no 632 (photo: Photothèque du Centre Camille Jullian, Aix-en-Provence).

palm tree and the horse on lamps of Roman Africa is guarantee enough that the Phoenician meaning of these symbols did not persist. Instead of signifying the origins of Africa's metropolis, these motifs became a household banality.

Yet the same figures could take on a different significance in other contexts. The same houses that contained lamps of the sort described here might also have mosaics on which horses and palm trees appeared, and these often bespoke a major preoccupation of Africa's Romans. A great mosaic discovered at Hadrumetum (Sousse) is the best example. Fragments in the National Museum of Sousse and modern drawings reveal two rectangular pavements, the first of which depicted medallions at each corner and a pastoral scene at the center. In each medallion stood two horses, each pair facing a fruited palm tree and bedecked with a palm branch. In each instance the horse's name appeared above its back. The second pavement also displayed a pastoral centerpiece and horses at the four corners. Here, however, only four horses, each confronting a palm tree and wearing a palm branch, bordered the landscape. The name of each horse flanked the palm tree. An Eros flew over each horse, ready to crown it with garlands. This Mosaic of the House of Sorothus (so named because the owner's name appears on the flanks of some of the horses) dates from the early third century A.D. The palm branches, garlands, horses' names, and owner's brand all proclaim Sorothus' occupation: this local dignitary raised horses for the circus races.[30] Public entertainment was an important dimension of life in Roman Africa. Other African mosaics composed between the second and the fourth century depict circus horses. The fourth-century mosaic of Carthage's Maison des Chevaux, for instance, contains a veritable gallery of horses, charioteers, and circus attendants.[31] The mosaic of the House of Sorothus, however, best exemplifies the Roman juxtaposition of the horse and the palm. The distant ancestor of these features is the horse-and-palm motif on the Siculo-Punic tetradrachms. But on this and similar mosaics Roman life thrust aside the original meaning of these symbols and instead brought to the viewer's mind the world of entertainment.

Four charioteers occupied a prominent place on the Byrsa Mosaic. The circus races were still a major preoccupation for the inhabitants of Vandal Carthage.[32] The horse motif also appears on bronze currency minted at Carthage during the Vandal century, but in this instance the symbol's meaning is in doubt. One series of large bronzes—municipals produced by the *curia* of Carthage with royal consent—has already received attention: Lady Carthage adorned the obverse.[33] Around the same time (again, the turn of the sixth century) the *curia* inaugurated under the Vandal king's auspices another bronze series. (See figs. 8.19 and 8.20.) This one bears a standing warrior on the obverse. Attired in cuirass and military cloak, the warrior relaxes his right arm and rests a long spear on the ground with his left. The legend KART-HAGO flanks him on the left and right. The exergue of the reverse displays

Fig. 8.19. Bronze coin of Carthage, valued at 42 *nummi*. Cambridge, Fitzwilliam Museum (photo: by permission of the Syndics, Fitzwilliam Museum).

Fig. 8.20. Bronze coin of Carthage, valued at 21 *nummi*. Paris, Bibliothèque Nationale, Cabinet des Médailles, Ancien Fonds no. 120 (photo: Bibliothèque Nationale, Paris).

the denominations XLII, XXI, or XII, but here (in contrast to the Lady Carthage Series) the clarifying N(VMMI) is absent. Above the reverse exergue is a bridled horse's head, facing left.[34] The modern critic will recognize in this representation a latter-day version of the left-facing horse's head on the reverses of some Siculo-Punic tetradrachms (cf. fig. 8.14 with figs. 8.19 and 8.20). But what did this motif mean to the Romans who sat on the *curia* of Vandal Carthage? The standing warrior presents no problem. He is an imitation of a standing emperor in military dress—a common feature on Western Roman coinage of the fifth century.[35] But what of the horse's head? Among the early Germanic peoples a horse's head fixed on a pole served as an announcement of future victory, an effort to deprive adversaries of their fighting spirit before battle. Did the Standing Warrior Series celebrate present and future victory for the Hasdingi? Did the Hasdingi manage to introduce some of their ancestral heritage into the culture of Roman Carthage?[36] Two considerations point toward negative answers to these questions. First of all, the Standing Warrior Series is a municipal issue and as such celebrates the grandeur of Carthage. The obverse legend KARTHAGO performs the same function as the personification of Carthage in the Lady Carthage Series.[37] Second, other bronze coins of late Roman, Vandal, or Byzantine Carthage display a horse's head with other symbols, and these enable the modern observer to approach an understanding of Phoenician motifs in a late Roman context.

In Late Antiquity Africa produced a maze of anonymous bronze *minimi*. The most common varieties bore obverses and reverses borrowed from imperial issues; a winged Victory was a favorite reverse type.[38] Early in this century the influential British Museum catalog tentatively assigned many of these bronzes to the Vandal century.[39] More-recent critics have found that this labyrinth of "Vandalic" currency contains pieces of Late Antique date to be sure, but of imperial, African, Egyptian, and uncertain provenance.[40] The modern observer who singles out specimens from this pile of small change must be prepared to show that the pieces held up for inspection originated from Vandal Carthage.

The present problem brings to view two coins whose origins are less certain than those of the Standing Warrior Series. In Copenhagen's Royal Collection of Coins and Medals there is a small bronze whose obverse carries a diademed figure (without identifying inscription) in military attire facing right (fig. 8.21). To the left stands a Cross Potent. The reverse shows an unbridled horse's head facing right.[41] The mint of Carthage probably produced this piece: recent excavations have unearthed a similar specimen in the city's southeast quarter.[42] But what authority caused this type to be produced? The

Fig. 8.21. Bronze coin of Carthage with a horse's head reverse. Copenhagen, National Museum, Royal Collection of Coins and Medals (photo: National Museum)

Fig. 8.22. Bronze coin of King Hildiric with a Cross Potent reverse. Paris, Bibliothèque Nationale, Cabinet des Médailles, Collection Schlumberger no. 2, 232 (photo: Bibliothèque Nationale, Paris).

Fig. 8.23. Bronze coin of Carthage with a palm tree reverse. Turin, Museo Civico, Reale Medagliere no. 28436 (photo: Medagliere delle Raccolte Numismatiche Torinesi).

texture and size are similar to those of bronze *minimi* which Vandal authorities produced in quantity.[43] The Standing Warrior Series is proof that some bronze currency minted during the Vandal occupation bore a horse's head on the reverse. King Hildiric issued small bronzes that utilized the Cross Potent. (See fig. 8.22.) The small bronze type under discussion may therefore date from the Vandal century. In any case, the intrusion of a standard imperial obverse carries the horse's head another step away from the Germanic heritage and places it in the milieu of late Roman, Vandal, and Byzantine Carthage.[44]

The second piece, part of the great collection that now resides in Turin's Museo Civico, is an enigma (fig. 8.23). It is a medium-sized bronze—its module is twenty millimeters—weighing about seven grams. An unbridled horse's head, facing right, adorns its obverse. On the reverse appears a palm tree with fruits. The coin bears no identifying inscription. Some of its basic characteristics—a die axis that verges upon ninety degrees, and the absence of centered obverse and reverse images—enable the modern observer to assign it to the mint of Carthage. The size of the piece resembles that of the twenty-one-*nummi* issues of the Standing Warrior Series, which also bears a horse's head.[45] On the strength of this consideration one can suggest, but not prove, that the specimen dates from the Vandal century. It is safer to state that moneyers of Carthage issued it around the fifth or sixth century.[46]

In Late Antiquity the mint of Carthage occasionally struck coins that juxtaposed the horse's head and the palm tree. Under the auspices of the Vandal kings the city's *curia* issued a large bronze series whose reverse displayed the horse's head. Such images last appeared on Carthaginian coinage in the fourth century B.C. What did they mean to the inhabitants of late Roman, Vandal, and Byzantine Carthage? The palm trees and horses on Roman imperial lamps and mosaics are warning enough that these symbols no longer commemorated the might of Tanit, protectress of the great Phoenician city-state. Yet it would be wrong to suggest that an inhabitant of fifth- or sixth-century Carthage would look at a Standing Warrior reverse and see in the horse's head depicted there a celebration of the circus races. During the Vandal century both kings and *curia* put Lady Carthage, a municipal badge, on some of the coins of Africa's metropolis. The horse's head, it seems, also advertised the city's greatness. The use of a Phoenician symbol with an approximation of the original meaning is, on reflection, not surprising. In the late fifth or early sixth century another *curia,* the Senate of Rome, issued with the approval of Odovacer or the Ostrogoths a series of large bronzes in denominations of forty and twenty *nummi.* The obverse and reverse bore a bust of Roma and the traditional Wolf and Twins. The Lady Carthage, Standing Warrior, and Wolf-and-Twins series are contemporary. Their emblems are expressions of municipal pride. They reflect the eastward contraction of Roman imperial authority and the consequent increase in the stature of the great cities of the western Mediterranean.[47] (See Fig. 8.24.)

3. THE YEAR OF CARTHAGE

Ostraka discovered near Bir Trouch, Algeria, demonstrate that during the reign of King Gunthamund (A.D. 484–96) the formula for dating by regnal year included the element "in the year N of Carthage." This convention also appears on silver coins of Carthage that have already received attention. They bear an obverse in the name of the emperor Honorius, and Lady Carthage adorns the reverse. The reverse also shows that the minting authority released the series in the fourth and fifth Years of Carthage. In addition to this silver issue there are five epitaphs—four from Africa Proconsularis and one from Numidia—that record deaths in the sixth, seventh, twentieth, and twenty-fourth Years of Carthage. The Bir Trouch ostraka make Gunthamund's reign a

Fig. 8.24. Bronze coin of Rome with Wolf-and-Twins reverse, valued at 40 *nummi*. Paris, Bibliothèque Nationale, Cabinet des Médailles, Ancien Fonds no. 79 (photo: Bibliothèque Nationale, Paris).

focal point of this method of dating. Other considerations make it likely, but not certain, that the formula originated early in Geiseric's kingship (439–77), soon after the Vandals captured Carthage. In any case, the insertion of the name of Carthage into a regnal formula means that the Vandal kings sought to link their own power with the stature of Carthage. The Year of Carthage is another Vandal celebration of the great metropolis of Africa.[48]

4. ANTHOLOGIA LATINA 371

The collection of Latin poetry known as the *Latin Anthology* has already received notice. Poets such as Florentinus, Felix, and Luxurius flourished at Carthage toward the end of the Vandal century and wrote verses that drew some of their inspiration from the classical past but also reflected contemporary life. Among their sponsors were the Vandal kings, other Hasding clansmen, and Vandal nobles who did not belong to the royal family. These patrons frequently persuaded their hired versifiers to celebrate the pleasures one could encounter in their private dwellings or in baths they had constructed.[49] A certain Fridamal, for instance, built a tower in the midst of a garden and then ordered a painting depicting him at the hunt to be placed in the tower. Luxurius wrote a poem saluting the painting.[50] King Thrasamund, to take another example, constructed baths equipped with hypocausts in a seaside suburb of Carthage called Alianae. Felix evidently sought to compose the dedicatory inscription for the baths. He gave Thrasamund, it seems, a choice of five dedications: three in elegiac couplets, and two in hexameters (the last with acrostics).[51]

Yet the Latin poets who celebrated the pleasures of Vandal Carthage also stood ready to proclaim state policy. The kings therefore had at their disposal not only coinage and public documents but also court poetry as a means of advertising their venture in Roman Africa. Of all the verses written at Carthage during the Vandal century, the hexameter poem attributed to Florentinus in the *Codex salmasianus* comes closest to a general statement of Vandal goals and aspirations.[52]

I will praise the royal celebrations made festive by yearly vows. The imperial splendor of Thrasamund, ruler of Libya, is the world's renown—just as the sun, glittering more brightly than the entire radiate universe, stands forth above all the stars. [5] Reverence and foresight converge in this man, as do good character, bravery, handsome appearance, distinction, spirit, vigorous education and a very adroit intelligence that watches over everything.

But why do I tarry further? Or why betake myself to a side path? Thrasamund alone has everything that is highly regarded in the whole earth's circuit. [10] Parthia glitters brilliantly with so many precious stones. Lydia's Pactolus furrows so many ruddy sands. The Silk People dye so many fleeces of changing color, granting by their precious garment—all vestments which blaze forth when purple dye is added—rewards to deserving rulers. [15] Africa pours forth profusely the fruits of the illustrious olive tree. The earth's produce—all that earns praise throughout the world—has entered your realm. The Creator on high has granted and allowed you alone to possess all these things.

With you as king the citadel of Carthage shines forth steadily. [20] Her offspring Alianae follows her with uneven step, her equal in esteem and distinction. The ruler's love for her caught fire most brightly. He built her, famous for her lovely site and her robust breezes. She deserved to bear the step of a deserving ruler. [25] Here the channel resounds beneath the marble-smooth swirl of the sea. Here the earth's riches rise up from the verdant soil, so that Our Master might enjoy the magnificence of land and sea.

Carthage, yes Carthage, retains her repute by her summits and by her king. Carthage the victress— [30] Carthage, the mother-city to the Hasdingi—triumphs. Carthage glitters. In all of Libya's lands Carthage, yes Carthage, is eminent. Carthage is adorned with learning. Carthage is embellished with teachers. Carthage is rich in peoples. Carthage is radiant. Carthage is well-endowed with houses. Carthage abounds with walls. [35] Carthage is savory. Carthage is nectar-sweet. Carthage flourishes, ruling in the name of Thrasamund. So that her empire might remain fortunate throughout the ages, we desire to observe yearly festivals for Our Master for many years, while he seeks anew the illustrious celebrations of his rule.

The ancient editors of the *Latin Anthology* correctly regarded these hexameters as a salute to royalty.[53] King Thrasamund (mentioned by name in verses 2 and 36) was the object of the praises that Florentinus composed in the classical idiom. There is only a hint (at lines 17 and 18) that Florentinus was a Christian.[54] Since the reign of Gunthamund, the Vandal rulers had appropriated some imperial titles in addition to the kingship, which they had held since the capture of Carthage. Florentinus was careful to note the "imperial splendor" (see verse 2) of Thrasamund. In lines 27 and 38 he spoke of Thrasamund as *dominus;* beginning with Gunthamund all Vandal kings adaopted the title *dominus noster.*[55] Annual vows and celebrations figure prominently at the beginning and end of the poem.[56] Here Florentinus was referring to the Vandal adaptation of the imperial *vota,* celebrations (most noticeable at five- or ten-year intervals) of the beginning date of an emperor's reign.[57] Neither Florentinus nor any other Latin poet who speaks about the regnal festivities of the Vandals indicates that the Vandal monarchs staged special observances every fifth year. The annual commemorations all seem to have been of equal intensity.[58] Finally, Florentinus (at lines 5 through 7) enumerated the many virtues of King Thrasamund. Of these, *pietas*—traditional reverence or dutiful respect toward the divine, one's fatherland, and one's family—was the most imperial.[59] During the dominate the obverses of Roman *solidi,* for instance, commonly gave the emperors the titles *Dominus Noster* and *Augustus* and characterized them as reverent (*pius*) and fortunate (*felix*). Florentinus and other Latin poets who saluted the dutiful respect of Vandal kings were seeking to place these monarchs near in spirit to the emperors.[60]

   Florentinus, then, composed a laudaïon that was the embryo of an imperial panegyric. A more explicit catalog of Thrasamund's virtues—an account of his ancestry, a narration of his deeds in war and peace, and a more robust peroration on the future glories of his reign—would have made the poem similar in content to Sidonius Apollinaris' hexameters in honor of the emperors Avitus, Majorian, and Anthemius.[61] Instead of developing further the theme of Thrasamund's imperial qualities, however, Florentinus introduced into his *In Praise of the King* another kind of encomium, the distant (and superior) ancestor of which was the *laudes Italiae,* the centerpiece of Virgil's *Georgics,* book 2. There the master had thrust aside the produce for which other regions were famous and had proclaimed Italy to be without rival in land, water, flora, fauna, and peoples.[62] In verses 8 through 18 Florentinus began to speak like Virgil, as he enumerated the world's wealth which flowed by trade into Thrasamund's Africa. Further reflection on Africa's fertility (beyond a spare notice of her olive trees, for which she was famous) might have produced a *laudes Africae.*[63] Instead, Florentinus turned aside and concluded his poem (lines 19 through 39) with a *laudatio Carthaginis.* In this section Carthage's "daughter," the suburb Alianae, first claimed the poet's attention. His notice of Thrasamund's construction there is less specific than the verses of Felix, who describes Thrasamund's baths in detail. On the other hand, Florentinus is more specific about the setting; references to a channel and the juxtaposition of fertile land and swirling sea bring to mind the shoreline north of Carthage, between today's Sidi Bou Saïd and Gammarth.[64] After this salute to an offspring of Carthage, however, Florentinus brought to view the metropolis herself. Carthage was the city of lofty summits, stately houses, walls, teachers, and advanced instruction. Florentinus here referred to the Byrsa (the site of the king's palace), the so-called Hill of Juno; the town houses and suburban

villas (of which other poets of the *Latin Anthology* and, recently, archaeologists have taken notice), the landward fortifications which the Roman authorities had constructed and the Vandal kings maintained; and the climate of
learning which persisted (albeit in diminished form) after the Age of Augustine.[65] Yet even as he praised Carthage, Florentinus associated the fortune
of the city with that of the Vandal king. Carthage, he proclaimed, was mother
to the Hasdingi, and the continued celebrations of Thrasamund's regnal year
were the guarantee that Carthage's "empire" would continue to prosper.[66] One
might say that Florentinus took the familiar motto that Thrasamund's successor
Hildiric placed on his silver coinage (FELIX KARTHAGO) and added a pro-
viso:[67] Carthage is fortunate indeed, so long as the Hasdingi are unconquered.

A salute to a king which became a *laudatio Carthaginis*, the introduction of
the Year of Carthage into regnal formulae, and the use of Phoenician and
tetrarchic badges of the city on currency place the Vandals' venture in Africa
some distance away from other Germanic sojourns on the Mediterranean
coast—for example, that of the Ostrogoths in Italy. In all the sources for Vandal Africa there is not a hint of the kind of apology that Cassiodorus wrote for
the royal house of the Amali. The abiding presence of Carthage in officially
sanctioned advertisements of Vandal greatness is a measure of the influence of
Roman civilization and Roman Africa's provincial elite during the Vandal
century.

APPENDIX: THE REGNAL YEAR OF THE VANDALS

In A.D. 537 the Emperor Justinian I ordered all official documents to be dated
by the years of his reign, the beginning of which he marked (according
to present-day reckoning) at 1 April 527, and by consulates and indictions.[68]
At the end of the last century Theodor Mommsen sought the origin of this
practice partly in Roman usage, and partly in the adoption of regnal years by
Germanic peoples. The Vandals were among the first to use regnal years.
Mommsen argued that soon after he captured Carthage Geiseric ordered time
to be measured from the beginning of his kingship, which he set at 19 October
439, the day of the city's capture.[69] Literary, epigraphical, and numismatic
evidence supports Mommsen's case and shows that the Vandal kings employed various formulae to publicize their regnal years.
   Before the Vandals came to Africa the inhabitants of the provinces of
Numidia, Africa Proconsularis, and Byzacium had abandoned the use of provincial and priestly eras in the third century and had thereafter dated public
documents by the names of the Roman consuls.[70] A funerary inscription of the

so-called Basilica of Cyprian attests the use of consular dating at Carthage as late as 438 or 439.[71] After this the Vandals changed the practice of chronological reckoning in their realm. The *Computus carthaginiensis,* a paschal composition drawn up when Deogratias was bishop of Carthage (454–57), bears the formula *anno decimo regis Geiserici* or *anno sextodecimo regis.*[72] The fourth and fifth editions of the *Liber genealogus* (a Donatist assemblage of biblical pedigrees and Christian events, based on the *Chronicle* of Hippolytus) are dated *ad annum sextum decimum regis* and *ad* (or *in*) *annum vicesimum quartum regis Geiserici,* respectively. The fifth edition of the *Liber genealogus* helps to locate these calculations in time. Fifty-eight years elapsed from the second consulate of Stilicho to the twenty-fourth year of King Geiseric; the year 463 came fifty-eight and twenty-four years after 405 and 439, respectively.[73] The *Laterculus regum Wandalorum* confirms: Thrasamund, who reigned from 496 until 523, died in the eighty-fourth year "from the entry into Carthage." [74] Again the year 439 emerges as a beginning point. The *Computus carthaginiensis* and *Liber genealogus* therefore show that as early as 455 inhabitants of Vandal Africa dated documents according to the regnal year of Geiseric, which indeed began on 19 October 439. The standard formula was *anno N regis Geiserici* ("in the year N of King Geiseric"). One funerary inscription of Sufetula in Byzacium bears the following concluding sentence: *natus anno XXVIII* / *regis Geseric pridie idus* / *septembres.* It is unclear whether this indicates the date of bith or death of the deceased.[75] In either case the literary sources discussed above render secure the use of Geiseric's name in dating formulae during his lifetime.

Geisiric's successors followed the practice of dating by regnal years. The preface to the *Notitia provinciarum et civitatum Africae* and documents inserted in Victor of Vita's history carry either full or abbreviated versions of the conventional phrase *anno N regis Hunirici.*[76] Gunthamund used more elaborate formulas. The *Tablettes Albertini* are dated *anno N domini* (or *domini nostri invictissimi*) *regis Gunthamundi;* Roman influence caused the king to adopt the imperial title *dominus noster* ("Our Master"). The ostraka discovered near Bir Trouch, Algeria, show that Gunthamund used another ingredient in the dating documents: *anno N K* (or *C*) *artaginis domni nostri regis Gunthamundi.*[77] Because the king's name is present here, the Year of Carthage is an elaboration of a regnal formula rather than a municipal era. Thrasamund, Hildiric, and Geilamir followed the example of their predecessors. A manuscript from Caralis (Cagliari) in Sardinia and funerary inscriptions from Vandal Africa bear variants of the formula *anno N domini nostri regis* for all three reigns.[78]

The Eastern Romans used existing and new methods of dating when they took control of Africa. Justinian's edict of 537 set the stage for the adoption of some new chronological indicators. In general, engravers who flourished during the Eastern Roman occupation employed combinations of regnal years and indictions or indictions alone when they dated their inscriptions.[79] Eastern Roman coins of Carthage bear indiction dates intermittently. Justinianic coins are sometimes dated *anno N*, but the obverse legend removes ambiguity.[80] These coins and certain inscriptions whose engravers carved the indiction as an afterthought show that Africans were at first slow to follow Justinian's order of 537.[81]

Sometime during the fifth or sixth century stonecutters and moneyers employed two methods of dating derived from the conventions noted above, but omitted the name of the current monarch. One of these—for convenience it may be called Type A—is the simple phrase *anno N*. Inscriptions from Madauros, Aquae Caesaris, and Tubernuc in Africa Proconsularis are dated *anno tertio, anno VII,* and *anno XXXIII,* respectively; whereas one epitaph of Leptis Minor in Byzacium bears the date *anno XXVIIII.*[82] The second method of dating (Type B) involved the use of the Year of Carthage. The moneyers who struck silver coins with the emperor Honorius on the obverse and Lady Carthage on the reverse dated this briefly lived series ANNO IIII K(ARTHAGINIS) and ANNO V + K(ARTHAGINIS).[83] Engravers carved on two funerary monuments of Madauros and two markers found at Hippo Regius in Africa Proconsularis the dates *anno VI K(arthagini)s, an(no) VII Karthag(i)n(is), anno XX Kartag(inis),* and *anno XXIIII Kartaginis,* respectively. Furthermore, an epitaph of Cuicul in Numidia bears the date *anno XXIIII K(arthaginis).*[84]

The interpretation of these two methods of dating is a matter of considerable debate. In his Paris dissertation Christian Courtois took Type A to be a regnal year of Geiseric and regarded Type B as an Eastern Roman era marking the reconquest of 533. In support of Courtois, Paul-Albert Février has assigned the Cuicul example of Type B to the Byzantine period on the grounds that Cuicul stands beyond eastern Numidia, the westernmost limit of a concentration of physical remains that can be dated to the Vandal century.[85] This attribution founders on indications that after 455 the Vandals imposed at least intermittent control over portions of Numidia and the Mauretanias.[86] Part of Courtois' reconstruction may therefore be rejected: there is no evidence that the Year of Carthage was in use during the Eastern Roman occupation of Africa. The interpretation of Noël Duval—the product of a systematic analysis of methods of dating in Numidia, Africa Proconsularis, and Byzacium— stands closer to the epigraphical and numismatic testimony assembled here. Duval has argued that types A and B are interchangeable, and that they both signify regnal years of Geiseric; only after Geiseric died did it become necessary to specify the name of the Vandal king.[87] Duval's case is not perfect. It involves a controversial interpretation of the epitaph of Sufetula, which records that the deceased "was born in the twenty-eighth year of King Geiseric." Furthermore, the *Computus carthaginiensis* and the fourth and fifth editions of the *Liber genealogus* demonstrate that Geiseric's subjects used the royal name and title to date documents during his reign.[88] Finally, Duval's reconstruction does not make sufficient allowance for inconsistencies of local stonecutters. It is safer to begin a test of Duval's argument with the supposition that Type A may record regnal years of any of the Vandal kings and—in view of indications that Africans were slow to begin dating by indiction[89]—Justinian I. The absence of Type B from the roster of Byzantine dating formulas restricts the search for the origin and nature of this convention. The Bir Trouch ostraka demonstrate that the Year of Carthage was in use during the reign of King Gunthamund (484–96).[90] If one allows for the possibilities that Gunthamund did not invent the formula and that his successors followed his example, Type B could have been in use from the reign of Geiseric to that of Geilamir. Can one be more precise than this?

Of the two conventions, Type A (with examples dated by the years 3, 7, 29, and 33) is the more cryptic. Early in this century Otto Seeck suggested a means of narrowing down the number of reigns during which the surviving examples could have been inscribed. All monarchs from Geiseric to Justinian I reigned three years, and all but Geilamir enjoyed seven years in power. Only Geiseric and Justinian I, however, ruled for twenty-nine and thirty-three years.[91] Therefore the four epitaphs that represent Type A may date from Geiseric's reign, as Duval has argued. Indeed, Type A's formula (*anno N*) stands close to *anno N regis* (without the king's name), a convention that the *Computus carthaginiensis* and the *Liber genealogus* used on occasion.[92] The application of Seeck's method to Type B, however, yields less clear-cut results. The coins and inscriptions representing Type B are dated in the fourth, fifth, sixth, seventh, twentieth, and twenty-fourth Years of Carthage. Once again, the greater number of years is a guide. Of all the Vandal kings, only Geiseric and Thrasamund reigned more than twenty or twenty-four years. At least one of these two monarchs shared with Gunthamund the use of the Year of Carthage, but the stonecutters who inscribed epitaphs in his (or their) twentieth and twenty-fourth years omitted the royal name. Furthermore, one Vandal king (not Geilamir, who reigned for three years) issued silver coinage during his fourth and fifth years.[93] Was Gunthamund the first Vandal king to introduce the Year of Carthage as an elaboration of regnal dating, or did he follow the example set by one of his predecessors?

Of the surviving attestations of Type B, only the silver coins minted in the name of the emperor Honorius are susceptible to further analysis. During Gunthamund's reign the mint of Carthage began to issue silver coinage with the king's name. Thrasamund, Hildiric, and Geilamir followed suit.[94] It is unthinkable that Gunthamund or his successors would have inaugurated an imperial imitation after the commencement of royal silver. Therefore the Honorius silver dates from no later than the fourth and fifth years of Gunthamund's reign (487/89). The reign of Honorius (393–423) sets the *terminus post quem;* the series began in 396/98 or later. Within the past generation critics have assigned these issues to Count Gildo (who rebelled against the Western Roman Empire in 397–98), and to the fourth and fifth regnal years of Huniric or Gunthamund (480/82 or 487/89). None of these dates can be proved beyond doubt to be correct. Nevertheless, it is possible to give credence to Baron Marchant's suggestion that Geiseric inaugurated the Year of Carthage in the fourth and fifth years of his reign.[95]

The first step in a modern exegesis of Baron Marchant's conjecture is to bring to view once again the full regnal formula utilized on the Bir Trouch ostraka: *anno N Karthaginis domini nostri regis Gunthamundi.* There is both tradition and innovation in this assemblage of conventions. Gunthamund was the first Vandal monarch to adopt the imperial title *dominus noster,* but other usages were in place before he became king. Geiseric was the first ruler to take the royal title (*rex*) and to order documents to be dated *anno N.* The *Computus carthaginiensis* and *Liber genealogus* demonstrate that he took these measures no later than A.D. 455.[96] The Byzantine chronicler Theophanes suggests that he did so soon after he and his soldiers captured Carthage in 439.[97] These considerations raise the possibility that the two methods of regnal dating, *anno N* and *anno N Karthaginis,* both originated during Geiseric's reign.

In an essay on the use of coinage for reconstructing events, A. H. M. Jones argues that modern critics have been too assiduous in detecting political motives for issuing money, and have thus been less attentive to economic reasons. Ancient minting authorities wanted first of all to have their coins circulate; political messages (in the form of badges and mottos) were of secondary importance.[98] Jones' approach to ancient coinage contributes in a general manner to the dating of the Honorius silver; it appeared during or soon after the reign of Honorius, when that emperor's currency enjoyed widespread circulation. It is interesting to note that the silver series under discussion is not the only Western provincial issue (beyond the pale of imperial coinage) to bear the name of Honorius. Two other silver types merit attention. The first of these, clearly minted at Carthage, is in two denominations. The more valuable of the two bears the inscription and bust of Honorius on the obverse, while the reverse displays a seated Roma and the legend VRBS ROMA. The obverse of the fraction is the same, while its reverse bears a winged Victory and the motto VICTORIA AVG(VSTI) or VICTORIA AVG(VSTORVM).[99] (Figs. 8.25 and 8.26.) The second series originated in northwestern Spain, in the lands of the Suevi. The familiar bust and inscription of Honorius appear on the obverse, and the reverse carries the unusual legend IVSSV RICHIARI REGES ("at the orders of King Richari").[100] (Fig. 8.27.) The first of these two series is more difficult to date, and discussion of it must therefore be postponed. The second issue, however, can be dated between A.D. 448 and 455,

Fig. 8.25. Silver coin of Carthage with VRBS-ROMA reverse. Washington, D.C., Dumbarton Oaks, acc. no. 48.17.3823 (photo: The Byzantine Collection, Dumbarton Oaks, Washington, D.C.).

Fig. 8.26. Silver coin of Carthage with Victory reverse. Cambridge, Fitzwilliam Museum (photo: by permission of the Syndics, Fitzwilliam Museum).

Fig. 8.27. Silver coin of Spain with a reverse bearing the name of the Suevic king Richari. Paris, Bibliothèque Nationale, Cabinet des Médailles, no. E/2770 (photo: Bibliothèque Nationale, Paris).

the years during which Richari was king of the Suevi.[101] The Richari silver, a regnal currency, appeared soon after the death of Honorius. The Honorius–*anno Karthaginis* silver is also regnal coinage. Did it too come into circulation around the middle of the fifth century?

If one calculates the dates on the Honorius–*anno Karthaginis* silver—the fourth and fifth Years of Carthage—from the known beginning of Geiseric's rule as king (19 Oct. 439), one places this silver issue in the years 443/44 and 444/45. If this chronology is accepted, it appears that Geiseric began using regnal years as a dating convention soon after his troops took Carthage. From what source might he have obtained the idea of a regnal year? Egypt, always a great influence on Roman Africa, had used the formula "the year N of Emperor N" since the beginning of the dominate. From the late fourth century until the reign of Justinian I, however, regnal dating fell into disuse there.[102] Egypt is therefore not a likely source for the Year of Carthage. Instead, an imperial inspiration may be sought. In the 440s the Eastern emperor Theodosius II ordered the production of two unusual *solidi* (figs. 8.28 and 8.29). The obverse of the first showed a facing portrait of the emperor in military dress, while the reverse carried a seated female figure (Constantinopolis?) and the legend IMP(ERATORE) XXXXII CO(N)S(VLE) XVII P(ATER) P(ATRIAE). The second type displayed on the obverse a left-facing bust of the emperor in consular robe, and on the reverse the emperor seated on a throne and the motto IMP(ERATORE) XXXXIIII CO(N)S(VLE) XVIII. The double dating in each case suggests that the two issues appeared in 442 and 444, respectively. The use of a single imperial year prefaced by the title *imperator* was a departure from prevailing custom; ordinarily, emperors of the

Fig. 8.28. *Solidus* of Theodosius II with reverse celebrating the emperor's forty-second year. Cambridge, Massachusetts, Fogg Art Museum, Whittemore Collection, acc. no. 1951.31.4 (on loan to Dumbarton Oaks) (photo: The Byzantine Collection, Dumbarton Oaks, Washington, D.C.)

Fig. 8.29. *Solidus* of Theodosius II with reverse celebrating the emperor's forty-fourth year. Washington, D.C., Dumbarton Oaks, acc. no. 62.73.2 (photo: The Byzantine Collection, Dumbarton Oaks, Washington, D.C.)

fifth century marked their years of rule on coinage with quinquennial or decennial *vota*.[103] The original occasion for this brief departure from tradition was perhaps Theodosius' attention to a Christian tradition that the Christ was born during the forty-second year of Caesar Augustus.[104] Theodosius' unusual *solidi* might well have influenced Geiseric's decision to date silver coinage of Carthage by his own regnal years.

The present reconstruction is only a working hypothesis. It encounters apparent difficulty in the Honorius–VRBS ROMA silver noted above. The recent catalog and analysis of Cécile Morrisson and James Schwartz have established beyond doubt that this extensive series was the work of the mint of Carthage, and that it antedated the more spare and derivative Honorius–*anno Karthaginis* silver. Since the British Museum catalog appeared around the turn of this century, it has become common to attribute both series to the Vandals; Morrisson and Schwartz adopt this standard reconstruction.[105] If Geiseric ordered the mint of Carthage to strike the Year-of-Carthage silver in 443/45, he would have been hard-pressed to bring the VRBS ROMA silver into production between 439 and 443, the years during which he and his people fought to retain the newly won metropolis of Roman Africa. The obstacle presented here, however, is not insuperable. In general terms, the two issues of silver from Carthage belong to the same span of time; the VRBS ROMA series came into production during or after the reign of Honorius (393–423) and no later than the early years of King Gunthamund. Morrisson and Schwartz have demonstrated that this silver issue dates from the fifth century, but I believe the decision to attribute it to the Vandals is open to question. Between about 390 and 430 the mint of Carthage enjoyed a brief spate of activity. At present mod-

Fig. 8.30. Bronze coin of Carthage with Victory and the legend CARTAGINE P(ER) P(ETVA) on the reverse. London, British Museum (photo: Trustees of the British Museum).

ern critics assign only a series of small bronzes (fig. 8.30) characterized by an ambiguous obverse (DOMINO NOSTRO, DOMINIS NOSTRIS, or DOMI-NIS NOSTRIS P[ER]P[ETVVIS] AVG[VSTIS]—all without the imperial names) and a variety of reverses (including some salutations of Carthage) to this period.[106] Yet a comparison of some imperial portraits in this series with some of those of the Honorius–VRBS ROMA silver reveals similarities: on Dumbarton Oaks and British Museum specimens of each issue, for instance, the pellet-shaped eyes and angular nose of the emperor resemble one another (Cf. figs. 8.25 and 8.30).[107] In the light of these comparisons one can suggest that a single authority ordered the mint of Carthage to issue full and fractional silver in Honorius' name, and small bronzes without the name(s) of the emperor(s). Who would have issued such an order? On the strength of the ambiguity of the legend DOMINO NOSTRO (etc.), modern critics have posited a dissident count of Africa as the inspiration of the small bronzes of Carthage. Count Gildo and Count Boniface (*rebellabant* 397–98 and ca. 422–29, respectively) are the favorite candidates.[108] Boniface is the more likely candidate of the two, for he remained at odds with parts of the imperial government for a longer time. Indeed, if one assigns to him the Honorius–VRBS ROMA silver, both economic and political motives for the series come to view: Boniface circulated coinage in the name of an emperor whose currency was common, and he advertised his well-known loyalty to the Western branch of the house of Theodosius after Honorius died in 423 and the bureaucrat John usurped the Western throne (423–25).[109]

The common date for the Honorius–VRBS ROMA series, then, rests on uncertain ground and does not spell doom for Baron Marchant's suggestion that Geiseric ordered the mint of Carthage to strike silver during the fourth and fifth years of his kingship. By the present reconstruction, Geiseric had both economic and political motives for placing Honorius' name and portrait on the obverse of his currency: Count Boniface had minted coinage in that emperor's name, and the new ruler of Carthage was not so secure that he could release money in his own name. Nevertheless, Geiseric did make bold to call himself king, and he dated this silver issue by his own years of reign. The beginning of the Vandal monarchy at Carthage and the commencement of the Vandal regnal year, it seems, are coterminous.[110]

NOTES

I presented an early version of this paper in the seminar of Noël Duval (University of Paris–Sorbonne) in 1978. At various stages of preparation I received helpful information and criticism from T. V. Buttrey, Randall Colaizzi, Jean Durliat, Noël Duval, Philip Grierson, Christian Habicht, T. L. Markey, Cécile Morrisson, Lellia Cracco Ruggini, and Susan Walker. Grants-in-aid from the American Numismatic Society (1969), the American Philosophical Society (1970), and the American Council of Learned Societies (1970 and 1983) enabled me to study the relevant coins in New York, Washington, D.C., London, Oxford, Cambridge, Paris, Copenhagen, Munich, Turin, Tunis, and Carthage. This paper first appeared in *Dumbarton Oaks Papers* 40 (1986): 1–16. Dumbarton Oaks has kindly granted permission to reprint the paper. The present version contains some new items which came to my attention after the earlier version went to press.

1   See the survey of F. M. Clover, "Carthage and the Vandals," *C. Mich.*, vol. 7 (1982), 1–22.

2   On the relations between the Amali and Italy's Roman aristocracy see, e.g., M. A. Wes, *Das Ende des Kaisertums im Westen des römischen Reichs* (The Hague, 1967).

3   Cf. Jord. *Get.* 1–3; and J. J. O'Donnell, *Cassiodorus* (Berkeley, 1979), 43–54.

4   See *PLRE*, 2:379–80, 462 (Felix 19), 476 (Florentinus 3), 695; and below, n. 22.

5   On the date of Victor's history, see Clover, "Carthage and the Vandals," 5, n. 26. In general, see *PCBE*, 1:1175–76 (Victor 64).

6   See *RIC*, 6:430, no. 46. In general, see *RIC*, 6:411–35.

7   Cf. P. Salama, "Un *follis* d'Alexandre tyran conservé à Madrid," *Numario hispanico* 9 (1960): 171–77; and *RIC*, 6:433, no. 62. The same motto appears on a third-century inscription of Rome: *CIL*, vol. 6, 29850a. On the date of Lucius Domitius Alexander's revolt, see T. D. Barnes, *The New Empire of Diocletian and Constantine* (Cambridge, Mass., 1982), 14–15.

8   Among the basic studies are A. H. M. Jones, *The Later Roman Empire, 284–602: A Social, Economic and Administrative Survey*, 3 vols. (Oxford, 1964), 3:347–80, D. Hoffmann, *Das spätrömische Bewegungsheer und die Notitia Dignitatum*, 2 vols. (Düsseldorf, 1969–70); and R. Goodburn and P. Bartholomew, eds., *Aspects of the Notitia Dignitatum* (Oxford, 1976).

9   On the interpretation of this illustration, see J. J. G. Alexander, "The Illustrated Manuscripts of the *Notitia Dignitatum*," in Goodman and Bartholomew, *Aspects of the Notitia Dignitatum*, 11–50, at 14; and P. C. Berger, *The Insignia*

of the Notitia Dignitatum (New York and London, 1981), 99–102. On the proconsul's residence at Carthage and the status of the city in the early fifth century, see F. M. Clover, "Carthage in the Age of Augustine," *C Mich.*, vol. 4 (1978), 1–14.

10 See Clover, "Carthage in the Age of Augustine," 9; and below, nn. 99 and 106.

11 In general, see *BMC Vand.*, 5. To my knowledge the Museo Civico of Turin and the Staatliche Museen zu Berlin hold the only surviving examples dated by the fifth Year of Carthage. On both these coins a Cross Potent stands between *anno V* and *K(arthaginis)*. On the reading of the obverse inscription, see R. Guéry, "Notes de céramique," *Bulletin d'archéologie algérienne* 3 (1968): 271–81, at 279–81; *contra* C. Morrison, "Les origines du monnayage vandale," *Actes du 8ème congrès international de nimismatique* (Paris and Basel, 1976), 461– 72, at 468, n. 29.

12 See the Appendix to this chapter.

13 See the discussion below, nn. 55–60.

14 See *BMC Vand.*, 13–14.

15 See *BMC Vand.*, 6–7. For the *curia* of Carthage as the possible minting authority see P. Grierson, "The *Tablettes Albertini* and the Value of the *Solidus* in the Fifth and Sixth Centuries A.D.," *Journal of Roman Studies* 49 (1959): 73–80, at 77–78. For the present consensus on the date of the large municipal bronzes of Carthage, see M. Hendy, *Studies in the Byzantine Monetary Economy, c. 300–1450* (Cambridge, 1985), 478–90.

16 Cf. F. Baratte and N. Duval, *Catalogue des mosaïques romaines et paléochrétiennes du Musée du Louvre* (Paris, 1978), 76–78, nos. 38a–c.

17 Cf. P. Gauckler, "La personnification de Carthage: Mosaïque du Musée du Louvre," *Mémoires de la Société nationale des antiquaires de France* 63 (1904): 165–78; and J. Salomonson, "Kunstgeschichtliche und ikonographische Untersuchungen zu einem Tonfragment der Sammlung Benaki in Athen," *Bulletin Antieke Beschaving* 48 (1973): 3–82, at 64–71.

18 Cf. R. P. Hinks, *Catalogue of the Greek, Etruscan and Roman Paintings and Mosaics in the British Museum* (London, 1933), 144–48, no. 57.

19 Cf. K. M. D. Dunbabin, *The Mosaics of Roman North Africa: Studies in Iconography and Patronage* (Oxford, 1978), 59, 62, and 250; and Dunbabin, "A Mosaic Workshop in Carthage around A.D. 400," in *New Light on Ancient Carthage*, ed. J. G. Pedley (Ann Arbor, Mich., 1980), 73–80.

20 For the reading of the inscription I follow Baratte and Duval, *Catalogue des mosaïques*, 77, no. 38a; *contra CIL*, vol. 8, 10539, which reads CVIR-IACVS.

21 Cf. K. M. D. Dunbabin, "The Victorious Charioteer on Mosaics and Related Monuments," *American Journal of Archaeology* 86 (1982): 65–89, at 75.

22 Luxurius 306 = *AL* 301. For the spelling of this poet's name I have followed the new editor, H. Happ, *Luxurius*, 1:142–58. At verse 1 both Bailey (*AL*, p. 248, *ad loc.*) and Happ (*Luxurius*, 1:26, 299) make a needless emendation: *Cyriace*. On the Latin Anthology in general, see Clover, "Carthage and the Vandals," 5–6, 20–22; and Averil Cameron, "Byzantine Africa: The Literary Evidence," *C Mich.*, vol. 7 (1982), 29–62, at 30–31.

23 Gauckler, "La personnification de Carthage," 170–71.

24   Cf. J. Bayet, "L'*omen* du cheval à Carthage: Timée, Virgile et le monnayage
     punique," in *Mélanges de littérature latine*, ed. J. Bayet (Rome, 1967), 255–80
     (esp. 256); and J. Ferron, "Le caractère solaire du dieu de Carthage," *Africa* 1
     (1966): 41–63.
25   See G. K. Jenkins and R. B. Lewis, *Carthaginian Gold and Electrum Coins*
     (London, 1963), p. 88, no. 117, and p. 128, nos. 27 and 18. On the significance
     of the caduceus, see Ferron, "Caractère Solaire," 50–52; and B. L. Trell,
     "Phoenician Greek Imperial Coins," *Israel Numismatic Journal* 6–7 (1982–
     83): 128–41.
26   See again Gauckler, "La personnification de Carthage," 165–78.
27   See H. B. Walters, *Catalogue of the Greek and Roman Lamps in the British Mu-
     seum* (London, 1914), nos. 85 and 95. I take the liberty of quoting a portion of a
     letter that Dr. Susan Walker of the British Museum sent to me on 6 Feb. 1985:
     "Lamp 85 was collected by Charles Townley and 95 was obtained from the col-
     lector Sir William Hamilton. It is likely, but not proven, that both lamps come
     from Italy."
28   Cf. R. Thouvenot, "Lampes en bronze," *Publications du Service des antiquités
     du Maroc* 10 (1954): 217–26; and J. Bussière, "Note sur la datation d'une
     lampe à tête de cheval trouvée à Renault (Oranie)," *Antiquités africaines* 3
     (1969): 237–42.
29   Cf. A. Ennabli, *Lampes chrétiennes de Tunisie* (Paris, 1976), 162–74, nos.
     762–76. An illustration of no. 771 appears in fig. 18.
30   Cf. Dunbabin, *Mosaics of Roman North Africa,* 93–94, and 270, no. 13.
31   Cf. ibid., 95–96, and 252–53, no. 33.
32   See above, nn. 20–23.
33   See above, n. 15.
34   See *BMC Vand.,* 3–4. On the minting authority and approximate date of this
     series, see above, n. 15.
35   See, e.g., A. S. Robertson, *Roman Imperial Coins in the Hunter Coin Cabinet,
     University of Glasgow,* 5 vols. (Oxford, 1962–82), 5:439, no. 20; 451, no. 1;
     and 462, no. 1.
36   Cf. T. L. Markey, "Nordic *Nídhvísur:* An Instance of Ritual Inversion?" *Stud-
     ies in Medieval Culture* 10 (1977): 75–85. Professor Markey brought this possi-
     bility to my attention.
37   See above, n. 15.
38   See, e.g., J. Lafaurie, "Trésor de monnaies de cuivre trouvé a Sidi Aïch
     (Tunisie)," *Revue numismatique,* 6th ser., 2 (1959–60): 113–30.
39   See *BMC Vand.,* 17–42.
40   See, e.g., J. G. Milne, "The Currency of Egypt in the Fifth Century," *Numis-
     matic Chronicle,* 5th ser., 6 (1926): 43–92.
41   See C. J. Thomsen, *Catalogue de la collection de monnaies de feu Chris-
     tian Jürgensen Thomsen,* 7 vols. (Copenhagen, 1866–76), 2:89, no. 1068;
     J. Friedländer, *Die Münzen der Vandalen* (Leipzig, 1849), 40.
42   Cf. T. V. Buttrey, "The Coins," *C Mich.,* vol. 1 (1976), 157–97, at 166–
     97 no. 120.
43   Thrasamund, for example, ordered some of the Victory *minimi* noted above

(nn. 38–39) struck in his name. Cf. *Sammlung Consul Eduard Friedrich Weber, Hamburg,* 2 vols. (Munich, 1908–9), 2:220, no. 3071 (now in Munich's Staatliche Münzsammlung, accession no. 27675); and M. Troussel, "Les monnaies vandales d'Afrique: Découvertes de Bou-Lilate et du Hamma," *Recueil des notices et mémoires de la Société archéologique, historique et géographique du Département de Constantine* 67 (1950–51): 147–92, at 172–87.

44   On Hildiric's bronzes with the Cross Potent, see *BMC Vand.,* p. 14, nos. 9–10. For recent reflections on the dating of the palm tree *nummi,* see W. E. Metcalf, "The Coins—1978," *C Mich.,* vol. 7 (1982), 63–168, at 64–67 and 150–52, no. 413.

45   Cf. figs. 20 (see n. 34, above) and 23.

46   For bronze *minimi* with similar or identical obverses and reverses, see Friedländer, *Münzen der Vandalen,* 40; and *BMC Vand.,* 26–27, nos. 68–72.

47   On the Wolf-and-Twins Series see Hendy, *Byzantine Monetary Economy,* 484–90. For the importance of Rome and Carthage in Late Antiquity see A. Audollent, *Carthage romaine, 146 avant Jésus-Christ–698 après Jésus-Christ* (Paris, 1901), 67–142; and R. Krautheimer, *Rome: Profile of a City, 312–1308* (Princeton, N.J., 1980), 3–87.

48   On the silver coins minted in the name of Honorius, see above, n. 11. It is difficult to separate the year-N-of-Carthage formula from other methods of dating employed by the Vandal kings. Consequently, I have placed a discussion of the Vandals' systems of regnal dating in the Appendix.

49   See above, n. 22.

50   Luxurius 304 = *AL* 299.

51   *AL* 201–5. Cf. E. Courtney, "Observations on the Latin Anthology," *Hermathena* 129 (1980): 37–50, at 39–40.

52   With one exception (see below, n. 64) I have followed Bailey's text of *AL* 371 (pp. 286–88). The translation of M. Chalon et al., "Memorabile factum," *Antiquités africaines* 21 (1985): 207–62, at 221–23, is based on the older Teubner text of Alexander Riese.

53   The *codex Salmasianus'* superscript: "Hi sunt uersus a florentino in laude(m) regis facto (Claude de Saumaise: *facti*)." Cf. Bailey, *AL,* p. 286, *ad loc.*

54   Blossius Aemilius Dracontius, a contemporary of Florentinus and a Christian, used classical characterizations similar to those of *AL* 371.17–18 to describe the God of the Christians in his *Satisfactio* to King Gunthamund (cf. vv. 55–92, et passim).

55   Cf. Drac. *Sat.* 107–12, and passim; and *BMC Vand.,* 8–15.

56   *AL* 371.1, 37–39.

57   Cf. A. A. Boyce, *Festal and Dated Coins of the Roman Empire: Four Papers* Numismatic Notes and Monographs, no. 153 (New York, 1965), 40–90.

58   Cf. *AL* 201.7–8 (Felix); and Drac. *Sat.* 45–52.

59   Cf. T. Ulrich, *Pietas (pius) als politischer Begriff im römischen Staate bis zum Tode des Kaisers Commodus,* Historische Untersuchungen, no. 6 (Breslau, 1930), passim.

60   For a similar use of the concept of *pietas,* see Drac. *Sat.* 109–12, et passim. For a general discussion of the Vandal kings' mixture of their own and imperial

titles, see H. Wolfram et al., *Intitulatio*, 2 vols. Mitteilungen des Instituts für Oesterreichische Geschichtsforschung, Ergänzungsbände 21, 24 (Vienna, Cologne, and Graz, 1967–73), 1:76–89; and M. McCormick, *Eternal Victory: Triumphal Rulership in Late Antiquity, Byzantium, and the Early Medieval West* (Cambridge, 1986), 261–66.

61 Cf. Sidon. *Carm.* 2, 5, and 7.

62 See Virgil *Georgics* 2.109–76.

63 Cf. *AL* 371.15. For similar sentiments, see *Expositio* 61.

64 Cf. *AL* 371.20–27. On Felix's view of the baths of Thrasamund, see *AL* 201–5. The title of *AL* 201 (*De thermis Alianarum;* cf. Bailey, *AL*, p. 150, *ad loc.*) leads me to reject the *Codex salmasianus'* reading *Alianas* in favor of the nominative plural *Alianae* at *AL* 371.20. Bailey (*AL*, p. 187, *ad loc.*) and Chalon, "Memorabile factum," 220–23, 231–41, retain the manuscript reading at this point. On Carthage's north shore during the Vandal century, see Clover, "Carthage and the Vandals," 7–8, 13–17.

65 For these features of Vandal Carthage see Clover, "Carthage and the Vandals," 1–22.

66 Cf. *AL* 371.30, 36–39. At v. 37 Florentinus uses the word *imperium* to describe the Vandal hegemony.

67 See *BMC Vand.*, 13–14; and fig. 7.

68 *CIC/NI* 47.

69 T. Mommsen, *Gesammelte Schriften*, 8 vols. (repr. Berlin, 1965), 6:342–58.

70 Cf. N. Duval, "Recherches sur la datation des inscriptions chrétiennes d'Afrique en dehors de la Maurétanie," in *Atti del terzo congresso internazionale de epigrafia greca e latina* (Rome, 1959), 245–62, at 245–49.

71 *IC Sainte-Monique* 46.

72 *Comp. carth.* 1.2, 5 and 2.4, 8 (ed. Krusch, pp. 279, 281, 287, 289). On Deogratias see *PCBE*, 1:271–73.

73 *Lib. gen.* 428, 499, 627, and 628c (*MGH:AA*, 9:181, 188, 196). On Stilicho's second consulate (405) see R. S. Bagnall and K. A. Worp, *The Chronological Systems of Byzantine Egypt* (Zutphen, 1978), 79. For the fourth and fifth editions of the *Liber genealogus* see P. Monceaux, *Histoire littéraire de l'Afrique chrétienne depuis les origines jusqu'à l'invasion arabe* (Paris, 1901–23), 6:247–58.

74 *Lat. reg. Wand.* 12–13 (*MGH:AA*, 13:459).

75 *ILCV* 3477. Cf. N. Duval, "Trois notes sur les antiquités chrétiennes d'Haïdra, l'ancienne Ammaedara (Tunisie)," *Bulletin de la Société nationale des antiquaires de France*, 1963, pp. 44–68, at 60–68.

76 *Not. prov., Praefatio;* and Vict. Vit. *HP* 2.39, 3.3–14.

77 C. Courtois et al., *Tablettes Albertini: Actes privés de l'époque vandale* (Paris, 1952), 313–14 (on the title *dominus noster* see above, nn. 53–60), J.-P. Bonnal and P.-A. Février, "Ostraka de la région de Bir Trouch," *Bulletin d'archéologie algérienne* 2 (1966–67): 239–49.

78 *Codex basilicanus* D. 182, fol. 288 in *CLA*, 1:1a); *ILCV* 1385 and 4452; and *IC Haïdra* 413, 419.

79 Cf. Duval, "Inscriptions chrétiennes d'Afrique," 250–52, 258–60; J. Durliat,

"La lettre L dans les inscriptions byzantines d'Afrique," *Byzantion* 49 (1979): 156–74; and N. Duval, "Comment distinguer les incriptions byzantines d'Afrique?" *Byzantion* 51 (1981): 511–32.

80   Cf. A. R. Bellinger, P. Grierson, et al., *Catalogue of the Byzantine Coins in the Dumbarton Oaks Collection and in the Whittemore Collection,* 3 vols. (Washington, D.C., 1966–73), 1:164–69, 2:1, 123–29; and C. Morrisson, *Catalogue des monnaies byzantines de la Bibliothèque nationale,* 2 vols. (Paris, 1970), 1:106–8.

81   Cf. Y. Duval, *Loca Sanctorum Africae: Le culte des martyrs en Afrique du IVᵉ au VIIᵉ siècle,* (2 vols., Collection de l'École française de Rome, no. 58 (Rome, 1982), 1:138–42, no. 64.

82   Cf. E. Albertini, "Quelques inscriptions de Madaure," *Bulletin archéologique du Comité des travaux historiques et scientifiques,* 1930–31, pp. 247–55, at 253, no. 13; *ILA,* vol. 1, 2959; *ILT* 819; and *ILCV* 3139.

83   See above, n. 11.

84   Cf. *ILCV* 1387, 1457, 1601A; E. Marec, "Epitaphe chrétienne d'époque byzantine trouvée aux environs d'Hippone," *Libyca: Archéologie-épigraphie* 3 (1955): 163–66 = *AE,* 1956, p. 125; and P.-A. Février, "Inscriptions chrétiennes de Djemila (Cuicul)," *Bulletin d'archéologie algérienne* 1 (1962–65): 207–26, at 214–22 = *AE,* 1967, p. 596.

85   C. Courtois, *Les Vandales et l'Afrique* (Paris, 1955), 369, 373, 375, 379; Février, "Inscriptions de Djemila," 214–22, cf. Courtois, 171–85.

86   See Vict. Vit. *HP* 1.13, 2.14; Prisc. frag. 27 (ed. Bornmann, p. 89); W. H. C. Frend's review of Courtois' *Vandales* in *Journal of Roman Studies* 46 (1956): 161–66, at 165; and A. Chastagnol and N. Duval, "Les survivances du culte impérial dans l'Afrique du Nord à l'époque vandale," in *Mélanges d'histoire ancienne offerts à William Seston* (Paris, 1974), 87–118, at 88–94.

87   Duval, "Inscriptions chrétiennes d'Afrique," esp. 252–56.

88   See above, nn. 75, 72–73.

89   See above, n. 81.

90   See above, n. 77.

91   O. Seeck, *Geschichte des Untergangs der antiken Welt,* 6 vols. (Stuttgart, 1897–1921), 6:330, 477. On the number of years the Vandal kings and Justinian I reigned, see Courtois, *Vandales,* 405–9; and *PLRE,* 2:645–48.

92   Cf. *Comp. carth.* 1.5, 2.8 (ed. Krusch, pp. 281, 289); and *Lib. gen.* 499 (*MGH:AA,* 9:188).

93   See above, nn. 11 and 84.

94   Cf. *BMC Vand.,* 8–16.

95   C. Courtois, "Les monnaies de Gildo," *Revue numismatique,* 5th ser., 16 (1954): 71–77; C. Morrisson, "Origines du monnayage vandale," 468–70; and C. Lenormant et al., eds., *Lettres du Baron Marchant sur la numismatique et l'histoire* (2d ed., Paris, 1851), 184–88.

96   See above, nn. 77, 55 and 60, 72–75.

97   Theoph. *Chron.* 5941 (ed. de Boor, 1:101), s.aa. 448/9, but recounting events that happened immediately after the Vandals captured Carthage. Since Geiseric became the leader of his people as early as A.D. 428 (cf. Hydat, *Chron.* 89),

Theophanes must be describing Geiseric's appropriation of the title of *rex*. Before 439 Geiseric probably held another form of chieftainship. On the complexities of early Germanic leadership and the resulting names for high magistracies, see J. M. Wallace-Hadrill, *Early Germanic Kingship in England and on the Continent* (Oxford, 1971), 1–20.

98 Cf. A. H. M. Jones, *The Roman Economy: Studies in Ancient Economic and Administrative History,* ed. P. A. Brunt (Oxford, 1974), 61–81.

99 See C. Morrisson and J. H. Schwartz, "Vandal Silver Coinage in the Name of Honorius," *American Numismatic Society Museum Notes* 27 (1982): 149–79.

100 See X. Barral i Altet, *La circulation des monnaies suèves et visigotiques* (Zurich and Munich, 1976), 51.

101 Cf. *PLRE,* 2:935.

102 Cf. R. S. Bagnall and K. A. Worp, *Regnal Formulas in Byzantine Egypt* Bulletin of the American Society of Papyrologists, suppl. 2 (Missoula, Mont., 1979), 42–44.

103 See Boyce, *Festal and Dated Coins,* 40–90 (esp. 73) and 99, nos. 116–18. On the date and the reverse legends of the two issues, see next note.

104 I follow here a new explanation of the IMP XXXXII and XXXXIIII *solidi* offered by Philip Grierson, "An Enigmatic Coin Legend: IMP XXXXII on *solidi* of Theodosius II," to appear in *Studia numismatica labacensia Alexandro Jeločnik oblata* (Ljubljana, forthcoming).

105 Morrisson and Schwartz, "Vandal Silver Coinage"; Cf. *BMC Vand.,* 2 and 5.

106 Cf. *LRBC,* p. 58, nos. 576–80. In 1970 I examined the specimen described in *LRBC,* p. 58, no. 580 (now in the possession of a private collector in Paris) at A. H. Baldwin and Son, London, and I offer here a reading of the obverse inscription which differs from that of the editors of *LRBC.* An illustration of a British Museum specimen (cf. *LRBC,* p. 58, no. 576) appears in fig. 30.

107 Cf. Morrisson and Schwartz, "Vandal Silver Coinage," 161–62.

108 Cf. *LRBC,* p. 58, nos. 576–80; and R. Turcan, "Trésors monétaires trouvés à Tipasa: La circulation du bronze en Afrique romaine et vandale aux Vᵉ et VIᵉ siècles ap. J.-C.," *Libyca: Archéologie-épigraphie* 9 (1961): 201–57, esp. 208–12 and 216.

109 On the career of Count Boniface see F. M. Clover, "The Pseudo-Boniface and the *Historia Augusta,*" in *Bonner Historia-Augusta-Colloquium 1977/78* (Bonn, 1980), 73–95; and *PLRE,* 2:237–40.

110 I owe the present reconstruction to conversations with Noël Duval and Philip Grierson. See now P. Grierson and M. Blackburn, *Medieval European Coinage,* vol. 1, *The Early Middle Ages (5th–10th Centuries)* (Cambridge, 1986), 20–22.

CHAPTER 9

Gelimer's Laughter:
The Case of Byzantine Africa

AVERIL CAMERON

It happened that Belisarius was spending some time in the suburb of Carthage called Anclae. When Gelimer came to him, he laughed out loud, a laugh that could not be concealed, and some of those who saw him assumed because of this excess that he had gone out of his mind, and was laughing for no reason. His friends however interpreted it this way: being clever and born of a royal house he had come to the throne, and been powerful and wealthy from childhood to old age; then having fallen into great fear and flight and suffering disaster at Mons Pappua, and now held as a prisoner, thus experiencing every species of good and bad fortune, he considered human life worthy only of laughter.[1]

So Procopius writes of the defeated Gelimer, king of the Vandals, taken soon after this incident to Constantinople to walk in his captor's triumphal procession. Procopius, the historian of the winning side, admired Gelimer as the noble barbarian while condemning his actual surrender as "womanish."[2] It came after the Vandal king had seen two small Vandal boys, one of them his own nephew, fighting over a piece of bread. The two stories, Gelimer's pity and Gelimer's laughter, symbolize the stark realities of the Byzantine conquest of North Africa. Can we get behind the stories to a sense of what that conquest meant for the province?

On the whole, Byzantine Africa has been left to the specialists. Although the reconquest of North Africa in A.D. 534 was the most spectacular of Justinian's military achievements, and although the reorganized province remained at least nominally under Byzantine control until the end of the seventh century, Africa has nevertheless often been completely omitted in general discussions of the transition from antiquity to the medieval world. Even within the specialist literature, the last major synthesis, still the standard work, was written as long ago as 1896.[3] Only now, with the major international program of excavation at Carthage, and with fresh epigraphic publications and reliable

171

work being done at certain other key sites, are sufficient interest and information accumulating to bring the rewriting of that book within sight. Even so,
the archaeological record is still so patchy for this period of North African
history that a full study remains at the moment an impossibility. On the other
hand, the impact of the Byzantine reconquest on North Africa, and especially
on the cities, must now obviously rank as a central issue in the light of the
growing body of archaeological evidence for Mediterranean cities generally in
the sixth and early seventh centuries, all the more so because North Africa is
treated in rich and circumstantial detail in a key literary source, Procopius'
Buildings.[4] Recent work on African towns in the late Roman period makes it
all the more necessary to ask what happened to them in the sixth and seventh
centuries.[5] Why, we must ask, did the province that Justinian acquired so
easily in A.D. 533, where a long history of Roman wealth and culture waited
to be reclaimed, succumb so completely to another invader hardly more than a
century later?

A history of Byzantine Africa lacking in colonial bias has yet to be written.
Charles Diehl's *L'Afrique byzantine* was, like most of the early archaeological
work, itself the product of a colonial regime.[6] But even now it is hardly possible to get away from such an approach, since the sources themselves present
us with an Africa seen through the eyes of the Byzantines, the invaders. Byzantine Africa was treated as a showpiece of the Justinianic empire. It was to
display the force of Byzantine arms with a massive program of building and
restoration, all in the name of liberation. The writers who have told us about it
do so from the Byzantine point of view. We can know what the local population thought about only from their recorded actions in the pro-Byzantine
sources.[7] Even the survey archaeology which might give us some compensat-
ing information has still to be done. Our own picture, therefore, will in the
meantime tend to be urban-based and unduly centered on the elites whose
doings feature in the sources. Only a large amount of new archaeological material of a different sort will enable this picture to be substantially altered. Finally, the history of the Berbers in the sixth century, previously seen only
obliquely through hostile Byzantine perceptions, is now itself attracting attention for ideological reasons.[8]

One relatively straightforward question that can be asked, however, is this:
Was the Byzantine reconquest of North Africa a stimulus to the province
which enabled it to hold out longer than most during the seventh century, or
was it on the contrary itself a factor which in the long run brought division and
weakness? Historians have often seen Byzantine rule in Africa as a thin veneer
superimposed over an indigenous culture that was, when the time came, extremely receptive to Islam; control and financial aid from Constantinople had
only to weaken, as both naturally did when the empire was hard-pressed on
other fronts during the reign of Heraclius (A.D. 610–41) and later, for the

suprastructure of Byzantine rule to fragment. The history of Byzantine Africa thus becomes the history of a colonial power unable to maintain its hold over its conquests.

But although there is something in this view, it is also much too simple. It fails to bring out the real diversity in the province, or the full complexities of the situation even before the problems of the seventh century. Because of the vagueness of the (later) Arabic sources for the later period, and their lack of interest in the Byzantines as opposed to the Berber opponents of the Islamic armies, together with the near-total silence of Byzantine sources on seventh-century Africa, we know very little of the internal relations of the province during the period before its "fall." [9] But our sources for the early part of Byzantine rule do allow us to form some idea of its effects on the province.

It must first be emphasized that however much it might be advertised as "restoration," this was in effect a conquest. [10] The small army led by the general Belisarius was not the Roman army familiar from pre-Vandal times. It was composed, in the main, of Greek-speaking Easterners. If the soldiers were not Greeks they might be Huns, Armenians, or Goths. Belisarius had to remind them that the town dwellers in the province were "Romans," and that he and his army had come to free them from the Vandal yoke. [11] The Byzantines also called themselves "Romans," but they spoke Greek. Their arrival underlined the fact that while the Vandals had been in North Africa, Rome had fallen. There was no reason to believe, when the Byzantine armies arrived, that Ostrogothic Italy would also be "restored" to the empire, and when, shortly afterward, Belisarius did move from Africa to begin the reconquest of Italy, Roman Africans were nevertheless forcibly reminded that Constantinople was the seat of power. There was no comparison, in any case, despite the early Byzantine successes, between the reconquests of Africa and Italy. The latter dragged on for nearly twenty years of fighting, and when it came, there was little left of Roman Italy. [12] In contrast, the Byzantines were able to hold the province of Africa and thus had the chance of imposing upon it an apparatus of rule from the East which made it unique in the sixth-century West. "Liberation" or no, Byzantine conquest meant the often harsh imposition of military rule from Constantinople. [13]

At the same time, the cities of Byzantine Africa, which were the targets of a vast imperial program of interrelated expenditure and taxation, did not fail to share in the general urban transformations of the century before Islam. From the rich urban civilization of Roman imperial Africa, which in a sense Justinian hoped to revive, the seventh-century province retained some of the form but much less of the substance; internal change preceded, and thereby facilitated, the coming of Islam. It is worth considering whether the shock of conquest and Eastern rule followed by a military decline did not actually precipitate urban change and alter the balance between town and country.

The Byzantines themselves were in no doubt about the nature of their presence in North Africa. Many had questioned the wisdom of the enterprise in the first place,[14] but after its remarkable success in the early stages what remained was the mechanics of conquest. Its chief elements were defense (a more formidable enemy than the Vandals revealed itself very soon in the Berbers), religious unity and if necessary conversion, and taxation. For all of these the towns were the essential units of organization. Justinian's generals and administrators had a clear idea of what a city should be like, founded on the Late Antique model: it would have large public areas, colonnades, baths.[15] Of course there were to be churches, and on a large scale; but we are still in a familiar classical setting, and the ideological importance of the restoration of the African cities comes out very strongly in the detailed accounts of the Byzantine intervention in North Africa in the *Wars* and the *Buildings* written by Belisarius's aid Procopius, who was himself present during the first phase. In Procopius' rhetoric, no less evident in the *Wars* than in the admittedly panegyrical *Buildings,* cities restored under the Byzantine administration stood for "culture" as opposed to "rusticity." He describes how at Caput Vada, the headland on the coast of Tunisia where Belisarius's force landed, a city was built, giving the rustics (*agroikoi*) the chance to change their way of life from *agroikia* (rusticity) to *asteia* (civilization).[16] The great city of Lepcis, home of the emperor Septimius Severus, was rescued, Procopius tells us, from the encroaching sand to become a showpiece of restoration and culture.[17] The cities symbolized the ideal of the reconquest policy, as it later became. They are opposed in Procopius' mind to two categories of Africans—the country dwellers (*agroikoi*), the rural population, of whatever origin, and the "barbarians," the marauding nomads and aggressive Berbers from the mountains. These are simple categories (Procopius has little if any sense of the true degree of assimilation between settled Berbers and the sub-Roman population in town and country), but then, the ideology of Byzantine reconquest was itself powerfully simple. It ignored, for instance, the extent to which the Vandal elite had permitted and even patronized Latin culture. The African poet Corippus, who enthusiastically supported the idea of reconquest, himself saw Carthage as representing sophistication in contrast to his own small-town background.[18] Paradoxically, it seems in fact to have been more of a center of culture in the late Vandal period than it was under Byzantine rule. Corippus himself may have realized something of this later, for he did not stay in Carthage: Constantinople seemed to offer better prospects.[19]

Procopius, then, portrays the intervention in crudely black and white terms: the Byzantines have God and the right on their side and the Roman Africans should be pleased to have their protection. More surprisingly, a similar model of the situation pervades the *Iohannis,* Corippus' panegyric on the campaigns of the general John Troglita against the Berbers in the late 540s. But the Africans themselves (that is, the townspeople) did not always see it this way, as

Procopius himself occasionally allows us to glimpse. It was a situation similar to that in contemporary Italy, where the Roman population was divided too. While some went to Constantinople to try to urge a more active war policy on Justinian, others, in Italy itself, found themselves caught between two military forces, the Goths and the Byzantines, and by no means always chose to support the latter.[20] In both cases there was also the religious factor. It was assumed in Constantinople that both Ostrogothic Italy and Vandal Africa were in need of liberation from the control of Arian heretics. The armies went in under the badge of religious intervention; it is hardly too much to call the reconquest a holy war. Even Procopius underlines the interconnection, to the Byzantine mind, between conquest and conversion, and the desire to spread the net of orthodoxy among the still-pagan Berbers through church building. Spreading orthodoxy is inherent in the Byzantine conception of urban renewal. At Lepcis, for instance, Procopius tells us that Justinian, that is, the Byzantine administration, built public baths, renewed the walls, and generally gave it the "form of a city"; the next sentence casually adds that the neighboring Gadabitani were then converted; and the paragraph concludes with a mention of Sabratha, where the only items singled out are fortifications and a church.[21]

Such an attitude naturally saw A.D. 534 as an unbridgeable divide in the history of North Africa. It imposed strong categories on the whole issue, chronologically and conceptually. The Vandals were alien, barbarian, and heretic; after the reconquest, the province (much smaller than Roman imperial Africa had been) was divided between friends and enemies, Romans (or so the Byzantines thought of them) and Berbers. Defense, in such a conceptual frame, would be a matter of maintaining a linear frontier between civilization and the alien "other." Our two main literary sources for the early reconquest period, Procopius and Corippus, both hold these views in their strongest form.

Procopius, at least, was seduced by the glamour of Belisarius' victories. He tells the story in the most dramatic sequence in his history: the anxious departure of the fleet from Constantinople, waved off by the emperor and empress and the patriarch; the arrival on the coast of Tunisia, marked by divine signs; Belisarius' entry into Carthage only a few months later; and the vivid scene when he and his officers, including Procopius himself, dined in the palace on food prepared for the Vandal king.[22] Procopius went on to record the less glorious phase that followed while Belisarius was away carrying the war to Ostrogothic Italy,[23] but he never had to address himself to the real problems of long-term control. Thus his account, even in the *Buildings,* written at latest in 560 but more probably in 553/54, reflects the confidence of the early years. The disillusion he felt when writing the last books of the *Wars* in the late 540s and early 550s is directed against the Byzantine government rather than the policy of conquest itself; it does not spring from a consideration of the real problems of the province.[24]

Furthermore, Africa was the first and easiest of Justinian's conquests. The Byzantines proceeded to apply there in purest form the techniques they assumed to be a necessary part of reconquest; whereas in Italy, as we have seen, the war dragged on for so long, and the resources on which the Byzantine army could draw were often so slender, that the impact of their presence was inevitably quite different. Among other factors, the ruin of most of the old Roman families, still immensely wealthy at the start of the Byzantine campaigns, deprived the Italian towns, many of them all but ruined in lengthy and sometimes repeated sieges, of their natural local patrons.[25] In North Africa, in contrast, few of the towns were severely damaged in the initial campaign, and even later, when they were subjected to raids from aggressive nomads whom the Byzantine forces could control only with great difficulty, they were neither besieged, like the Italian towns, nor virtually destroyed, like the towns of Asia Minor during the Persian inroads of the early seventh century. Thus North Africa provided Justinian with a unique opportunity, and it is here that we see in sharpest form the difference that reconquest might make.

Nevertheless, it was probably less than Procopius believed. His detailed account of the Byzantine building work at Carthage, for example, implies that under the new system the city was dramatically different from its former self.[26] And since he was present at the reconquest and stayed in Carthage when Belisarius went off to conduct the Italian campaign, why not believe him? After all, he seems to have been confirmed by the recent British and Canadian excavations.[27] But only in part: other building works he mentions have not been revealed, and, more seriously, he can be shown to have been selective, on what principles we do not know. Elsewhere in both the *Wars* and the *Buildings* he can be shown to have structured his set descriptions for reasons other than exact accuracy; even here he perhaps knowingly ascribes to the Byzantines a chapel of the Virgin on the Byrsa which had been there already under the Vandals.[28] There are then serious potential problems with the simple reliability of our most important literary source. But even if he were to be taken wholly at face value, there is still the matter of the perception, which he shared with Byzantine official propaganda, that there was a rigid dividing line between "Vandal" and "Byzantine" North Africa, both in buildings and in other matters. In the former case, archaeology can rarely be so precise in its dating, and there are certainly examples of building work being carried out in the later Vandal period.[29] Similarly, many forms of Roman public life continued into the Vandal period, and it would be absurd to suppose that there was not similar continuity into the Byzantine phase.

Just as difficult is the attempt to decide what proportion of the public buildings of this period was officially inspired or financed. The body of Byzantine official inscriptions is small; many buildings, even major ones, have none, or else are on a smaller scale altogether.[30] Clearly the great fortresses, and the barracks that existed in many towns, will have been centrally commissioned, as indeed Procopius' lists suggest. But many smaller works, repairs and alterations of existing buildings, fortified houses, and farms, will have been carried out by local effort. It is the same with the churches, frequently restored or altered during the sixth century or in some cases the seventh, and often on the base of a much earlier foundation. The great Kelibia basilica on Cap Bon, for example, now once again covered by the sand, was in full use during the Vandal period; it is unknown whether the apse restoration and remodeling of the baptistery that took place during the sixth century owed anything to official directives.[31] Similarly, it is often next to impossible to distinguish between Byzantine and Arab work, especially where the same structures went on being used over a lengthy period. There was no clear-cut dividing line, and for this purpose A.D. 698, the year of the final fall of Carthage, is no more than a date in a textbook. The year A.D. 534 was different: it saw the beginning of a very deliberate policy by the imperial government. All the same, it was probably not so drastic a break in all spheres as Procopius would have us believe.

Yet Byzantine Africa was exceptional, even in the context of Justinianic building, for the amount of public building carried out. The imperial government adopted a high profile. It was the same in religious matters. Again, the extreme unevenness of the evidence makes a complete picture impossible to achieve. For instance, although Procopius tells us that new churches dedicated to the Virgin (as at Augila and Septem) were considered crucial to the conversion policy of the imperial government, they have not survived; and the epigraphic record is thin indeed on the cult of the Virgin in this period, our chief evidence coming from seals, which of course tell us more about the Byzantine officials than about the local population.[32] On the other hand, certain Eastern saints do seem to have become more popular, though Procopius does not mention them; these cults are more likely the result of a spontaneous development than of any deliberate policy.[33] The chief impact of the new regime in religious matters was, so far as the already Christian population was concerned, mainly a strongly negative one. Its first act was to condemn Arianism and restore Catholics to all their lost privileges; one of the most striking passages in the *Wars* is that in which Procopius describes how the basilica of St. Cyprian at Carthage was recovered by the Catholics after it had been decorated for a saint's feast day by the Arians. But perhaps the government had not realized the likely effects of these laws on the army—at any rate, there were many Arians in the Byzantine army itself, and the harsh measures led to a serious mutiny that was a major source of trouble for the Byzantine administration in the early years. It is very likely that there were also more Arians in the population at large than the government would have liked to admit, and that it was not only in the army that division was created. The danger was that the mutineers would command widespread support in the population and that the administration would be unable to hold its gains.[34]

With great difficulty the mutiny was put down, but a new gulf opened up between the imperial government and the Africans. Justinian began as early as A.D. 543 to issue directives insisting that certain theological writings favored on the whole in the West but heartily condemned in the Monophysite East be officially rejected.[35] To the African bishops, whose natural ties were with Rome rather than Constantinople, this was devastating. They were being asked by the very "Romans" who were claiming to have liberated them from religious oppression to take up a position that they considered to be the equivalent of heresy. The events that followed were of profound importance for the church in Africa. Its bishops, especially Facundus of Hermiane, took the lead in opposing the emperor. Many of them traveled in a body to Constantinople in A.D. 550 to argue with him in person, among them the bishop of Carthage and the chronicler Victor of Tonnena, to whom we owe much of our knowledge of the affair. They met with a harsh reception: Victor was imprisoned and wrote his chronicle in exile; Bishop Verecundus of Iunca died at Chalcedon with Pope Vigilius; the bishop of Carthage was deposed, like many others, and replaced by a character who resorted to a strong-arm tactics to get the bishops who had stayed behind in the province to toe the government line. In A.D. 554 there followed the Fifth Ecumenical Council in Constantinople, used by the emperor as an instrument for enforcing his policies designed to conciliate Monophysites and orthodox.[36] Many bishops who objected were exiled to Egypt, while those who remained in Numidia and Proconsular Africa tended to fall in with the new bishop of Carthage rather than submit to beating or imprisonment.

This was a rude shock, not merely for the African church, but also for the Roman elite in the province from whose ranks the bishops tended to come. They had found a way of accommodation under the Vandals; now their adjustment to the new regime was sharply halted by this open breach with Constantinople. Moreover, there was an uncanny replay of this mass exodus of 550 a century later, when many African bishops left the province for Rome for the Lateran Council of A.D. 649, again in complete breach with the Eastern government.[37] On neither occasion have we much idea of how many ever returned to Africa. It is certain, however, that each of these episodes, separated by a century, served to deprive the province of its natural leaders and made it harder to formulate a securely pro-Byzantine elite. The evidence does not permit an impression of the degree of assimilation between Byzantines and Africans in the running of the province in the intervening period, but one can imagine that these passionate reactions and the harsh treatment of the objectors made the acceptance of Byzantine rule much more difficult.

Another factor that told against smooth acceptance was the level of warfare in the province after the arrival of the Byzantines, and which their aggressive military installations seemed to provoke rather than to contain. The pro-Byzantine poet Corippus writes as if to persuade his fellow Africans that the

Byzantines are after all a good thing even though African homes have become a battleground for the Byzantine and Berber soldiers who sweep through their cities and overrun their land.[38] It is unlikely that the Byzantines anticipated the strength of the Berber tribes when they decided to invade; all their attention was given to what proved the easy task of defeating the Vandals. But after the Vandals had been safely deported, the Byzantines had to meet a more persistent and intractable opponent in the Berber alliance, against whose camels, and on unfamiliar semidesert terrain, they were at a complete disadvantage.[39] The Byzantine regime in North Africa did not merely have to face the problem of the local, sub-Roman, sedentarized population; it was also confronted by the aggressive camel nomads and the Berbers of the Aurès. Governors and governed alike were thus taken by surprise. Inevitably, given the rhetoric of the reconquest policy, the Byzantines saw their task in terms of erecting boundaries. Even by Corippus, an African himself, and ironically a main source for Berber ethnography, the Berbers are presented as outside civilization: their hallmark (and the whole explanation for their actions) is treachery; their boorishness is revealed in their language (like the barking of dogs), their dress (dirty rags), and their religion (a bull-god with horrid rites).[40] Naturally it was no different for Procopius, though not being personally involved he is perhaps slightly less vehement. In the short term the Byzantines managed, after serious losses on their side over more than a generation (the most notable being Belisarius' successor, the great general Solomon), to maintain formal control—or perhaps it was rather that the danger abated for a while of its own accord. In the longer term, they could do nothing to prevent the balance of power from passing to the Berber tribes. Byzantine rule was not, as had been the hope, bounded by a linear defense system holding the enemy at bay. The "enemy" was within, and Byzantine rule a matter of pockets of control surrounded by a larger exposed hinterland. The strengthening of the towns, more cosmetic than practical, in no way enabled them to extend their control of the countryside around them.

The arrival of the Byzantines presented a linguistic problem as well. The culture of the North African towns was a Latin culture. In Carthage, under the Vandals, Latin letters still flourished; a contemporary poem could praise Carthage as the home of learning,[41] and there was an audience for occasional verses on secular themes. The Byzantines found a panegyrist who naturally wrote for them in Latin: Corippus' *Iohannis,* in eight books of hexameters, begins by complimenting the literary culture of Carthage.[42] Funerary inscriptions continued to be written in Latin, a Latin which, to judge from a seventh-century commemoration, was admittedly by then on the decline but which was still Latin nonetheless.[43] Yet the officials of the new regime, as we know from their seals, used Greek,[44] and by the early seventh century Africa was a haven for Greek-speaking exiles from the East who found an easy acceptance not only among the Greek administration but also from the African bishops. The most significant figure in Carthage during this period was Maximus the Confessor, who came to North Africa as a safe refuge from invasion and became the leader of the second African ecclesiastical resistance to Constantinople.[45] He wrote to the exarch about the impending arrival of Sophronius from Egypt, commenting on the richness of the library he would bring with him. It is striking that the two men evidently assumed that they would still find in Carthage a developed intellectual milieu, and that the language of their interchange would be Greek. When Maximus held a public debate on doctrinal matters with the deposed patriarch of Constantinople Pyrrhus, who had also found his way to Africa, this too seems to have been conducted in Greek.[46] Just as the disturbed conditions in the East in the seventh century brought an influx of Greek speakers and with them a spread of Greek culture into Sicily, so the Byzantine presence in North Africa carried a degree of Greek culture at least to the African elite, and more particularly to the African church.[47] For this was an ecclesiastical culture. The arrival of the Byzantines coincided with the virtual end of secular writing in the province, at least so far as we know. After Corippus (who left for Constantinople after the writing of the *Iohannis*), there is no surviving secular work. The bustling world revealed in the *Latin Anthology* does not seem to have outlasted the Vandals—an ironic comment on Byzantine pretensions to be bringing the blessings of culture to a country oppressed by barbarians.

For the first few decades, while the reconquest was new and great effort was being put into urban revival, there was nevertheless continuity in the style of urban life. In A.D. 523 the return of Bishop Fulgentius from exile imposed by the Arian Vandals resembled a familiar late Roman *adventus*—if we can believe his biographer—with torches, lamps, and a procession through streets strewn with foliage. Eleven years later, Belisarius led the captive Vandal king Gelimer in triumph through Constantinople to do homage to Justinian, and in the following year celebrated the opening of his consulship with a triumphal entry into Syracuse in Sicily. In 547 the general John Troglita entered Carthage in triumphal procession at the head of his army, leading Berber women prisoners riding on camels.[48] Carthage thus took its place, in the eyes of the Byzantine administration, as one of the great cities of the empire, not far behind Constantinople in splendor. At the end of the sixth century it enjoyed its most settled and prosperous period during the exarchate of the elder Heraclius, and it was the launching pad for the successful expedition of his son to depose the usurper Phocas and make himself emperor in Constantinople.[49]

But by the seventh century, North African towns were beginning to show the same signs of change as can be found elsewhere in the Mediterranean.[50] The large public spaces increasingly gave way to crowded buildings and shops, built in, over, and around the now-otiose classical monuments. Stones

from the latter were used for other purposes, especially for defensive structures erected or cobbled up even inside the town area, as at Sbeitla, Maktar,
and elsewhere. In Carthage the circus had now fallen out of use and was perhaps even built over for housing.[51] The spacious houses of former days were
subdivided with hastily constructed walls.[52] Burials began to be found within
the urban area.[53] If there was new building on a more substantial scale, it
tended to be either defensive or ecclesiastical, the former private and small-
scale; the great fortresses belong to the first flush of Byzantine conquest.[54] It is
not easy to get a general picture of urban development in seventh-century Africa, even in those few towns that have been well excavated.[55] But the change
was more profound than could be explained simply by the arrival of refugees
from the Arab invasion of Egypt crowding into the towns, as may have been
the case with Carthage. It may at times represent a retreat to the towns from an
increasingly dangerous countryside. But it is also a matter of change of use,
implying a change in the style of urban life. This change does not always signal economic decline, for church building continues, if on a reduced scale.[56] It
was instead part of a transformation in urban life that can be seen in many
parts of the Mediterranean, at least by the mid seventh century, and in many
cases well before. The speed of and the immediate reasons for this change
naturally varied from region to region. In its most dramatic form, in Asia
Minor, where urban life came almost to a standstill in the seventh century, the
Persian invasions of the second decade were a major cause of local disruption.[57] But in North Africa, as in very many other places, the towns contracted
gradually and took on a medieval appearance, with crowded streets and housing huddled round a fortified center. This development coincided with serious
difficulties for the government in Constantinople which drastically reduced
the interest it could take in North Africa.[58] If, as seems likely, the network of
secular officials was weakened, this was to give more power to the bishops,
whose key urban role was reflected in the prominence of churches, often large
and numerous, in the urban context. The renewed conflict of these bishops
with Constantinople in the mid seventh century, therefore, and their subsequent departure for Rome in A.D. 649 with Maximus the Confessor, left many
of the cities without their most-essential figures. The urban development carried out by the Byzantines in their early years had been a mushroom growth,
enlarging the superstructure without at the same time enlarging the economic
base, and such growth was accompanied, to make matters worse, by a heavy
imposition of tax.[59] Even so, the restored towns of the Byzantine period were
smaller than their Roman imperial predecessors, just as the province itself was
smaller than Roman Africa. The initiatives of Belisarius and Solomon and
their successors, impressive though they were, did not in the end reverse the
slow tendency toward ruralization or restore to the towns a secure economic
future.

The relation of town and countryside in North Africa in the later Byzantine phase is at present extremely hard to determine. Hardly any of the necessary survey work has been attempted, and much of the building, even on the best-excavated sites, can only be dated approximately. For this part of the period, moreover, there is an almost total lack of relevant literary sources, and the epigraphic record is almost as limited. Nevertheless, there are ample signs of continued intense olive production.[60] It seems to be urban life in the old sense that declines, not agricultural prosperity. The Arab invaders saw olive oil as the wealth of Africa. Meanwhile the towns were taking on a more "rural" character; Sbeïtla (Sufetula) in the seventh century consisted of small houses, some of them fortified, clustering round the large and impressive churches.[61] An oil press straddled what had once been the main highway. The last stand of the Byzantines before the fall of Carthage itself took place near here, when the army led by the exarch Gregory, who had declared himself emperor in desperation at the gulf that now existed between Africa and Constantinople, was defeated by the Arabs in 647 and Gregory himself killed. It is unlikely that either the Byzantine army or the extent of Gregory's power was anything like as great as the Arab sources claim, and in the confused years that followed, the Arab writers on whom we depend for all our information pay much more attention, when describing their opponents, to the Berbers than to the "Romans," who are pale and shadowy by comparison.[62] The breakdown that preceded the defeat of Gregory had been a breakdown in relations, and no doubt also in military and economic ties, with Constantinople, the product of the distraction of the central government by its much more serious problems in the eastern provinces and at home, and then confirmed by the Monothelite religious policies of the last years of Heraclius' reign and their aftermath.[63] There were few reasons now for the provincials in North Africa to feel loyalty to Constantinople, but there was no alternative local elite or system of organization that could offer greater security. The natural leaders were the bishops, but after Gregory's defeat they followed Maximus to the Lateran Council in Rome. We may guess that in this situation the loyalties of the rural and town populations were anything but united.

Some absorption of Eastern ideas had inevitably taken place. Eastern saints—Theodore, Menas, Pantaleon—gained some new popularity, even if they had not arrived, like Tryphon, with the Byzantines.[64] But local African martyrs remained the most deeply venerated, and in the case of North Africa it was not, as elsewhere, that the population in the seventh century was viewed by the central government as heretic, but rather the reverse—the African church retained its traditional identification with Western ideas and found itself a church in opposition to an Eastern government it viewed as dangerously pro-Monophysite.

Certainly by the second half of the seventh century, and probably already before that, serious hope of practical help from Constantinople had melted away. One must assume that, as was already the case in Syria in the sixth century, many of the defenses stood unmanned, the great fortresses half-empty. The small defensive works of this period speak of self-help in an uncertain situation. Many must have chosen perforce the path of accommodation. No opposition was put up to the building of Qayrawān, and when Carthage eventually fell in 697, it had probably already yielded its place as the center of what small element of the Byzantine administration still remained. The legendary figure who appears in the Arab sources as the last opponent of the Arab armies in North Africa, the woman leader known as the Kāhina, was neither a Byzantine nor a "Roman African."

That fact alone points to one of the major factors in the Islamicization of the Maghrib. It is often asked how it was that Christianity in North Africa, with its great traditions, could succumb, apparently so easily, to the Arab conquest. Christianity has left no epigraphic traces in the Maghrib after the seventh century until a few remains from the eleventh, and although the sources for North Africa in the intervening period do tell us more about the surviving Christian communities than has perhaps been realized, it is clear that Christians were on the whole a diminishing and underprivileged class within the state.[65] Most striking of all, we know of no bishops in Africa after the well-documented episode with Maximus the Confessor until an odd name turns up three centuries later. Part of the explanation for this spectacular decline from former splendor must lie as far back as the seventh century, and in the situation at that time of the Berber tribes. Poised on the edge of Christianization, they now found themselves caught between the Byzantines, becoming weaker by the hour, and the incoming Arabs. It was in fact the Berbers who led the resistance to the latter, and as J. Cuoq argues, as long as they did, the Arabs encountered difficulty. The eventual success of the Arabs in the province was achieved not least by their ability, after the defeats of Kusayla and the Kāhina, the two Berber leaders of the late seventh century, to attract the allegiance of the Berbers away from the Byzantine remnant. One may suspect that this process was aided by a degree of emigration of the Byzantine population, as had happened in the eastern provinces during the first wave of Arab conquests. Those who remained, in the first century of Arab rule, clustered in the towns, a paradoxical reversal of the ruralization that had recently been in progress, while the majority of the Berbers found it easier to convert to Islam.

It is not so much a question of why the Arab conquest of the Maghrib came so easily, therefore, as of why the great military and urbanizing initiatives of the first phase of Byzantine reconquest were unable to produce long-term stability. Many factors were conducive to their ultimate failure, both internal and external: the rise of the Berber kingdoms stressed by historians insistent on charting decolonialization; oppressive taxation by the Byzantines, accompanied by a religious policy that only stimulated local opposition; the apparent failure to consolidate a local elite, whether secular or ecclesiastical, on which stable government could depend; and the increasing weakness of Constantinople in the seventh century.[66] A fundamental problem in the early days, which was partly surmounted later but never completely resolved, was simply that the "reconquest" was in practice the imposition of rule by an Eastern over a Western culture; the historic connection of the province was with Rome, and it was to Rome that the Africans turned in the seventh century. A much slower and longer term change lay behind the whole story of the Byzantine presence in North Africa—the gradual transformation of city life that was obscurely taking place in provinces all over the Mediterranean, and which marked a change far more widespread and far-reaching than the replacement of Byzantine by Arab rule in the Maghrib. There was no "fall" of Byzantine Africa but instead the combination of countless smaller changes that had been quietly taking place over a long period, connected with some specifiable conditions and events.

The main problem in writing about Byzantine Africa, and especially about its history in the seventh century, is the lack of evidence. The general pool of knowledge has been increased only in fitful patches since Diehl wrote his major work in 1896. Nor did the early archaeological investigations, carried out in an era before rigorous methods were known and often inadequately published, focus on the aspects that now seem important and interesting. The recent extensive international excavations at Carthage, though they have produced a good deal of evidence for the Byzantine period, are hard to set into a wider context even for Carthage itself, since the excavations were inevitably selective and since the literary and epigraphic record is so meager. At the latter end of the period, there are severe problems of dating of seventh-eighth-century work, making any sense of a dividing line between Byzantine and "Arab" occupation highly deceptive. Above all, we have almost nothing from the local people themselves to tell us how they saw their situation. The Greek and Latin sources, such as they are, are seriously skewed toward the Byzantines and the ecclesiastical elite; perhaps the Arab writers, with their disinterest in the Byzantines (natural enough in view of the chronological gap between the seventh century and the earliest accounts), after all indicate a more realistic emphasis.

Exploitation of the local population by the invaders, whether or not in the name of liberation, undoubtedly played a part in undermining the prospects for a realistic future. But we know far too little about the real relations of the administration and the locals to be able to judge how far this was really the case. By the later sixth century the province appears to have been enjoying a distinct prosperity. Nor do we find in our sources the constant allusions to local disaffection or lack of cooperation with the Byzantine army that are evident in Procopius' account of Justinian's wars, in Italy, or that are recorded for Egypt in the Arab invasions.[67] The case of Byzantine Africa was both different and, had we only the evidence to trace it in full, more complicated.

The reconquest of Africa was one of Justinian's great success stories, perhaps his greatest of all. It was followed by a program of expenditure and public works more elaborate than any attempted elsewhere, again because it was the first and the most complete of his conquests. Naturally it is tempting to look for dramatic reasons that this great achievement should in the end have failed—that the revitalized Roman and Christian Africa should have "fallen," apparently so easily, to the Arabs. It is understandable that Marxist, nationalistic, or decolonializing explanations should all be offered in discussing this problem.[68] But the problem itself has been posed in the wrong terms. Viewed from the perspective of Constantinople and the eastern empire in the seventh century, it does not seem at all surprising that Africa too was lost. Much has been written on the seventh century from the point of view of the break in urban continuity in Asia Minor and the origins of the theme system, but far too little on what was evidently a major disruption affecting all aspects of the east Roman state, including inevitably its relations with the western provinces, its economic base, its capacity to maintain its administrative and fiscal structures, and of course its military capability. Given this serious situation, Africa could have survived, or offered any plausible long-term resistance to the Arab armies, only if it had been able to develop sufficient internal resilience during the Byzantine phase. We have seen that for many reasons this was not the case. Despite a period of quiet prosperity in the late sixth century, Africa compared badly in the longer term with Italy, which after all did not have to deal with Arab invaders. It had depended too much, we may suspect, on the input of Constantinople and was left vulnerable when that input ceased to be maintained. Its own elite was undermined by the alienation of its ecclesiastical leaders, even though it managed to maintain its oil trade overseas for longer than might have been expected. Could it be told, the story would prove to be less dramatic, but more complex, than its usual presentation either in ancient or in modern accounts. It might also prove to have as much to do with the world outside Africa as with the Maghrib itself.

NOTES

Material from this paper has previously been presented in lectures given at the Warburg Institute, London, and the Antiquary seminar, University of Edinburgh.

1   *Vandal Wars* 2.7.13–15.
2   Ibid., 1–9, esp. 6.
3   C. Diehl, *L'Afrique byzantine* (Paris, 1896). The most useful recent general study, breaking much new ground, is D. Pringle, *The Defence of Byzantine Africa from Justinian to the Arab Conquest,* 2 vols. (Oxford: B.A.R., 1981). There are chapters on Byzantine Africa in two recent general works: W. H. C. Frend, in

J. D. Fage and R. Oliver, eds., *Cambridge History of Africa,* vol. 2 (Cambridge, 1978), 478ff.; and P. Salama, in G. Mokhtar, ed., *UNESCO General History of Africa,* vol. 2 (London, 1981), 499ff. See also Averil Cameron, "Byzantine Africa: The Literary Evidence," in *Excavations at Carthage Conducted by the University of Michigan,* ed. J. Humphrey (Ann Arbor, 1982), 7: 29–62.

4   On the *Buildings* in general, see Averil Cameron, *Procopius and the Sixth Century* (London, 1985), chap. 6, and on Procopius' treatment of Africa there and in the *Vandal Wars,* chap. 10; also, M. Janon, "L'Aurès au VIe siècle: Note sur le récit de Procope," *Antiquités africaines* 15 (1980): 345–51. For a survey of Mediterranean urbanism in the sixth century in relation to current archaeological work see R. Hodges and D. Whitehouse, *Mahommed, Charlemagne and the Origins of Europe* (London, 1983).

5   C. Lepelley, *Les cités de l'Afrique romaine au Bas-Empire,* 2 vols. (Paris, 1979–81), emphasizing the thriving state of African cities in the fourth century.

6   See on this N. Duval, "Etudes d'architecture chrétienne nord-africaine," *Mélanges de l'Ecole française de Rome* 84 (1972): 1071–1172.

7   For instance, the *Iohannis* of Corippus, a panegyric on the Byzantine military presence, despite being the work of a local poet: see Averil Cameron, "Corippus' *Iohannis:* Epic of Byzantine Africa," *Papers of the Liverpool Latin Seminar* 4 (1983): 167–80; and Y. Modéran, "Corippe et l'occupation byzantine d'Afrique: Pour une nouvelle lecture de la *Johannide,*" *Antiquités africaines* 22 (1986): 195–212, written independently but with similar conclusions. Apart from this work, local literary sources are extremely limited, and mainly confined to two periods, the years of the Three Chapters dispute (see below, and Cameron, "Byzantine Africa," 45ff.) and the stay of Maximus the Confessor in Africa in the seventh century (ibid., 53ff.).

8   For survey archaeology see, however, R. Bruce Hitchner, "The Kasserine Archaeological Survey, 1982–1986," *Antiquités africaines* 24 (1988). On the Berbers see Mokhtar, *UNESCO General History of Africa,* vol. 2, and recent work by E. Gellner, P. Bourdieu, and others. So far the period of the transition from Byzantine to Arab rule has been relatively neglected in these studies, but for useful discussion of the methodological (and ideological) problems involved in handling the evidence see G. Vitelli, *Islamic Carthage: The Archaeological, Historical and Ceramic Evidence* (Tunis, 1981). For the concept of "two Africas" and its effect on the historiography of Roman Africa see C. Courtois, *Les vandales et l'Afrique* (Paris, 1955); Lepelley, *Les cités de l'Afrique romaine* 1 : 11ff., 49ff.

9   There is an excellent discussion of these sources by H. Slim in R. Guéry, C. Morrisson, and H. Slim, *Recherches archéologiques franco-tunisiennes à Rougga,* vol. 3, *Le trésor de monnaies d'or byzantines* (Rome, 1982), 76–94.

10   For the details, see E. Stein, *Histoire du Bas-Empire,* vol. 2 (Paris, 1949; repr. Amsterdam, 1968), 311ff.; Cameron, *Procopius,* chap. 10.

11   Procopius *Vandal Wars* 1.16.3–6.

12   The comparison between the aftermath of the two "reconquests" is instructive. The victory in Africa was easy, and the Byzantine presence more widely imposed; in Italy the long struggle, especially followed as it was by renewed invasion from outside Italy, severely damaged both the cities and the Italian elite, bringing about

an earlier and different transformation: see T. S. Brown, *Gentlemen and Officers: Imperial Administration and Aristocratic Power in Byzantine Italy* A.D. *554–800* (London, 1984); and Chris Wickham, *Early Medieval Italy* (London, 1981).

13 In both Italy and Africa the Byzantine rule was termed an "exarchate." See P. Goubert, *Rome, Byzance et Carthage,* vol. 2, pt. 2 of *Byzance avant l'Islam* (Paris, 1965); M. Hendy, *Studies in the Byzantine Monetary Economy c. 300– 1450* (Cambridge, 1985), 406f.

14 Procopius *Vandal Wars* 1.10.2–6.

15 *Buildings* 6.6.13–16 (Caput Vada), cf. 4.1.22–24 (Justinianopolis/Čaričin Grad). See D. Claude, *Die byzantinische Stadt im 6 Jahrhundert,* Byzantinisches Archiv, no. 13 (Munich, 1969); urban change in Italy: B. Ward-Perkins, *From Classical Antiquity to the Middle Ages: Public Building in Italy* A.D. *300–850* (Oxford, 1984).

16 *Buildings* 6.6.15. No trace of this city has been found, and the whole description makes the reader suspicious (I owe this observation to Julia Clayton).

17 Ibid., 4.1–5, 11–13.

18 Corippus, *Iohannis,* pref.

19 See Cameron, "Byzantine Africa," 37, 43.

20 *Vandal Wars* 1.20.18–19 (Belisarius' harangue); for Italy see n. 67 below.

21 *Buildings* 6.4.11–13.

22 *Vandal Wars* 1.10–21.

23 Ibid. 2.14f. For an analysis of Procopius' Vandal war narrative see Cameron, *Procopius,* chap. 9.

24 Signs of critique in Procopius' sections on Africa: *Vandal Wars* 2.28.52; *Gothic Wars* 4.17.21; cf. *Secret History* 18.27.29. (with 9–12). The *Secret History* passage is particularly important: Africa is presented as the chief example of Justinian's destructive policies. But the earlier parts of the war narrative, in particular, accept the aim of reconquest unquestioningly. On Procopius' attitudes in general to the ideology of reconquest see M. Cesa, "La politica di Giustiniano verso l'occidente nel giudizio di Procopio," *Athenaeum,* n.s., 59 (1981): 389–409.

25 See Brown, *Gentlemen and Officers;* Cameron, *Procopius,* chap. 11.

26 *Buildings* 6.5.8–11; see Cameron, "Byzantine Africa," 33–34.

27 See H. Hurst, S. Roskams, et al., eds. *Excavations at Carthage: The British Mission,* vol. 1, *The Avenue du Président Habib Bourguiba, Salammbo,* pt. 1: *The Site and Finds Other than Pottery,* by Hurst and Roskams, 21, 63f; pt. 2: *The Pottery and Other Ceramic Objects from the Site,* by M. G. Fulford and D. P. S. Peacock (Sheffield, 1984); C. M. Wells, "Carthage 1976; La muraille théodosienne," *Echos du monde classique* 21 (1977): 15–23; C. M. Wells and E. Wightman, "Carthage 1978: La muraille théodosienne," ibid. 23 (1979): 15–18; Wells and Wightman, "Canadian Excavations at Carthage 1976 and 1978: The Theodosian Wall, Northern Sector," *Journal of Field Archeology* 7 (1980): 43–63.

28 *Buildings* 6.5.9., on which see Cameron, "Byzantine Africa," 33, n. 34.

29 At Sbeïtla, for instance (n. 61 below). A similar uncertainty exists in the case of structures dating from the last phase of Byzantine or first phase of Arab rule: Vitelli, *Islamic Carthage,* 1ff.

30   See J. Durliat, *Les dédicaces d'ouvrage de défense dans l'Afrique byzantine*, Collection de l'Ecole française de Rome, no. 49 (Rome, 1981); and Pringle, *Defence of Byzantine Africa*.

31   J. Cintas and N. Duval, "L'église du prêtre Félix (région de Kélibia)," *Karthago* 9 (1958): 155–265.

32   Procopius *Buildings* 6.2.20 (Augila); 7.16 (Septem). See now Y. Duval, *Loca Sanctorum Africae: Le culte des martyres en Afrique du IVᵉ au VIIᵉ siècle*, 2 vols. (Paris, 1982), 2:616f., 760, for the rather faint indications of an actual spread of the cult of the Virgin in Africa, despite Procopius' emphasis (for which see also *Buildings* 1.3.1). See Duval, 2:568, for the abandonment of Christian sites in the seventh century and the correspondingly high rate of preservation of inscriptions relating to the deposition of relics; p. 760, "l'interruption brutale de la chrétienté d'Afrique."

33   Duval, *Loca sanctorum Africae*, 2:657ff., 759.

34   Church of St. Cyprian: *Vandal Wars* 1.21.17–25 (a highly wrought dramatic passage). Arians: ibid., 2.14.21ff.; see W. E. Kaegi, "Arianism and the Byzantine Army in Africa, 533–45," *Traditio* 21 (1965): 23–53; Procopius *Secret History* 18.10.

35   See Cameron, "Byzantine Africa," 45ff., for all these events; and, e.g., W. Pewesin, *Imperium, Ecclesia universalis, Rom: Der Kampf der afrikanischen Kirche um die Mitte des 6. Jahrhunderts* (Stuttgart, 1937); P. Champetier, "Les conciles africaines durant la période byzantine," *Revue africaine* 95 (1951): 103–19.

36   For the council, see Stein, *Histoire du Bas-Empire*, 2: 660f.

37   The departure of the bishops for Rome: Cameron, "Byzantine Africa," 57. J. Cuoq, *L'église d'Afrique du Nord du IIᵉ au XIIᵉ siècle* (Paris, 1984), 119f, stresses the importance not only of the departure of the bishops but also of emigration of other Christians in the seventh century.

38   Cameron, "Corippus' *Iohannis*." For the level of militarization in the province, see Pringle, *Defence of Byzantine Africa*, 1:55ff. Numbers and costs: Hendy, *Byzantine Monetary Economy*, 164ff.

39   The emergence of the Berber threat is strongly emphasized by P. Salama, in G. Mokhtar, ed., *UNESCO General History of Africa*, 2:499ff. Corippus' *Iohannis* describes Byzantine campaigns against the Berbers in the late 540s and well illustrates the difficulties the Byzantines encountered (though that campaign actually ended in success—see below).

40   Cameron, "Corippus' *Iohannis*," 173; cf. *Ioh.* 4.350f. with 2.26f., 125f.; *perfidia:* e.g., 4.222f., and for the bias of the whole poem, further Cameron, "Byzantine Africa," 38–39.

41   *Anth. Lat.* 371. For the collection of poems of the Vandal period in the so-called "Latin Anthology," see M. Rosenblum, *Luxorius: A Latin Poet among the Vandals* (New York, 1961); J. Szöverffy, *Weltliche Dichtungen des lateinischen Mittelalters* (Berlin, 1970), 177–90. Some evidence of continuing rhetorical education in Latin in the sixth century: Pringle, *Defence of Byzantine Africa*, 1: 116–117.

42   Corippus *Ioh.*, preface.

43See esp. L. Ennabli, *Les inscriptions funéraires chrétiennes de la basilique dite de Saint-Monique à Carthage* (Rome, 1975) (listed under the abbreviation *IC Sainte-Monique* in *Works Cited*).

44Seals: C. Morrisson and W. Seibt, "Sceaux de commerciaires byzantins du VII⁰ siècle trouvés à Carthage," *Revue numismatique*, 6th ser., 24 (1982): 222–40.

45See Cameron, "Byzantine Africa," 53ff., on Maximus and Sophronius.

46*PG* 91.287–354. At least, it is preserved in Greek. See J. M. Garrigues, *Maxime le Confesseur* (Paris, 1976), 51ff. Sophronius' library: *PG* 91.534.

47Seventh-century Sicily: L. Ruggini, "La Sicilia fra Roma e Bisanzio," in *Storia della Sicilia*, vol. 3 (Naples, 1980), 1–96; A. Guillou, "La Sicile byzantine: Etat de recherches," *Byzantinische Forschungen* 5 (1977): 95–147.

48The *Life* of Fulgentius by Ferrandus, ed. and trans. G. G. Lapeyre, *Vie de Saint Fulgence de Ruspe* (Paris, 1929), see esp. 26ff; Belisarius' triumph: Procopius, *Vandal Wars* 2.9; John Troglita: Corippus, *Ioh.* 6.54ff.

49See A. N. Stratos, *Byzantium in the Seventh Century*, vol. 1 (Amsterdam, 1968), 80ff.

50For the general phenomenon see Hodges and Whitehouse, *Mahommed, Charlemagne,* with brief comments on Africa at 67ff. For orientation see N. Duval, "Etudes d'architecture," and "Comment distinguer les inscriptions byzantines d'Afrique?" *Byzantion* 51 (1981): 511–32.

51I am grateful to Simon Ellis for information on this point.

52Attested in the British, Canadian, and Michigan sectors. See esp. S. P. Ellis, "Excavations in the Canadian Sector (2CC9)," *CEDAC Carthage* 5 (1985): 21–22; E. M. Wightman, "Geological Research and Excavation in the Northern Sector of Carthage, June–July 1983," ibid., 19.

53E.g., H. Hurst, "Excavations at Carthage 1975: Second Interim Report," *Antiquaries Journal* 56 (1976): 195ff.; Hurst and Roskams, *Excavations at Carthage,* vol. 1, pt. 1, pp. 31, 46. See now the important review by J. Humphrey, in *Journal of Roman Studies* 77 (1987): 230–36.

54Some prestige building continued (N. Duval, "Les églises d'Haïdra, III," *CRAI,* 1971, pp. 160–66. But the later Byzantine constructions concentrate on low-quality housing or ad hoc defenses (for the tendency of modern scholars to label these as Islamic see Vitelli, *Islamic Carthage,* 1ff).

55For some of the problems see the article of Simon Ellis cited above, n. 52. For the questions posed by the coinage, see R. Reece, in Hurst and Roskams, *Excavations at Carthage,* vol. 1, pt. 2, pp. 171–81, esp. 175, postulating a drastic effect on the monetary economy as a result of the reconquest.

56See Duval, "Eglises d'Haïdra."

57See the works of C. Foss, notably "The Persians in Asia Minor and the End of Antiquity," *English Historical Review* 90 (1975): 721–47, and "Archaeology and the 'Twenty Cities' of Byzantine Asia," *American Journal of Archaeology* 81 (1977): 469–86; also, Hodges and Whitehouse, *Mahommed, Charlemagne,* 61ff. and passim.

58For this see Cameron, "Byzantine Africa," 58ff.; there is an almost total absence of references to Africa in Byzantine sources of the period. But see Guéry, Morrisson, and Slim, *Recherches archéologiques;* and Morrisson, "Un trésor de solidi de Constantin IV de Carthage," *Revue numismatique*, 6th ser., 22 (1980): 155–60 (evidence of coin hoards suggesting Byzantine efforts directed toward Africa in the late seventh century unrecorded in literary sources).

59 Pringle, *Defence of Byzantine Africa*, 1:109ff.; Hendy, *Byzantine Monetary Economy*, 167f. The British team paint a very gloomy picture of Carthage in the seventh century, see Reece, in Hurst and Roskams, *Excavations at Carthage*, vol. 1, pt. 2; M. Fulford, in *ibid.*, 261; and Fulford, "*Carthage: Overseas Trade and the Political Economy*, A.D. 400–700," *Reading Medieval Studies* 6 (1980): 66–80.

60 Oil production: Pringle, *Defence of Byzantine Africa*, 1:115. For the pottery evidence see F. Zevi and A. Tchernia, "Amphores de Byzacène au Bas-Empire," *Antiquités africaines* 3 (1969): 173–214; A. Carandini, "Pottery and the African Economy," in *Trade in the Ancient Economy*, ed. P. Garnsey, K. Hopkins, and C. R. Whittaker (London, 1983), 145–62. C. R. Whittaker, "Late Roman Trade and Traders," in ibid., 163–80, discusses the general nature of trade in the late Roman period. See also W. H. C. Frend, "North Africa and Europe in the Early Middle Ages," *Transactions of the Royal Historical Society*, 5th ser., 5 (1955): 61–80; Frend, "The North African Cult of Martyrs," in *Jenseitsvorstellungen in Antike und Christentum; Gedenkschrift für Alfred Stuiber*, ed. E. Dassmann (Münster, 1982), 154–67; and Frend, "The End of Byzantine Africa: Some Evidence of Transitions," *Bulletin archéologique du Comité des travaux historiques et scientifiques*, n.s., 19 (1983), fasc. B, *Afrique du Nord* (Paris, 1985), 387–97.

61 For Sbeïtla see N. Duval, "Observations sur l'urbanisme tardif de Sufetula (Tunisie)," *Cahiers de Tunisie* 12 (1964): 87, 105; and N. Duval and F. Baratte, *Les ruines de Sufetula: Sbeitla* (Tunis, 1973). See also R. A. Markus, "Country Bishops in Byzantine Africa," *Studies in Church History* 16 (1979): 1–15.

62 For an analysis of the Arab sources see H. Slim, in Guéry, Morrisson, and Slim, *Recherches archéologiques*, 75–94; also M. Brett in J. D. Fage and R. Oliver, eds., *Cambridge History of Africa*, 2:490ff.; Pringle, *Defence of Byzantine Africa*, 1:45ff.; and Cuoq, *L'église d'Afrique du Nord*, 106ff.

63 See Cameron, "Byzantine Africa," 56ff. for these complex events and their repercussions in Africa.

64 See Y. Duval, *Loca sanctorum Africae*, 2:657ff.

65 Though not a work of primary research on the Roman and Byzantine periods, as the author himself admits, Cuoq's book, *L'église d'Afrique du Nord*, provides not only valuable discussion of the sources for the continuation of Christianity under Islamic rule but also thoughtful discussion of the position of Byzantines, Romans, and Berbers in the seventh century and later (see esp. 173ff.).

66 When the state was undergoing "an economic and financial crisis of fundamental proportions and long-standing nature in addition to a political one" (Hendy, *Byzantine Monetary Economy*, 619, and see in general 619–26 for the military and fiscal aspects of that crisis).

67 Italy: E. A. Thompson, *Romans and Barbarians: The Decline of the Western Empire* (Madison, Wis., 1982), 98ff.; and J. Moorhead, "Italian Loyalties during Justinian's Gothic War," *Byzantion* 53 (1983): 575–96. Egypt and Syria: G. E. M. de Ste. Croix, *The Class Struggle in the Ancient Greek World* (London, 1981), 483f.

68 Similarly Lepelley, *Cités de l'Afrique*, writing of the fourth century.

CHAPTER 10

Variable Rates of Seventh-Century Change

WALTER EMIL KAEGI, JR.

First, it is necessary to begin with a cautionary note about the direction of these observations and their somewhat paradoxical conclusions. The emphasis is upon continuity and tends to argue against any quickening of change with respect to culture and institutions in the initial decades of the seventh century. The subject is change not exclusively with respect to culture, but in a broader perspective, with an emphasis on institutions. The Byzantine Empire experienced unprecedented change in Europe and Asia in the seventh century. Yet it is increasingly evident how much continuity still persisted at the beginning of the seventh century with features of the late Roman experience of previous centuries. Indeed the seventh century is unintelligible without reference to conditions in the preceding two centuries.[1]

In the summer of 1969 during a delightful visit to Thessaloníki, I asked A. H. M. Jones why he decided to terminate his masterful *Later Roman Empire* in 602, and whether his choice of that terminus involved a conscious determination that a period and group of institutions ended in 602. He replied to me that he selected that date because Theophylact Simocatta ended his history at that point, and it was for him a convenient place to halt his own study.

Scholars may choose some early seventh-century date to establish a chronological terminus for other reasons of convenience—perhaps to begin or end a university course.[2] Yet there was no sharp institutional or social or economic or cultural break in 600 or 602 or 610, or even in the last decades of the sixth century. There was increasing interpenetration and adjustment of classical literary and Christian forms and values, which Averil Cameron has so sensitively analyzed on a number of occasions, for example, in the case of Agathias. Yet despite the shocks of invasions, movements of refugees, and even physical destruction of buildings and agriculture, with potentially shattering cultural

191

effects, the essential elements of an elite classical culture remained intact, at least at Constantinople and in some of the eastern provinces, until the end of the reign of Heraclius in 641; it had not already died in the late sixth century. Although new cults and new formulations of imperial authority appeared in the reign of Heraclius, as Averil Cameron and Irfan Shahid have ably demonstrated, the battered physical and institutional environment in which the culture and thought existed, although under great strain, still survived. It was, it appears ever more increasingly clear, still late Roman throughout the first four decades of the seventh century.

With respect to culture, one may note that individuals such as Theophylact Simocatta, George of Pisidia, and the physician Paul of Aegina were still demonstrating, far into the reign of Heraclius, that they had acquired and knew how to use elements of elite classical culture. This may reflect education acquired much earlier, but there are no comparable intellectuals who demonstrate, or perhaps choose to demonstrate, the trappings of that traditional classical culture in the years that follow the death of Heraclius. There may have been individuals who did acquire a very solid education, such as the historian Trajan who wrote now-lost works in the reign of Justinian II, but there is no conclusive evidence. Indeed there were learned men, such as Anastasius the Sinaite, but they do not choose to write works in the high, rather artificial and pedantic style of a Theophylact or George of Pisidia. The explanation may lie in the gradual deterioration of the older system of education under the pressures of crisis, fiscal and otherwise, or a change of values in the course of the seventh century, or both. These tendencies may have already been taking effect earlier in the reign of Heraclius but did not become evident until exceptional individuals with traditional elite classical educations and values had died off and were not or could not be replaced by others with comparable training. The dearth of sources, of course, may muddle historical understanding of seventh-century cultural realities.

Even the Persian invasions do not appear to have disrupted life and culture and cult everywhere as severely as Clive Foss has shown them to have done in Asia Minor.[3] In Byzantine Mesopotamia, Syria, and Palestine—with the notable exception of Jerusalem—the Persian occupation does not appear to have resulted in comparable destruction or even the interruption of Christian cult practices.[4]

Institutional change had been very slow in the late Roman Empire, "imperceptible," as A. H. M. Jones described it.[5] That tendency persisted until the beginning of the seventh century, when the process of change began to accelerate. The successful overthrow and execution of the emperor Maurice by the centurion Phocas in 602 is easily the most visible symbol of a new and violent period in which there was a quickening of the pace of change. The confident and comfortable assertions and assumptions that it had been so easy for the ecclesiastical historian Evagrius Scholasticus to make in the 590s were no longer possible after 602.[6] It would be erroneous to claim, as Paul Goubert once did, that Maurice was an excellent emperor who would have been able to reorganize the eastern provinces and develop satisfactory diplomatic relations with Persia if only he had not met death at the hands of the usurper Phocas. Goubert asserted the thesis that "602 equals 622," that it was the overthrow and execution of Maurice that gave historical significance to Muḥammad's hijra, that only the events of 602 made possible the emergence of Islam as a major religion and factor.[7] Goubert's thesis involves erroneous leaps of logic. There were many deficiencies in Maurice's policies with the Arabs long before his own overthrow. Goubert never developed his thesis fully, perhaps because he came to realize that Maurice had so many faults that its principal original tenets were unsustainable. His Byzantinocentric thesis was so flawed that it no longer deserves serious consideration. Very few Islamicists are probably even aware of his publications expressing his points.[8]

The Persian invasions under King Chosroes II exposed, between 603 and 628, the grave vulnerabilities of the Byzantine Empire. The overthrow of Maurice brought in its wake other attempts at violent rebellion within the empire, including the one under Heraclius that successfully overthrew Phocas, in early October 610. The execution of Phocas brought no stabilization. The virtual collapse of the Byzantine armies between late 610 and 615, the Persian invasion and occupation of Syria, Palestine, and Egypt, all revealed the extremely dangerous new condition of the empire.[9]

The shattering of the old norm that there had been no violent overthrow of emperors at Constantinople since the reign of Constantine I, that the essential borders of the empire had held firm, that there was no sharp cultural or economic or social or institutional break with earlier classical and Roman structures, exposed an altered world. It included shocks of invasions, displaced refugees, unevenly distributed physical destruction of buildings and agriculture. Change came quickly, violently, and drastically in the wake of rebellion and war. Most tangible was the truncation of the physical dimensions of the empire because of the Persian, Avaric, and Slavic invasions, however temporary that truncation was.[10] Yet the old, familiar maritime links between the various Mediterranean ports in Africa, Cyprus, Egypt, Syria, and Constantinople—at least up to the middle of the seventh century—continued to provide a means by which inhabitants could share the experiences of those from other areas and still remain somewhat broad in their perspectives. Those links perpetuated, for a while, late Roman continuities.

The slow rate of change in so many dimensions between the fourth and early seventh century may have contributed to the intensification, violence, speed, and vast scope of the change that finally happened in the seventh century. Although some contemporary sources definitely perceived that a great change was taking place (especially poignant is the *Doctrina Jacobi nuper baptizati*), it is less certain whether villagers, townspeople, and rural inhabitants experienced any drastic change in their physical environment and daily lives, if they escaped the destruction of war.[11]

The contemporary sources report great fluctuations and contrasting moods of despair and joy on the part of the populace in response to news of the changing fortunes of the Byzantine Empire and its armies. The *Doctrina Jacobi nuper baptizati* and the *Miracula* of Saint Anastasius the Persian (who died in 628) contain contemporary reports of swings in mood.[12] The empire had experienced defeats and victories in the sixth century and before, but the heights and depths of such moods appear to have been much greater among at least some parts of the population in the years that immediately preceded the Muslim invasions. These were a symptom of growing perceptions of instability and uncertainty.[13]

The empire's worldview had been decisively shaken in 602 and remained off balance throughout the ensuing three decades of crisis. Heraclius, after overthrowing and executing Phocas, never had a chance for a respite.[14] The timing of the abortive revolt of Phocas' brother Comentiolus in October 610 perpetuated the crisis and permitted the Persians to make their decisive breakthrough on the eastern front in 611. The Muslim invasions followed Heraclius' victory over the Persians too swiftly to permit restabilization. The rapid succession of internal and external crises created insecurity and volatility, which kept Heraclius and his government perpetually off balance. This disorder is reflected in the mood of some of the sources. Before the end of the century apocalyptic visions will emerge as one part of the reaction to these circumstances, but their provenance lies outside the borders of the empire.[15] How much inhabitants of the empire perceived events in apocalyptic terms is more complicated, and the conclusive evidence is slightly later, in the form of the Pseudo-Daniel vision.[16]

Institutional change appears to have been very slow, in contrast to the extreme swings of popular moods. It is inappropriate here to provide a complete description of the present state of scholarly knowledge of late Roman and Byzantine institutions in the early seventh century—and many controversial and obscure problems remain challenges—but scattered evidence indicates that they remained essentially late Roman ones, modified only slightly from their character in the Justinianic era. In the early decades of the seventh century, the institutional mechanisms through which the Byzantines developed their responses to external military challenges were for the most part very old ones.

The slow evolution of late Roman institutions included titulature of offices and ranks. Yet no seventh-century *Notitia dignitatum* exists. The geographical texts of George of Cyprus and the *Synekdemos of Hierocles* show no important and radical changes. Even more important, Heraclius appears to have retained or restored parts of the old administrative structure that existed before the interruption of the Persian occupation in some eastern provinces such as Palestine and Syria. Older provincial nomenclature, such as Palaestina Prima, Palaestina Secunda, and Palaestina Tertia persisted, as did such older nomenclature for military units as the *equites Illyriciani* and other *numeri,* which is impressive.[17] Old recruiting practices continued in parts of the empire, like the use of officers of the excubitors for recruiting.[18] How unchanged the actual provincial bureaucracies' operations were is debatable: that is, did bureaucrats still function and think in the same manner as in previous decades and centuries?

The evidence indicates a continuation of the late Roman or early Byzantine practice of concentrating troops in and around towns where warranted, although, as R. M. Price satisfactorily demonstrated in his Oxford dissertation, there had been a tendency already in the late fourth and early fifth century in Syria to distribute many of them in the north Syrian countryside to avoid potential friction with townspeople.[19] This rural distribution of troops—contrary to Zosimus' emphasis on their concentration in cities—in northern Syria is an anticipation of what happened when precisely the same troops moved north into Anatolia in the wake of the Muslim conquest of Syria and Byzantine Mesopotamia. That is, it is an anticipation of the kind of distribution of soldiers that will take place in the more mature theme system, with important differences in forms of compensation.[20]

The inperial post still operated in Bithynia as late as October 610, but it is unclear what happened to it in the eastern provinces after that time.[21] *Phabrikēsioi* or *fabricenses,* or workers in state arms factories, which were a fundamental part of the late Roman military and financial structure (under the *magister officiorum*), were still in existence in the early seventh century in Bithynia and at Seleucia, in northern Syria, but it is unclear whether any of them or their factories, *fabricae,* still existed elsewhere in Syria at that time or in the 630s.[22]

In summary, accumulating evidence indicates conclusively that the institutional structure of the Byzantine Empire at the moment of the initial Muslim invasions was still basically a late Roman one, but not, of course, an unchanged version of Constantinian or Justinianic structures. There had been no comprehensive transformation of Byzantine military institutions in the 620s. The parenthetical and circumstantial traces in the primary sources reveal a substantially unaltered group of institutions, practices, and terminology.

The *Parastaseis syntomoi khronikai,* which is a late source, indicates that money was used in recruiting in the 620s, whether on an exceptional or a regular basis is uncertain. Imperial excubitors were exercising their traditional role of scrutinizing and organizing military recruitment, although it is impossible to state confidently whether this was the case throughout the empire; and furthermore, they were employing some kind of monetary payment or bounty as an inducement.[23] Governmental land grants were not yet the instrument for raising and financing armies. The relevance of this for understanding Heraclius' relations with the Arabs is that it complements other information on the importance of money for the recruitment and the maintenance of Arabs in Byzantine service. It makes more comprehensible the significance of the payment and nonpayment of money for the armies of Arabs and non-Arabs alike whom Heraclius raised to fight the invading Arab tribes from the peninsula. Problems in paying soldiers regularly wracked the Byzantine armies and bureaucracy, and they complicated and hindered the efforts to find and develop a conherent and effective defense of the provinces that the Muslims threatened. The old system was still in place but it was strained to the utmost, and urgent expedients were being taken in the effort to make it still function.[24]

Heraclius' appointment of a *sakellarios* or treasurer, whose name was Theodore Trithourios, to command the Byzantine armies in Syria is important, not only because it is an explicit early reference to the mature office of *sakellarios,* but also because it underlines the Byzantine government's need to assure its soldiers of its commitment to the regular and full payment of promised funds. It should be remembered, however, that Justinian I had appointed Narses as *sakellarios* to command the Byzantine armies in Italy; there was a sixth-century precedent. There is no evidence that such appointments had any connection with the creation of "soldiers' properties" or *stratiōtika ktēmata,* the existence of which is securely attested only much later. Heraclius decided to appoint a *sakellarios* to command soldiers because monetary payments were still crucial in the raising and maintenance of soldiers, and because it appears that there had been problems in assuring the prompt, regular, and full payment of what soldiers expected.[25] All of this is consistent with the continuing role of money in the financing of Heraclius' armies, including those Arabs who were recruited to help to defend Byzantine Palestine and Syria.[26]

One neglected case of late Roman institutional continuities into the seventh century is that of the *annona militaris,* which included ration allotments of grain, oil, wine, vinegar, and meats, as well as *capitus* or fodder. A number of distinguished late Roman specialists, for example, D. Van Berchem, A. H. M. Jones, R. MacMullen, and L. Cracco Ruggini, have studied the *annona militaris,* including its controversial origins. Many questions remain unsolved, however, including its ultimate fate in the Byzantine period.[27] Scholars such as Jones have noted its eventual conversion or commutation into monetary payments in gold or other coin, during and after the fourth century. This process is known as *adaeratio.* A close reading of various early seventh-century primary sources reveals, however, that the norm for soldiers' revenues was not exclusively monetary payment. Payments in kind continued.[28] It was some of the great early scholars of Islamic institutions, most notably

C. H. Becker, who observed that the *annona* persisted up to and beyond the initial Islamic conquest.[29] Jean Maspero, the distinguished specialist on Byzantine military institutions in Egypt, agreed that the *annona militaris* persisted in Egypt to the end of Byzantine rule and beyond.[30]

The situation in Byzantium's more poorly documented provinces, however, has not received any scholarly notice. The *annona militaris* also persisted in Byzantine Syria and Mesopotamia and Armenia in the reign of Heraclius. It was not always commuted by *adaeratio* to monetary payment. It was a mechanism by which Heraclius expected to pay and supply the soldiers whom he raised. It is essential to understand that in the 620s and 630s the Byzantine— and allied Christian Arab—soldiers depended on the smooth functioning of the *annona militaris.* Byzantine soldiers who concentrated for the defense of Syria expected the localities, their officials, and their inhabitants to furnish them with provisions. Thus al-Balādhurī reports that when the inhabitants of Byzantine Emesa (Ḥimṣ) capitulated to the Muslims, they "offered them food for their animals and for themselves." [31] At Buṣrā or Bostra the leading official offered the Muslims "food, oil and vinegar." Al-Balādhurī states that "for some time, oil and vinegar and food were taken for the benefit of the Muslims in Mesopotamia, which tax was later reduced." [32] He also reported that ʿIyāḍ b. Ghanm, the conqueror of Byzantine Mesopotamia, assessed, in addition to a head-tax of one dinar per person, some taxes in kind: "He levied on them *qafīzes* of wheat, and some oil, vinegar and honey." [33] Al-Balādhurī recounts one tradition that the caliph ʿUmar "ordered that in the way of providing the Moslems with wheat and oil, they have to give every Moslem in Syria and Mesopotamia two *modii* of wheat and two *qisṭs* of oil per month. He also assessed on them grease and honey, the quantity of which I do not know." [34] Naturally, the Muslim recipients of such payments in kind at that early date were soldiers.

The statements of al-Balādhurī can be identified with *annona militaris* by comparison with references in the *Codex Theodosianus* and the *Corpus juris civilis,* although there may be some additional sources. The Byzantines did not regard it as hopeless to rely on the *annona militaris* on the eve of and during the Muslim invasions. No thorough alteration of the fiscal system had taken place by the early 630s.[35] It is not surprising that the *Miracula* of Saint Anastasius the Persian reveals that the position of *optio* or paymaster of the traditional *annona militaris* still existed in Palestine in approximately 631.[36] This is another indication of the survival of the old fiscal system for the essentially late Roman Byzantine army.

It appears that the Armenian historian Sebeos provides evidence for the continuing use of the *annona militaris* at a critical point late in the reign of Emperor Heraclius. In his narration of the return of Heraclius' victorious army from Persia to Byzantine Armenia, namely, "Asorestan," the region be-

tween the Tigris and Euphrates rivers west of the city of Amida (modern Diyarbakir, Turkey), presumably in late 628 or early 629, Sebeos reports that
the Armenian Catholicos Ezr, after entering into religious communion with
Heraclius, engaged in important activities. Sebeos explains, "From then on
he resided in the land of the Greeks. The general was pleased [and] at his will
regulated the conditions of the soldiers and the distribution of the storehouses
over the whole land." [37] The general who is mentioned here was the famous
Mnez Gnuni.

Sebeos is probably referring to storehouses that were intended for military
provisions for the distribution or allocation of the *annona militaris* to soldiers.
D. Van Berchem has demonstrated that storehouses were important for the
functioning of the *annona militaris*. This indicates that far into the reign of
Heraclius the soldiers depended upon the *annona militaris* and that its equitable distribution was a controversial but important question for local taxpayers.[38] The region was one in which Heraclius had previously been active,
during his wars with the Persians. It is another possible indication that the
system of *stratiōtika ktēmata* had not yet become the principal means for
maintaining soldiers. This is a precious and rare piece of evidence from the
period between the end of the Persian war of Heraclius and the commencement of the Muslim invasions. Yet Constantine VII and a tenth-century Muslim geographer report the existence of Byzantine military warehouses near the
frontier in the tenth century, so the institution persisted in some form.[39] The
Byzantine use of monetary payments to soldiers in the sixth century, for example, in Italy, can in no way be invoked to deny the existence of payments in
kind to some soldiers in the seventh century, in the midst of different circumstances and the different policies, options, and resources that were available to
the changing imperial fiscal administration.

Problems in distributing the *annona militaris* probably contributed to Byzantine military unrest during the Byzantine effort to create a viable defense
against the Muslims.[40] Difficulties in the equitable and efficient and fiscally
rational distribution of the *annona militaris* cease to receive mention in the
truncated Byzantine Empire after the loss of Palestine, Syria, Byzantine
Mesopotamia, and Egypt. There are hazards, of course, in arguing *ex silentio,*
but it is probable that a logistical and military system of compensation that
depended on the *annona militaris* was modified or transformed somehow in
the later part of the seventh century. That process appears to have accelerated
as a result of the reduction in the distances that the Byzantine troops needed to
travel after those major territorial losses. It was less necessary to make provi-
sioning depend on distribution of *annona militaris* in the late seventh century
and beyond. The change had consequences for imperial taxpayers and for imperial finances, although the sparseness of the primary sources underlines the
need for caution.[41]

The question of the *annona militaris* is far from clarified. It is clear that it had not been universally employed in the great wars of the sixth century. It is similarly unclear just how widely it was used in the early seventh century. Was it adequate for the nutritional needs of fighting men and their mounts (some have questioned whether anyone could have lived on a single allotment, although many soldiers succeeded in receiving more than one share)? Precisely which bureau was still responsible for collecting and distributing it, now that the old praetorian prefecture was less visible? Did it survive somehow in a modified form, and if so, precisely what was that form? Perhaps the Byzantine government's shortage of money and precious metals contributed to the greater use of this system of payment in kind, which still remained nominally the legally authorized system of accounting. Much more research is necessary before historians can offer very satisfactory answers.

The unpreparedness of Byzantine officials to handle unprecedented large numbers of Byzantine and allied soldiers and supply them with the *annona militaris* in an area—Syria south of Chalkis (Qinnasrīn) and in Palestine—where no such large Byzantine armies had previously held precisely comparable positions in the late Roman and early Byzantine periods helps to explain the background to the logistical crisis and breakdown that transformed into military indiscipline and unrest on the eve of the battle of the Yarmūk in 636. It probably contributed to the destruction of the cohesion of the Byzantine soldiers and their eventual disintegration as fighting units. Arabs who served in groups as Byzantine allies had been entitled to allotments of *annona militaris* late in the sixth century.[42]

The reason for the survival of the payments in kind that al-Balādhurī mentions in his *Kitāb futūḥ al-buldān* at the time of the Muslim conquests is that these were survivals of older late Roman fiscal and logistical institutions for the maintenance of the Roman (Byzantine) army.[43] A. Noth examined these traditions of payments in kind from the perspective of Islamic traditions and found them to be authentic.[44] He did not, however, understand their continuity with late Roman fiscal institutions. Yet that is why they receive mention in Egypt, Syria, and areas of former Byzantine Mesopotamia. The late Roman system of taxation and of the distribution of military pay and supplies was under strain but it had not yet disappeared in the 630s. The very strains under which the old system labored probably contributed to its demise after the Byzantine withdrawal to Anatolia. The system of *annona militaris* was not functioning well. There were complaints, such as those mentioned by the Coptic historian John of Nikiu (who is preserved in an Ethiopic translation), about the heavy costs of the *annona* system.[45]

The existence of the *annona militaris* and older systems of military recruitment does not by itself indicate that the entire older system of military and fiscal institutions was still operating, let alone operating smoothly. Each of these components will require specific analysis. But the direction of research is clear: a rigorous examination of the primary sources around the middle of the seventh century in order to determine just how many of the Justinianic (or modified Diocletianic-Constantinian) institutions were still functioning.[46] It will be important to check whether the survival of the identical or similar names necessarily proves the existence of identical institutions. If anything, the accumulating evidence about the *annona militaris* reinforces the case for gradual institutional change through the early decades of the seventh century, at least well into the third decade of the reign of Heraclius.

The *annona* system probably made it more difficult for the Byzantines to pursue the Muslims in open country. The Byzantines were dependent, and their mobility suffered accordingly, because of their logistical system. The logistical problems of the Byzantines in Syria in the 630s differed from their problems during the campaigning in Syria in 613 and 614. In 613 Heraclius unsuccessfully attempted to halt the Persians in northern Syria, outside Antioch.[47]

The persistence of old institutional and fiscal institutions into the seventh century probably contributed, although in a very modest way, to the persistence of older habits of thought and culture as well. It is incorrect, however, to believe that intellectual patterns are always dependent on material conditions.[48] Seventh-century military history can receive illumination from the investigation of seventh-century social and economic history, yet military history deserves study in its own right, and not merely as the reflection of social contexts.[49] It is equally hazardous to assume that military unrest represents otherwise undocumented popular sentiment in various provincial localities. This fallacious line of reasoning is reminiscent of the excesses of Rostovtzeffian theory of the meaning and causes of soldiers' actions in the third century, which received decisive refutation long ago.[50] With respect to Byzantine thought and culture, however, as with Byzantine institutions, there is no perceptible or sharp break with earlier late Roman forms until after the end of the reign of Heraclius. In particular, the evidence does not indicate that there had been any profound replacement of older forms of classical thought, at least within the elite, in the late sixth century.[51] Any sharp cultural or intellectual break, as well as any institutional one, occurred after 641, regardless of how much earlier slow trends and events may have contributed.[52]

The continuities that do exist between Late Antiquity and the seventh century can help to clarify some of the many obscure and controversial questions of seventh-century history. There has been a justifiable skepticism among some Islamic historians about any reflexive assumption that Byzantine or Christian oriental sources are inherently more trustworthy than Muslim ones concerning the seventh century. They rightly point out, as I often have, that

Byzantine sources such as Theophanes may well derive some of their material from oriental Christian sources that in turn depend on Muslim sources for their information and accordingly cannot be regarded as strictly independent authorities. That is often true. Theophanes and Nicephorus require use with caution. But there is a much larger group of late Roman and early Byzantine materials, such as *notitiae,* inscriptions, place names, specific fiscal practices, nomenclature, offices, and institutions, whose existence does not depend upon the vagaries of *Quellenforschung* and its hypothetical reconstructions, nor upon any one tradition. There is a sufficient corpus of information about Late Antiquity that those Muslim traditions about early seventh-century conditions that find close corroboration with the larger late Roman–early Byzantine context are worthy of credence for some of their other information about conditions and events. Absence of correlations in itself does not impugn the veracity of other Muslim sources on subjects and regions that have no relevance for late Roman and early Byzantine affairs. All information on Byzantium in the seventh century is not unreliable; there is a solid base, and that is the broader and well-established specifics of late Roman and early Byzantine official and private life. Many gaps remain in our knowledge, but it can help, within specific limits, to check some information in some Muslim sources on the early seventh century. These continuities help the historian to understand seventh-century change. It is necessary to refine the methodology for evaluating sources, and this will require cooperation between late Roman, Byzantine, and Islamic specialists. It will not be an easy task.

In conclusion, it seems that the slowness of cultural and institutional change was a cause of both strength and weakness to the Byzantine Empire at the start of the seventh century. Because the rate of change had been so slow, it was extremely difficult for people to adjust flexibly and rapidly to the sudden stream of new developments and challenges. The slowness of change made the seventh-century shocks all the worse. Yet the slowness of institutional change was testimony to the strength inherent in those old institutions even at the start of the seventh century, when they still were an asset of Byzantium.[53]

The lack of sufficient institutional change earlier in the seventh century may help to explain the quickness, violence, and sharpness of the changes that did take place later. The postponement of change intensified the ultimate changes when they came. There is no doubt that the scraps of sources show that some contemporaries—such as Saint Anastasius the Sinaite and Maximus the Confessor, and subsequent Byzantines such as Constantine VII—did perceive that violent and comprehensive change took place and accompanied the loss of former Byzantine territories. The truncation of the empire was the most tangible manifestation of change to contemporaries and subsequent Byzantines. Whether the inhabitants of those lost territories experienced any immediate drastic change in their physical environment, culture, and daily life is a different question, which properly requires investigation by those scholars who are specialists in Islamic history and literature.[54]

NOTES

I wish to acknowledge my gratitude for the assistance of a grant in 1985 from the Penrose Fund of the American Philosophical Society, which helped to make possible the research for and publication of this paper.

1   John Haldon, "Ideology and Social Change in the Seventh Century: Military Discontent as a Social Barometer," *Klio* 68 (1986): 139–90, has written a provocative article in which he questions the relevance of examining materials from preceding centuries. But there are substantial continuities with the immediately preceding centuries of Late Antiquity, especially with respect to institutions and culture, and especially with respect to the soldiers. Haldon himself, although claiming to insist on the rigorous and explicit definition and explanation of his assumptions, fails in his learned volume *Byzantine Praetorians* (Bonn: Habelt, 1984), to explain what at all the study of the Opsikion and Tagmata has to do with earlier Roman Praetorians. His use of the title is likely to distort Byzantinists' understanding of the Praetorian Guard in its classic centuries. The Tagmata and Opsikion receive much illumination from Haldon, but his introduction of the word "Praetorians," without any explanation in his book or elsewhere, will create scholarly misunderstanding and is an example of the most dangerous and misleading type of cross-referencing to earlier institutions. Marcel Durry, *Les cohortes prétoriennes* (Paris: E. de Boccard, 1938), wrote the classic and enduring analysis of the Praetorian Guard. In it he strove to eradicate the kinds of pejorative assumptions and misconceptions about the Praetorian Guard that Haldon's title injudiciously reintroduces to Byzantine studies. Haldon is yielding to modern political scientists' highly inaccurate term "praetorianism," which they have not cross-checked with historical material of the first through third centuries. Military historians should avoid this inaccurate twentieth-century term: "praetorianism," as used by political scientists, has no place in Byzantine studies. There are continuities of Byzantine military institutions and military unrest with conditions in the third through sixth centuries, but any relationship with the realities of the Praetorian Guard of previous centuries remains to be demonstrated rigorously and remains unproved at this time.
2   As I do, at the University of Chicago, in 610.
3   Clive Foss, "The Persians in Asia Minor and the End of Antiquity," *English Historical Review* 90 (1975): 721–47.
4   See Robert Schick's important dissertation, which will contribute to understand-

ing the transition between Byzantine and Muslim societies and cultures in the
seventh-century Levant: "The Fate of the Christians in Palestine during the
Byzantine-Umayyad Transition, A.D. 600–750" (Ph.D. diss., Dept. of Near
Eastern Languages and Civilizations, Univ. of Chicago, 1987), chap. 2.

5 A. H. M. Jones, *The Later Roman Empire* (Oxford: Blackwell, 1964), 1:vi. See
also, Philip Freeman and David Kennedy, eds., *The Defence of the Roman and
Byzantine East,* British Institute of Archaeology at Ankara, monograph no. 8,
British Archaeological Reports, International Series, no. 297 (1 & 2) (Oxford,
B.A.R., 1986), for various contributions on this topic.

6 Evagrius Scholasticus *HE* 3.41. (ed. J. Bidez and L. Parmentier [London, 1898],
144). See, in general, the thesis of W. E. Kaegi, *Byzantium and the Decline of
Rome* (Princeton, N.J., 1968).

7 Paul Goubert, *Byzance avant l'Islam,* 2 vols. (Paris, 1950), 1:23–27, 269–72.

8 Cf. remarks of W. E. Kaegi, *Byzantine Military Unrest 471–843: An Interpretation* (Amsterdam and Las Palmas: Hakkert, 1981), 118–19.

9 W. E. Kaegi, "New Evidence on the Early Reign of Heraclius," in *Army, Society
and Religion in Byzantium* (London: Variorum, 1982), esp. 319–30. Also, David
Olster, "The Politics of Usurpation in the Seventh Century: The Reign of Phocas" (Ph.D. diss., Dept. of History, Univ. of Chicago, 1986).

10 W. E. Kaegi, "Heraklios and the Arabs," *Greek Orthodox Theological Review* 27
(1982): 109–33; Kaegi, "The Frontier: Barrier or Bridge?" in *Major Papers, the
17th International Byzantine Congress* (New Rochelle, N.Y.: A. D. Caratzas,
1986), 279–303.

11 *Doctrina Jacobi nuper baptizati* (63, 77 Bonwetsch).

12 *Doctrina Jacobi nuper baptizati* (63, 70, 77 Bonwetsch); *Acta M. Anastasii Persae* (12–13 Usener). Note also the exhilaration of Pantaleon in his speech (ca.
634–37) on the exaltation of the cross: "Un discours inédit du moine Pantaléon
sur l'élévation de la Croix [*BHG* 427 p]," ed. F. Halkin, *Orientalia christiana
periodica* 52 (1986): 257–70. On this oration and its date: E. Honigmann, "La
date de l'homélie du prêtre Pantaléon sur la fête de l'Exaltation de la Croix (VIIᵉ
siècle) et l'origine des collections homiliaires," *Bulletin de la classe des lettres et
des sciences morales et politiques, Académie royale de Belgique,* 5th ser., 36
(1950): 547–59.

13 See W. E. Kaegi, "Initial Byzantine Reactions to the Arab Conquest," chap. 13
in Kaegi, *Army, Society and Religion in Byzantium* (London: Variorum, 1982)
(repr. with corrections from *Church History* 38 [1969]: 139–49).

14 Kaegi, "New Evidence on the Early Reign of Heraclius," passim.

15 On seventh-century apocalyptic visions, see the pioneering work of Paul J. Alex-
ander, *The Byzantine Apocalyptic Tradition,* ed. Dorothy de Ferrante Abrahamse
(Berkeley and Los Angeles: Univ. of California Press, 1985); Francisco Javier
Martinez, "Eastern Christian Apocalyptic in the Early Muslim Period" (Ph.D.
diss., Catholic Univ., 1985); Harald Suermann, *Die geschichtstheologische Re-
aktion auf die einfallenden Muslime in der edessenischen Apokalyptik des 7.
Jahrhunderts.* Europäische Hochschulschriften, Reihe 23, Theology, Band. 256.
(Frankfurt, Bern, and New York: Peter Lang, 1985).

16 *Die griechische Daniel Diegese: Eine altkirchliche Apokalypse,* ed. Klaus
    Berger, Studia Post-Biblica, vol. 27 (Leiden: Brill, 1976). This important text
    deserves more research.

17 M. Avi-Yonah, s.v. "Palaestina," *RE,* Supplementband 13 (1974): 321–454. *Le*
    Synekdémos d'Hieroklès et l'Opuscule géographique de Georges de Chypre, ed.
    and trans. E. Honigmann, Corpus Bruxellense Historiae Byzantinae, Forma Im-
    perii Byzantini, no. 1 (Brussels, 1939) 66–68, for George of Cyprus, ca. 600,
    and pp. 41–44, for the sixth-century *Synekdemos.* F. Abel, *Histoire de la Pa-*
    lestine, 2 vols. (Paris: J. Gabalda, 1952), 2:388–93, on period of Persian inva-
    sion and occupation, 2:393–406, on Muslim invasion and conquest. *Acta M.*
    Anastasii Persae, Thaumata (13 Usener). On old nomenclature for provinces of
    Palestine, see: al-Balādhurī, *Futūḥ al-buldān* (109 de Goeje); W. E. Kaegi,
    "Notes on Hagiographic Sources for Some Institutional Changes and Continuities
    in the Early Seventh Century," *Byzantina* 7 (1975): 59–70; Kaegi, "Some
    Seventh-Century Sources on Caesarea," *Israel Exploration Journal* 28 (1978):
    177–81 (repr., in *Army, Society and Religion in Byzantium*).

18 W. E. Kaegi, "Two Studies in the Continuity of Late Roman and Byzantine Mili-
    tary Institutions," *Byzantinische Forschungen* 8 (1982): 87–111, esp. 90–98.
    The reservations of Haldon in *Byzantine Praetorians,* 627–28, deserve rejection
    because of the improbability of the "scouts" being entrusted with the melting
    down of the bronze ox of Constantinople at Constantinople, where the excubitors
    normally were located; second, the occupation of the site of the Forum of the Ox
    by the excubitors in official ceremonies, as cited in the *De ceremoniis* of Con-
    stantine VII Porphyrogenitus, is important additional proof for their participation
    in the destruction of the bronze ox, which their ceremonial post memorialized.

19 R. M. Price, "The Role of Military Men in Syria and Egypt from Constantine to
    Theodosius II" (D.Phil. diss., Oxford Univ. 1974), conclusion on 375, cf. 71.
    General background: E. W. Gray, "The Roman Eastern Limes from Constantine
    to Justinian," *Proceedings of the African Classical Associations* 12 (1973):
    24–40. Classic is V. Chapot, *La frontière de l'Euphrate* (Paris, 1907). Some of
    the logistical problems of an earlier era were still relevant at the beginning of the
    seventh century. Therefore it is worthwhile to consult John P. Adams, "The Lo-
    gistics of the Roman Imperial Army: Major Campaigns on the Eastern Front in
    the First Three Centuries A.D." (Ph.D. diss., Dept. of History, Yale Univ.,
    1976); S. Thomas Parker, *Romans and Saracens: A History of the Arabian Fron-*
    tier, Dissertation Series, no. 6 (Winona Lake, Ind.: American Schools of Oriental
    Research, 1985).

20 Zosimus *Hist.* 2.34.1–2 (ed. L. Mendelssohn [Leipzig, 1887], 91–92). A hypo-
    thetical reconstruction of the functioning of the themes: J. Haldon and H. Ken-
    nedy, "The Arab-Byzantine Frontier in the Eighth and Ninth Centuries," *Zbornik*
    Radova, Vizantoloshki Institut (Belgrade) 19 (1980): 79–116. There is no justi-
    fication, however, for attributing the origin of the Byzantine themes or the word
    thema to an Altaic root. There are no reasons to doubt that the origin of the word
    is Greek, and there is no need to seek a foreign etymology or institutional inspira-
    tion. The theory of J. Howard-Johnston, "Thema," in *Maistor* (Canberra: Aus-
    tralian Association for Byzantine Studies, 1984), 189–97, must be rejected. For

possible relationships with the *ajnād,* see Irfan Shahid, "Heraclius and the Theme System: New Light from the Arabic," *Byzantion* 57 (1987): 391–406, which is an important, valuable, and provocative contribution to the understanding of this issue. Shahid provides the fullest case for the existence of districts with "theme-like" characteristics in Syria before the Muslim conquest. I have not yet seen the doctoral dissertation of Alan G. Walmsley, "Administrative Structure and Urban Settlement in Filasṭīn and Urdunn" (Ph.D. diss., Univ. of Sydney, Australia, 1987). From preliminary reports on the thesis of Walmsley I infer that he argues that the *ajnād* (Muslim military districts) began in the caliphate of ʿUmar. I must suspend judgment on this controversy until I can study the logic and documentation of Walmsley's conclusions, which are said to include extensive references to archaeological data.

21 *Vie de Théodore de Sykéôn,* c. 152.4–9 (ed. and trans. A.-J. Festugière, Subsididia Hagiographica, no. 48 [Brussels, 1970], 1:121–22); G. Zacos and A. Veglery, *Byzantine Lead Seals,* 2 vols. (Basel, 1972–85), no. 1136, vol. 1.2, p. 727, seal from Seleucia, dated to about 617.

22 *Vie de Théodore de Sykéôn,* c. 159.45–47 (1:134–35 Festugière). Broader background on production: M. C. Bishop, ed., *The Production and Distribution of Roman Military Equipment* (Oxford: B.A.R., 1985).

23 *Parastaseis syntomoi khronikai* 42, ed. and trans. Averil Cameron et al., *Constantinople in the Eighth Century* (Leiden: Brill, 1984), 115–17, 228–30; Kaegi, "Two Studies in Continuity," 90–98; and Kaegi, "Late Roman Continuity in the Financing of Heraclius' Army," *Kurzbeiträge/Communications, 16e congrès international des études byzantines; Jahrbuch der öesterreichischen Byzantinistik,* 1982, pp. 53–61.

24 Kaegi, "Two Studies in Continuity," and "Late Roman Continuity," passim.

25 *Theoph. Chron.* A. M. 6125–26 (337–38 De Boor). Cf. N. Oikonomides, *Les listes de préséance byzantines des IXᵉ et Xᵉ siècles* (Paris, 1972), 312.

26 Arab and Greek sources stress the monetary incentive for Byzantine troops.

27 See W. E. Kaegi, "The Annona Militaris in the Early Seventh Century," *Byzantina* 13 (1985): 591–96. On the background: D. Van Berchem, "L'annone militaire dans l'empire romain au IIIᵉ siècle," *Mémoires de la Société des nationale antiquaires de France,* 8th ser., 10 (1937): 117–202; Jones, *Later Roman Empire* 458–60, 626–30, 634, 644, 651, 671–77; R. MacMullen, *Roman Government's Response to Crisis* (New Haven, Conn., 1976) 268–71; L. Cracco Ruggini, *Economia e società nell 'Italia annonaria': Rapporti fra agricoltura e commercio dal iv al vi secolo d.c.* (Milan: Giuffrè, 1961), 268, 281, 284, 291, 320, 324, 325, 342, 350, 367, 377, 470, 474, 523. On qualifications to and reservations about this terminology of *annona,* see André Cerati, *Caractère annonaire et assiette de l'impôt foncier au Bas-Empire* (Paris: Librairie Générale de Droit et de Jurisprudence, 1975), 22–27, 40–53, 87–115, 120–51. For more criticisms see Jean-Michel Carrié, "L'Esercito, trasformazioni funzionali ed economie locali," in *Società romana e impero tardoantico,* vol. 1, *Istituzioni, ceti, economie,* ed. Andrea Giardina (Rome and Bari: Editori Laterza, 1986), 454–56.

28 Jones, *Later Roman Empire,* 207–08, 235, 254, 258, 326, 448, 460–61, 566. See André Cerati, *Caractère annonaire et assiette de l'impôt foncier,* esp.

153–89, on qualifying conceptions of *adaeratio*. Karl Leo Nöthlichs, "Spätantike Wirtschaftspolitik und *Adaeratio,*" *Historia* 34 (1985): 102–16, gives some
arguments for the continuation of the possibility of payment in kind instead of in
money. Starting from another direction, M. Hendy, *Studies in the Byzantine Monetary Economy, c. 300–1450* (Cambridge: Cambridge Univ. Press, 1985), 646,
argues that *annonae* and *capitus* "were by the sixth century largely adaerated according to customary rates," see also 647–48, 165–67, 294–95. The drain on
cash that Hendy believes, p. 647, to have been so heavy that Emperor Maurice
had to try to reduce it, could have been changed in several ways, one of which
was simply to resort to less adaeration and pay the rations in kind. This may not
have been the general solution to the cash problem, but in the reign of Heraclius,
to judge by Muslim sources, some actual payment in kind of ration allowances
took place in some areas. The answer to the cash drain was not wholesale land
grants at that time. Hendy's attempt to use the *apothēkai* as a proof for a new
fiscal system for the army is unpersuasive, as N. Oikonomides has shown, "Silk
Trade and Production in Byzantium from the Sixth to the Ninth Century," *Dumbarton Oaks Papers* 40 (1986): 35, n. 12.

29   Carl H. Becker, *Beiträge zur Geschichte Ägyptens unter dem Islam* (Strasbourg,
      1902), 83–85.

30   J. Maspero, *Organisation militaire de l'Egypte byzantine* (Paris, 1912), 112, esp.
      n. 10.

31   al-Balādhurī, *Futūḥ al-buldān* (131 de Goeje). Translation from *The Origins of
      the Islamic State,* vol. 1, trans. Philip K. Hitti (New York, 1916), 200.

32   al-Balādhurī (152, 178 de Goeje); trans. from 234, 278, Hitti.

33   al-Balādhurī (173 de Goeje); trans. 271 Hitti.

34   al-Balādhurī (125 de Goeje); trans. 191 Hitti. Cf. de Goeje 124 and 191 concern-
      ing terms that Khālid ibn al-Walīd imposed on the Damascenes.

35   *Codex Theodosianus* 7.4.4–11, 7.4.23; *Codex Justinianus* 12.37.1; Vegetius
      Epitome rei militaris 3.3.

36   *Miracula, Acta M. Anastasii Persae,* c. 13 (25 Usener). Cf. *Colt Archaeological
      Expedition: Excavations at Nessana,* vol. 3, no. 79, line 59, on p. 230.

37   Sebeos, *Histoire d'Héraclius,* trans. F. Macler (Paris, 1904), 92. The actual
      translation here is by R. W. Thomson, on the basis of the 1979 Abgaryan ed.,
      p. 161. I thank him for all of his advice in its interpretation. On the location of
      Asorestan, C. Toumanoff, *Studies in Christian Caucasian History* (Washington,
      D.C.: Georgetown Univ. Press, 1963), 131–32, with maps. See also the transla-
      tion by Robert Bedrosian of Sebeos' *History* (New York, 1985), 117, "Subse-
      quently he [Ezr] resided with the Byzantine army, doing as the general wished.
      He arranged the orders of soldiers and the distribution of granaries for the entire
      country."

38   D. Van Berchem, "L'annone militaire," 156–88, 193–99. But see the discus-
      sion of late Roman granaries by Geoffrey Rickman, *Roman Granaries and Store
      Buildings* (Cambridge: Cambridge Univ. Press, 1971), 264–70, 278–92, who
      includes some modifications of the theories of Van Berchem. But D. Van Berchem,
      "L'annone militaire est-elle un mythe?" *Armée et fiscalité dans le monde an-
      tique,* Colloques Nationaux du Centre National de la Recherche Scientifique, no.
      936 (Paris: Editions du C.N.R.S., 1977), 331–36, and discussion, 337–39.

39   Constantine VII, *De cerim.*, ed. J. Reiske, pp. 477, 491, 658–59. Cf. James Howard-Johnston, "Studies in the Organisation of the Byzantine Army in the Tenth and Eleventh Centuries" (D.Phil. diss., Oxford Univ., 1971), 181–82. For more usual warehouses: Cyril Mango, *Le développement urbain de Constantinople*, Travaux et mémoires du Centre d'histoire et civilisation de Byzance, Collège de France (Paris: Diffusion de Boccard, 1985), 54–55, 59.

40   Kaegi, *Byzantine Military Unrest*, 148–53. Eutychius, *Das Annalenwerk des Eutychios von Alexandrien*, 128 (ed. Michael Breydy, *CSCO*, vol. 471, *Scriptores Arabici*, tome 44 [Louvain, 1985], 135–36); Azdī 151–52, 175–77.

41   Hendy, *Byzantine Monetary Economy*, 619–62, is somewhat over-optimistic in his evaluation of the speed of the process of institutionalization of land grants, for which the documentation is lacking. Nevertheless, it is probable that Constans II and his immediate successors did initiate improvisations in the payment and maintenance of troops. There is a question, however, of the degree to which the imperial government maintained tight control over the process of change or found it necessary to bend to the demands of soldiers at moments of governmental vulnerability.

42   John of Ephesus *Hist. eccl.* 3.3 (trans. E. W. Brooks, *CSCO, Scriptores Syri*, ser. 3, vol. 3 [Louvain, 1936], 132). On this passage, see also E. Stein, *Studien zur Geschichte des byzantinischen Reiches vornehmlich unter den Kaisern Justinus II. und Tiberius Constantinus* (Stuttgart, 1919), 94.

43   Yet there are many vexatious questions about the origins of Islamic taxation; see now T. Khalidi, ed. *Land Tenure and Social Transformation in the Middle East* (Beirut, 1984), for various contributions.

44   A. Noth, "Die literarisch überlieferten Verträge der Eroberungszeit als historische Quellen für die Behandlung der unterworfenen Nicht-Muslims durch ihre neuen muslimischen Quellen," in *Studien zum Minderheitenproblem im Islam*, ed. T. Nagel, Bonner Orientalische Studien, n.s., 27, (1973), 1:297–301.

45   John, Bishop of Nikiu, *Chronicle* 119.12 (trans. R. H. Charles [Oxford: Oxford Univ. Press, 1916], 190).

46   For a discussion of some problems, Kaegi, "Notes on Hagiographic Sources," 61–70.

47   A. N. Stratos, "La première campagne d'Héraclius contre les Perses," *Jahrbuch der österreischischen Byzantinistik* 28 (1979): 63–74, (repr. in his *Studies in Seventh-Century Byzantine Political History* [London: Variorum, 1983]).

48   That is a principal error in the assumptions and approaches to the relationship of culture and society in Haldon's article "Ideology and Social Change in the Seventh Century" (discussed in n.1), in which too much twentieth-century ideology is overconfidently read back into the seventh century. His is an interpretation without a sound and rigorous foundation in the primary sources of the seventh century. His interpretation of culture and ideology rests on wishful thinking. He does not show the relevance to understanding the seventh century of much of the modern social scientific literature and models that he cites.

49   Haldon, "Ideology and Social Change in the Seventh Century," 177, claims, e.g., that " 'Military unrest,' like many other forms of social action, was obviously determined by its form and its content by the context of the times." His remarks smack too much of Marxist determinism for my tastes. No true under-

standing of military unrest or other aspects of military activity in the seventh or other centuries can emerge from such a narrow deterministic approach. Social contexts may illumine, but in themselves they will not exclusively determine military actions.

50   E.g., ibid., 185, 187, 188.

51   I cannot accept the date for the end of classical thought proposed by P. Brown in his otherwise stimulating book, *The World of Late Antiquity* (New York, 1971), 177–84, esp. 182; the late sixth century is too early.

52   I benefited from the discussions of aspects of this topic at the Ninth Annual Byzantine Studies Conference at Duke University, October 1983.

53   Slow institutional change continued even later in the seventh century and beyond: Ralph-Johannes Lilie, "Die zweihundert jährige Reform: Zu den Anfängen der Themenorganisation im 7. und 8. Jahrhundert," *Byzantinoslavica* 45 (1984): 27–39.

54   On some of this see Schick, "The Fate of the Christians in Palestine." See also the important studies of Hugh Kennedy: "From *Polis* to *Madina:* Urban Change in Late Antique and Early Islamic Syria," *Past & Present* 106 (1985): 3–27; "The Last Century of Byzantine Syria: A Reinterpretation," *Byzantinische Forschungen* 10 (1985): 141–85; "The Melkite Church from the Islamic Conquest to the Crusades: Continuity and Adaptation in the Byzantine Legacy," in *Major Papers, The 17th International Byzantine Congress* (New Rochelle, N.Y.: A. D. Caratzas, 1986), 325–43. Also, W. E. Kaegi, "The Strategy of Heraclius," *Proceedings of the Second Symposium on the History of Bilād al-Shām during the Early Islamic Period Up to 40* A.H.,/640 A.D.; Fourth International Conference on the History of Bilād al-Shām (English and French Papers), vol. 1, ed. Muhammad Adnan Bakhit (Amman, Jordan, 1987), 104–15.

CHAPTER 11

The Arabesque, the Beveled Style, and the Mirage of an Early Islamic Art

TERRY ALLEN

No development in material culture is entirely without precedent. It is literally, even today, impossible to create something totally new. Yet what we call Islamic art (primarily the art of those lands conquered by the Arabs in the seventh and eighth centuries), and especially early Islamic art, has been regarded very nearly as something totally new. It has been seen as fundamentally different from Western art, as a drastic mutation created by the confluence of Sassanian and early Byzantine traditions with some amorphous but distinctively Islamic taste. Even those art historians who have stressed the contributions of Byzantine and Sassanian art to Islamic art have been at pains to distinguish Islamic art as a radically new development. Ernst Herzfeld saw the very combination of Western and Eastern motifs as a mark of a new taste (figs. 11.1 and 11.2):

> What then characterizes these Umayyad buildings in Jerusalem [the Dome of the Rock and the Aqṣā Mosque] as monuments of Islamic art? . . . The collaboration of foreign masters and artisans, who were summoned together from afar. And in the decoration: the unmediated juxtaposition of Western and Eastern, local and imported elements; the free play of fantasy, the invention of new [hybrid] forms and combinations out of variation, which has now become a principle.[1]

Oleg Grabar has advanced the notion of an "Islamic overlay" on preexisting arts and has written that "Islamic art . . . can be imagined as a sort of graft on other living entities."[2] Richard Ettinghausen, following Louis Massignon, tied the nature of Islamic art directly to the nature of Islam as a religion.[3]

Thus, paradoxically, it is a cliché to say both that the Dome of the Rock is

Fig. 11.1. Dome of the Rock, exterior. Jerusalem (courtesy Foundation Max van Berchem).

entirely Byzantine in conception, *and* that it is fundamentally new in some syncretic, "Islamic" way.

This attitude is historically understandable. To a degree hardly appreciated it reflects traditional Western images of the Near East—and the discipline of art history is inextricably part of Western culture. Partly it generalizes backward in time from the relatively more abundant and better preserved art of later Islamic civilization—that of the Mamluks, Timurids, Safavids, and Ottomans, which dates from many centuries after the origins of Islam and Islamic culture. Ironically the idea of the "Islamicness" of Islamic art has been picked up by Muslims unaware of how deeply rooted it is in a highly culture-bound Western view of the "East." Here I wish to show that this traditional attitude toward early Islamic art requires revision; that early Islamic art, while it naturally grows away from its sources, is still a branch of the art of Late Antiquity, coordinate in its aesthetic logic with Byzantine art and with Western medieval art from the Merovingians to the Gothic age. Further, I shall argue that the direction taken by Islamic art is an extension of, not a radical change of course from, the aesthetic trends of Late Antiquity (the fourth through sixth centuries A.D.). To this end I wish to consider the two most-distinctive developments of early Islamic art, the arabesque and the beveled style.[4]

Fig. 11.2. Dome of the Rock, interior. Jerusalem (courtesy Foundation Max van Berchem).

The very word *arabesque* suggests an arbitrary Western approach to Islamic art—there is no Arabic equivalent for the term, unless one has been formed as a calque. Yet there is no question that from the earliest European contacts with Islamic art (the *Oxford English Dictionary* gives citations back to 1786, and European artists have been interested in arabesques since the fifteenth century at least[5]), something distinctive has been seen about these vegetal designs. There is no real definition of the term either, although Alois Riegl, the Austrian art historian (1858–1905) who seems to have been the first to take up seriously the question of what constituted the arabesque (in *Stilfragen*, 1893), attempted a characterization. For Riegl the principal features of the arabesque were the geometrization of the stems of its vegetation,

Fig. 11.3. Mosque of Ibn Ṭūlūn, soffit of arcade on court-
yard. Cairo (photo: Terry Allen).

the particular vegetal elements used, and the growth of these elements un-
naturalistically from one another rather than from a single continuous stem.
But above all Riegl pointed out that the arabesque had *unendliche Rapport,* or
infinite correspondence, meaning that the design can be extended indefinitely
in any direction.[6] Vegetal decoration can be geometrized unsystematically,
and its elements can grow from one another, without being arabesque. It is the
unendliche Rapport of the arabesque that is crucial, and it is this notion, rather
than Riegl's obsessive pursuit of particular vegetal forms, that has been developed by Herzfeld and a host of others. Writing of the stucco ornament of the
Mosque of Ibn Ṭūlūn in Cairo, Herzfeld said (fig. 11.3), "As Riegl has
already established, the difference between late antique and arabesque orna-

Fig. 11.4. Detail of façade. Mushattā, Jordan (after
K. A. C. Creswell, *The Muslim Architecture of Egypt*,
1952, repr. 1978; courtesy Oxford University Press).

ment is only a gradual, not a habitual one." But then he immediately continued:

It is in the specific transformation of their formal elements that their arabesque character lies. The play of fantasy; the principle of variety, which creates new combinations
and variations; the composition on the basis of infinite correspondence along one or
two axes; the dematerialization of the elements, which completely transforms their
original vegetal or objective sense and creates new, abstract decorative values, and
with which is connected the amalgamation of the elements of the vase, stem, leaf,
blossom, and fruit without the accentuation of distinctions—all this characterizes this
ornament as arabesque.[7]

For Herzfeld, the carved stone facade of Mushattā (fig. 11.4) was the first
monument in which the arabesque occurs, although not in its fully developed
form. While it is clear from the passage quoted that Herzfeld's ideas on the

Fig. 11.5. Temple of Bacchus, ceiling between peristyle and cella. Baalbek.

arabesque were not entirely focused, the famous triangles of Mushattā can hardly be claimed as arabesques, even on Herzfeld's terms. For example, Mushattā has no *unendliche Rapport,* since the designs filling the triangles formed by the zigzag cornice are generally composed within the limits of those triangles and are not cropped by them. Nor is its vegetal ornament "dematerialized," though here Herzfeld was onto an important point. Only the supposedly new combination of Eastern and Western motifs puts Mushattā within Herzfeld's loose definition, and in fact that combination was the reason he gave for assigning Mushattā an Islamic date—that such combinations

Fig. 11.6. Floor mosaic from Thina, third century. Tunis, Musée du Bardo (photo: Terry Allen).

Fig. 11.7. Museum, floor mosaic. Al-Jīm, Tunisia (photo: Terry Allen).

215

Fig. 11.8. Khirbat al-Mafjar, bath, small apsed room (dīwān), reconstruction drawing. Palestine (after R. W. Hamilton, *Khirbat al-Mafjar*, 1959; courtesy Oxford University Press).

Fig. 11.9. Khirbat al-Mafjar, bath, dīwān, fragment of a stucco panel. Palestine (after R. W. Hamilton, *Khirbat al-Mafjar*, 1959; courtesy Oxford University Press).

could only be a result of bringing together workmen from different lands.[8]

Axial correspondence or symmetry—*unendliche Rapport*—is the result of extending a geometric construction. Complex geometric frameworks seem to have developed in antique architecture in the decoration of ceilings, especially the cofferings, though their exact origin is not important here. I offer as an example the ceiling of the peristyle of the Temple of Bacchus at Baalbek (fig. 11.5).[9] These ceiling frameworks, it appears, were reflected onto floors and occur in greater variety in the better preserved technique of floor mosaics, of which new examples come to light every year (figs. 11.6, 11.7). We are accustomed to thinking of classical architecture as rationalist, and so it was, from the base of the walls up. But even as early as the second century A.D., geometric and illusionistically geometric mosaics appear as floor decoration in such buildings. By the fourth and fifth centuries mosaic floors had developed designs that could make one's head swim.[10] Anna Gonosová has shown how floor patterns (most of them far more sober than these examples) were adapted for use in wall decoration according to a logical compositional scheme. In early Islamic monuments such as Khirbat al-Mafjar geometric frameworks appear in panels of wall decoration as well as on floors (figs. 11.8, 11.9).[11]

Fig. 11.10. Khirbat al-Mafjar, reconstruction drawing of a stucco panel. Palestine (after R. W. Hamilton, *Khirbat al-Mafjar*, 1959; courtesy Oxford University Press).

Fig. 11.11. Khirbat al-Mafjar, reconstruction drawing of a stucco panel. Palestine (after R. W. Hamilton, *Khirbat al-Mafjar*, 1959; courtesy Oxford University Press).

Fig. 11.12. Temple of Baal, lintel. Palmyra, Syria (photo: Terry Allen).

Fig. 11.13. Ara Pacis, decorative panel, 13 B.C. Rome.

Now the point of these patterns is that they are complex geometric constructions that are infinitely extensible (figs. 11.10, 11.11). They have *unendliche
Rapport*. But they are not arabesques; they are merely frames constructed
from a variety of motifs, often enclosing various filler elements, including the
grape vine.[12] The vine had been geometrized in antique and Late Antique art,
too, along with the acanthus (figs. 11.12, 11.13), but only as a formalization

Fig. 11.14. Mosque of al-Ḥākim, frieze on north side of gate, 990–1013. Cairo (photo: Terry Allen).

of nature; anyone who has tended grape vines will appreciate how determinedly they spiral and curve.[13]

What Herzfeld saw in the Mushattā facade (fig. 11.4), I think, is that the simple geometric schemes on which the stems of its still-traditional vines were laid out were becoming more complex, with further addition of overlapping and intertwining. This is the basic insight Riegl reached through the study of vegetal forms.[14] Herzfeld pointed out that in the stucco decoration of the Mosque of Ibn Ṭūlūn in Cairo foliate fragments are compartmentalized in geometric frames; this is still only juxtaposition of geometry with vegetation. But by the tenth century vine ornament came to be arranged in or in conjunction with complex patterns drawn from the same repertoire as the mosaic floors (figs. 11.14, 11.15). By this time the vine scroll could interlace with geometric frames—and this was new. Eventually, as a still-later step, the pattern of the vine scroll was assimilated to the geometric framework: the stems of the vine were given the shape of what had formerly been a nonvegetal pattern, or conversely, the geometric framework came to life and the vine leaves sprouted directly from it. This visual shift created a highly variable and adaptable system of vegetal decoration whose *method of construction* is of *intrinsic* interest. This for me is the arabesque, the most distinctive and fascinating contribution of Islamic art.

This development took centuries to unfold—it was no sudden event. The arabesque (on my terms) appears not to have existed until the tenth century. Yet there is nothing in it that was not inherent in the art of Late Antiquity.[15]

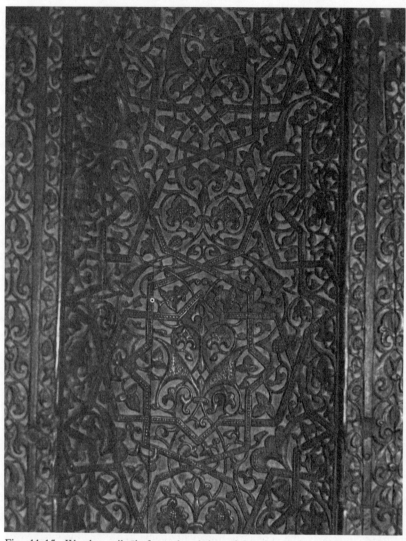

Fig. 11.15. Wooden miḥrāb from the shrine of Sayyida Nafīsa, Cairo, 1138–46. Cairo, Museum of Islamic Art (photo: Terry Allen).

Fig. 11.16. Hagia Sophia, southwest corner, square capital. Istanbul (photo: Terry Allen).

Fig. 11.17. Hagia Sophia, nave, spandrel of the first-floor nave arcade. Istanbul (photo: Terry Allen).

Fig. 11.18. Church of St. Polyeuctos, excavated niche head. Istanbul (photo: Terry Allen).

The arabesque is, indeed, a development of Late Antique art in a direction that art was already going. The crucial assimilation of vegetal ornament to complex geometric systems was made possible intellectually by the abstraction in Late Antique art of vegetal ornament (and the vine scroll in particular), and the divorce of shape or outline from texture, one of the characteristics Herzfeld saw, I think prematurely, in the carved decoration of Mushattā.

This abstraction of shape from texture goes back a long way in Byzantine architecture; certainly, as Cyril Mango has noted, to the days of the emperor Justinian, builder of Hagia Sophia, and Anicia Juliana, the patron of the Church of St. Polyeuctos.[16] The acanthuses in capitals excavated from Constantine's Hagia Sophia of A.D. 325 have already lost all leafy texture and are involuted in a way that confuses the unity of the individual leaves. In the square capital from Justinian's Hagia Sophia shown in figure 11.16 not only have the acanthus leaves adopted the distinctive lacy texture remarked by Mango; they also have lost the traditional arrangement in tiers.

When one considers the capitals of Hagia Sophia or the decoration of its first-floor nave spandrels (fig. 11.17), it is easy to see that abstract ornament has been used to cover architectural solids so as to give them uniform textures. Texture is used to articulate components of the design; the vine leaves no longer have the texture of actual leaves but look as if they were made of soap

Fig. 11.19. Church of St. Polyeuctos, excavated capital. Istanbul (photo: Terry Allen).

or chalk. Once the vine had lost its realistic character and adopted this literal approach to volume, it could be adapted to any framework, and in one such adaptation it became the arabesque. (It is notable that in the arabesque the vine loses its viny character exceedingly slowly; it is not until the fifteenth century that such related forms as flowers are introduced into it.)

For lack of material, the beginnings of the artistic changes that led to the arabesque can only be sketched. It is clear that in the Church of St. Polyeuctos an exotic (perhaps "Eastern"?) effect was sought, one at odds with the classical heritage of Byzantine art. Fragments from the building show a disconcerting combination of naturalism and exotic vegetal decoration suited to an age in which an acanthus leaf could be an outline instead of a palpable physical reality (figs. 11.18, 11.19). "Sassanian" elements such as the fanciful vegetal forms found in the capitals at Ṭāq-i Bustān (fig. 20) are not copied outright in this Constantinople church, as they are in the Dome of the Rock.[17] But it almost seems that the Polyeuctos capitals were attempts at forming such exotic designs with pieced-together Late Antique forms.

Having arrived at this point, Byzantine architects and artisans would have been prepared to adopt vegetal motifs of a comparable level of abstraction from reality, and it is easy to imagine a period in the late sixth and early sev-

Fig. 11.20. Capital. Ṭāq-i Bustān, Iran (after E. Herzfeld, *Am Tor von Asien: Fels-denkmale aus Irans Heldenzeit*, 1920; courtesy Dietrich Reimer Verlag, Berlin [FRG]).

Fig. 11.21. Aqṣā Mosque, roof timber, detail. Jerusalem (after R. W. Hamilton, *The Structural History of the Aqsa Mosque*, 1949; courtesy Oxford University Press).

enth centuries when such motifs as those found at Ṭāq-i Bustān were learned by the architects and artisans who followed on in the tradition of St. Polyeuctos and Hagia Sophia. Despite the virtual lack of evidence, it seems to me likely that this development may have been centered in Palestine and Syria, and in fact the earliest appearance of these frankly "Sassanian" forms is in one of the roof timbers of the Aqṣā Mosque in Jerusalem (fig. 11.21), a piece of woodwork that probably should be dated to the second half of the seventh century A.D.[18] In this example, each inwardly spiraling tendril of the acanthus scroll is turned into a pearl band like the circles of pearls so common in Sassanian art. But this is an adaptation, not an imitation, because the band does not close to form a circle; instead it spirals one full turn, throwing off leaves like the vegetation it replaces, a subtle and delightful transformation.

The historical sequence that leads to the arabesque, then, is an initial shift in attitude within Late Antique art in the Byzantine Empire toward the canons of architectural decoration and its effects. At the same time there was a demonstrable interest in unconventional motifs of "Eastern" origin. This shift in taste would naturally have been followed by a closer study of the motifs actually used in the East (motifs that were often but reflections of Western models anyway). The juxtaposition of apparently Eastern and Western motifs in the mosaics of the Dome of the Rock (fig. 11.22) would then be no novelty, but the natural outcome of an intelligible artistic process.[19] It was also natural for this fantastic vine-based vegetation to be linked with the geometric frameworks with which the vine had long been associated, although it was centuries before the frameworks actually became the stems of the vine ornament. Thus the arabesque is the outcome of artistic movements set in motion centuries before it appears, not the immediate result of the cultural split that created the Islamic world. The vine was assimilated to geometric frameworks in the Islamic world and not (or not to the same degree) in Byzantine art, but it is methodologically vacuous to attribute that difference to something "Islamic."[20] Art historical conclusions must be drawn from the evidence itself and cannot be based on the blind application of ideas that have no basis in

Fig. 11.22. Dome of the Rock, mosaic revetment of octagonal arcade, inner face of pier 5, left side. Jerusalem (after K. A. C. Creswell, *The Muslim Architecture of Egypt*, 1952, repr. 1978; courtesy Oxford University Press).

229

Fig. 11.23. Balkuwārā Palace, stucco dado. Samarra, Iraq (after E. Herzfeld, *Der Wandschmuck der Bauten von Samarra und seine Ornamentik*, 1923; courtesy Dietrich Reimer Verlag, Berlin [FRG])

visual material. It is because of the division of the Late Antique world by the Arab conquest, not because of the details or "spirit" of the new religion (whatever "spirit" means when applied to art), that developments could occur in the Islamic world and not elsewhere. The art of the Islamic world, especially in Syria and Egypt, simply grew apart from its former connection with Constantinople. Byzantine art, and Western medieval art too, had the same potential as Islamic art but took different courses. A parallel assimilation of vegetation to geometry happened entirely separately in Ireland: the designs in the Book of Kells are very much like arabesques based on a different set of geometric constructions and using different motifs. The arabesque itself, though not a form characteristic of European art, is just as much a part of the Western artistic tradition as the Gothic style is.

If it is unjust to art historical logic to see the arabesque as somehow "Islamic," the beveled style of architectural decoration has been treated in a way that can only be called a miscarriage of justice.[21] The first securely dated examples come from the ʿAbbasid dynasty's new capital of Samarra (838–92), though Herzfeld believed that certain capitals in this style, probably from Raqqa, Hārūn al-Rashīd's capital, should be dated as early as A.D. 800.[22] In any event, the beveled style flourished in Greater Mesopotamia in the early

Fig. 11.24. Balkuwārā Palace, stucco dado, detail. Samarra, Iraq (after E. Herzfeld, *Der Wandschmuck der Bauten von Samarra und seine Ornamentik*, 1923; courtesy Dietrich Reimer Verlag, Berlin [FRG]).

decades of the ninth century. The most famous examples come from Samarra (figs. 11.23, 11.24) and the Mosque of Ibn Ṭūlūn in Cairo, derived from a Samarran model, although the Ibn Ṭūlūn stucco reflects its sources in placement and motifs and is not really beveled much at all. Ettinghausen has defined the beveled style concisely:

In it . . . identical designs are delineated and at the same time separated from each other by various types of curved lines with spiral endings; occasionally, small marginal notches, short slits, dots, and applied surface decorations are added for further accentuation. The designs are purely abstract, although Herzfeld has pointed out that they derive from border designs of Hellenistic architecture and from floral forms such as acanthus, buds, flowers and rinceaux. The sense of complete stylization is enhanced by another characteristic feature, the slant style of carving, that is, the beveling of the surface toward the curved outlines of the design, which creates a sculptured plane with a soft, flat modulation. The total impression is that of a uniform, abstract pattern with no background between the individual designs.[23]

I would reverse the emphasis here: despite the impression of a uniform, abstract pattern, the designs are not purely abstract but are consciously derived from Hellenistic prototypes. In two capitals, probably from northern Syria

Fig. 11.25. Alabaster capital said to be from Syria. New York, Metropolitan Museum of Art (36.68.1, Samuel D. Lee Fund, 1936; photo: Metropolitan Museum of Art).

(figs. 11.25, 11.26), it is easy to see the transformation that has occurred: the vegetal elements of the prototype, already abstracted from larger patterns and presented individually or recombined—a feature very common in Sassanian and Umayyad stucco decoration—are reinterpreted in this new style. It is a transformation of treatment, of manner, not of subject matter.

The beveled style forms what might be called an artistic horizon in virtually all media: interpretations of the beveled style appear in pottery, glass, and rock crystal.[24] It must have been very fashionable, the latest thing. It replaced earlier styles in woodwork, in which it continues up to the twelfth century, and continued to be employed and transformed in architectural stucco in Iran through the fourteenth century. In both media the importance of the technique and its habitual forms is signaled by the inclusion of these beveled forms in the standard repertoire of border designs.

There has been a lot of loose talk about the origins of the beveled style. Attention has naturally focused on the technique of beveling itself. Astonishing as it may seem, the only theory that has ever been widely accepted, and

Fig. 11.26. Alabaster capital said to be from Syria. New York, Metropolitan Museum of Art (36.68.3, Samuel D. Lee Fund, 1936; photo: Metropolitan Museum of Art).

that is still repeated as though it were plausible, is that the Turkish slave soldiers of the ʿAbbasid caliphs brought with them from Central Asia horse trappings resembling the well-known Scythian metalwork, which is similarly beveled. We are asked to believe that in the new Islamic world of Iraq these inconsequential items were seized upon as the source of a new style.[25] (Herzfeld, on the other hand, felt that beveling, which facilitates the mass production of stucco by the use of molds, was devised simply so that the acres of stucco dadoes required in Samarra and the settlements that were to become Cairo could be executed rapidly, which is a more sensible if equally implausible notion.)[26]

In fact, the principles of the beveled style—complete contiguity of decorative motifs, and the adjustment of surface relief to form an undulating surface—already existed in Late Antique art, as the square capital from Hagia Sophia (fig. 11.16) shows. This complete contiguity is a natural result of the divorce of shape or outline from realistic form and texture. And so is the ad-

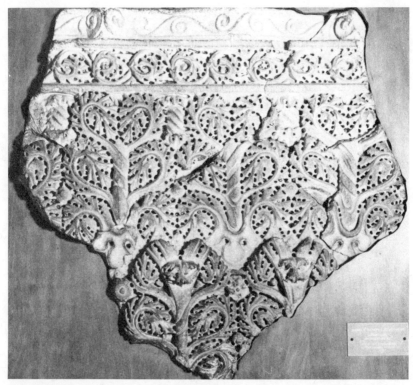

Fig. 11.27. Fragment of marble parapet revetment excavated at Antioch. Baltimore, Baltimore Museum of Art (65.4 cm. high; BMA 1940.170.a, Antioch Subscription Fund; photo: Baltimore Museum of Art).

justment of the contour of the decoration so that it forms an undulating surface not directly related to the real forms of the vegetation represented. The carved stucco dadoes from Samarra, one of which Herzfeld believed to have been derived from Mushattā,[27] are actually translations into stucco of Late Antique stone dado revetments, as is shown by a stone fragment from fifth-century Antioch (fig. 11.27).[28] This fragment, probably from a dado, is composed of acanthuses arranged in tiers with offset axes, as in a typical Corinthian capital. But the vegetation has been compressed in depth to form an undulating surface completely covered with contiguous ornament. This vegetal ornament is of some interest aside from its surface contour. The topmost row of acanthuses consists of doubled pairs of inward-curling leaves growing from a short, thick, and prominent stem. The stem is set in a separate base that sprouts two leaves itself. The heart-shaped outline of the uppermost pair of leaves must represent the source for a design such as the stucco dado from the Balkuwārā Palace at Samarra (fig. 11.24). At Samarra the top row of heart-shaped leaf forms rises from and forms the base for more bulbous stems, and the base form of the Antioch fragment has been wrapped around the base of the stem from which the leaves grow, creating a curved lozenge shape. This lozenge is connected to a simpler but similar lozenge below by another stem-like form. The correspondence between the two pieces is not exact, but it exists. Taken together with the evidence of the sequence of capitals already presented, this compositional correspondence strengthens the case for considering the Antioch fragment's undulating surface as an early stylistic prototype for the beveled style.

I believe that nearly all the hundreds of decorative motifs found at Samarra were derived in this same way: dado revetment designs were transposed into the beveled style (or one of the other two "Samarra styles"). Herzfeld recognized this connection but failed to appreciate how systematic the transpositions are: there is very little new at Samarra in terms of patterns, and, given the background I have been tracing, the technique in its essentials must have been applied to at least some of these patterns much earlier than the ninth century. What is significant about the first half of the ninth century is that a kind of decoration that had been just one of many substyles in the Late Antique and early Islamic Near East blossomed and became dominant in a cultural milieu that drifted away from the antique past and by the Samarra period most likely knew that past only very dimly. Evidently vegetal ornament had no reality or physicality for the ʿAbbasid beveler. No Late Antique artist could have imagined so complete a transformation, because in his sources vegetal ornament was still construed literally. But that vegetal ornament had been greatly abstracted through the steps I traced earlier in talking about the arabesque: emphasis on outline over texture, addition of fantastic forms from Sassanian art, increasing complexity of geometric frameworks for vegetal ornament, and emphasis on the method of construction of the vegetal ornament rather than on its literal representation of vegetation. It was thus possible to give this ornament a completely new slant. This is the way new art forms come into being: what later artists see in an object or monument they take as their prototype is different from what its creators and their contemporaries saw in it, and the artistic product of that new perception is in turn seen by later artists in a way still further removed from the original understanding of the first work. One cannot draw straight lines between extant monuments widely separated in time without considering this entirely human and very familiar process of transformation. The beveled style is several steps away from Late Antique art but fully its descendant.

Even the two-dimensional patterns formed by sawing veined marble into four matching panels for revetment (fig. 11.2) were adopted into the repertoire of the beveled style as apparently abstract vegetation.[29] This flat dado revetment was copied in a corresponding location, but in three dimensions, at Sa-

Fig. 11.28. House XIII, room 11, west wall. Samarra, Iraq (after E. Herzfeld, *Der Wandschmuck der Bauten von Samarra und seine Ornamentik*, 1923; courtesy Dietrich Reimer Verlag, Berlin [FRG]).

marra (figs. 11.28, 11.29). That shows how far removed from its origins the beveled style had become; it is no wonder that in such an age it could be applied to all sorts of objects in all media. Eventually the forms created in the beveled style were regrouped into new configurations, completely divorced from any source, giving rise to such fantasies as the well-known beveled bird panels.

Currently, lack of material makes it impossible to trace the development of the beveled style between fifth-century Antioch and ninth-century Samarra; there is no way of knowing whether it "grew up," so to speak, in Byzantine Syria or in Sassanian and early Islamic Mesopotamia. Certainly it blossomed in Mesopotamia when that region was the artistic center of the Islamic Empire. But like the arabesque, it is an offshoot of Late Antique art, not an utterly original and thus somehow "Islamic" creation. It is the natural result of a series of transitions, begun in the fifth or early sixth century, in which at each stage artisans saw the sources they used differently from the way those objects and buildings had been seen by their creators.

In both the arabesque and the beveled style, forms that existed within Late Antique art became extremely popular and underwent relatively rapid but

Fig. 11.29. House XIII, room 11, west wall, detail. Samarra, Iraq (after E. Herzfeld, *Der Wandschmuck der Bauten von Samarra und seine Ornamentik*, 1923; courtesy Dietrich Reimer Verlag, Berlin [FRG]).

nonetheless orderly and intuitively comprehensible modifications. I think one would be hard-pressed to demonstrate that either Byzantine art or medieval European art was any more closely linked with antiquity, though of course they are linked with it in other ways. We are inclined by habit to see the connection of medieval Western art to its antique heritage largely in terms of subject matter, and we tend to see the lack, or loss, of figural art in Islamic culture as a distinguishing and distancing feature of Islamic art, when it is only a characteristic of the shape of that culture's taste and interests, not of its artistic development. Similarly, the overabundance of figures in Buddhist religious art has no direct and obvious connection with the style of that art. The apparent iconophobia of Islamic art is greatly exaggerated by the destruction of figural art by iconoclasts (more often in recent centuries and with a cumulative effect) and by the preservation of a disproportionate number of religious monuments in which figural art was not employed after the seventh century. (Consider, too, that the pre-Islamic churches of north Syria seem to be completely aniconic.) One can find antique subject matter in Islamic art, though generally in the tenth to twelfth centuries. Thus there is no temporal parallel in Islamic art to the early date of the Carolingian Renaissance of the eighth to ninth centuries. But then Islamic art had a late start, so to speak, and when it did arrive at a classical revival in such buildings as the Great Mosques of Harrān and Diyarbakir, it was much more thorough than, though achieved by precisely the same process as, the Carolingian Renaissance.[30] These two revivals are two time-warped sides of the same coin. The Islamic world and the two Christian worlds, Europe and Byzantium, saw themselves as continuers of antiquity rather than as changers of it, though of course all three cultures took "antiquity" in different senses.

There is another difference between Islamic art and its Byzantine and Western siblings, and it is the reason I have left the qualifier "*an early* Islamic art" in my title. Europe and Byzantium continued their relationships with antiquity, Europe winding up with the Renaissance and a fixation with antiquity that is still deeply ingrained, and Byzantium with its fantasy that it was simply carrying on the culture of antiquity. The Islamic world, on the other hand, continued to absorb new nations and cultures and to develop strong regional variations whose recombinations produced the most striking results. Islamic art became increasingly varied and at the same time self-referring, developing its own broad identity. It is important to see that the arabesque and the beveled style, and more broadly, the diverging of the three major artistic traditions of the early Middle Ages, come about not because of the intrusion of new cultural factors such as Islam, but because of the breakup of a former cultural unity, that of the decaying Roman Empire, and the isolation of the new cultural entities from each other. The same breakup of a unitary or at least coherent cultural system with similar divergent results occurred later in the history of the Islamic world, with the decay of the caliphate and the eventual sundering of the Islamic world by the Mongols: the art of the Mamluks is as different from that of the Timurids as Byzantium's is from France's.

This divergence is the most interesting aspect of the Late Antique origins of these three artistic traditions: although all three proceeded in accord with a common human nature, within a few centuries they had grown apart so much that they never grew back together again. The Islamic Empire included lands that retained only the froth from the repeated waves of antique art that washed the nearer East. Along with the eventual cultural dominance of Mesopotamia, whose Hellenism had always been eccentric, this expansion of the Late Antique Near East shifted the basis of cultural patronage away from the heavily Hellenized provinces of Syria and Egypt. Thus the steps away from Late Antique prototypes were swifter and longer in the Islamic world than elsewhere, and even more rapid in the eastern parts of the Islamic world. One may compare this rate of change with what happened in the slow-moving art of Byzantium, immersed in reveries of its antique past.[31]

So although the arabesque and the beveled style come directly out of Late Antiquity, their distinctly unclassical character and the degree to which they treat vegetal ornament differently from their Late Antique sources show the extent to which the culture that produced them had moved away from its own Late Antique sources, where it had them at all. And it is clear that at some point, say the end of the twelfth century for the sake of argument, Islamic art had become a distinct entity, not proceeding along the same general lines as European or Byzantine art, and no longer related very much to antiquity of any kind. It is later Islamic art—of the thirteenth through seventeenth centuries—that we tend to think of when we form a mental picture of Islamic art. This later art, of course, is no more "Islamic" than the earlier one, and it stands in the same relationship to its immediate past as early Islamic art does to Late Antique art. But by 1200 Islamic art had settled in its own tracks; and at least for now I reserve the epithet "mirage" for the early period.

Let me underline my point. It is not necessary to appeal to the secret inner workings of some "Islamic mind" that revels in the "free play of fantasy" in order to explain the development of early Islamic art. Like all art, it follows the rules of human nature and human perception, rules that can be applied to its entire course. We tend to see early Islamic art as radically new not because it was, but because we tend to collapse the time scale over which it developed new forms and to identify the end product, later Islamic art, with its origins. It would be idle to argue that Islam had no effect on the art of the Islamic world. But there is nothing "Islamic" about Islamic art. Such a term—which, like it or not, we are stuck with—is drawn from the wrong list of adjectives.

NOTES

1 Ernst Herzfeld, "Die Genesis der islamischen Kunst und das Mshatta-Problem,"
   Der Islam 1 (1910): 27–63, 105–44, on 32, my translation. Note that at this
   early date Herzfeld argued that the beveled style was invented in Egypt; Samuel
   Flury, "Samarra und die Ornamentik der Moschee des Ibn Tūlūn," *Der Islam* 4
   (1913): 421–32, corrected this Egyptocentric view and made Ibn Ṭūlūn (properly) dependent on Samarra; Herzfeld picked up the point in *Der Wandschmuck
   der Bauten von Samarra und seine Ornamentik,* Forschungen zur islamischen
   Kunst, ed. Friedrich Sarre, vol. 1 of ser. 2, Die Ausgrabungen von Samarra
   (Berlin, 1923), 7–8.

2 Oleg Grabar, *The Formation of Islamic Art* (New Haven, Conn. 1973), 19, delet-
   ing an errant comma that found its way between "other" and "living" in the
   printed text.

3 Richard Ettinghausen, "The Character of Islamic Art," in *The Arab Heritage,*
   ed. N. A. Faris (Princeton, N.J.: 1944), 251–67. Ettinghausen expanded on this
   viewpoint in "Interaction and Integration in Islamic Art," in *Unity and Variety in
   Muslim Civilization,* ed. Gustave E. von Grunebaum (Chicago, 1955), 107–31; it
   was anticipated by, among others, Carl Johan Lamm, in "The Spirit of Moslem
   Art," *Bulletin of the Faculty of Arts* (Cairo Univ.) 3 (1935): 1–7. Cf. Mehmet
   Ağa-Oğlu, "Remarks on the Character of Islamic Art," *Art Bulletin* 36 (1954):
   175–202, which is still unrivaled in its common sense. Massignon's essentially
   romantic viewpoint is responsible at second- and thirdhand for much of the non-
   sense that has been written, even at the scholarly level, about the "spirit of Islamic art." Ernst Kühnel, *Die Arabeske: Sinn und Wandlung eines Ornaments*
   (Wiesbaden, 1949), has a similarly romantic introduction, omitted in his article
   "Arabesque" in the *Encyclopaedia of Islam,* 2d ed. Kühnel emphasized the vegetal peculiarities of the arabesque's vine scroll, but these characteristics occur in
   Late Antique vine scrolls as well. The scholarly treatment of Islamic art as "Islamic" may consciously parallel the interpretation of Early Christian art as "a
   new spiritual art," a viewpoint discussed by Kurt Weitzmann in his introduction
   to *Age of Spirituality: Late Antique and Early Christian Art, Third to Seventh
   Century: Catalogue of the Exhibition at The Metropolitan Museum of Art, November 19, 1977, through February 12, 1978* (New York, 1979).

4 It is my pleasure to note the many instructive conversations I have had on these
   and related topics with my colleagues Anna Gonosová, Eva Hoffman, and Chris-
   tine Kondoleon. They may not agree with all of what I have to say here, but much
   of whatever clarity it may have is the result of their substantial contributions.

5 A phenomenon nicely documented in the ornamentation of books: Stanley Morison, "Venice and the Arabesque Ornament," *Selected Essays on the History of
   Letter-Forms in Manuscript and Print,* ed. David McKitterick, 2 vols. (Cambridge, 1980–81), 142–58.

6 Alois Riegl, *Stilfragen* (Berlin, 1893), 302–3, for the first three features; *unendliche Rapport* is introduced at the conclusion of his discussion of the arabesque, 308.

7 Herzfeld, "Genesis," 44–45, my translation; I have omitted Herzfeld's footnote

in the first sentence, which refers to Riegl, *Stilfragen*, 306. On Mushattā see Herzfeld, "Genesis," 36–37; for him the arabesque exists fully in the decoration of Samarra. Cf. also *Wandschmuck*, 6.

8 Herzfeld, *Wandschmuck*, pt. 2, passim.

9 Consider also the examples adduced in *ibid.*, 137; including a ceiling from the Temple of Bacchus at Palmyra.

10 See references in the following note; perhaps the best assortment of designs is to be found in the large collections of mosaics from Tunisia displayed in Tunis, al-Jīm, and elsewhere. These represent designs that naturally would have circulated throughout the Roman and, later, the Byzantine world.

11 Irving Lavin, "The Ceiling Frescoes in Trier and Illusionism in Constantinian Painting," *Dumbarton Oaks Papers* 21 (1967): 97–133, briefly discusses the illusionistically architectural schemes from which the nonarchitectonic and relentlessly literal decoration of such monuments as Khirbat al-Mafjar descends. In "The Hunting Mosaics of Antioch and Their Sources: A Study of Compositional Principles in the Development of Early Mediaeval Style," *Dumbarton Oaks Papers* 17 (1963): 179–286, Lavin discusses a well-known series of these mosaics and reviews the literature. See also Ernst Kitzinger, "Stylistic Developments in Pavement Mosaics in the Greek East from the Age of Constantine to the Age of Justinian," *La mosaïque gréco-romaine*, Colloques Internationaux du Centre National de la Recherche Scientifique, Paris, 29 Aug.–3 Sept. 1963 (Paris, 1965), 341–52, esp. 345–50, repr. in *The Art of Byzantium and the Medieval West: Selected Studies by Ernst Kitzinger*, ed. W. Kleinbauer (Bloomington, Ind., 1976). For the aesthetic logic of Late Antique and early Byzantine mosaics, on walls and vaults as well as floors, see Anna Gonosová's Ph.D. diss., "The Role of Ornament in Late Antique Interiors with Special Reference to Intermedia Borrowing of Patterns" (Harvard Univ. 1981).

12 Cf. Herzfeld, "Genesis," 41ff.

13 J. B. Ward-Perkins, "Nicomedia and the Marble Trade," *Papers of the British School in Rome* 48 (n.s. 35) (1980): 23–69, on 61, cites evidence indicating that as early as ca. A.D. 120 sculptors traced out geometric frameworks to aid in the symmetrical execution of foliate patterns. This practice may well underlie the Islamic assimilation of vegetation to complex geometric patterns, but did not in itself produce that assimilation.

14 Riegl, *Stilfragen*, 266–87, 308.

15 As Riegl saw, ibid., 309ff.

16 Cyril Mango, *Byzantium, the Empire of New Rome* (New York, 1980), 260–63, describes these developments. For comparative material see Otto Feld, "Zu den Kapitellen des Tekfur Saray in Istanbul," *Istanbuler Mitteilungen* 19–20 (1969–70: 360–67.

17 The capital illustrated was found at Bīsutūn; similar ones have been found at other sites in western Iran. See Heinz Luschey, "Zur Datierung der sasanidischen Kapitelle aus Bisutun und des Monuments von Taq-i Bustan," and Wolfram Kleiss, "Dis sasanidischen Kapitelle aus Venderni bei Kamyaran nördlich Kermanshah," *Archaeologische Mitteilungen aus Iran*, n.s., 1 (1968): 127–47. As Luschey remarks in his discussion of dating, many scholars have seen that the shape of these

capitals is a Byzantine import into Sassanian architecture; indeed, the whole idea
of a stone building is a "Romanizing" one. Cf. Ṭāq-i Girrah, published most recently by Hubertus von Gall, "Entwicklung und Gestalt des Thrones im vorislamischen Iran," *Archaeologische Mitteilungen aus Iran,* n.s., 4 (1971): 220–23.
Further on the Ṭāq-i Bustān capitals, there is interesting comparative material in
Kurt Erdmann, "Die Kapitelle am Taq i Bostan," *Mitteilungen der Deutschen
Orient-Gesellschaft,* no. 80 (1943): 1–24. Note his figs. 6*b* and particularly 8*b*,
where the damaged condition of the capital shows the use of a regular framework
(cf. fig. 9) for laying out the vegetal decoration.

18   R. W. Hamilton, *The Structural History of the Aqsa Mosque: A Record of Archaeological Gleanings from the Repairs of 1938–1942,* Department of Antiquities in Palestine (London, 1949), 83ff., discusses the cypress roof timbers span-
ning the central nave (which he calls tie beams, thus causing some confusion with
the tie beams of the arcades). He argues convincingly that they are reused. One of
the timbers (pl. XLVIII, 3, discussed 89–90) differs markedly in style from the
rest. Hamilton, seeing the trace of a cross in the central wreath, implies a Christian source. I see (in the published plate) the trace of hexaform rosettes in all these
wreaths, suggesting to me that now-lost metal fittings were once attached at these
points, probably, as Hamilton says, for chains. I also suggest as an idea for con-
templation that this beam may belong to the building, or at least to its site—perhaps to the mosque that the Western pilgrim Arculf saw, or to some repair or alteration made to that mosque when the Dome of the Rock was constructed. (There
is no textual evidence for such work or other archaeological evidence that I know
of to suggest it directly, but it is reasonable to suppose that the mosque was refur-
bished at a time when attention was manifestly focused on the site, and it is useful
to keep such possibilities in mind.)

19   On the interchange of motifs between East and West in Late Antiquity see Lavin's
thoughtful analysis, "Hunting Mosaics," 197–99, and on classical architecture
in northern Mesopotamia, see Marlia Mundell Mango, "The Continuity of the
Classical Tradition in the Art and Architecture of Northern Mesopotamia," in
East of Byzantium: Syria and Armenia in the Formative Period, ed. Nina G.
Garsoïan, Thomas F. Mathews, and Robert W. Thomson (Washington, D.C.
1982), 115–34. The Sassanian occupation of Syria, Palestine, and Egypt in the
early seventh century came long after the beginning of the changes in Late Antique art discussed here. It may have had some effect on Byzantine art, but it is
likely to have been far more influential on the impoverished art of the Sassanian
world. In connection with Sassanian art, Herzfeld's remarks in "Damascus: Studies in Architecture," *Ars Islamica* 10 (1943): 60–61, come to life:

Oriental buildings like the Ṭāk-i Kisrā [Ctesiphon] are not links of the chain of Western
movements. No date can be derived from [comparing them]. . . . One must not transfer to
the contrary situation principles and notions abstracted from the study of ascending evolu-
tions, where art grows step by step to greater achievements [as in the West]. He who studies
Hellenistic art in the Arsacid empire does not study movement, but stagnation, not evolution, but decomposition; he makes autopsies, and the livid spots may appear any time in a
body in which life blood ceases to pulse. Time is a quality of life, death, beyond chronology, is eternity. Hellenistic architecture in the East begins with and goes on using hybrid

forms, and it is only in Syria and not before our era that canonical forms are introduced, apparently as an effect of western study, such as embodied in Vitruvius' *De Architectura*.

One need not agree with this evaluation to appreciate its force: antique elements in Parthian (and Sassanian) brick architecture are mannerisms, not fundamental aspects of the way the architecture was conceived.

20 Or as Riegl did, to "orientalische Geist," 267.

21 The term *beveled* is thoroughly embedded in the literature. I discovered when I gave the talk on which this paper is based, however, that it is confusing to most people, to whom *beveled* is synonymous with *chamfered*—that is, a beveled surface would be one broken up into oblique facets, whereas the beveled style involves smoothly curving surfaces. Perhaps *beveled style* should be considered a technical phrase; at any rate it is an accepted one.

22 Friedrich Sarre and Ernst Herzfeld, *Archäologische Reise im Euphrat- und Tigris-Gebiet*, 4 vols. (Berlin, 1911–20), 2:347–53.

23 Richard Ettinghausen, "The 'Beveled Style' in the Post-Samarra Period," in *Archeologia Orientalia in Memoriam Ernst Herzfeld*, ed. George C. Miles (Locust Valley, N.Y., 1952), 72–83, on 73; and Herzfeld, *Wandschmuck*, 8–9. Cf. also 5–6, emphasizing the linear nature of the designs and their supposed *horror vacui*, but also pointing out their origins in Hellenistic architecture. In closing his introduction to *Wandschmuck*, 9, Herzfeld wrote:

> The art of Samarra built itself on a foundation that was Hellenistic in all its components. On this foundation Aramaeans and Iranians had built further. Then when Islam came into its inheritance it completed this work. This art is no offspring of any particular landscape, no expression of the deepest nature of a complete national identity. But it reflects in its universality the supranational, universal world regime [of Islam]; in its limitation to pure ornament the aversion of the Islamic religion to the living world; and in its unnaturalistic abstraction it clearly bears the stamp of the Semitic spirit [*Geist*]. And in this way something eminently Arabic reposes in it; it is also in this sense arabesque. Just as the Arab Kingdom of the Caliphs set the scope that the Islamic world has encompassed as long as it has lived, and still does today; just as the Arabic religious conception slings a united bond around Islam's many-sided world of ideas, which flow from many of the strangest sources; so this arabesque art is the ground on which all later arts of peoples known to Islam have grown. (My translation)

Herzfeld's elaboration of these points and further analysis of the Samarra stucco dadoes, 10–14, is essential reading on the beveled style.

24 Ettinghausen, "The Beveled Style," passim.

25 A development of ideas put forward by Riegl in *Die spätrömisches Kunst-Industrie nach den Funden in Österreich-Ungarn*, vol. 1 (Vienna, 1901). Ettinghausen, in a posthumously published article, scouted both Late Antique and Central Asian sources for the beveled style and suggested instead Sassanian metalwork and seal rings: "Medieval Islamic Metal Objects of Unusual Shapes and Decorations in the Metropolitan Museum of Art," *Islamic Archaeological Studies* (Cairo) 1 (1978 [1982]): 27–77, including plates, at 31; see n. 32 giving an example in the British Museum: "A. D. H. Bivar, *Catalogue of the Western Asiatic Seals in the British Museum. Stamp Seals II. The Sassanian Period*, London,

1969, p. 143: Decorated Ellipsoids (shape II)." While this is an improvement on the argument from Central Asian metalwork (stated in modified form by Maurice Dimand, "Studies in Islamic Ornament, II. The Origin of the Second Style of Samarra Decoration," *Archeologia Orientalia in Memoriam Herzfeld*, ed. Miles, 62–68), it still preserves the fundamentally mistaken notion that small objects are plausible sources for architecture.

26   Cf. also Herzfeld, "Genesis," and esp. "Mshattā, Ḥīra and Bādiya: Die Mittelländer des Islam und ihre Baukunst," *Jahrbuch der preuszischen Kunstsammlungen* 42 (1921): 104–46, esp. 138–40. Herzfeld saw the Mushattā decoration as descended from Assyrian orthostat reliefs (*Wandschmuck,* 2), and this is doubtless true in a sense. But there were, of course, intermediaries, and not only in northeastern Mesopotamia, as Herzfeld believed.

27   Herzfeld, "Mshattā, Ḥira und Bādiya," fig. 14.

28   First published by Richard Stillwell in *The Excavations 1937–1939,* vol. 3 of *Antioch-on-the-Orontes,* 5 vols. in 6 (Princeton, N.J., 1934–72), 169–70 and pl. 42, no. 231; more recently in Weitzmann, *Age of Spirituality,* 667–68. The piece has also been published, I believe mistakenly, as a pilaster capital by J.-P. Sodini et al., "Dénès: Campagnes I–III (1976–1978), recherches sur l'habitat rural," *Syria* 57 (1980): 1–304, fig. 302 (cf. also the useful comparative material). Thus Herzfeld's Samarra comparison, far from deriving its design from Mushattā, actually documents an earlier, Late Antique format of dado decoration not preserved in the extant material, which also appears at Mushattā, where it was embellished with antique architectonic elements that probably did not exist in the prototype. For architectural stone fragments related to both the Church of St. Polyeuctos and the Antioch fragment, see Otto Feld, "Bericht über eine Reise durch Kilikien," *Istanbuler Mitteilungen* 13–14 (1963–64): 88–107, esp. 91–92, 106, pl. 43, 4–6, and cf. pl. 46, 4, all dated between 550 and 650 on stylistic grounds.

29   The example illustrated is from Tunisia; one might compare a later painted dado excavated at Nishapur (Metropolitan Museum of Art 40.170.176, illus. as fig. 29 in Walter Hauser and Charles K. Wilkinson, "The Museum's Excavations at Nīshāpūr," *Bulletin of the Metropolitan Museum of Art* 37, no. 4 [April 1942]: 83–119) in which the left-hand panel is a rather distant imitation of veined marble. For earlier painted imitations of marble dadoes, see Lavin, "The Ceiling Frescoes in Trier," 108.

30   Eva Hoffman, "The Emergence of Illustration in Arabic Manuscripts: Classical Legacy and Islamic Transformation" (Ph.D. diss., Harvard Univ., 1982), documents a revival of antiquity in manuscript illustration that roughly parallels the architectural revival. For Harran see K. A. C. Creswell, *Early Muslim Architecture,* 2 vols. (Oxford, 1932–40, vol. 1 rev. and pub. in 2 parts, 1969). On Diyarbakir, Max van Berchem, Josef Strzygowski, and Gertrude Bell, *Amida* (Heidelberg, 1910), is still the basic source. The architectural tradition that encompasses the classical revival is described in Terry Allen, *A Classical Revival in Islamic Architecture* (Wiesbaden: Ludwig Reichert, 1986).

31   See Cyril Mango, "Byzantinism and Romantic Hellenism," *Journal of the Warburg and Courtauld Institutes* 28 (1965): 29–43.

PART IV

Models for a New Present: The *Qurʾān*

CHAPTER 12

The ʿAbbasid Dawla: An Essay on the Concept of Revolution in Early Islam

JACOB LASSNER

Following three decades (A.D. 718–47) of clandestine revolutionary activity, the descendants of the Prophet's uncle al-ʿAbbās co-opted a provincial insurrection, overthrew the dynasty that had displaced the Prophet's family from power, and established a political order that would endure for half a millennium.[1]

Contemporaries referred to the advent of the ʿAbbasids as the *dawla,* a word Arabic lexicographers endowed with a wide range of meanings, including a turn that signifies dramatically changed times or fortunes. By extension it also came to mean a turn at rule, and only later, probably in the tenth century, a dynastic polity.[2] For the ʿAbbasids and their early adherents *dawla* meant, more specifically, a turn of the wheel of fortune resulting in total victory over their predecessors, the house of Umayya, and concurrent with that triumph the formation of an entirely new order. The *dawla* was no rebellion of ambitious kinsmen displacing close relatives in search of their own gain. Nor was it a coup of restless praetorians seeking personal aggrandizement at the expense of established rulers. No parochial interests were championed. No simple rotation of palace occupants was anticipated. Eagerly awaited by a significant cross section of Islamic society, the onset of ʿAbbasid rule, true to its underlying conception, was looked upon by contemporaries as a substantive and dramatic break with the recent past.

Such expectations of change were reflected in ʿAbbasid apologetics and in formal gestures made by the new rulers.[3] Advocates of the dynasty thus proclaimed the era of the Banū ʿAbbās in hyperbolic language rich in metaphor and heavily spiced with apocalyptic symbols. In response, the ʿAbbasid sovereigns adopted regnal titles suggesting that the messianic age was at hand and that they were the chosen instruments of this manifest destiny.[4] The new Commanders of the Faithful deliberately cultivated images that made them larger than their Umayyad predecessors, if not life itself—in short, images that were

well suited to an age of exaggerated expectations. A shrewd observer of the
incipient regime likened the ʿAbbasid caliph to a man riding a lion to power, a
leader who in the eyes of his subjects could move mountains from their place.
Even if the caliph were to order a change in the orientation of prayer (away
from Mecca), this observer thought that the ʿAbbasid legions would follow
him blindly.[5] As fate would have it, the ʿAbbasids were not called upon actually to ride lions or restructure massive geological formations or change the
time-honored direction of worship. But the capacity to inspire belief that the
caliph could transcend the laws of nature and religion would have been remarkable in and of itself. The author was, no doubt, given to exaggeration,
and the picture of the caliph riding a wild beast to power was clearly a rhetorical device. However, neither hyperbole nor metaphor can disguise what should
have been obvious. There was little question of the caliph's capacity, and even
less question of his intention, to alter irrevocably the political landscape.

Broadly speaking, the expectations of decisive change were fulfilled by ensuing events. The exemplary fashion in which the new rulers attempted to
eradicate every last vestige of the Umayyad house was unprecedented in the
experiences of the Faithful.[6] There had been assassinations, random killings,
and even executions, but never before had it been the declared policy of
an Islamic ruler to exterminate an extended Muslim family, much less one
of Meccan origins. The Banū Umayya, leaders among those opposing the
Prophet, had been granted pardons when he returned to Mecca in triumph.
Similarly, Muʿāwiya, the founder of the Umayyad dynasty, guaranteed safety
to the family and allies of his rival, the Prophet's son-in-law ʿAlī b. Abī
Tālib—this after six years of extremely bitter civil strife. In both instances
blood spilled in rage was not allowed to serve as a cause of further bloodshed.
The interests of the larger community demanded cool attitudes and continued
forbearance; the need was to heal wounds past and present and set the stage
for future accommodation.[7]

In contrast, the ʿAbbasids pursued the last Umayyad ruler, Marwān II, as
they would have hunted an animal. And having caught up with Marwān as he
fled, they killed him and then mutilated him beyond recognition.[8] When Abū
al-ʿAbbās, the newly proclaimed ʿAbbasid caliph, received the severed head
of his adversary, he found it emptied of contents and stripped clean. Nothing
remained in the cavity except a small snake that undulated its way through
sockets where eyes and mouth had been.[9] Not content with having made an
example of the Umayyad sovereign, the ʿAbbasids rounded up the leading notables of the former ruling house and executed the lot. One version of this
event indicates that the Umayyads had been invited to Abū al-ʿAbbās' table to
partake of his food and company. Disarmed by this amicable gesture, the invited guests soon learned the caliph's true purpose. A literate prince among
them deciphered the cryptic verses of the poet Sudayf, who pronounced their

death sentences as part of the entertainment; the others, spared briefly by their lack of sophistication, discovered Abū al-'Abbās' intentions only with the appearance of the executioners. When the true purpose of the meal was fulfilled, mats were laid over still-warm bodies and the caliph calmly sat down to his dinner, entertained by a chorus of moans from the wounded and maimed who had not yet succumbed.[10]

It is doubtful that this macabre story portrays accurately the details of that fateful last supper, but the reported savagery of the 'Abbasids toward their predecessors clearly captured the mood of the occasion and the changing times. Even the dead were not spared; having disposed of the living, the 'Abbasids violated the graves of the Umayyad caliphs. Like the head of Marwān, the family cemetery was emptied of its contents and stripped clean. Only the pious 'Umar II, the so-called Best of the Banū Umayya, who had been kindly in his dealings with the Prophet's family, was allowed to repose as he had been buried.[11] It was as though a defiled body politic had been given a purgative and, in consequence, had eliminated all traces of the Umayyad usurpers.

The annihilation of the leading Umayyads was but the first step in many changes to come. With unexpected swiftness the Prophet's kinsmen set about transforming an Islamic state that had been narrowly based on Arab privilege and beset by tribal xenophobia into a broadly based polity aspiring to universal outlook and recognition. A detailed analysis of this transformation can be found elsewhere. Suffice it to say that viewed *in toto* the restructuring of society attempted by the 'Abbasids seems radical and far-reaching. Whether one speaks of new networks of social relationships, a complete overhaul of the military structure, innovations in provincial administration, or the creation of a highly centralized and massive bureaucracy, encased by monumental architecture and reflected in lavish court ceremonial, the changes instituted by the 'Abbasids represent an ambitious departure from both the style and the substance of Umayyad rule.[12] In this sense at least, Arabic *dawla,* derived from a root meaning "to turn" or "come about," is the semantic equivalent of the English word *revolution,* which since the Renaissance has come to mean political upheaval as well as rotation. One could add parenthetically that this is a rare case in which the translation of Arabic political vocabulary into European languages enhances comprehension more than it distorts meaning.

THE 'ABBASID *DAWLA* AS IRANIAN REVIVAL

As a rule, historians should be cautious when using heavily charged terms and value-laden concepts of a more recent age to analyze events and institutions far removed in time and place. In choosing a familiar vocabulary, they may inadvertently shape the past in the light of their own experiences and parochial interests, creating thereby a picture of men and events that is at best misleading. Modern scholars may be quite correct in describing the advent of the 'Abbasids as a revolution, but many of them have tended to misread the broader significance of the *dawla*.

Until quite recently investigators concerned with the formation of 'Abbasid political institutions tended to rely on a flawed conventional wisdom derived from European scholarship of the nineteenth century. Many orientalists of that age tailored their data to fit a conceptual framework strongly influenced by the growth of nationalism and current theories of race and society.[13] They therefore depicted the emergence of the 'Abbasid dynasty as the culmination of a long struggle between the "Arab kingdom" of the Umayyads and the conquered population of a shattered Iranian Empire. Or, put somewhat differently, the conflict they perceived was between a ruling institution predicated on the special privilege of a relatively small Arab aristocracy and an Iranian populace disadvantaged by Arab rule. According to this view, the disadvantaged Iranians coalesced into a broadly defined revolutionary force whose outlook and ethnic origins were largely rooted in the former Sassanian provinces to the east—that is, in the districts known collectively as Khurāsān.

An exaggerated emphasis was thus given to the role played by the indigenous population of Khurāsān during the years of clandestine operations and, especially, during the open revolt that followed. Moreover, concurrent with this enlarged role for the native Khurāsānīs there developed the rather seductive notion that Islamic government became increasingly Iranized under the 'Abbasids. For in order to ensure the continued support of the eastern provinces, and more particularly the Khurāsān army, the sovereigns of the 'Abbasid realm, who were themselves Arabs, responded sympathetically to the echoes of an Iranian past. The demand for radical change was thus tempered by the need if not the necessity to look backward. Seen in this light, the revolutionary triumph heralded the creation of a new order in which narrowly defined political structures of Arab origins were replaced by revived Iranian institutions. The Arab kingdom therefore gave way to a polity still led by Arabs, but more universal in outlook and composition.

At the extreme, such views led to the picture of an 'Abbasid state that was essentially a new Iranian empire, albeit one dressed in the formal attire of a Persianized Islam. Throwing caution to the winds, one could argue that— from this perspective at least—the early 'Abbasid state might be considered the last political order of Late Antiquity. Although no formal consensus emerged among these modern scholars about whether this picture of the revolution suited their notions of progress, one can detect sympathies that seem to echo a bias favoring the new regime.[14] One has the feeling that, given the values of the age, some nineteenth-century scholars may have preferred nationalist spirit to foreign domination, or the universalism of the Iranian peoples to the particularism of the Arabs. There were also possibilities for cruder formulations. Being Aryans, the Persians might have seemed more admirable than the Arabs, who were Semites, although, to be sure, the former would have been considered inferior to the Aryan inhabitants of the European milieu.

Cautious scholars described the Arab contribution to the ideological and military struggle against the Umayyads and recognized that the ʿAbbasids, whose cause was embraced by the populace, were themselves blood relatives of the Prophet, the most distinguished Arab of all. Nevertheless, even such a meticulous and sensitive researcher as J. Wellhausen could not resist concluding that "under the guise of International Islam, Iranianism triumphed over the Arabs." [15] Although the author's following remarks imply that he had no clear idea of what this statement meant in substantive terms, the apparent sentiments embodied in this statement and others like it took on a formulaic significance, and the alleged Iranization of ʿAbbasid rule was generally regarded as orthodox doctrine by subsequent generations of scholars. [16] Even those who preferred the "manly, frugal, and hardy Arabs" felt it necessary to acknowledge that the ʿAbbasid revolution signified the triumph of Persian arms and ideals. [17]

Any search for influences that invokes memories of ancient Iran should be treated with much caution, as more often than not the attribution of eastern origins serves only to explain the obscure by that which is still more obscure. Although this methodology retains a certain compelling attraction, it does not make for a tight analysis of the events in question, and, indeed, it has recently come under critical review. Revisionist historians, armed with hitherto unknown sources, have attacked the idea of a native uprising against the Umayyads in Khurāsān, with all that this implies for the alleged creation of an Iranian style of government under the early ʿAbbasids. Present conceptualizations dramatize instead the critical role of eastern-based Arab tribal armies in the ʿAbbasid victory and, at the same time, emphasize the intricate development of ʿAbbasid political ideology in the context of early Shiʿism, a movement deeply rooted in the Arab past. [18] It is recognized that the Iranized Arab settlers in the villages of Khurāsān played a role disproportionate to their numbers in directing the military and administrative affairs of the emergent regime, but these partially assimilated elements of local society are viewed as retaining their Arab identity. Moreover, the settlers' conception of the struggle between the new order to come and the entrenched Umayyad state was firmly based on the events of an earlier Islamic history. The revolutionary mandate, as they understood it, was to restore the Islam that had existed in the time of the Prophet, and not to reverberate to the echoes of a dim foreign past. Although this does not preclude a susceptibility to lingering Persian influences, a deliberate restoration of Iranian institutions in the nascent ʿAbbasid state seems highly problematic at best. Readers of the historical literature, early

Islamic as well as modern Western, will have enough trouble finding a firm link between Iranian ideals and those who brought the ʿAbbasids to power, let alone a connection between the revolution and the alleged Iranization of government that was said to follow. The concept of *dawla* implied dramatic change, but no changes in favor of Iranization were contemplated by the ʿAbbasid revolutionaries nor were any carried out by their immediate successors.

The presumptive case for a revolutionary ideology that drew upon Iranian sentiments and heterodox beliefs has been based largely on evidence obtained from the Arabic heresiographers. However, the authors of this genre had a vested interest in dramatizing the impact and distribution of "extremist" views. The sources describe a process of fragmentation and proliferation among a bewildering variety of sects and subsects, many of which seem to be, and indeed might have been, indistinguishable from one another. On the whole, the picture of extremist groups opposed to the Umayyads seems rather confused and raises many more questions than it answers. Was there a floating constituency of revolutionaries who appeared at different times under different names, or were there discrete groups of disciplined sectarians? Were practices and beliefs broadly based or confined to a limited following? Can the extremist tendencies described by the heresiographers be traced back to established systems of belief that flourished in an earlier political setting? Or, to put it somewhat differently: Is there any indication that Iranian influence was widespread among those fanning the embers of revolution? And if it was spread among groups of potential rebels, would the ʿAbbasids have encouraged such views during the clandestine or active phases of their own revolution? Would they have continued to do so after the Prophet's family was returned to power? Above all, was this extremist activity linked by nationalist sentiments and perceived by contemporaries as having a decisive influence on the course of events?[19]

With questions of this sort in mind, one is obliged to focus on the Rāwandīya, a shadowy group of ʿAbbasid supporters originally from Khurāsān.[20] It seems that the Rāwandīya were drawn to the doctrine of metempsychosis, which had a particular appeal among the contemporary proto-Shiʿites, and that they eventually linked this concept to an ʿAbbasid eschatology. They thus believed that the transmigration of souls (*tanāsukh al-arwāḥ*) specifically defined ʿAbbasid claims to rule. A propagandist called al-Ablaq (as fate would have it, a leper, who spoke in hyperbole) maintained that the spirit (*rūḥ*) attached to Jesus passed on to the Prophet's son-in-law ʿAlī b. Abī Ṭālib and then, successively, to several divine figures, until it came to rest with the ʿAbbasid patriarch and revolutionary leader Ibrāhīm b. Muḥammad. Like other radical Shiʿite groups, the Rāwandīya also espoused extreme libertine views and thus felt free to indulge in acts that were not permissible (*istaḥallū al-ḥuramāt*). As if to reinforce this last point, al-Ablaq combined the new reli-

gious sentiments with traditional Near Eastern hospitality and invited his colleagues to partake of his food, his drink, and, not least, his wife. The Umayyad
authorities who were charged with the defense of public morality and order
were, however, more conventionally inclined, and the Rāwandī and his followers were killed and their bodies hung in public display.

The lamentable fate that befell this group did not, however, write an end to
the saga of the Rāwandīya. With the rise of the ʿAbbasids, a branch of the sect
turned its attention to the new order; and Ibrāhīm's brother, the caliph Abū
Jaʿfar al-Manṣūr, took his turn as the object of their veneration. It was perhaps
inevitable that the Rāwandīya should have come to visit "their Lord" in order
to receive food and drink at his court in the capital. Although there is no indication that they wished to express their deep-felt convictions by partaking
also of the caliph's wives and concubines, their public acclaim of al-Manṣūr's
divinity, which was quite heretical, and their general behavior, which was
quite unruly, led to a serious altercation. Between leaping from the top of the
caliph's palace (perhaps in the hope of obtaining a better transmigration) and
liberating the prison in which their leaders had been quickly and quite under-
standably incarcerated, the overzealous Khurāsānīs forced the entry of the security forces and the ensuing slaughter of their group.[21]

The references to extreme communalism that appear in accounts of the
Rāwandīya seem to suggest the kind of radical propaganda spread by the
ʿAbbasid agent (*dāʿī*) Khidāsh among the villagers of Khurāsān.[22] The circumstances of his career are, however, shrouded in mystery and confused by
contradictory traditions. In the end, the ʿAbbasid version made a point of dis-
crediting this early director of revolutionary activity in Khurāsān. The bill of
particulars against him included, among other things, that he advocated religious license, and that he endorsed certain extremist tendencies on behalf of
the ʿAbbasid patriarch without seeking the latter's approval. For his efforts
Khidāsh was seized by the local authorities and, after being brutally tortured,
was killed and crucified. However, other reports state that the ʿAbbasids themselves killed him, presumably because of his independent, if not heretical,
actions.

As with the Rāwandīya, the negative response of the ʿAbbasids to extremist
views—in both instances views that were expressed in support of their leadership—may be taken as an indication of ʿAbbasid attitudes during and after the
revolution. This is not to say that anti-Umayyad sentiments, no matter how
bizarre, could not have served the ʿAbbasid cause, or even received their indirect endorsement. There was nothing to prevent ʿAbbasid propagandists from
assuming a multitude of poses during the period of clandestine operations,
especially during its formative stages; they could then appear as all things to
all people. Moreover, the marriage of a radical outlook to an ʿAbbasid eschatology was not without advantages in an age of messianic expectations.

From this perspective, the extreme views held by certain sectarian groups regarding the violability of the inviolable should not be understood as a simple manifestation of excessive behavior. They may indeed refer to a much more pervasive concept, that of redemption through sin in preparation for the messianic age. In any case, there is no compelling evidence to link the sectarians and their beliefs with a resurgent Iranian nationalism.

Would it have made any difference if nationalist sentiments were indeed embedded in heterodox beliefs? The ʿAbbasids did not embrace the wide spectrum of proto-Shiʿite views nor, despite l'affaire Khidāsh, did they attack them forcefully. What the ʿAbbasids feared most during the clandestine phase of their activities was that their intentions would be disclosed prematurely, and, conversely, that their lack of militant activity would cause supporters to turn to more-militant opponents of the Umayyad regime. As a rule, the ʿAbbasids reacted toward extremism of any kind with great caution, lest they or their followers be implicated in an ill-conceived venture that was destined for failure. After the emergence of the dynasty, ʿAbbasid concern shifted dramatically and they worried about solidifying their hold on the diverse revolutionary constituencies that had brought them to power. Nevertheless, the watchword remained caution. Having become responsible for public order, the ʿAbbasid caliphs would hardly have permitted, let alone encouraged, views of extreme permissiveness. Excesses may have served some useful purpose in anticipation of the millennium, but as the ʿAbbasids came and the millennium did not, the current need was to discourage thoughts that could fire the imagination of disappointed activists—particularly those hotheads who might be inclined to go off in search of a more rewarding revolution. Once entrenched in power, the new dynasts dealt swiftly and severely with heterodox groups, including those who might have been earlier supporters of the cause. Needless to say, they were particularly severe with those whose activities were tinged with sedition, if not marked by open rebellion.[23]

Although quickly crushed by the imperial armies, several obscure and apparently inconsequential native uprisings in the eastern provinces were endowed with dramatic importance by later medieval and modern authors.[24] The picture they paint is that of native Khurāsānīs taking up arms against the new ʿAbbasid state after failed messianic expectations—in this case, expectations linked to an Iranian revival, and perhaps even the replacement of traditional Islam with a syncretistic national religion. The insurrections are thus seen as the cutting edge of widely held nationalist sentiments. A recent scholar goes a step further.[25] Echoing sympathy for a self-determination that is born of class consciousness, he depicts ʿAbbasid rule in the east as colonialist and a betrayal of revolutionary ideals. ʿAbbasid agents in Khurāsān thus "precipitated a true mass revolt by exploiting the traditional antagonism between the Khurāsānī peasant and feudal classes to the advantage of the new 'Muslim' [read

ʿAbbasid] urban and military/landowning (or controlling) elite.'' [26] Choosing a vocabulary that, if nothing else, is highly charged, he further describes the local rebels, about whom precious little is known, as a sort of national liberation front for Khurāsān. Despite the considerable learning that is evident throughout his weighty argument, this historiography should be recognized for what it actually is: the conceptual residue of more-recently proposed models of revolution and revolutionary change. That this view has much in common with the orientalist outlook of the nineteenth century is deliciously, if unintentionally, ironic.

Given the uncertainty that surrounds early Islamic history, let us assume, for the sake of argument, that a revolutionary ideology, permeated by Iranian beliefs and fueled by local anti-Arab sentiments, in fact took root in the districts of Khurāsān. Would such an ideology have electrified the ʿAbbasid revolutionary army, and would it have subsequently influenced the caliphs when they were called upon to shape the nascent ʿAbbasid state? That is to say, might there have been an Iranization of Islamic government as a result of pressures brought to bear against the reigning dynasts by the very instruments of their control?

The indigenous Khurāsānīs, who as a group lacked experience in warfare as well as personal loyalty to the ʿAbbasid family, are not prominently mentioned among the contingents of the revolutionary army. But the Arab settlers of the seventh century ardently supported the revolutionary cause and were represented in the ranks by a disproportionately high number of field commanders and political operatives. Sent from Iraq to Khurāsān, these Arabs settled in the local villages and became assimilated, in many respects, to their new environment. They married with the local populace, accommodated themselves to local customs, and even lost the capacity to speak good Arabic, feeling more at ease instead with a bastardized language or dialect known as *lughat* or *lisān* (*ahl*) Khurāsān, "the language" or "speech of [the men of] Khurāsān." Occasionally, in the heat of battle, troops of the revolutionary army are quoted by the chroniclers as speaking some form of Persian to one another. An erosion of tribal sensibilities among the older settlers seems to have created some sense of regional loyalty. There were contingents of the army who may have identified themselves not only as Arabs but also as Khurāsānīs. When the formal structure of the revolutionary army was established, the old settlers received their service pay according to a military roll arranged by village rather than by tribal affiliation. [27]

Given these circumstances, might the older settlers have been susceptible to the same revolutionary ideology that allegedly motivated the native inhabitants of the region—that is, the indigenous population whose displeasure with Arab rule exceeded their capacity to take action? However seductive this line of enquiry might be for scholars wedded to earlier conceptions, it does not fit the facts as we now know them. There is at present no reason to suppose that the partially assimilated Arabs who joined the rebellion against Umayyad rule did so in order to restore Iranian privileges, let alone to establish a political order that conjured up fond memories of an Iranian empire. On the contrary, the old settlers, who were represented by a large number of commanders and political activists (*naqīb*) were so privileged because of their early and sustained commitment to the 'Abbasid house. This was, as we shall see, a commitment rooted in an Islamic and, more particularly, an Arab past.

As a group, the old settlers contributed much more to the military success of the revolution than did the indigenous Khurāsānīs, but even a mixed force of old settlers and native villagers would not have been able to overthrow the local Umayyad authorities, let alone defeat the battle-tested imperial armies under the command of such able generals as 'Āmir b. Dubāra and Nubāṭa b. Ḥanẓala. The settlers no doubt retained some martial skills, but on the whole they could not be relied upon as first-rate soldiers, for they had long ceased to function as cohesive military units in the employ of the state. To defeat the Umayyads, the 'Abbasids had to find an army capable of undertaking an extended campaign in a highly disciplined and professional manner. They did this by co-opting the tribal soldiers of the east, who were among some forty to fifty thousand Arab tribesmen brought to Khurāsān in the eighth century to fight in the campaigns of Qutayba b. Muslim. This was a force that honed its fighting skills in yearly forays along the frontier—that is, when the tribesmen did not fight among themselves or with the local authorities. Only the support of these divisive regular forces enabled the 'Abbasids to triumph on the field of battle. And lest one forget, this was an army of Arabs, led by Arabs and organized along Arab tribal lines. Only much later, when the Khurāsān army was resettled in Iraq, primarily at the new capital, Baghdad, did these regiments cease to function as discrete tribal units.[28]

Can one seriously believe that the tribesmen who came to Khurāsān in the eighth century would have been responsive to Persian influence shortly thereafter, and that in turn they would have exerted pressure on the 'Abbasids to reintroduce institutions of a glorious Iranian past? On the whole, the tribal armies seemed to lack ideological fervor. At the outset of their involvement with the revolution, they had no real commitment to the 'Abbasid family. Certainly there had been no long-standing tie to the 'Abbasid cause. Indeed, when the tribesmen first took up arms for the revolution, it was in support of an unnamed leader, the so-called preferred one from the house of the Prophet.[29] Hopelessly divided, the tribal units succumbed to skillful political (and financial) manipulations that drew them and the other rebels together against common enemies: the local Umayyad authorities, rival tribesmen, and those regiments of the Umayyad standing army currently stationed in Khurāsān.

Facing the formidable Umayyad forces, the professional soldiers of the revolution, who later formed the military backbone of the 'Abbasid state, were seemingly less impressed with political doctrine than with the pragmatic elements of their newly established relationship with the revolutionary leadership: namely, regular service pay and patronage dispensed to the mutual benefit of the army and its patrons. Early and sustained military successes are thus more likely to have enhanced esprit de corps among the forces co-opted by the revolutionary leadership than any ideological pronouncements of the ʿAbbasid propagandists. There was nothing particularly Iranian about the pragmatic concerns of the tribal armies, nor is there any evidence to link the tribesmen with nationalist sentiments tinged with an anti-Arab bias.

A string of victories brought the Khurāsān army to Iraq, and eventually the soldiers were settled in the military cantonments of the new ʿAbbasid capital, Baghdad.[30] Transplanted from the east into an alien environment, the mixed forces that made up the ʿAbbasid standing army strove for a new identity that would engender pride and create a sense of unity that transcended the narrowly defined affiliations of the past. They found this identity by recalling events and places associated with the ʿAbbasid era. Thus the first generation of Khurāsānīs born in Iraq referred to themselves as the "sons [*abnāʾ*] of the *dawla*" or the "sons of the revolutionary calling [*al-daʿwa*]." With evident pride, they pointed to Khurāsān as the root (*aṣl*) of their lineage, that is, the region from which the ʿAbbasid revolution burst forth to bring about a new age. However, if Khurāsān was the root, then Baghdad, the so-called Khurāsān of Iraq, was the branch (*farʿ*). The *Abnāʾ* considered themselves more firmly rooted in the *dawla* than their fathers and more a part of it than their grandfathers. The expression "more rooted" (*aʿraqu*) appears to be a play on words to indicate more Iraqi, that is Baghdadi, for it is the tie with the ʿAbbasid capital and hence the caliphs themselves that allowed the *Abnāʾ* to claim their distinction.[31]

In this case the heavy, indeed almost exclusive emphasis on a newly acquired geographical affiliation is a clear sign of muted tribal sensibilities. There is, in fact, not a single topographical description of Baghdad that shows firm evidence of military cantonments organized along Arab tribal lines. The sources suggest that the full transformation from tribal to regional and then imperial army was accomplished within a single generation—an exemplary sign of the profound changes brought about by the ʿAbbasid *dawla*.[32] However, in no way does this dramatic change from tribal to imperial force suggest an Iranization of military structure or a resurgence of Iranian national feeling. Such as it was, the loyalty of the ʿAbbasid army was governed by highly personalized ties that generally transcended ideological concerns.[33] The *Abnāʾ* themselves put it succinctly: "We recognize only them [the ʿAbbasids] and will [allow ourselves to] be recognized only by them."[34] This is not to say that the ruling family did not attempt to indoctrinate the armed forces with official views, or that the latter were totally unreceptive to any such program. The legitimacy of the ʿAbbasids was certainly defended on ideological grounds, but these arguments were always rooted in an Arab and Islamic past.

THE *DAWLA* AS ISLAMIC REVIVAL

For all the emphasis on radical change suggested by the term *dawla,* the central theme of ʿAbbasid propaganda, before and after the revolution, was the regeneration of Islamic society by returning to the ethos of an earlier age.[35] The reference is not to the era of an Iranian empire but to the halcyon days of early Islam when the Prophet himself guided the community of the Faithful. The far-reaching changes that completely overturned the existing political and social order thus tend to mask another meaning of *dawla,* a meaning that extends beyond the semantic range of revolution when it is used as a political term. As regards the ʿAbbasids, *dawla* had the additional nuance of a historical process that had come full cycle. Simply put, it was the Islamic past and not visions of a radically new future that shaped the political outlook of Muslims during the formative years of the ʿAbbasid regime.

There is, perhaps, no text where this signification is explicit, but it is implied throughout the historiography of the period. Even as they promoted the onset of a new era, apologists for the recently established dynasty focused their attention on events of earlier Arab-Islamic times. Beginning with a survey of Mecca on the eve of Islam, and continuing through the revolution, they carefully searched the past record for inspiration, guidance, and above all evidence of their patron's legitimacy. Arguments thus linked the forebears of the ʿAbbasids, and also those of their opponents and would-be opponents, to events of dramatic importance that were indelibly etched in the historical consciousness of contemporary Muslims. It was intended, of course, that the performances of the ʿAbbasid ancestors should be seen as authentic models of proper moral and political behavior, and conversely that the ancestors of their opponents should be found lacking. In such fashion the past became the standard by which the chroniclers of the Banū ʿAbbās measured the family against its principal rivals and interpreted the dynasty's rise to power for contemporaries and generations of Muslims yet unborn.

The paradigm adopted by the dynastic historians was, in essence, quite simple: The ʿAbbasid family was made the most fitting analogue to their kinsman the Prophet, and the recently proclaimed age of the ʿAbbasids was heralded as a return to the days of the proto-Islamic community. The ʿAbbasid era was thus seen as the mirror image of a time when God's Messenger presided over the affairs of the Muslims. The Prophet's authority had been unquestioned among his Muslim contemporaries, and the community (*umma*) of his time was characterized by an Islam as yet unsullied by internal political strife. In any event, this was the idealized view of Prophet and *umma* that shaped historical consciousness for successive generations. But history often has a way of creating difficulties for those who invoke it on behalf of a partisan cause. The ʿAbbasid performance during the Umayyad interregnum— the ninety years in which the Prophet's family had been displaced from the leadership of the community—was unimpressive and elicited caustic comments from those who put a high premium on principle and personal courage. As a result, the revolutionary record of the ʿAbbasids often had to be rewritten, or at least reinterpreted, to make it consonant with the ideals and circumstances of an earlier age. More recent times were therefore recorded as if they were the exact images of the historic past. The perceptions occasioned by this revision of history ultimately blurred, and sometimes obliterated, distinctions between generations and events.

Citing the past to legitimate the present and future is commonplace. In this instance, circumstances forced the dynastic chroniclers to go a step further in their appeal to history. When the analogy to the past was clumsy—that is, when the evidence that could be drawn from historical precedents was inconclusive, if not totally inappropriate to contemporary ʿAbbasid claims—the apologists for the ruling house simply reversed the historiographical process. Returning to earlier periods, they again rewrote history; however, this time they recorded the past as a back projection of more-current events. As a result, critical moments of Islamic experience were idealized and then recorded as distant echoes of one another. At times, accounts of diverse periods are almost indistinguishable. The dramatic personae are interchangeable and their utterances tend to be variations of one another. The labels and organizational structures of loyal followers are almost, if not in fact, identical. Even the description of the external forces that shaped ʿAbbasid policy produces a sense of déjà vu.

Complex realities were thus endowed with a compelling, if highly artificial, sense of symmetry. It was as though the apologist-cum-historian threw stones into the turbulent waters of history, creating with each toss perfectly concentric circles. Again and again basic patterns were made to repeat themselves. In account after account, almost without variation, there are links, sometimes real but more often than not contrived, between the formative stages of Islam and later developments of political and religious importance. A piquant example of this stew of past and present is the account of an important ʿAbbasid mission to Khurāsān after the death of the aforementioned Khidāsh.[36]

It appears that the Khurāsānīs had grown restive. Two decades of clandestine activities had shown few results. Prehaps the time was now ripe to undertake an initiative of their own, or to look elsewhere for a new revolutionary leadership, one that was willing to take on the considerable challenge of removing the Umayyads. In order to forestall unwanted premature actions, or a possible slippage in support, the ʿAbbasid patriarch Muḥammad b. ʿAlī dispatched one of his most trusted emissaries, Bukayr b. Māhān, on a delicate mission to the east.[37] His task was to reconstitute the revolutionary apparatus in Khurāsān, thus giving the impression that a more active challenge to Umayyad rule was in the offing. The details of this episode are reported in the *Akhbār al-dawla,* a work generally characterized by its unblushing support for the ʿAbbasid cause.[38]

Bukayr's meeting with the Khurāsānīs—or to be more precise, the apologist's version of this meeting—clearly recalls descriptions of the Prophet's negotiations with the Medinese at the second (conclave of) al-ʿAqaba, an event that took place in Mecca in A.D. 622.[39] A first gathering between the Prophet and twelve Medinese had taken place the previous year, when the latter, who were visiting the holy city, pledged allegiance to God's Messenger according to an oath that merely invoked broad moral principles (*bayʿat al-nisāʾ*). During the pilgrimage of the following year, the Medinese, now numbering some seventy individuals from the tribes of the Aws and Khazraj, again met with the Prophet at the wooded area of al-ʿAqaba. This later meeting, reportedly conducted amid great secrecy, focused on a second oath. Serving as his nephew's spokesman, the Prophet's uncle al-ʿAbbās (the great-grandfather of the revolutionary Muḥammad b. ʿAlī) asked the Medinese to make a choice between a more specific commitment to his nephew or severing negotiations. When the Prophet, in turn, asked for their protection, the leader of the Medinese, stressing his people's long and meritorious service in combat, agreed enthusiastically.

According to tradition, this agreement heralded a major change in the policies of the Islamic community. Before the second conclave at al-ʿAqaba, God had not given the Prophet permission to fight or shed blood. He was thus ordered to endure insults and ignore provocations. His enemies, the oligarchs of Quraysh, persecuted his followers, causing some to abandon their faith and others to choose exile. All this was now changed. The second oath taken by the Medinese was not a restatement of broad moral principles, it was a pledge of war (*bayʿat al-ḥarb*). God had finally given the Prophet permission to enter into combat, and his Medinese supporters, the so-called *Anṣār,* were enjoined to help him in this effort, regardless of circumstances.

Abū al-Haytham al-Tayyihān, one of the Medinese, interrupted the proceedings and questioned the Prophet about his (that is, the Prophet's) commitment. He pointed out that, in answering the Prophet's call, his people would have to sever their ties with others, and wondered whether the Prophet would continue to remain with his new converts after God granted him victory. The Prophet answered that the new oath would be mutually binding and asked for twelve leaders (*naqīb,* pl. *nuqabāʾ*) to take charge of affairs at Medina. The *nuqabāʾ,* in turn, arranged for Muḥammad's acceptance among their brethren, paving the way for the hijra, the event that was to change the course of Islamic history. That is, ensconced at Medina with growing support, the Prophet was soon able to take the offensive against his long-standing opponents, the forebears of the Umayyad dynasts that his ʿAbbasid kinsmen would later seek to replace.

Any similarities between the two series of meetings (i.e., the Prophet and the Medinese during the pilgrimages of A.D. 621 and 622, and Bukayr and the Khurāsānīs the following century) may strike us as entirely coincidental; but the analogy between the Prophet at Mecca, shortly before the hijra, and the 'Abbasid patriarch's situation some 115 years later was not lost on Bukayr b. Māhān. In this highly tendentious account, the patriarch's emissary is portrayed as vividly recalling the second meeting at al-'Aqaba. Sent by Muḥammad b. 'Alī to revitalize support on behalf of the 'Abbasid leadership, Bukayr proposed a revolutionary apparatus that invoked memories of a glorious past.

He spoke to the Khurāsānīs of how the Prophet had chosen twelve leaders (*naqīb*) to organize his following in Medina. Then (as did al-'Abbās for his nephew) Bukayr gave his listeners the choice of accepting the imām or breaking off the negotiations. Acceptance in this case meant renewing allegiance to the 'Abbasid patriarch and, following a proposal set forth by Bukayr, establishing an organizational structure similar to the one employed by the Prophet. Like the Medinese before them, the Khurāsānīs are described as responding affirmatively and with enthusiasm. A so-called charter of the newly formed revolutionary units (which was dictated by Bukayr b. Māhān) thus recalled that "seventy men of the Aws and Khazraj met with the Prophet the night of al-'Aqaba and pledged allegiance to him; whereupon he appointed twelve leaders [*naqīb*] from among them." [40] The charter then affirmed that the way (*sunna*) of the Khurāsānīs was surely the *sunna* established earlier by the Prophet. Not surprisingly, Bikayr organized an inner council of twelve *nuqabā'*, chosen from a more inclusive group of seventy, and empowered them all to proceed with the business of planning a revolution. Keeping in mind the patriarch's reservations, he also enjoined them to observe the strictest caution, lest they disclose their intentions prematurely.

By describing the revolutionary apparatus according to a time-tested model, the apologist showed the 'Abbasids bestowing their supporters with the authority that had previously accrued to the agents chosen by God's Messenger. The historic past relived was thus meant to ensure Muḥammad b. 'Alī's legitimacy as well as that of those who took up his cause. Seen in retrospect, the 'Abbasid effort in Khurāsān mirrored the effort of their celebrated predecessors in Medina, guaranteeing thereby the eventual success of Bukayr's revolutionaries. The Prophet's triumph over the oligarchs of Quraysh and the 'Abbasid triumph over their descendants were intended to be seen as mirror images of one another.

This paradigmatic rendering of the past remained part and parcel of later Arabic historiography. A ninth-century litterateur, speaking of the virtues of the caliph's Khurāsānī forces—and through a Khurāsānī interlocutor, no less—preserves echoes of early 'Abbasid propaganda when he points out that there were in reality two groups known as "the supporters" (*al-Anṣār An-*

ṣārān).[41] The identity of the first group would have been clear to all his readers. These were the tribesmen of the Aws and Khazraj who coalesced to form *the* supporters, those who first protected the Prophet when he dwelt in their midst at Medina and then supported him in a subsequent campaign against his Meccan opponents. However, readers with strong historical memories would also have determined the identity of the second group referred to here as *Anṣār*. These were the ʿAbbasid revolutionaries from Iran, that mixed force of Arab tribesmen spoken of earlier, who coalesced to form the *ahl Khurāsān* and then swept the Umayyad descendants of the Qurayshite oligarchs from power. The Khurāsānī, or more correctly the author, puts it rather well: "The Aws and Khazraj supported the Prophet in the early days [*fī awwal al-zamān*] and the army of Khurāsān [*ahl Khurāsān*] will support his inheritors on the last day [*fī ākhir al-zamān*]." This reference to the end of time originally signified the long-awaited ʿAbbasid revolution that was to usher in the messianic era, when history would come full cycle and the pristine Islam of the early days would once again become manifest in the realm of the believers.

When the Khurāsānī goes on to claim that "the twelve agents [*nuqabāʾ*] are from us," he refers both to the twelve *nuqabāʾ* from the Aws and Khazraj, the agents established by the Prophet at Medina to facilitate his acceptance in that community, and to the twelve agents—also called *nuqabāʾ*—who, in the time of Muḥammad b. ʿAlī, fanned out into the various districts of Khurāsān to foment a rebellion that would once again bring the Prophet's kinsmen to power.[42] And when the Khurāsānī boasts, "We are the people of the moat and the sons of the people of the moat," he again refers to two events. The first is rooted in the age of the Prophet, when Salmān al-Fārisī, the original Islamic hero of Iranian origin, rescued victory from the jaws of defeat by suggesting that the Prophet dig a trench around the oasis of Medina. By doing this, the Prophet befuddled the opposing Meccan cavalry, who, having never experienced such a stratagem, were unable to solve the defenses arrayed before them. This was a critical moment in a series of great victories leading eventually to the capitulation of Mecca and the return of the Prophet's family, the Banū Hāshim, to preeminence in political affairs. Similarly, the latter-day Khurāsānīs dug moats around their encampments to signify the beginning of an active and successful resistance against Umayyad authority. Their defiant action was seen as heralding the emergence of the ʿAbbasid family, their triumph on the field of battle as bringing the ʿAbbasids to power, and their continued support as providing the backbone of the dynastic order.

REVOLUTION AS REENACTMENT OF THE PAST

One should not be misled by the concurrent privileging of past and present. Contrived as they are, the proposed links between actors and events of different eras are not always without foundation. In practice as well as theory, revolution was seen as a reenactment of the Islamic past. Earlier images and forms, particularly those that conjured up powerful memories, were consciously imitated in real life. If, for example, modern readers of the Arabic sources note obvious similarities between the ʿAbbasid effort to overthrow the Umayyads and the Prophet's struggle against the Umayyad forebears, the Qurayshite oligarchs of Mecca, it is because the ʿAbbasid operatives deliberately imitated the past in choosing their slogans, in constructing their revolutionary apparatus, and, more generally, in establishing an agenda for action.

Nor should one conclude that imitating the past was an exercise in which historical memories were cynically distorted and presented to a gullible public for political gain. To retrace the steps of the Prophet had an almost magical quality. A former truth proclaimed was a truth recreated. The strategies that led to previous triumphs were the guarantees of future success. It was as though invoking memories of the past was sufficient to overcome the most discouraging of contemporary obstacles. Moreover, the ruling family and its supporters were not alone in retracing the steps of the Prophet. The need to emulate God's Messenger was deeply embedded in the consciousness of contemporary Muslims and was endorsed by a broad cross section of society, including the main rivals of the new regime, the house of the Prophet's son-in-law ʿAlī b. Abī Ṭālib. One cannot overestimate the widespread effects occasioned by this way of viewing the world.

The behavior of the ʿAlid Muḥammad b. ʿAbdallāh al-Maḥḍ during his historic moment of crisis is a case in point.[43] Besieged in Medina and facing insurmountable odds, the ʿAlid rebel rejected the wise counsel of a trusted adviser. Rather than flee to Egypt where he could have raised an army, Muḥammad b. ʿAbdallāh chose instead to remain in the Prophet's city, and in order to contain an enemy force far superior to his own he gave orders to dig out the aforementioned trench that had given the Prophet victory more than a century earlier. Muḥammad b. ʿAbdallāh thus drew attention to his claim of having inherited the sacred authority of his namesake and blessed ancestor. But this alone would not explain his decision to remain and defend the city. He was surely aware that military tactics had evolved over the course of a century and that the method for breaching the kind of defensive position first suggested by Salmān to the Prophet was known to the commanders of the eighteen thousand men who encircled him.

It was this specific trench, highlighting concrete memories of the past, that could not be crossed. As if by magic the audacious plan that had repelled the Meccan alliance would save the current defenders of Medina from the superior force confronting them. Seeking a proper metaphor, Muḥammad b. ʿAbdallāh likened the Prophet's trench to impenetrable armor. Although his sentiments may have been entirely consistent with a lesson drawn from the early history of the Faithful, his decision to defend Medina ultimately proved disastrous. The enemy, no less respectful of the Prophet's past role, nevertheless laid planks across the barrier and then sent their cavalry charging into the city; Muḥammad b. ʿAbdallāh was dispatched shortly thereafter to a better world.

The eagerness of some ʿAlids for martyrdom may have struck a responsive chord among elements of the population, but the conspicuous failure of militant ʿAlid revolutionaries when confronting the Umayyads fully justified the quiet strategy opted for by the ʿAbbasid leadership—a strategy clearly designed for a long but successful campaign. For once control of the Islamic community was attained, it would always be possible to rewrite history and establish retroactively a more active role for the ʿAbbasids during the clandestine years of the revolutionary struggle. The ʿAbbasids therefore tended to be a good deal more circumspect than their ʿAlid cousins when applying the lessons of history. With their low profile during the long years of the clandestine struggle—a rather charitable way of describing their lack of revolutionary zeal—they sought images from the past that accentuated the need for prudent behavior. Patience was a virtue they readily proclaimed. They pointed out that the Prophet, and more particularly his less fortunate followers, had been subjected to numerous indignities over an extended period of time before the historic migration that led him to forsake Mecca for Medina. Even then he did not initially call for a military campaign against his enemies, the oligarchs of Quraysh. Such a request of his new supporters at Medina would have been inappropriate and counterproductive considering the preponderance of power that his enemies could bring to bear against them. A politically astute observer knows how to delay gratification and design a policy that discourages risky ventures for the sake of long-range gains.

There was no denying, however, that it was the military challenge that brought the Meccans to their knees and the Muslims to power. The ʿAbbasid propagandists were therefore in a quandary. Caution had its place, but memories of active resistance to an unwanted and illegitimate authority roused great fervor within the broad community of the Faithful. The ʿAbbasid leadership would not have been well served if their official chroniclers pictured them as less willing than their ʿAlid counterparts to stand up and be counted as active revolutionaries. A delicate balance was therefore required of ʿAbbasid apologists. The dynastic propagandists argued that the family leadership had indeed challenged the Umayyads politically, and on occasion had actually paid the price for confronting the ruling regime; but they sought to temper their resistance with caution, until that proper moment when a full-fledged revolt toppled the usurpers from power.

A semiofficial ʿAbbasid tract describes a conversation between a leading revolutionary agent (Bukayr b. Māhān) and the ʿAbbasid patriarch Ibrāhīm b. Muḥammad.[44] The event seemingly took place some five years after Bukayr's earlier mission to Khurāsān.[45] Once again, the eastern revolutionaries had grown restive. Indeed, they had urged the new ʿAbbasid patriarch to throw caution aside and take decisive action against the usurping Umayyads; so, apparently against his better judgment, the patriarch announced the year of the impending revolt. Although the designated rebellion was four years off, the leader of the ʿAbbasid family nevertheless ordered his loyal agent to carry black battle flags to the various revolutionary stations in Khurāsān, presumably to give them the feeling that a more militant stance had been taken. The choice of black, which was to become the official color of the revolution and then the dynasty, was obviously deliberate.[46] The account recalls a long history linking black to the Prophet's grandfather (who wore the color contesting the ancestors of the Umayyads for leadership in Mecca) and similarly to young David, who wore black when he went against Goliath (no doubt an analogue to the current Umayyad tyrants, who like Goliath seemed unbeatable). The author then points out that the Prophet's supporters at Medina, the aforementioned *Anṣār,* would also have covered themselves in black following the battle of Uḥud, where they suffered a serious setback at the hands of the Umayyad forebears, but they were dissuaded from doing so by the angel Gabriel, who indicated to the Prophet that the (latter-day) *Anṣār* and their ʿAbbasid patrons would be the ones to redeem all the sufferings of the past.

The tradition thus underscores the military preparations for the open revolt and the prediction of its ultimate success. There is, however, an additional message subtly embedded within this highly contrived account. As was customary among the Arab tribesmen, the wearing of black would have signified sentiments associated with calamitous occasions (*maṣāʾib*) and related to that, the desire for revenge. God's angel nevertheless suggested that the *Anṣār* put aside their garments for some future time when the wearing of black would give them strength, and hence victory. When asked about the black battle flags, he remarked that faith was better (for the present) than fragments of iron. The heavenly visitor was thus asking the Prophet's supporters to put aside the public expression of their feelings and delay gratification until the ʿAbbasid revolt. In essence, the militants among the ʿAbbasid supporters are portrayed as having been asked to follow the example of their predecessors and wait until the moment designated for them to fulfill this time-honored prophecy.

Such calls for patience could only have given rise to mixed emotions, particularly when the time seemed propitious to redress old grievances. This ambivalence over a proper course of action is seemingly reflected in the message conveyed to the Khurāsānīs by the patriarch's agent carrying the black flags. After recounting the episode of Gabriel and the *Anṣār,* the patriarch's emissary reportedly exclaimed to a gathering of local revolutionary agents, "Calamities [*maṣāʾib*] have continued to follow the family of the Messenger of God. Nevertheless the wearing of black will ultimately be approved of, so that the [revolutionary] factions [*ashyāʿ*] supporting the [Prophet's] family will attain their revenge."[47] The historical echoes preserved in similar accounts clearly illustrate the tension produced by the conflicting strategies of boldness and caution, and further suggest that these tensions were a continuing source of concern for the revolutionary leadership until the revolt was well under way and the victory assured.

The long-awaited triumph of the Prophet's family arrived in due course, but despite public expectations, the millennium did not. There was therefore the danger that some disappointed Muslims might undertake still another revolution on behalf of still another pretender from the Prophet's family. Taking stock of the situation, the ʿAbbasids reversed course. It was time to cool messianic ardor and advocate a return to political normalcy. The desire for stability, which was keenly felt throughout the realm, left its subtle imprint. *Dawla*, which had signified revolutionary change, became the "ʿAbbasid turn at rule," and ultimately when contemporaries spoke of the ʿAbbasid *dawla* they referred to a dynasty that continued for five stormy centuries. When the Mongols conquered Baghdad, sounding a death knell to the regime, the power that had been vested with the dynasts of the realm had long since passed to others outside the ruling family. And yet, although the ʿAbbasid caliph was no longer ruler de facto, many held it inconceivable that the body politic could exist without his formal presence. Clearly, failed messianic expectations did not lead to a new *dawla*.

Tradition has it that when the Mongol Hülegü planned to end the dynasty by executing the caliph al-Mustaʿṣim he was initially dissuaded from doing so by warnings that an act of such magnitude might tamper with the cosmic order of the universe.[48] The sun might be veiled, the rains might cease to fall, and the earth might fail to give rise to vegetation. Whether the grandson of Chingiz Khan actually experienced the dread mentioned in this tendentious account is of small concern. The point is, until this moment in history the presence of the caliph, no matter how chosen or how legitimate, had long been recognized by the majority of the Faithful as a prerequisite for established order. Rebellions against centralized authority were commonplace, but aside from an ʿAlid counter-caliphate in Egypt there had been no challenge to ʿAbbasid rule worthy of being labeled a *dawla*.

A sharp critic of the ʿAbbasids who saw all this in retrospect caught the full irony of the situation. Citing the former opponents of the regime, Ibn Ṭabāṭabā drew particular attention to the Buyids, the Seljukids, and the Khwārizm Shahs, all of whom dominated Baghdad while the ʿAbbasid caliph seemed powerless. However, the question of who holds power and how it is held can be subtle, if not puzzling, as the author indicates in a rather piquant aside:[49]

All of this [tribulation] and yet their [ʿAbbasid] rule continued. No dynasty was powerful enough to put an end to their rule and obliterate the traces of their existence. On the contrary, one of the aforementioned rulers would assemble and lead large armies before arriving at Baghdad. And when he arrived, he would seek an audience with the Caliph; and when admitted to the Caliph's presence, he would kiss the ground before him. His utmost wish was that the Caliph appoint him to some position and present him with a standard and the robe of honor. When the Caliph did that, the ruler would kiss the ground before him and walk astride the Caliph's stirrup, the latter's saddlecloth tucked under his arm.

Palace coups enabled Turkish praetorians to control various caliphs behind the scenes, military victories enabled the Buyids, Seljukids, and Khwārizm Shahs to dominate them more directly, but none dared tamper with society's expectations by replacing the ʿAbbasid caliph as ruler *de jure*. In this sense their triumphs on the field of battle and in court intrigues did not signify a *dawla*. Whatever power the conquerors of Baghdad wielded, the symbols of authority and the universal recognition that accompanied this authority were beyond their grasp.

A Buyid amīr reportedly spent much time studying the caliphal enclave in Baghdad in an attempt to emulate the physical surroundings of those designated Commanders of the Faithful. To that end he built his own palace complex, the magnificent Dār al-Mamlaka in the Mukharrim quarter of the capital.[50] But at the moment of his greatest triumph, and in full public view, the ruler de facto in Baghdad was, in accordance with protocol, asked to kiss the ground before his acknowledged sovereign. Given the impotence of the caliph in contrast to the real power at his own disposal, the amīr was first inclined to refuse. He yielded, however, for he was a man who fully appreciated the consequences of proper social, hence political, behavior. In the end, the only *dawla* this Buyid could aspire to was the honorific title granted him by the caliph: "ʿAḍud al-Dawla"—that is, the one who assists the ʿAbbasids in their turn at rule.[51] There is an additional paradox to ʿAḍud al-Dawla's behavior. The Buyids, themselves Shiʿites, had become the props upon which ʿAbbasid sovereignty had come to rest. It would seem that diverse elements of society had concluded that the body politic was better served by continuity than change, so strongly ingrained was the perceived need for symbols of political stability.

In the end, the murder of al-Mustaʿṣim and the brutal sack of Baghdad hardly occasioned cosmic disorder. The sun was not veiled; the rains did not cease; the earth did not refuse to yield its bounty. Indeed, the collapse of the ʿAbbasid caliphate in Baghdad did little at first to alter the daily course of politics and religion. However much it affected the public mood and the vivid imagination of historians, the immediate results of the Mongol conquest were hardly earthshaking. The grandson of Chingiz Khan found it necessary to return to Central Asia, and two years later the vanguard of his army was defeated trying to extend Mongol control to the west. Thus even Hülegü's great victory over the caliphate produced something less than a *dawla*, if we are to understand by that a cataclysmic upheaval followed by the universal recognition of a new ruling order.

NOTES

I have chosen to deal with this subject in the form of a lightly annotated essay. The essay draws heavily on two works of mine. For a larger view of early ʿAbbasid government and more detailed references to original sources see J. Lassner, *The Shaping of ʿAbbāsid Rule* (Princeton, N.J., 1980). The historiography of the ʿAbbasid revolution is discussed in *Islamic Revolution and Historical Memory,* American Oriental Series, Vol. 66 (New Haven, Conn., 1986), which was in preparation at the time of the conference.

1 The definitive history of the early ʿAbbasids is yet to be written. Indeed, with the sources currently available, it is not likely that a detailed descriptive history is possible. Useful surveys are: H. Kennedy, *The Early Abbasid Caliphate* (London, 1981); F. Omar, *The ʿAbbāsid Caliphate 132/750–170/786* (Baghdad, 1969)—a shortened version of the two-volume Arabic original *Al-ʿAbbāsiyūn al-awāʾil* (Beirut, 1970). For the revolution itself, see G. van Vloten, *De Opkomst der Abbasiden in Chorasan* (Leiden, 1890) and his *Recherches sur la domination arabe, le chiitisme et les croyances messianiques, sous le khalifat des Omayades* (Amsterdam, 1894); J. Wellhausen, *Das arabische Reich und sein Sturz* (Berlin, 1902) trans. M. G. Weir as *The Arab Kingdom and Its Fall* (Calcutta, 1927), 492–566; C. Cahen, "Points de vue sur la révolution Abbāside," *Revue historique* 230 (1963): 295–338; M. Shaban, *The ʿAbbāsid Revolution* (Cambridge, 1970); D. Dennett, "Marwān b. Muḥammad and the Passing of the Umayyad Caliphate" (Ph.D. diss., Harvard Univ., 1939); E. Daniel, *The Political and Social History of Khurasan under Abbasid Rule 747–820* (Minneapolis and Chicago, 1979), 25–72; T. Nagel, *Untersuchungen zur Entstehung des abbasidischen Kalifates* (Bonn, 1972); and esp. M. Sharon, *Black Banners from the East* (Jerusalem and Leiden, 1983), which is a partial translation of his Ph.D. diss., "Alīyat ha-ʿAbbāsīm la-sh-shilṭōn" (Hebrew Univ., 1970). The translation has a slightly altered format and contains much new information. Note also Lassner's *Islamic Revolution and Historical Memory.*

2 E.g., Ibn Manẓūr, *Lisān,* s.v. "*d-w-l*"; *EI²,* s.v. "*dawla*"; B. Lewis, "Islamic Concepts of Revolution," *Revolution in the Middle East,* ed. P. J. Vatikiotis (London, 1972), 25–26. See also Lewis, "On Revolutions in Early Islam," *Studia Islamica* 32 (1970): 215–31; Sharon, *Black Banners,* 22–27.

3 See Lassner, *Islamic Revolution and Historical Memory.*

4 B. Lewis, "The Regnal Titles of the First ʿAbbāsid Caliphs," in *Dr. Zakir Husain Presentation Volume* (New Delhi, 1968).

5 Ibn al-Muqaffaʿ, *Risāla fī al-ṣaḥāba* (Beirut, 1966), 347.

6 S. Moscati, "Le massacre des Umayyades dans l'histoire et dans les fragments poétiques," *Archiv Orientální* 18 (1950): 88–115.

7 Note the appreciation of Muʿāwiya's position in so strident an ʿAlid source as Ibn Ṭabāṭabā, *Fakhrī* (Beirut, 1966), 103ff.

8 See, e.g., Ṭabarī, *Annales,* ed. M. de Goeje et al., vol. 3, pt. 1, pp. 44ff.

9 For this incident see Ibn Ṭabāṭabā, *Fakhrī,* 148.

10 Ibid., 151. See also n. 6 above.

11 The role of ʿUmar II in ʿAbbasid eschatology is discussed in Lassner's *Islamic Revolution and Historical Memory*. For a survey of ʿUmar II's reign see J. Wellhausen, *Arab Kingdom*, 267–311; also see H. A. R. Gibb, "The Fiscal Rescript of ʿUmār II," *Arabica* 2 (1955): 1–16.

12 See Lassner, *ʿAbbāsid Rule*.

13 In particular Count Gobineau's influential *Essai sur l'inégalité des races humaines* (Paris, 1853–55).

14 The bias is most pronounced in the twentieth century among Western-trained Iranian scholars investigating the ʿAbbasid revolution. See M. Azizi, *La domination arabe et l'épanouissment du sentiment national en Iran* (Paris, 1938), 2–127; G. H. Sadighi, *Les mouvements religieux iraniens au IIᵉ et au IIIᵉ siècles de l'hégire* (Paris, 1938). The cause of Iranian nationalism has been taken up more recently by Daniel, *Khurasan under Abbasid Rule*, in particular 189ff.

15 Wellhausen, *Arab Kingdom*, 558.

16 Note B. Spuler's "Iran: The Persistent Heritage," in *Unity and Variety in Muslim Civilization*, ed. G. von Grunebaum, (Chicago and London, 1955), 167–81; and H. Massé, "Reconstitution d'une aristocratie iranienne," *Cahiers d'histoire mondiale* 1, no. 4 (1954): 815–26.

17 The view of Sir W. Muir, *The Caliphate* (London, 1898). That is, corrupted by the civilization around them the Arabs lost the capacity for rule.

18 See esp. Sharon, *Black Banners*, 231–38.

19 See van Vloten, *Recherches sur la domination arabe*, 48ff. M. G. S. Hodgson, "How Did the Early Shīʿa Become Sectarian?" *Journal of the American Oriental Society* 75 (1955): 1–13; M. W. Watt, *The Formative Period of Islamic Thought* (Edinburgh, 1973), 36–82; Cahen, "Points de vue"; and *EI²*, s.v. "Khurramiyya."

20 Ṭabarī, *Annales,* ed. M. de Goeje et al., vol. 2, pt. 3, p. 1953, and vol. 3, pt. 1, pp. 129ff. and 418–19; *Fragmenta historicorum arabicorum,* 227–28; Ibn Ṭabāṭabā, *Fakhrī,* 160–61. Dīnawarī, *Akhbār* (Leiden, 1888), 380; Yāqūt, *Muʿjam*, 6 vols. (Leipzig, 1866–73), 2:129–30; Ashʿarī, *Maqālāt*, 3 vols. Istanbul, 1929–33), 1:22–23; also A. B. Halkin's translation of Baghdādī's *al-Farq bayn al-firaq* (*Moslem Schisms and Sects,*) 2:74–75, 87–98.

21 The most detailed description of this event is in Ṭabarī, *Annales,* ed. de Goeje et al., vol. 3, pt. 1, pp. 129ff., 418–19.

22 *EI²*, s.v. Khidāsh; Lassner, *ʿAbbāsid Rule,* 111; Sharon, *Black Banners,* 165–74, 180–86, 189ff.

23 A survey of these activities is found in Daniel, *Khurasan under Abbasid Rule,* 78ff.

24 E.g., ibid., 90–93, 125–56. Daniel's conclusions are to be treated with considerable caution, as discussed below.

25 Ibid., esp. 189–200.

26 Ibid., 9.

27 For the composition of the revolutionary army see Sharon, "ʿAlīyat," 264–91, esp. 276–80.

28 The most detailed treatment of the military campaign is found in ibid., 206–60.

29 See M. Sharon, "The ʿAbbāsid Daʿwa Re-examined on the Basis of the Discov-

ery of a New Source," *Arabic and Islamic Studies* (Bar-Ilan Univ.) 1 (1973); and his *Black Banners*, 75.

30 The most recent treatment of ʿAbbasid military settlement is found in Lassner, *ʿAbbāsid Rule*, 139–62, 184–241.

31 Ibid., 129–36: Jāḥiẓ, *Manāqib*, in A. M. Hārūn, *Rasāʾil al-Jāḥiẓ*, 2 vols. (Cairo, 1964–65), 1:25–26.

32 Lassner, *ʿAbbāsid Rule*, 208–23.

33 Ibid., 102–15.

34 Jāḥiẓ, *Manāqib*, 26.

35 The theme of the *dawla* as Islamic revival is explored in great detail in Lassner's *Islamic Revolution and Historical Memory*.

36 See n. 22.

37 For this mission see Sharon, *Black Banners*, 183ff, who dates the event to A.H. 126. A rather different view of this event is found in Lassner, *Islamic Revolution and Historical Memory*, who dates it ca. A.H. 120. There is much confusion about this mission. It is likely that Bukayr was obliged to make a trip to the east on more than one occasion.

38 *Akhbār* (Beirut, 1971), 213ff.

39 For an ʿAbbasid version of Muḥammad's negotiations with the Medinese, see Ibn Hishām, *Sīra*, 2 vols. (Göttingen, 1858–60) vol. 1, pt. 1, pp. 293ff.

40 *Akhbār*, 215ff.; also Sharon, *Black Banners*, 191ff.

41 Jāḥiẓ, *Manāqib*, 15.

42 A general description of ʿAbbasid revolutionary movements in Khurāsān is found in Sharon, *Black Banners*, 155ff.

43 Ṭabarī, *Annales*, ed. de Goeje et al., vol. 3, pt. 1, pp. 227–28; Iṣfahānī, *Maqātil* (Teheran, 1365/1946), 267–68; Lassner, *ʿAbbasid Rule*, 69–79; T. Nagel, "Ein früher Bericht über den Aufstand des Muḥammad b. ʿAbdallāh im Jahre 145 h.," *Der Islam* 46 (1970): 227–62; *EI*, s.v. "Muḥammad b. ʿAbdallāh."

44 *Akhbār*, 240–42, 245–47.

45 See n. 37.

46 On the color black, see F. Omar, *ʿAbbāsīyāt: Studies in the History of the Early ʿAbbasids* (Baghdad, 1976), 148–54. This is derived from his somewhat lengthier article in Arabic, "Al-Alwān wa dalālatuhā al-sīyasīyah fī al-ʿaṣr al-ʿAbbāsī al-awwal," *Bulletin Faculty of the Arts* (Baghdad Univ.) 14 (1971): 827–36.

47 *Akhbār*, 247.

48 See Ibn Ṭabāṭabā, *Fakhrī*, 140ff.

49 Ibid., 142.

50 Regarding the palaces of the Buyid amīrs see J. Lassner, *The Topography of Baghdad in the Early Middle Ages: Text and Studies* (Detroit, 1970), 271.

51 Ṣābiʾ, *Rusūm* (Cairo, 1963), 31.

CHAPTER 13

Qur'anic Myth and Narrative Structure in Early Islamic Historiography

R. STEPHEN HUMPHREYS

Since the last decades of the nineteenth century, scholars have been at least generally aware of partisanship and ideological shaping in the textual sources for the first 150 years of Islamic history. In several works, Julius Wellhausen drew particular attention to the compilers of the late eighth and early ninth century who were the direct sources for our extant texts, composed roughly a century later. It is due to him that Abū Mikhnaf (d. 774), Sayf b. ʿUmar (d. ca. 800), al-Wāqidī (d. 823), and al-Madāʾinī (d. 855) became, so to speak, household names.[1] The purpose of Wellhausen's criticism was to locate the most authentic account, that one version of events that most accurately preserved the objective historical reality. In general, he seems to have taken little interest in the intentions and literary strategies of the later compilations through which we know these writers, apparently regarding them as relatively neutral repositories of historiographic fragments. On the other hand, he explicitly discounted the significance of the sources from which Abū Mikhnaf, Sayf, and others (all of whom lived at least a century after the events they recounted) had drawn their information; he was content simply to identify it as oral tradition, either tribal, factional, or theological in character.[2]

Until the past two decades, there was little advance in method or precision over Wellhausen, whose work in fact still shapes our understanding of the first Islamic century. But in the 1960s we began to see some major efforts to rethink the terms in which Arabic historical writing of the eighth and ninth centuries should be approached. Here it will suffice to mention only two especially significant contributions.

In *ʿAlī and Muʿāwiya in Early Arabic Tradition*, E. L. Petersen tries to trace the labyrinthine evolution of the principal narratives that recount the crucial years between the murder of ʿUthmān (656) and the abortive arbitration of the conflict between the pretenders ʿAlī and Muʿāwiya (658).[3] In spite of a number of significant errors, his work is extremely important.[4] Petersen suggests that the earliest traceable accounts go back only to the first quarter of the eighth century—that is, at least a half century after the events they purport to describe. (This dating is supported in the parallel field of ḥadīth studies by a recent study by G. H. A. Juynboll, who conducts his inquiry according to a different methodology and with a much more solid documentation.)[5] In addition, Petersen argues that later authors—including Wellhausen's favorite, Abū Mikhnaf—are only responding to or embroidering upon the primitive accounts. That is, the accounts composed in the late eighth and early ninth centuries have no independent evidentiary value. Following a line of argument first advanced by Ignaz Goldziher a century ago, Petersen links each of the accounts he discusses to current political circumstances and to some major religiopolitical orientations in early Islam.

In an important group of studies, Albrecht Noth looks at the constituent elements of early historical writing—the limited repertory of topoi, forms, and motifs that shape all the narratives transmitted to us by this literature.[6] His approach shows that the innumerable discrete narratives that make up early Islamic historiography can be interpreted as highly formalized set pieces. From this perspective, the supposedly historical accounts in our sources are properly literary fictions that have only a loose and indeterminate affiliation with the external reality they purport to describe.

Radical as their conclusions may be, however, Petersen and Noth are ultimately concerned with old issues: the authenticity of allegedly early reports, the factual accuracy of these narratives, and the influence of partisanship and ideology on Islamic historiography. In what follows, I would like to put aside the question of whether we can use this historical tradition to construct a valid picture of what really happened. Instead, I hope to identify the general interpretive frameworks that early Muslim historians used to lend form, cohesion, and meaning to the disparate and fragmented materials available to them. I thus hope to draw attention away from the earliest writers, whose work we know only indirectly, and even then in bits and pieces, and instead to focus on the historians of the late ninth and tenth centuries, whose works survive more or less in their original form. We will look in particular at three chronicles. These differ greatly in scale and structure but share certain basic attitudes toward the meaning of history: (a) al-Yaʿqūbī (d. 897), al-Taʾrīkh (Chronicle); (b) al-Masʿūdī (d. 956), Murūj al-dhahab wa-maʿādin al-jawhar (The Meadows of Gold and Mines of Jewels); and (c) al-Ṭabarī (d. 923), Taʾrīkh al-rusul waʾl-mulūk (The Chronicle of Prophets and Kings)—the largest and most influential of all.[7]

When these scholars set about reconstructing the history of early Islam, what historiographic models were available to them? Plainly they did not draw on the resources of late Roman culture—either the profane political tradition represented by Ammianus Marcellinus and Procopius or the ecclesiastical chronicle tradition, which seems to have begun with Eusebius of Caesarea and was now the dominant mode of historical writing in the Christian East. Works of the former type they did not know at all. Although they were almost certainly aware of the latter tradition, its precise impact is very hard to assess, nor are we yet certain which works they used or how they came to know of them. Translations did occur, obviously: Bishop John of Nikiu's famous chronicle was translated from Greek into Arabic, for example—but when? The Christian Arabic chronicle literature, by Eutychius of Alexandria (Saʿīd b. al-Baṭrīq, 877–940), Agapius of Manbij (Maḥbūb b. Qusṭanṭīn, d. ca. 940), Severus b. al-Muqaffaʿ (fl. 950–1000), and others, seems to have started in the tenth century, too late to have had any impact on early Islamic historical writing. We are left with the assumption, plausible enough but undocumented, that a few Syriac chronicles were translated or summarized for the use of Muslim scholars.[8]

Whatever the channels of transmission, the churchmen's chronicles clearly supplied Muslim writers with some data on biblical, Greek, and Roman history. On the other hand, they made very sparing use of whatever they learned about Rome; Ṭabarī has only three pages on the Roman emperors, as opposed to five hundred pages on biblical figures and two hundred pages on the Sassanian kings of Iran. On the level of structure, the ecclesiastical chronicle almost surely established the model of universal history (stretching from Creation to the present) used by Yaʿqūbī and Ṭabarī, and it may also have suggested the annalistic framework used by so many Muslim historians from the tenth century on. (The earliest extant Islamic example of annalistic structure is the chronicle of Khalīfa b. Khayyāṭ al-ʿUṣfurī [d. 854], while the most elaborate and influential is again Ṭabarī. Note however that these works impose an annalistic framework only on the Islamic era; Ṭabarī makes no effort to use the elaborate comparative chronologies devised by the Christian chroniclers for the ages before Islam.)[9] But none of this throws any light on the ways in which Muslim historians perceived and tried to convey the meaning of their community's past.[10]

Sassanian Iran ought to have contributed far more than did Christian Rome.[11] Many of the leading Muslim historians of the late ninth and early tenth centuries were of Iranian background. Moreover, the Iranian political tradition was not only well known in this period but also deeply assimilated into Islamic culture—in art and court ceremonial as well as literature. In addition to general concepts of government and political prudence, the half-legendary, half-historical narratives of Iran's kings were a part of the mental equipment of most educated Muslims in Iraq and Iran. In short, had Muslim historians desired to integrate the history of Islam with that of ancient Iran, they could easily have done so; Chosroes could well have played the same role in Ṭabarī as Augustus did in Eusebius.

Precisely this would happen soon enough, in the court-centered histories that began to be written (both in Arabic and Persian) in the late tenth and eleventh centuries. These are imbued with a political ethos and a sense of historical process that consciously sink their roots in Sassanian tradition. But with the possible exception of Abū Ḥanīfa al-Dīnawarī (d. 875), that tradition is hard to find in the historians of a century earlier. The work of the earlier historians does not focus on contemporary events, but on the first century and a half of Islam. Nor do they regard this period of origins as flowing from or integrally connected with the Sassanian past. On the contrary, they look at Islam as a radically new phase in world history, supplanting what had previously existed. This concept is reflected in the sharp disjunction in the kinds of materials they present and in the way they structure these materials when they come to Islamic times. Tarif Khalidi is particularly struck by the abrupt shift in Masʿūdī's presentation:

In contrast to his treatment of the ancient nations, Masʿūdī's account of the rise of Islam and of the Umayyad and Abbasid Caliphates is largely political and literary in nature. A disparity becomes immediately apparent between his cultural account of earlier nations and the political character of his Islamic history which is dynastic/annalistic in form. . . . This disparity . . . was not peculiar to Masʿūdī's histories but is also found in Yaʿqūbī and Maqdisī, both of whom were approximate contemporaries of Masʿūdī and wrote histories with a similar structure.[12]

Where then should we look for the source of the interpretive framework, the patterns of process and change, which inform early Islamic historiography? One would suppose that we might find some guidance in the Qurʾān—not only Islam's founding charter, after all, but also the most powerful force in the shaping of Islamic thought and culture. The hypothesis of a Qurʾanic underpinning for Islamic historiography, however plausible in principle, is admittedly difficult to demonstrate. Decisive proof would require us to find explicit statements of method and purpose in our texts, but these seldom occur and are quite unrevealing when they do. On the other hand, certain structural features in this literature do point to a consciousness of the past which has been decisively shaped by the Qurʾān.

First, as we noted above, every Muslim chronicler presents Islam as a decisive break in world history. The mission of Muhammad opens a new age in which the development of the Islamic community is the only important theme, and in which non-Muslim peoples (insofar as they are mentioned at all) are no longer treated as having an autonomous history of their own.[13]

Second, the narrative of the community's development constructed by early Muslim historians is based upon a limited and remarkably stable repertory of key events, which remain much the same among writers of all different religious and political persuasions. Evidently the early Muslims, however bitter their disputes among themselves, developed a strong consensus about the few incidents and persons in their history which demanded serious scrutiny and evaluation. Around this narrowly defined repertory of events cluster the bulk of reports and anecdotes; the same few stories are told and retold in a myriad of different forms. In contrast, other events (which from our perspective might well have seemed more significant) are passed over in silence or with terse allusions.

It is thus reasonable to suppose that the paradigm (or paradigms) governing early Islamic historiography are somehow embodied in this set of events. If that is so, we could recover this paradigm by identifying the core events within this literature and analyzing how they are related to one another. We cannot attempt to identify here the whole set of these events; clearly, however, it comprises those incidents that were regarded as the central crises in the community's evolution—incidents that assured its triumph, or that threatened its integrity and even its very existence. A knowledge of the external facts of these crises will not allow us to grasp their role in Islamic historical consciousness. Instead, we need to understand the interpretations that Muslim historians applied to them.

On this level, to be sure, the early historians seldom spoke for themselves. Rather, they preferred to convey their interpretations through the actions and words they attributed to the protagonists in their narratives. An alert reader quickly sees that these protagonists typically describe or justify their behavior by appealing to religious themes or principles. That is, the events constituting the core of Islamic history are presented in a specifically religious framework, and other elements—tribal quarrels, economic frictions, and so on—are severely subordinated if not altogether absent. Predictably but nonetheless significantly, statements of the religious issues at stake are grounded in citations from or unmistakable allusions to the Qur'ān. It is the sacred text that seems to provide the definitive criterion for understanding and judging these events.

This argument is not mere speculation, for we possess a particularly clear and explicit example of the Qur'ān's power to define the meaning of a critical moment. Ṭabarī reproduces a lengthy letter, which purports to have been written by the caliph ʿUthmān (644–56), besieged by rebels and desperately seeking support from loyal elements in the community, to the commander of the annual Pilgrimage caravan, ʿAbdallāh b. ʿAbbās.[14] The context of this letter lends it a special weight, for it comes very near the end of Ṭabarī's account of ʿUthmān's life. In this setting (doubtless carefully chosen), the aged caliph's account of the crisis seems not merely an *apologia pro vita sua* but a summing-up of the theological significance of the community's history down to that moment.

The letter opens with a series of nine direct citations from the Qur'ān. These stress several related themes: that God had made the Believers into a single community, bound together in unity in obedience to Him; that obedience to God equally demanded obedience to those who held authority over the community; that to sow dissension and disunity within this divinely ordained community was a violation of a Believer's covenant with God; finally, that those who broke faith with God, whether individuals or communities, must expect severe punishment. ʿUthmān's own statements are simply an elaboration of these themes, as he attempts to show how the scheme of things presented in divine revelation is being worked out in the current crisis. He points to the immense rewards that God has so far lavished upon the Muslims and warns them of catastrophe if they persist in rebellion; their religion will be shattered into quarreling sects, and in the end they will suffer the fate of the people of Noah. His enemies have claimed to be the advocates of true religion, but they are no more than hypocritical sowers of dissension. Those who are trying to bring him down are violating their oaths of absolute obedience both to him and to God. On his side, he has made every effort to adhere to God's commandments and to established precedent and repents of any unwitting errors. In any case he could not accede to the demand that he abdicate; his office belongs to God, and in carrying it out he does the work of God rather than of men.

It is important to understand that the Qur'anic citations in "ʿUthmān's" letter are no mere ornament or illustration. They provide the logic and vocabulary—the conceptual apparatus—through which he perceives, interprets, and presents the crisis confronting him and the community. They are the very essence of his argument.

The way in which this letter uses the Qur'ān suggests the kind of historical paradigm that early Muslim historians might have found there. Clearly the Qur'ān is not a book of history in any conventional sense. It makes no attempt to recount the events through which the Muslim community established itself in Mecca and Medina. Insofar as contemporary events occur at all in the text, they are not narrated but simply alluded to (often in frustratingly oblique ways), with the aim of demonstrating their moral and theological significance.[15] Certainly we find nothing resembling the highly structured narratives that are so crucial an element in the Old and New Testaments. On the other hand, the Qur'ān does identify a recurrent pattern in human history—a pattern applicable to almost every nation (umma) or people (qawm).

The Qur'ān puts great emphasis on the covenant between man and God (a concept expressed by the words ʿahd or mīthāq). This covenant consists of

God's promise of salvation in return for man's full acceptance of the obligation to obey His commandments and to worship Him alone. This promise-and-obligation has existed since the very creation of man and is binding on every person, as expressed in the following verse (vii, 172):

Your Lord brought forth descendants from the loins of Adam's children and made them testify against themselves. He said, "Am I not your Lord?" They replied, "We bear witness that you are." This He did, lest you should say on the Day of Resurrection, "We had no knowledge of that," or, "Our forefathers were indeed idolaters, but will you destroy us, their descendants, on account of what the followers of falsehood did?"

Man is by nature careless, however, and God in his mercy has periodically sent messengers to various nations and peoples to remind them of their covenant. Most peoples contemptuously reject these prophets, however, and are severely punished *as a collectivity* for this denial of their freely accepted obligation. (In the Qur'anic view of things, to accept God and his commandments is an obligation not merely for individuals but also for communities. Both are fully accountable for their obedience or disbelief—individuals at the Day of Judgment, communities in this world.) Here the story of Noah is paradigmatic: the community that rejects the messenger recalling it to its covenant is abruptly and violently obliterated.[16]

A few peoples, however, do accept the prophetic challenge and renew their covenant with God. Among these saved communities, the Jews and Christians are the most prominent. Even they, however, have soon enough corrupted—though they have not utterly abandoned—their renewed covenant and must now live under the threat of divine chastisement.[17]

Finally, Muḥammad was chosen as the apostle to his people, and some few, called Muslims or Believers (*mu'minūn*), have heeded his summons. However, the Qur'ān does not give a wholly idealized account of Muḥammad's people. They may be called "the best community ever brought forth to mankind, bidding to honor and forbidding dishonor, and believing in God" (iii, 110), and "a midmost community, that you might bear witness before men and the Messenger bear witness before you" (ii, 143). On the other hand, they are constantly hectored by the Qur'ān to stand fast, to submit to God and His messenger, not to quarrel and divide into sects, and so on. Like all their predecessors, the Muslims constantly confront the temptation to slacken and turn away from the rigors of obedience to God. *Sūra* x, 14 implies a threat as well as a promise: "We destroyed many generations before you when they did wrong and denied the true signs which their messengers had given them. Thus shall the guilty be rewarded. Then We made you their successors in the land, to see how you would act."

On a certain level, in fact, the issue is now graver than ever, for Muḥammad is the seal of the prophets, the last messenger whom God will send before the Day of Judgment. If his people fail to fulfill their covenant, the last hope of salvation will vanish. In this light, the obligation of the Muslim community is extremely heavy, and the Qur'ān gives no assurance that it will be equal to the task it has assumed. And if that was so even for men living in the Prophet's presence and under his guidance, how will it be for later generations?

All this suggests that in the Qur'ānic paradigm of repeated prophetic challenge, followed either by rejection and punishment or (more rarely) by acceptance and prosperity, we may find what we are looking for. A pattern of this kind can be seen as the kernel of a powerful myth informing the whole body of early Islamic historical writing. Consider the perspective of Muslims looking at their society from the standpoint of the mid eighth century, after the long agony and unhealable wounds of the second civil war (680–700). They would see a community that had begun by accepting the call to return to their primeval covenant with God and had been rewarded as no other people had ever been. But then this community had somehow, somewhere fallen prey to man's innate flaw of heedlessness and ingratitude, and now it was rent by bloodshed and schism. These facts confronted thoughtful Muslims with agonizing questions. Could this betrayal of the covenant be repaired? Could the Muslim community ever again take up its obligations wholeheartedly? And if this were possible, how and at whose hands might such a redemption come about? In the opinion of some, admittedly, it was not the whole body of Muslims who had failed, but only the ignorant and heedless masses. But in that case, did there remain a saving remnant able to fend off God's wrath until the community could at last be restored to the path of righteousness?[18]

Issues of this sort were of course hardly new, since they imbue the historical and prophetic books of the Hebrew Bible. Among early Muslims, the soul-searching provoked by the dialectic of scripture and historical experience crystallized in the form of an almost universally shared myth, one which we can call the myth of Covenant, Betrayal, and Redemption.

For those who contemplated the Islamic past, it was crucial to determine both the circumstances in which the betrayal of the Muhammadan covenant had occurred and the nature of that betrayal. The official interpretation propounded by the ʿAbbasid court—which had the delicate task of both insisting on its own Prophetic lineage and legitimizing the first three (non-Hashimite) caliphs—laid the entire blame for the community's disasters on the cynical and corrupt Umayyad clan (in particular the tyrant and usurper Muʿāwiya).[19] Outside the court, however, almost all factions agreed that the crisis had occurred in the reign of the third caliph, ʿUthmān ibn ʿAffān (644–56), although every other issue was bitterly disputed. In particular, debate centered on whether the ultimate guilt for the catastrophe lay with ʿUthmān himself, with the rebels who had put him to death, or with other elements in the community.

We find the simplest, most clearly defined views on these issues in two pro-'Alid writers, Aḥmad b. Wāḍiḥ al-Ya'qūbī and 'Alī b. al-Ḥusayn al-Mas'ūdī.[20]

Mas'ūdī's account may reflect the ancient Iranian notion that the ruler is the exemplar for his subjects, and that on his personal justice and integrity depends the good order of the world. In any case he clearly portrays 'Uthmān as the fountainhead of all the ills of his time. In Mas'ūdī's presentation, the Muslim community had remained essentially faithful to its covenant under the first two caliphs, who were clumsy and prone to error but generally well-meaning. 'Umar's personal piety and austerity, for example, were broadly imitated by the mass of Muslims. But 'Uthmān was corrupt and a tyrant. Whereas Abū Bakr and 'Umar had properly deferred to the prestige and religious authority of 'Alī, 'Uthmān would follow the counsel only of his own corrupt kinsmen. Through him such dissension and malice were sown in the community that its integrity could never afterward be fully restored. Even 'Alī (656–61), the noblest of mankind and truly God's elect, could not achieve the task.

Ya'qūbī presents a very different view of the link between the caliph and the Muslim community. He seems to regard the corruption of 'Uthmān's rule as a consequence of the inner rot already existing in the Muslim community at large. From this corruption only a tiny saving remnant (symbolized most dramatically by the austere and pathetic figure of Abū Dharr al-Ghifārī) was immune. Ya'qūbī lays particular stress on the way in which 'Uthmān was elected to the caliphate.[21] His presentation of this event argues that 'Uthmān was elected only because the leaders of the community rejected 'Alī, whom they knew to be the Prophet's designated heir, for a man of known moral weakness. For Ya'qūbī, then, once the community was deprived of Muḥammad's personal guidance, it almost at once turned its back on his teaching. Indeed, in electing and submitting to 'Uthmān the community was reinstating the social and moral order of the Jāhiliyya, and offering mere lip service to the covenant it had solemnly assumed. In short, the Muslims as a body were hardly better than the Jews and Christians.

Far more complex and nuanced than either of these accounts is the presentation of Muḥammad b. Jarīr al-Ṭabarī. To a far greater extent than other historians of his time, Ṭabarī allows—and even requires—his readers to frame their own conclusions about the true meaning of the events he recounts. There is here a studied ambiguity, a determination to show that the religious and political problems posed by 'Uthmān's reign might be resolved in a number of different ways.

To start with, Ṭabarī presents two disparate and in fact irreconcilable versions of events, each of them reflecting a distinct interpretation of the guiding myth of Covenant, Betrayal, and Redemption. These two interpretations are perhaps most clearly visible in his account of the murder of 'Uthmān.[22] The first interpretation holds that the covenant has in fact been continuously and faithfully maintained by the community as a whole, in spite of the falling away and malice of some few members. The community has not fallen into disobedience, and its members can be confident that its relationship with God remains whole and unbroken. In contrast, the interpretation imbedded in the second version of events asserts that the covenant has certainly been betrayed, though redemption and the restoration of the covenant may still be hoped for.

The first interpretation is conveyed primarily by a long set of narratives compiled by Sayf ibn 'Umar (d. ca. 800).[23] Sayf's account stresses several central points, all of which were hotly contested by other compilers and transmitters: (a) the personal piety of 'Uthmān; (b) the unity and concord of all the Prophet's leading Companions in his defense; and (c) the vile character of 'Uthmān's assailants, a rabble of dissidents aroused by the basest motives, who violated the clear will of those who really embodied the community's tradition. There is a hidden agenda in this account, of course: the intense desire to assert the unbroken unity and integrity of the Muslim community. Sayf's approach can perhaps be linked to the ideas of the ahl al-ḥadīth, which began to find a clear formulation by the ninth century. In particular, it stems from the notion that the Prophet's Companions must be regarded as substantially equal in religious merit, and that all of them should be revered by Muslims as models of correct belief and practice. The true Islam is enshrined in their statements and actions; though later generations may have fallen away from this ideal standard, they can always appeal to it and try to revivify it in their own lives.[24]

Ṭabarī gives pride of place to the account of Sayf ibn 'Umar; it is put at the very climax of the drama and is presented as a coherent unit rather than being chopped into the short, scattered segments used for the accounts of other reporters. Even so, I believe that Ṭabarī means to reject it. He seems to use it as a kind of idealized core account, which he flanks with selected reports from other traditions (especially those of Wāqidī and Ibn Isḥāq) which both are far more realistic in tone and contradict Sayf on almost every point.[25] These are not just alternate versions, included to place all the relevant testimony before the reader, but commentaries on and critiques of Sayf. Faced with these challenges to Sayf's account, a critical reader would realize that he could accept the latter's interpretation only as a matter of religious faith, not as established knowledge.

The versions of Wāqidī, Ibn Isḥāq, and others, state that 'Uthmān was defended by *no* reputable Companions against his assailants, but only by his own disreputable kinsmen. Nor was 'Uthmān personally guiltless, for his own conduct at critical junctures had done much to stir up revolt against him. But even if the revolt against 'Uthmān seemed justifiable on a certain level, it had shattered the unity of the community for at least the next century and riven it with constant rebellion and civil strife. A refrain repeated over and over throughout these accounts is ʿUthmān's plea: "If you kill me, you will never pray together again."

How and by whom could redemption come? Ṭabarī must surely have accepted the notion that the community's sin was not irrevocable, that many Muslims had remained faithful to their covenant. Otherwise, his own life's work as a jurist and Qur'anic exegete would have been a sham. In his account of the reign and death of ʿUthmān, however, he does not address this issue directly. In view of his political affiliations, we might expect him to say that the event that at last expunged the tyranny and dissension engendered by the death of ʿUthmān was the ʿAbbasid revolution. But with Ṭabarī such expectations are very often misleading. His ironical and sometimes paradoxical juxtaposition of accounts means that we should resist conclusions that are not based on a close analysis of the texts he presents and their relationships to one another. It is due mostly to him, after all, that we know how many hopes were disappointed by the ʿAbbasids, how many revolts they faced, how many stresses arose within their own family.

This point brings us to our conclusion. Some commentators, such as Franz Rosenthal and John Wansbrough, have suggested that the Muslim view of early Islamic history was static and unproductive. Wansbrough says that Islamic culture generated "not history but nostalgia."[26] I would disagree. The Covenant-Betrayal-Redemption myth analyzed here is a very productive one indeed, though it was no doubt anxiety provoking as well. People who perceive themselves to be living in a state of sin, but who hope to recover a state of grace, must contend not only with their past but also with the future. They are in the midst of a dynamic process in which hope and striving are still relevant. Only when redemption no longer seemed a real possibility, and hope had receded into a remote messianic future, would the history of the early community become a stale exercise in nostalgia.

An awareness that redemption was not something that could be achieved by the Islamic community became increasingly widespread in the second half of the ninth century, and could only have been confirmed by the inexorable decline and ultimate humiliation of the ʿAbbasid caliphate in the tenth. (The rise of the Fatimids and the Carmathian revolt rallied only a minority.) In these circumstances, the myth of Covenant, Betrayal, and Redemption was bound to seem less and less applicable to the flow of events. Certainly it was not capable of bestowing meaning, order, and value on the sordid court intrigues of petty and evanescent military dynasties. In this perspective, it is not surprising that no one tried to redo Ṭabarī's *summa* of early Islamic history. After him, historians increasingly focused on recent and contemporary events, interpreting them in a decisively non-Qur'anic framework. For such historians, the beginnings of Islam could be mourned and longed for, but few any longer believed that they could be recovered and done anew.

APPENDIX: THE LETTER OF 'UTHMĀN
TO THE INHABITANTS OF MECCA

The following text is given in Ṭabarī, 1:3040–45, and purports to be a letter written by the besieged 'Uthmān and given to 'Abdallāh b. 'Abbās, commander of the Pilgrimage in this year, to present to the people of Mecca. As to whether the letter is in any way authentic, one can only speculate. Our only direct evidence for its provenance is the *isnād*, "Ibn Abī Sabra says: 'Abd al-Majīd b. Suhayl informed me that he had made a copy [*intasakha*] from 'Ikrima of the letter which 'Uthmān had written." If this *isnād* is genuine (always a matter of dispute), it would indicate that the letter entered into circulation not later than 723–24, the date of 'Ikrima's death. 'Ikrima was a *mawlā* of 'Abdallāh b. 'Abbās and was regarded as one of the principal transmitters of the latter's Qur'ān commentary.[27] It is thus conceivable that 'Ikrima had actually seen the original letter handed to Ibn 'Abbās. Even on a more skeptical view—that is, that the letter came into circulation after 'Ikrima's death and was attached to his name in order to lend it a spurious authenticity—the *terminus ad quem* would be 823, the death date of Wāqidī, who is Ṭabarī's direct source here.

The letter's supposed connection with Ibn 'Abbās and 'Ikrima throws little light on its origins. The former's name might imply a link with the 'Abbasid dynasty, but Ibn 'Abbās' relations with the Umayyad dynasty were amicable, whereas 'Ikrima was accused of Kharijite sympathies. In fact there is nothing pro-'Abbasid or pro-Kharijite in the text. Its plea for Muslim unity recalls a basic theme of Umayyad ideology, and the letter has certain formal and substantive parallels with one written by al-Walīd II (d. 744) and recently studied by Crone and Hinds.[28] I do not believe that it is of Marwanid provenance, however; there would be far greater stress on caliphal sanctity and prerogatives if it were. Perhaps, if the letter is not authentic (either *verbatim* or in substance), we should look to Murji'ite circles in the mid eighth century. The utter lack of Prophetic *ḥadīth* in the text hardly permits a later date, while the stress on unity and obedience to legitimately constituted authority would be consistent with their determinedly "neutralist" outlook. Further discussions of attribution must be postponed. In any event, this letter demonstrates that the myth of Covenant and Betrayal was firmly implanted in Muslim culture by late Umayyad or early 'Abbasid times.

In the translations, I have used Arberry's translation of the Qur'ān, with minor modifications. For many citations, the text gives only the opening and closing verses. Since educated Muslims would know the Qur'ān by heart and fill in the missing verses, I have inserted such ellipses between brackets in order to bring out the full meaning of the citations in question.

In the name of God, the Compassionate, the Merciful. From God's servant 'Uthmān, Commander of the Faithful, to the Believers and Muslims. Peace be with you, and to you I praise God—there is no god but He.

To proceed. Verily I call on you to remember Almighty God, who has bestowed benefits // {3041} upon you, taught you Islam, guided you away from error, delivered you from unbelief, shown you clear proofs, lavished sustenance upon you, and given you victory over the enemy. "And He has lavished on you His blessings." (xxxi, 19) For verily Almighty God says, and His saying is the truth, "If you count God's blessing, you will never number it; surely man is sinful, unthankful," (xiv, 37)

The Almighty also says, "O believers, fear God as He should be feared, and see you do not die save in surrender [i.e., as Muslims]. And hold you fast to God's bond, together, [and do not scatter: remember God's blessing upon you when you were enemies, and He brought your hearts together, so that by His blessing you became brothers. You were on the brink of a pit of Fire, and He delivered you from it; even so God makes clear to you His signs; haply so you will be guided. Let there be one nation of you, calling to good, and bidding to honor, and forbidding dishonor; those are the prosperers. Be not as those who scattered and fell into variance after the clear signs came to them;] those there awaits a mighty chastisement." (iii, 97–101)

He has also said, and His saying is the truth, "O believers, remember God's blessing upon you, and His compact [*mīthāq*] which he made with you, when you said, 'We have heard and we obey.'" (v, 10)

He has also said, and His saying is the truth, "O believers, if an ungodly man comes to you with a tiding, [make clear, lest you afflict a people unwittingly, and then repent of what you have done. And know that the Messenger of God is among you. If he obeyed you in much of the affair, you would suffer; but God has endeared to you belief, decking it fair in your hearts, and He has made detestable to you unbelief and ungodliness and disobedience. Those—they are the right-minded,] by God's favor and blessing; God is Allknowing. All-wise." (xlix, 6–8)

[Remember also] the saying of the Almighty, "Those that sell God's covenant (*'ahd Allāh*) and their oaths for a little price, [there shall be no share for them in the world to come; God shall not speak to them nor look at them on the Resurrection Day, neither will He purify them;] and for them awaits a painful chastisement." (iii, 71)

He has also said, and His saying is the truth, "So fear God as far as you are able, [and give ear, and obey, and expend well for yourselves. And whosoever is guarded against the avarice of his own soul,] those—they are the prosperers." (lxiv, 16)

He has also said, and His saying is the truth, "Break not the oaths after they have been confirmed [and you have made God your surety; surely God knows the things you do. And be not as a woman who breaks her thread, after it is firmly spun, into fibres, by taking your oaths as mere mutual deceit, one nation being more numerous than another nation. God only tries you thereby: and certainly He will make clear to you upon the Day of Resurrection that whereon you were at variance. If God had willed, He would have made you one nation; but He leads astray whom He will and guides whom He will; and you will surely be questioned about the things you wrought. Take not your oaths as mere mutual deceit, lest any foot should slip after it has stood firm and you should taste evil, for that you barred from the way of God, and lest there should await you a mighty chastisement. And do not sell the covenant of God for a small price; surely what is with God—that is better for you, did you but know. What is with you comes to an end, but what is with God abides,] and surely We shall recompense those who were patient their wage, according to the best of what they did." (xvi, 93–98)

He has also said, and His saying is the truth, "Obey God, and obey the Messenger and those in authority among you. [If you should quarrel on anything, refer it to God and the Messenger, if you believe in God and the Last Day; that is better,] and fairer in the issue." (iv, 62)

He has also said, and His saying is the truth, "God has promised those of you who believe and do righteous deeds [that He will surely make you successors in the land, even as He made those who were before them successors, and that He will surely establish their religion for them that He has approved for them, and will give them in exchange, after their fear, security: 'They shall serve Me, not associating with Me anything.'] Whoso disbelieves after that, those—they are the ungodly." (xxiv, 54) // {3042}

He has also said, and His saying is the truth, "Those who swear obedience to thee[29] swear obedience in truth to God; [God's hand is over their hands. Then whosoever breaks his oath breaks it but to his own hurt; and whoso fulfills his covenant made with God,] God will give him a mighty wage." (xlviii, 10)

To continue, Almighty God desired for you absolute obedience and unity [al-sam' wa'l-ṭā'a wa'l-jamā'a], and warned you against rebellion, schism, and discord. He informed you about what your predecessors had done, presenting it to you so that He might have it as proof against you. If you rebel against Him, then accept the counsel of Almighty God and beware of His punishment, for you will never find a community [umma] which has been destroyed save after it has fallen into discord. [Such a community can be saved] only if it has a head who can unite it. If ever you do that, you will not perform the prayer together, your enemy will be given power over you, and you will disagree as to what is lawful or forbidden. If you do that, no true religion [*dīn*] will remain before God—glory be to Him—and you will be divided into sects. Now Almighty God has said to His Messenger, "Those who have made divisions in their religion and become sects, thou art not of them in anything; their affair is unto God, then He will tell them what they have been doing." (vi, 160) Verily I enjoin upon you what God has enjoined, and I warn you of His chastisement. For [the prophet] Shuʿayb said to his people [*qawm*], "O my people, let not the breach with me move you, so that there smite you the like of what smote the people of Noah, [or the people of Hūd, or the people of Ṣāliḥ; and the people of Lot are not far away from you. And ask forgiveness of your Lord, then repent to Him; surely my Lord is] All-compassionate, All-loving." (xi, 91–92)

To continue. Verily certain groups [*aqwām*] among those who have been talking in this way have maintained to the people that they are only summoning [them] to the Book of Almighty God and to the truth, and that they desire neither this world nor any strife over it. When the truth was presented to them, behold the people were at variance concerning it: among them are those who accept the truth when it is presented to them and [then] turn away from it, and among them are those who abandon the truth and renounce it in this matter, desiring to snatch it without any right. My life has seemed long to them and their hopes of governing have been deferred, and so they seek to hasten [God's] decree [viz., by murdering me].

They have written you that they returned [to their homes] on the basis of (certain promises) I gave them; I am not aware that I have neglected any of my promises to them. They have been seeking, so they allege, [the enforcement of] God's ordinances [*al-ḥudūd*]. I said, "Apply them against whomever you know to have violated any one of them. Enforce them against anyone near or far who has wronged you." They have said, "The Book of God is to be recited aloud." I replied, "Then let him who recites do so, except for anyone who inserts in (the text) something which God has not revealed in the Book." They said, "The deprived man ought to be provided for, and the public wealth [*al-māl*] should be expended in such a way that sound precedent [*al-sunna al-ḥasana*] may be followed thereby. The [caliph's] one-fifth share and the [fixed] alms tax should not be exceeded. Capable and trustworthy men should be placed in authority. The wrongs [suffered by] the people should be charged against those who have committed them." Now I am content with this and have persevered in doing it. I came to the Prophet's wives to speak with them, saying, "What do you command me [to do]?" They answered, "You should assign governorships [*tuʾammiru*] to ʿAmr b. al-ʿĀṣ and ʿAbdallāh b. Qays [viz. Abū Mūsā al-Ashʿarī] and leave Muʿāwiya [in office]. An *amīr* [ʿUmar?]

made him governor before you; he sees to the well-being of his territory and his army is content with him. Send ʿAmr back [to Egypt], for his army is content with him. Make him governor and he will restore good order in his territory." Now I did all that, and [ʿAmr] has since then transgressed against me and violated right conduct.

I have written to you and to my associates who have made allegations concerning the matter. They have sought to hasten God's decree, barred me from the prayer, and blocked me from the mosque. They have stolen what they could in Medina. I have written this letter to you at a time when they are giving me one of three choices. First, they will retaliate against me for every man whom I have struck, rightly or wrongly, except that some portion of it will be forgone. Alternatively, I will resign the caliphate [al-amr] and they will assign it to someone else. Or finally, they will send to the provincial garrisons [al-ajnād] and to the inhabitants of Medina who obey them, and thus declare themselves free of the absolute obedience to me which God has enjoined upon them.

To them I have replied [as follows]. As for my exacting retaliation against myself, caliphs before me used to strike [men] in error and retaliation was not demanded against any of them, and I know that they are aiming only against // {3044} me. As for my abdicating sovereignty [al-imāra], I would rather they strike me than to resign from the work of Almighty God and His caliphate. As for your statement—"they will send to the provincial garrisons and the inhabitants of Medina and thus be quit of obedience to me"—I am not an agent of yours, nor did I compel them to obey beforehand. Rather, they voluntarily accepted [obedience to me], seeking to please Almighty God and to resolve discord. As to him among you who desires only this world, he shall obtain of it only what Almighty God has prescribed for him. He who desires only God's face, the Abode hereafter, the well-being of the community [al-umma], the seeking of Almighty God's pleasure, and the sound precedent [al-sunna al-ḥasana] laid down by the Messenger of God and the two caliphs after him, (that man) shall surely be rewarded for that by God.

Your reward is not in my hands. If I bestowed upon you the whole world, it would not be a fair price for your religion nor would it compensate you in any way. So fear God and take into account His reward. I am not content—nor will God (Glory be to Him!) be content—that anyone among you should violate His covenant [ʿahd]. As for what [the rebels] will force me to choose between, it adds up simply to deposing [me] and naming a new caliph [al-nazʿ waʾl-taʾmīr]). I have been master of myself and those with me, I have seen to [the enforcement of] God's judgment [ḥukm] and [avoided] altering the benefits [bestowed] by God—Glory be to Him. I have hated evil precedent, division within the Community, and the shedding of blood. I adjure you by God and by Islam to take only what is right—and you will be given that by me—

and to abandon wrongdoing against those with rightful claims. Deal justly between us, as Almighty God has commanded you. I adjure you by God—Glory be to Him—who has appointed for you the covenant and mutual support in God's affair—for God //{3045} has said, and His saying is true, "Fulfill the covenant ['*ahd*]; surely the covenant shall be asked of." (xvii, 36) This is an excuse before God; perhaps you will be mindful.

To continue, "Yet I claim not that my soul was innocent—surely the soul of man incites to evil—except inasmuch as my Lord has mercy; truly my Lord is All-forgiving, All-compassionate." (xii, 53) If I have chastised certain groups [*aqwām*], I have desired only good thereby, and I turn in repentance to Almighty God from every [evil] deed I have committed and seek His forgiveness. Verily none forgives sins but He. Surely the mercy of my Lord comprehends everything. Only the nation [*al-qawm*] which has gone astray despairs of God's mercy, and He accepts repentance from His servants and pardons evil deeds and knows what they do. I ask Almighty God to forgive me and you, and to reconcile the hearts of this Community [*yu'allif qulūb hādhihi al-umma*] upon what is good, making sin hateful to it.

Peace be upon you and the mercy of God and His blessings, O Believers and Muslims.

NOTES

1 Julius Wellhausen, *Prolegomena zur ältesten Geschichte des Islams,* vol. 6 (1899) of *Skizzen und Vorarbeiten,* 6 vols. (Berlin, 1884–99); Wellhausen, "Die religiös-politischen Oppositionsparteien im alten Islam," in *Abhandlungen der Königlichen Gesellschaft der Wissenschaften zu Göttingen,* Phil.-hist. Klasse, n.s., 5, no. 2 (1901), trans. R. C. Ostle and S. M. Walzer as *The Religio-Political Factions in Early Islam* (Amsterdam, Oxford, and New York, 1975); and Wellhausen, *Das arabische Reich und sein Sturz* (Berlin, 1902), trans. M. G. Weir as *The Arab Kingdom and Its Fall* (Calcutta, 1927).

2 Wellhausen, *Prolegomena,* 4.

3 E. L. Petersen, *'Alī and Mu'āwiya in Early Arabic Tradition: Studies in the Genesis and Growth of Islamic Historical Writing until the End of the Ninth Century* (Copenhagen, 1964). See also two articles by him: "'Alī and Mu'āwiyah: The Rise of the Umayyad Caliphate, 656–661," *Acta Orientalia* 23 (1959): 157–96; "Studies on the Historiography of the 'Alī-Mu'āwiyah Conflict," *Acta Orientalia* 27 (1963): 83–118.

4 On these errors see in particular Martin Hinds, "The Ṣiffīn Arbitration Agreement," *Journal of Semitic Studies* 17 (1972): 93–129, esp. 105.; and Ursula Sezgin, *Abū Miḥnaf: Ein Beitrag zur Historiographie der umaiyadischen Zeit* (Leiden, 1971), 25–31 et passim.

288   IV. MODELS FOR A NEW PRESENT: THE QUR'AN

5 G. H. A. Juynboll, *Muslim Tradition: Studies in Chronology, Provenance, and Authorship of Early Hadīth* (Cambridge, 1983), chap. 1, see esp. 70–76.

6 Albrecht Noth, *Quellenkritische Studien zu Themen, Formen, and Tendenzen in frühislamischen Geschichtsüberlieferung* (Bonn, 1973); Noth, "Isfahan-Nihavand: Eine quellenkritische Studie zur frühislamischen Historiographie," *Zeitschrift der Deutschen morgenländischen Gesellschaft* 112 (1968): 274–96; and North, "Der Charakter der ersten grossen Sammlungen von Nachrichten zur frühen Kalifenzeit," *Islam* 47 (1971): 168–99.

7 al-Yaʿqūbī, *al-Taʾrīkh*, ed. T. Houtsma, 2 vols. (Leiden, 1883). al-Masʿūdī, *Murūj al-dhahab wa-maʿādin al-jawhar*, ed. and trans. C. Barbier de Meynard and Pavet de Courteille as *Les prairies d'or*, 9 vols. (Paris, 1861–77); rev. and trans. Charles Pellat (Ar. text: 7 vols., Beirut, 1965–79; trans.: 5 vols., Paris, 1965–74. al-Ṭabarī, *Taʾrīkh al-rusul waʾl-mulūk*, ed. M. J. de Goeje et al., 15 vols. (Leiden, 1879–1901); rev. by M. A. F. Ibrahim, 10 vols. (Cairo, 1960–69). English trans., *The History of al-Tabari*, ed. Ehsan Yar-Shater, 38 vols. projected, with various translators (Albany, N.Y., 1985–).

8 On these authors see Georg Graf, *Geschichte der christlichen arabischen Literatur*, 5 vols. (Vatican City, 1944–53), 2:32–41, 300–306. In fact, Masʿūdī may have consulted the recently composed work of Eutychius of Alexandria during the last decade of his life, which he spent in Egypt, for Roman and Byzantine history. But for early Islamic history, even Masʿūdī sticks strictly to Islamic sources and models.

9 Khalīfa b. Khayyāṭ al-ʿUṣfurī, *al-Taʾrīkh*, recently discovered, survives in a single Moroccan MS: ed. Akram Ḍiyāʾ al-ʿUmarī, 2 vols. (Najaf, 1967).

10 The links between the eastern Christian and early Muslim historiographic traditions remain to be explored. A comprehensive survey of the sources for seventh-century Iraq produced by all the region's cultural traditions can be found in M. G. Morony, *Iraq after the Muslim Conquest* (Princeton, N.J., 1984), 537–654, esp. 620ff. Some useful indications can be gotten from two articles in B. Lewis and P. M. Holt, *Historians of the Middle East* (London, 1962): Franz Rosenthal, "The Influence of the Biblical Tradition on Muslim Historiography," 35–45; J. B. Segal, "Syriac Chronicles as Source Material for the History of Islamic Peoples," 246–58. See also Sebastian Brock, "Syriac Views of Emergent Islam", in *Studies on the First Century of Islamic Society*, ed. G. H. A. Juynboll (Carbondale, Ill., 1982), 9–22.

11 Ignaz Goldziher thought so: "Historiography in Arabic Literature," in *Gesammelte Schriften*, 5 vols. (Hildesheim, 1967–73), 3:359–94. He is plainly wrong here, however. In contrast to most of his work, this piece is speculative and ill documented.

12 Tarif Khalidi, *Islamic Historiography: The Histories of Masʿudi* (Albany, N.Y. 1975), 114.

13 There is an important exception to this statement in Masʿūdī, who displays a genuine interest in and considerable understanding of Byzantine history since the rise of Islam. See Ahmed Shboul, *al-Masʿūdī and His World* (London, 1979), 227–84.

14   Cited in Ṭabarī, 1:3040–45. For a translation of the text and discussion of its provenance, see the Appendix to this paper.

15   See *sūras* iii, 117–24 and viii, 1–9, 42–46 (Badr, 624); ix, 25–29 (Ḥunayn, 630); xxx, 1–4 (Perso-Byzantine Wars, probably the Persian occupation of Syria and Egypt, 614–19); xxxiii, 9–27 (Battle of the Ditch, 627); xlviii, 1–2, 17–27 (Truce of Ḥudaybiyya, 628, and the Occupation of Mecca, 630). These are probably the clearest and most unambiguous references, and even they may be open to question on several counts.

16   The Noah story is cited many times, but is most fully given in *sūra* xi, 25–48.

17   This theme is especially reiterated in *sūras* ii and v; a good concise statement is v, 12–14.

18   The Covenant motif in early Islamic historiography has also been discussed by John Wansbrough, *The Sectarian Milieu: Content and Composition of Islamic Salvation History* (Oxford, 1978)–e.g., p. 87: "The scriptural theodicy was essentially covenantal, a characteristic fundamental also to the literary forms of both *Sīra* and Sunna, in which is stressed the oracular and paradigmatic role of the agent of covenant renewal." Even so, there are significant differences between Wasnbrough's interpretation and mine. (1) He believes that the Qur'ān in its present form was generated over the first two Islamic centuries around a core of prophetical *logia*, whereas I follow Islamic tradition in placing the redaction of the text in the two decades following Muḥammad's death. (2) His analysis focuses entirely on texts (whether Qur'ān, Sunna, or *Sīra*) dealing with the life of Muḥammad, while I am equally concerned with the early caliphal era. (3) He overlooks the themes of Betrayal and Redemption, and insists that in Islamic culture the covenant restored by Muḥammad was perceived as a closed, static moment rather than as an ongoing process—see pp. 46, 88. In accordance with long-established orientalist tradition, he does admit the notion of decline from the initial perfection of the Prophetic community (p. 148), but "decline" is a far less challenging, even traumatic, concept than "betrayal." In my judgment, "decline" is an attitude that emerges only in later times (the fifth/eleventh century on).

19   The official ʿAbbasid version is developed in the formal edict calling for the cursing of Muʿāwiya which was issued by the ʿAbbasid caliph al-Muʿtaḍid in 897 (d. 902). This statement was allegedly based on a far older version issued by al-Maʾmūn (*regn.* 813–33), whose own pro-ʿAlid bent was well-known. Ṭabarī (ed. de Goeje), 3:2166–77; trans. Franz Rosenthal, *The Return of the Caliphate to Baghdad. History of al-Tabari*, vol. 38 (Albany, 1985), 48–63. The themes of al-Muʿtaḍid's decree are closely paralleled in several polemical treatises by al-Jāḥiẓ (d. 869): *Faḍl Hāshim ʿalā ʿAbd Shams, K. taṣwīb ʿAlī fī taḥkīm al-ḥakamayn, al-ʿUthmāniyya,* and *al-Nābita.* Bibliographic data and translations of selected passages from these are given in Charles Pellat, *The Life and Works of Jahiz*, trans. D. M. Hawke (Berkeley and Los Angeles, 1969), 16–18, 58–62, 66–86.

20   Yaʿqūbī, *al-Taʾrīkh* (ed. Houtsma), 2:186–206; Masʿūdī, *Murūj al-dhahab* (ed. Pellat), 3:75–92.

21   On the *shūrā*, see Yaʿqūbī, *Taʾrīkh* (ed. Houtsma), 2:186–87.

22   Ṭabarī (ed. de Goeje), 1:2980–3025. M. G. S. Hodgson, *The Venture of Islam,*

3 vols. (Chicago, 1974), 1:350–58, esp. 354–56, seems to have been the first to identify these. My own interpretation is obviously indebted to his analysis, though I have developed some points differently than he.

23 Ṭabarī (ed. de Goeje), 1:3007–20.

24 On the *ahl al-ḥadīth*, see Hodgson, *Venture of Islam*, 1:386–92. The insistence that Muslims should revere all the Companions equally has its roots in the Murjiʾite movement of the mid eighth century; in extant texts this idea can perceived as early as the *Fiqh Akbar I*, a late eighth-century credo linked to the teaching of Abū Ḥanīfa (d. 767). See A. J. Wensinck, *The Muslim Creed: Its Genesis and Historical Development* (Cambridge, 1932), 102–24. Important material also in Charles Pellat, "Le culte de Muʿāwiya au IIIᵉ siècle de l'hégire," *Studia Islamica* 6 (1956): 53–66; and Gérard Lecomte, *Ibn Qutayba: L'homme, son oeuvre, ses idées* (Damascus, 1965), 243–47.

25 I cannot give a detailed account here of Ṭabarī's "variant traditions." Briefly, Ibn Isḥāq and Jaʿfar al-Muhammadī convey a strongly pro-ʿAlid point of view and seem to justify the revolt against ʿUthmān, who is portrayed as weak, treacherous, and corrupt. Wāqidī's accounts, taken as a whole, are much more ambivalent; they are both critical of ʿUthmān's failings and acutely aware of the political and ethical dilemmas created by the revolt against him. That Wāqidī's tradition could support a vindication of ʿUthmān's legitimacy, whatever his weaknesses, can be seen in the account of Balādhurī (d. 892), who relies on Wāqidī for some four-fifths of his material: *Ansāb al-Ashrāf*, vol. 5, ed. S. D. Goitein (Jerusalem, 1936), 1–105.

26 Wansbrough, *Sectarian Milieu*, x. Cf. Rosenthal, "Influence of the Biblical Tradition," 39–40, 45. Wansbrough's stress on nostalgia has deep roots in Western orientalism: cf. C. Snouck Hurgronje, *Selected Works*, ed. G.-H. Bousquet and J. Schacht (Leiden, 1957), 248, 265–66.

27 J. Schacht, "'Ikrima," *EI²*, 3:1081–82; Juynboll, *Muslim Tradition*, 55–57, 139–40.

28 P. Crone and M. Hinds, *God's Caliph: Religious Authority in the First Centuries of Islam* (Cambridge, 1986), 116–26.

29 *Yubāyiʿūnaka*—a crucial word in this context, for it also means "to render the oath of allegiance" (the *bayʿa*) to a new caliph. Contemporary readers could not have missed the allusion.

WORKS CITED

INDEX

Works Cited

This list is divided into two sections, the second of which, "Modern Scholarship," begins on page 305. Books of the Bible and the Greek and Latin classics are available in numerous editions, and they have therefore been omitted from this list.

A. ANCIENT SOURCES AND OTHER WORKS CITED BY ABBREVIATION OR SHORT TITLE

	Acta M. Anastasii Persae. Edited by H. Usener. Programmschrift, University of Bonn. Bonn, 1894.
	Acts of Thomas. Translated by R. McL. Wilson. New Testament Apocrypha. Philadelphia: Westminster Press, 1965.
AE	*L'année épigraphique: Revue des publications épigraphiques relatives à l'antiquité romaine.* Paris: Presses Universitaires de France, 1888–.
Akhbār	*Akhbār al-dawla al-ʿabbāsiyya.* Edited by A. A. al-Dūrī and A. J. al-Muṭṭalibī. Beirut: Dār al-Ṭalīʿa, 1971.
AL or *Anth. Lat.*	Shackleton Bailey, D. R., ed. *Anthologia Latina.* Vol. 1, *Carmina in codicibus scripta;* Fasc. 1, *Libri salmasiani aliorumque carmina.* Stuttgart: B. G. Teubner, 1982.
Ambros. *De off. min.*	*Ambrosii Episcopi Mediolanensis De officiis ministrorum.* Edited by J. G. Krabinger. Tübingen: H. Laupp, 1857.
Ambros. *Hex.*	*Sancti Ambrosii Exameron.* Edited by C. Schenkel. *CSEL* 32, pt. 1 (1897): 3–261.
Amm. Marc.	*Ammiani Marcellini Rerum gestarum libri qui supersunt.* Edited by C. U. Clark, 2 vols. Berlin, 1910–15.
AnonRB	*Anonymus De rebus bellicis.* In *A Roman Reformer*

and Inventor, edited by E. A. Thompson. Oxford: Clarendon Press, 1952.

Anon. Val. — *Excerpta valesiana.* Edited by J. Moreau and V. Velkov. Leipzig: B. G. Teubner, 1968.

Aristotle. *The Works of Aristotle.* Translated by J. A. Smith and W. P. Ross. 12 vols. Oxford: Clarendon Press, 1908–52. Also, *The Complete Works of Aristotle.* Translated by Jonathan Barnes. Oxford, 1912–54. Reprint. Princeton, N.J.: Princeton University Press, 1984.

Arrian. *Periplus Ponti Euxini.* In *Periplo del Ponto Eusino,* edited by G. Marenghi. Naples: Libreria Scientifica, 1958.

Ashʿarī, *Maqālat* — al-Ashʿarī, Abū al-Ḥasan. *Maqālāt al-islāmiyyīn waʾikhtilāf al-muṣallīn.* Edited by Hellmut Ritter. 3 vols. Istanbul: Deutsche Morgenländische Gesellschaft, 1929–33.

Athanasius. *Apologia ad Constantium.* Edited by J.-M. Szymusiak. Sources chrétiennes, no. 56. Paris: Editions du Cerf, 1958.

Augustinus or Aug. *De civitate Dei* or *CD* — *Sancti Aurelii Augustini De civitate Dei.* Edited by B. Dombart, A. Kalb, et al. *CCL* 47–48 (1955).

Augustinus *De Gen. ad litt.* — *Sancti Aureli Augustini De Genesi ad litteram libri xii.* Edited by J. Zycha. *CSEL* 28, pt. 1 (1894): 3–435.

Aug. *De Trin.* — Augustinus. *De Trinitate. CCL* 50–50A.

Aug. *Ep.* — *Sancti Aureli Augustini hipponiensis episcopi epistulae.* Edited by A. Goldacher. *CSEL* 34, 44, 57, 58.

Aug. *E. Psalm.* — Augustinus. *Ennarationes in Psalmos. CCL* 38–40.

Aug. *Serm.* — Augustinus. *Sermones. PL* 38–39.

Azdī — Muhammad b. ʿAbdullāh Abū Ismaʿīl al-Azdī al-Baṣrī. *Taʾrīkh futūḥ al-Shām.* Edited by William Nassau Lees. Bibliotheca Indica. Calcutta, 1857. Also edited by ʿAbd al-Munʿim ʿAbd Allāh ʿĀmir. Cairo: Muʾassasat Sijill al-ʿArab, 1970.

al-Baghdādī, *al-Farq baʾyn al-firaq* — al-Baghdādī, ʿAbd al-Qāhir. *Al-Farq bayn al-firaq wa-bayān al-firqa al-nājiya.*
  a) Edited by M. Badr. Cairo: Maṭbaʿat at-Maʿārif, 1910.
  (*b*) Edited by M. ʿAbd al-Ḥamīd. Cairo: Muḥammad ʿAlī Sabīḥ, n.d. [1964?].
  (*c*) Translated as *Moslem Schisms and Sects.* Vol. 1, by Kate Seelye. New York: Columbia

University Press, 1920. Vol. 2, by A. B. Halkin. Tel Aviv: Palestine Publishing Co., 1935.

al-Balādhurī, Aḥmad ibn Yaḥyā. *Ansāb al-ashrāf.* Vol. 1 edited by M. Hamidullah. Cairo: Dār al-Maʿārif, 1959. Vol. 2 edited by M. al-Maḥmūdī. Beirut: Dār al-Taʿāruf li'l-Maṭbūʿāt, 1974. Vol. 3 edited by A. A. al-Dūrī. Wiesbaden: Franz Steiner Verlag, 1978. Vol. 4 edited by Max Schloessinger and M. J. Kister. Jerusalem: Magnes Press, 1971. Same as vol. 4, pt. 1, edited by Iḥsān ʿAbbās. Wiesbaden: Franz Steiner Verlag, 1979. Vol. 4B edited by Max Schloessinger. Jerusalem: Hebrew University Press, 1938. Vol. 5 edited by S. D. Goitein. Jerusalem: Hebrew University Press, 1936.

————. *Futūḥ al-buldān.* Edited by M. J. de Goeje. Leiden: E. J. Brill, 1866. Translated by Philip K. Hitti and Francis Murgotten as *The Origins of the Islamic State.* 2 vols. Columbia University Studies in History, Economics, and Public Law, vol. 68, nos. 163, 163a. New York: Columbia University Press, 1916–24.

B.A.R.   British Archaeological Reports. Oxford, 1974– .

Basil *Hexaemeron*   *Basile de Césarée: Homélies sur l'Hexaéméron.*
(*Hom. in hex.*)   Edited by S. Giet. Sources chrétiennes, no. 26. Paris: Editions du Cerf, 1949.

Basil *Hom. in Div.*   Basilius Caesariensis. *Homilia in divites.* PG 31: 227–304.

BMC Vand.   Wroth, Warwick, *Catalogue of the Coins of the Vandals, Ostrogoths and Lombards and of the Empires of Thessalonica, Nicaea and Trebizond in the British Museum.* London: British Museum, 1911. Reprinted. Chicago: Argonaut, 1966.

CCL   *Corpus Christianorum: Series latina.* About 250 volumes projected. Turnhout: Brepols, 1954– .

Cedrenus   *Georgii Cedreni Historiarum compendium.* Edited by I. Bekker. *CSHB* 34–35 (1838–39).

CIC/CI or Cod. Just.   *Corpus iuris civilis.* Vol. 2, *Codex iustinianus.* Edited by P. Krueger. Reprint. Dublin and Zurich: Weidmann, 1967.

CIC/Dig.   *Corpus iuris civilis.* Vol. 1, *Institutiones; Digesta,* 29–926. Edited by Theodor Mommsen et al. Reprint. Dublin and Zurich: Weidmann, 1973.

CIC/NI   *Corpus iuris civilis.* Vol. 3, *Novellae Iustiniani.*

Edited by R. Schoell et al. Reprint. Dublin and Zurich: Weidmann, 1972.

CIL   *Corpus inscriptionum latinarum.* Berlin: G. Reimer, 1862–.

CLA   Lowe, E. A. *Codices latini antiquiores: A Palaeographical Guide to Latin Manuscripts Prior to the Ninth Century.* 12 vols. Oxford: Clarendon Press, 1934–71.

C Mich.   Humphrey, J. H., ed. *Excavations at Carthage Conducted by the University of Michigan.* Several volumes. Tunis and Ann Arbor, 1976–.

Comp. carth.   Krusch, B., ed. *Computus carthaginiensis sive de ratione Paschae.* In *Studien zur christlichmittelalterlichen Chronologie: Der 84-jahrige Ostercyclus und seine Quellen,* 279–97. Leipzig, 1880.

Constantine VII *De cerim.* *Constantini Porphyrogeniti imperatoris De caerimoniis aulae byzantinae libri duo.* Edited by J. Reiske. *CSHB* 9–10 (1829–30).

Consultatio   *Consultatio veteris cuiusdam iurisconsulti.* In *Fontes iuris romani antejustiniani,* edited by S. Riccobono et al., 2:594–613. 3 vols. 2d ed. Florence, 1940–43.

Corippus *Iohannis* or *Ioh.* *Flavii Cresconii Corippi Iohannidos libri viii.* Edited by J. Diggle and F. R. D. Goodyear. Cambridge: Cambridge University Press, 1970.

Courtois, Christian, Louis Leschi, et al., eds. *Tablettes Albertini: Actes privés de l'époque vandale (Fin du Vᵉ siècle).* Paris: Arts et Métiers Graphiques, 1952.

CRAI   *Comptes rendus de l'Académie des inscriptions et belles-lettres.* Paris, 1857–.

CSCO   *Corpus scriptorum christianorum orientalium.* Subseries: *Scriptores Arabici* and *Scriptores Syri.* Louvain, 1903–.

CSEL   *Corpus scriptorum ecclesiasticorum latinorum.* Vienna: C. Gerold, 1866–.

CSHB   *Corpus scriptorum historiae byzantinae.* 50 vols. Bonn: E. Weber, 1828–97.

CTh   *Codex Theodosianus. TL* 1, pt. 2.

Dessau   Dessau, Hermann, ed. *Inscriptiones latinae selectae.* Berlin, 1892–1916.

Dīnawarī, *Akhbār* al-Dīnawarī, Abū Hanīfa. *al-Akhbār al-ṭiwāl.* Edited by V. Guirgass. Leiden: E. J. Brill, 1888.

Doctrina Jacobi nuper baptizati. Edited by N. Bonwetsch. Berlin: Weidmann, 1910.

Drac. *Sat.*   *Blossi Aemili Draconti Satisfactio, una cum Eugeni*

	recensione. Edited by F. Speranza. Rome: Bretschneider, 1978.
EI or *EI²*	*Encyclopaedia of Islam.* 1st ed. Leiden: E. J. Brill, 1913–1938. 2d ed. Leiden: E. J. Brill, 1954–.
Ennodius *Panegyricus*	*Magni Felicis Ennodii Panegyricus dictus clementissimo Regi Theoderico.* Edited by F. Vogel. *MGH:AA* 7, pt. 1 (1885): 203–14.
	Eunapius. *Chronikē historia.* Edited and translated by R. C. Blockley in *The Fragmentary Classicising Historians of the Later Roman Empire,* 2:1–150. Liverpool: F. Cairns, 1983.
Eusebius of Caesarea *Onomasticon*	*Eusebius Werke: Das Onomasticon der biblischen Ortsnamen.* Edited by E. Klostermann. *GCS* 11, pt. 1. Leipzig: J. C. Hinrichs, 1904. Reprint. Hildesheim: G. Olms, 1966.
	Eutychius. *Das Annalenwerke des Eutychios von Alexandrien.* Edited by M. Breydy. *CSCO* 471, *Scriptores Arabici,* 44. Louvain, 1985.
Evagrius Scholasticus *HE*	*The Ecclesiastical History of Evagrius.* Edited by J. Bidez and L. Parmentier. London: Methuen, 1898. Reprint. Amsterdam: A. M. Hakkert, 1964.
Exposito	Rougé, J., ed. *Expositio totius mundi et gentium.* Sources chrétiennes, no. 124. Paris: Editions du Cerf, 1966.
Ferrandus *Vita Fulgentii*	*Ferrand, diacre de Carthage: Vie de Saint Fulgence de Ruspe.* Edited and translated by G. G. Lapeyre. Paris: Lethielleux, 1929.
FHG	Müller, C., ed. *Fragmenta historicorum graecorum.* 5 vols. Paris: Firmin Didot, 1841–84.
Fragmenta historicorum arabicorum	Goeje, M. J. de, ed. *Fragmenta historicorum arabicorum.* From *al-ʿUyūn waʾl-ḥadāʾiq fī akhbār al-ḥaqāʾiq.* Leiden: E. J. Brill, 1869.
GCS	*Die grieschischen christlichen Schriftsteller der ersten Jahrhunderte.* Berlin: Akademie-Verlag, 1897–.
Greg. Naz. *Or.*	Gregorius Nazianzenus. *Orationes. PG* 35:395–1252, 36:12–664.
Gregory of Tours *Historia Francorum*	*Gregorii episcopi turonensis Libri historiarum X.* Edited by B. Krusch and W. Levison. *MGH: SRM* 1, pt. 1 (1937–65).
	Die griechische Daniel Diegese: Eine altkirchliche Apokalypse. Edited by Klaus Berger. Studia Post-Biblica, vol. 27. Leiden: E. J. Brill, 1976.
HA	Hohl, E., et al., eds. *Scriptores Historiae Augustae.*

                          2 vols. 2d/3d ed. Reprint. Leipzig: B. G.
                          Teubner, 1971.
HdA   Müller, Iwan von, and Walter Otto, eds. *Handbuch
                          der Altertumswissenschaft.* Volumes in prog-
                          ress. Munich: C. H. Beck, 1923–.
Hydat. *Chron.*   *Hydace: Chronique.* Edited by Alain Tranoy. 2 vols.
                          Sources chrétiennes, nos. 218–19. Paris: Edi-
                          tions du Cerf, 1974.
Ibn al-Muqaffaʿ   Ibn al Muqaffaʿ, ʿAbd Allāḥ. *Risāla fī al-ṣaḥāba.*
                          (*a*) Edited by Muhammad Kurd ʿAlī in *Rasā'il al-
                          bulaghāʾ*, 120–31. Cairo, 1331/1913.
                          (*b*) Edited by ʿUmar Abū al-Naṣr in *Āthār Ibn al-
                          Muqaffaʿ*. Beirut: Dār Maktabat al-Ḥayāt,
                          1966.
                          (*c*) Translated by Charles Pellat as *Ibn al-Muqaffaʿ*,
                          "conseilleur" du calife. Paris: G. P. Maison-
                          neuve et Larose, 1976.
Ibn Hishām, *Sīra*   Ibn Hishām, ʿAbd Allāh. *Sīrat Rasūl Allāh.* Edited
                          by F. Wüstenfeld. 2 vols. Göttingen: Dietrich,
                          1858–60.
Ibn Manẓūr, *Lisān*   Ibn Manẓūr. *Lisān al-ʿArab.*
                          (*a*) 20 vols. Būlāq, 1300–1308/1882–83.
                          (*b*) 15 vols. Beirut: Dar Ṣādir, 1374–76/1955–56.
Ibn Qutayba   Ibn Qutayba, ʿAbd Allāh b. Muslim. *ʿUyūn al-
                          akhbār.* 4 vols. Cairo: Dār al-Kutub al-
                          Miṣriyya, 1925–30. Book 1 translated by
                          Josef Horovitz as "The Book of Govern-
                          ment." *Islamic Culture* 4 (1930): 171–98,
                          331–62, 487–530; 5 (1931): 1–27.
Ibn Ṭabāṭabā, *Fakhrī*   Ibn Ṭabāṭabā (=Ibn al-Ṭiqṭaqā), Muhammad b. ʿAlī.
                          *al-Kitāb al-fakhrī fī al-ādāb al-sulṭāniyya
                          waʾl-duwal al-islāmiyya.* Edited by E. Deren-
                          bourg. Paris, 1895; Beirut, 1386/1966. Trans-
                          lated and annotated by E. Amar as *Histoire
                          des dynasties musulmanes depuis la mort de
                          Mahomet jusq'à la chute du khalifat ʾabbāside
                          de Baghdad.* Paris, 1910.
I C Haïdra   Duval, Noël, and Françoise Prévot, eds. *Recherches
                          archéologiques à Haïdra.* Vol. 1, *Les inscrip-
                          tions chrétiennes.* Collection de l'École fran-
                          çaise de Rome, no. 18. Rome: École Française
                          de Rome, 1975.
IC Sainte-Monique   Ennabli, Liliane, ed. *Les inscriptions funéraires
                          chrétiennes de la basilique dite de Sainte-
                          Monique à Carthage.* Collection de l'École
                          française de Rome, no. 25. Rome: École Fran-
                          çaise de Rome, 1975.

ILA   Gsell, S., et al., eds. *Inscriptions latines de l'Al-*
                        gérie. 2 vols. Paris: Champion, 1922–57.
ILCV   Diehl, E., et al., eds. *Inscriptiones latinae chris-*
                        tianae veteres. 4 vols. Reprint. Berlin: Weid-
                        mann, 1961–67.
ILT   Merlin, A., ed. *Inscriptions latines de la Tunisie*.
                        Paris: Presses Universitaires de France, 1944.
Irenaeus *Adv. haer.*   Irenaeus Lugdunensis. *Adversus haereses*. Edited by
                        A. Rousseau et al. as *Irénée de Lyon: Contre*
                        les hérésies. 9 vols. Sources chrétiennes, nos.
                        100, 152, 153, 210, 211, 263, 264, 293, 294.
                        Paris: Editions du Cerf, 1965–82.
Iṣfahānī, *Maqātil*   al-Iṣfahānī, Abū al-Faraj. *Maqātil al-Ṭālibiyyīn*.
                        Teheran, 1307/1889–90 (lithographed edi-
                        tion); Teheran, 1365/1946.
Itin. Eg.   *Itinerarium Egeriae*. Edited by Ezio Franceschini
                        and R. Weber. *CCL* 175 (1965): 29–103.
                        Translated by John Wilkinson as *Egeria's*
                        Travels. London: Society for Promoting Chris-
                        tian Knowledge, 1971.
JAC   *Jahrbuch für Antike und Christentum*. Münster:
                        Aschendorff, 1958– .
Jāḥiẓ, *Manāqib*   al-Jāḥiẓ, ʿAmr b. Baḥr. "Risāla ilā Fatḥ b. Khāqān
                        fī manāqib al-Turk wa-ʿāmmat jund al-
                        khilāfa."
                        (*a*) In *Tria Opuscula*, edited by G. van Vloten,
                        1–56. Leiden: E. J. Brill, 1903.
                        (*b*) In *Rasāʾil al-Jāḥiẓ*, edited by A. M. Hārūn, 1:
                        1–86. Cairo: Maktabat al-Khanjī, 1964.
                        (*c*) Translated by C. T. Harley-Walker as "Jahiz of
                        Basra to al-Fath ibn Khaqan on the 'Exploits
                        of the Turks and the Army of the Caliphate in
                        General.'" *Journal of the Royal Asiatic So-*
                        ciety, 1915, pp. 631–97.
Jerome *Chronicon*   *Die Chronik des Hieronymus*. Edited by Rudolf
                        Helm. 2d ed. *GCS/Eusebius Werke*, vol. 7.
                        Berlin: Akademie-Verlag, 1956.
————. *Ep.*   *Sancti Eusebii Hieronymi Epistulae*. Edited by Isidor
                        Hilberg. *CSEL* 54–56 (1910–18).
John Chrysostom or Joh. Iohannes Chrysostomus. *De laudibus sancti Pauli*
    Chrys. *De laudibus*   *apostoli homiliae*. *PG* 50:473–514.
    Pauli
John Chrysostom or Joh. Iohannes Chrysostomus. *In acta apostolorum homi-*
    Chrys. *Hom. in ac.*   *liae*. *PG* 60:13–384.
John Chrysostom or Joh. Iohannes Chrysostomus. *In Matthaeum homiliae*.
    Chrys. *In*   *PG* 57, 58.
    Matt. hom.

John Chrysostom or Joh. Chrys. *Serm. in Gen.* — Iohannes Chrysostomus. *Sermones in Genesim. PG* 54:581–630.

John of Ephesus *Hist. eccl.* — Joannes, bishop of Ephesus. *Historiae ecclesiasticae Pars tertia.* Translated by E. W. Brooks. *CSCO, Scriptores Syri*, ser. 3, vol. 3 (1936).

John, bishop of Nikiu. *Chronicle.* Translated by R. H. Charles. Oxford: Oxford University Press, 1916.

Jord. *Get.* or Jordanes *Getica* — *Jordanis de origine actibusque Getarum.* Edited by Theodor Mommsen. *MGH:AA* 5 (1882): 53–138.

JRS — *Journal of Roman Studies.* London: Society for the Promotion of Roman Studies, 1911–.

Julian *Mis.* — *Misopogon.* In *L'empereur Julien: Oeuvres complètes*, edited by J. Bidez et al., vol. 2, pt. 2, pp. 141–99. Paris: Belles Lettres, 1964.

Khalīfa b. Khayyāṭ al-ʿUṣfurī. *al-Taʾrīkh.* Edited by Akram Ḍiyāʾ al-ʿUmarī. 2 vols. Najaf: Maṭbaʿat al-Adab, 1967.

Lat. reg. Wand. — Mommsen, Theodor, ed. *Laterculus regum Wandalorum et Alanorum. MGH:AA* 13 (1898): 456–60.

Leges Visigothorum — Zeumer, Karl, ed. *Leges Visigothorum.* Monumenta Germaniae historica, Legum sectio 1: Legum nationum germanicarum, vol. 1. Hannover: Hahn, 1902.

Lib. gen. — Mommsen, Theodor, ed. *Liber genealogus. MGH: AA* 9 (1892): 154–96.

Libanius. *Libanius: Selected Works.* Edited and translated by A. F. Norman. 3 vols. Loeb Classical Library. Cambridge, Mass.: Harvard University Press, 1969–77.

Libanius *Or.* — *Orationes.* In *Libanii opera*, edited by R. Foerster, vols. 1–4. Leipzig: B. G. Teubner, 1903–19.

Le livre de la couronne: Kitāb at-tāj. Translated by Charles Pellat. Collection Budé, Traductions d'auteurs arabes. Paris: Belles Lettres, 1954.

LRBC — Carson, R. A. G., P. V. Hill, and J. P. C. Kent, eds. *Late Roman Bronze Coinage, A.D. 324–498.* London: Spink and Son, Ltd., 1960.

Luxurius. Edited by Heinz Happ. 2 vols. Stuttgart: B. G. Teubner, 1986.

al-Masʿūdī, ʿAlī b. al-Ḥusayn. *Murūj al-dhahab wa-maʿādin al-jawhar.*
(a) Edited and translated by C. Barbier de Meynard

and Pavet de Courteille as *Les prairies d'or*. 9 vols. Paris: Imprimerie Impériale and Imprimerie Nationale, for the Société Asiatique, 1861–77.

(*b*) Revised edition and translation by Charles Pellat, under same title. Arabic text: 7 vols. Beirut: al-Jāmiʿa al-Lubnāniyya, 1965–79. Translation: 5 vols. Paris: Société Asiatique, 1965–74.

(*c*) Edited by Y. A. Dāghir. 4 vols. Beirut: Dār al-Andalus, 1956–66.

Merobaudes *Carmina*   *Fl. Merobaudis Reliquiae*. Edited by Friedrich Vollmer. *MGH:AA* 14 (1905): 3–20. Translated by F. M. Clover, *Flavius Merobaudes: A Translation and Historical Commentary*. Transactions of the American Philosophical Society, vol. 61, pt. 1. Philadelphia, 1971.

MGH:AA   *Monumenta Germaniae historica: Auctores antiquissimi*. 15 vols. Berlin: Weidmann, 1875–1919.

MGH:SRM   *Monumenta Germaniae historica: Scriptores rerum merovingicarum*. 7 vols. Hannover: Hahn, 1885–1965.

ND   *Notitia dignitatum: Accedunt notitia urbis constantinopolitanae et laterculi provinciarum*. Edited by Otto Seeck. Berlin: Weidmann, 1876.

NMaj   *Novellae Maioriani. TL* 2:155–78.

Not. prov.   *Notitia provinciarum et civitatum Africae*. Edited by C. Halm. *MGH:AA* 3, pt. 1 (1879): 63–71.

NTh   *Novellae Theodosii. TL* 2:1–68.

NVal   *Novellae Valentiniani. TL* 2:69–154.

OGIS   Dittenberger, Wilhelm, ed. *Orientis graeci inscriptiones selectae*. 2 vols. Leipzig: S. Hirzel, 1903–5.

Olympiodorus. *Historikoi logoi*. Edited and translated by R. C. Blockley in *The Fragmentary Classicising Historians of the Later Roman Empire*, 2:155–220. Liverpool: F. Cairns, 1983.

Pantaléon   Halkin, F., ed. "Un discours inédit du moine Pantaléon sur l'élévation de la Croix [*BHG* 427 p]." *Orientalia Christiana Periodica* 52 (1986): 257–70.

Parastaseis syntomoi khronikai. In *Constantinople in the Early Eighth Century*, edited by Averil Cameron et al. Leiden: E. J. Brill, 1984.

Passio Sancti Sabae   In "Saints de Thrace et de Mésie," edited by H. Dele-

haye. *Analecta Bollandiana* 31 (1912): 161–
300, at 216–21.

Pauli Historia Langobardorum. Edited by L. Beth-
mann and G. Waitz. Monumenta Germaniae
historica: Scriptores rerum langobardicarum et
italicarum saec. VI–IX. Hannover: Hahn,
1878.

Paul Med. *V Ambr.*   *Paulinus Mediolanensis: Vita di S. Ambrogio.* Edited
by M. Pellegrino. Rome: Ed. Studium, 1961.

PCBE   Mandouze, A., et al., eds. *Prosopographie chrétienne du Bas-Empire.* Vol. 1, *Prosopographie
de l'Afrique chrétienne (303–533).* Paris: Editions du Centre Nationale de la Recherche
Scientifique, 1982.

Periplus Maris Erythraei. Translated by W. H.
Schoff. New York: Longmans, Green and Co.,
1912.

PG   Migne, J. P., ed. *Patrologiae cursus completus: Series graeca.* 161 vols. Paris, 1857–66.

Philostorgius *Hist. eccl.*   *Philostorgius: Kirchengeschichte.* Edited by J. Bidez
and F. Winkelmann. 2d and 3d eds. Die
christlichen Schriftststeller der ersten Jahrhun-
derte. Berlin: Akademie-Verlag, 1972, 1981.

Photius *Bibliotheca*   *Photius: Bibliothèque.* Edited by R. Henry. 8 vols.
Paris: Belles Lettres, 1959–77.

PIR   *Prosopographia imperii romani.* 2d ed. Volumes in
progress. Berlin and Leipzig: de Gruyter,
1933–.

PL   Migne, J. P., ed. *Patrologiae cursus completus: Series latina.* 221 vols. Paris, 1878–87.

PLRE   Jones, A. H. M., J. R. Martindale, et al., eds. *The
Prosopography of the Later Roman Empire.*
Volumes in progress. Cambridge: Cambridge
University Press, 1971–.

Porphyry. *Life of Plotinus.* In *Plotinus, with an
English Translation,* translated by A. H.
Armstrong, vol. 1. Loeb Classical Library.
Cambridge, Mass.: Harvard University Press,
1966.

Prisc. or Priscus   *Prisci panitae fragmenta. FHG* 4 (1868): 69–110; 5
(1870): 24–26. Also edited by Fritz Bornmann
Florence: Le Monnier, 1979. Edited and translated by R. C. Blockley in *The Fragmentary
Classicising Historians of the Later Roman
Empire,* 2:221–400. Liverpool: F. Cairns,
1983.

Procopius *Buildings;*
Secret History;
Wars
In *Procopii caesariensis opera omnia.* Edited by J. Haury and G. Wirth. 4 vols. Leipzig: B. G. Teubner, 1963–64. Translated by H. B. Dewing in *Procopius, with an English Translation.* 7 vols. Loeb Classical Library. New York, 1914–40.

Prudentius *Contra Symmachum*
Aurelii Prudentii Clementis Contra orationem Symmachi libri duo. Edited by Johann Berman. *CSEL* 61 (1926): 215–88.

RAC
Reallexikon für Antike und Christentum. Stuttgart: Hiersemann, 1950–.

RIC
Mattingly, H., et al. *The Roman Imperial Coinage.* 9 vols. to date. London: Spink and Son, 1923–81.

RE
Pauly, A. von, G. Wissowa, et al., eds. *Real-Encyclopädie der classischen Altertumswissenschaft.* Stuttgart: J. Metzler, etc., 1893–1980.

Rufinus *Hist. eccl.*
Die Kirchengeschichte: Die Lateinische Übersetzung des Rufinus. Vol. 2 of *Eusebius Werke,* edited by Theodor Mommsen. *GCS* 9, pts. 1–3. Leipzig: J. C. Hinrichs, 1903–9.

al-Ṣābi', *Rusūm*
al-Ṣābi', Hilāl. *Rusūm dār al-khilāfa.* Edited by Mikhā'īl ʿAwād. Cairo, 1963; Baghdad: Maṭbaʿat al-ʿĀnī, 1964. Translated by Elie A. Salem as *The Rules and Regulations of the ʿAbbasid Court.* Beirut: American University of Beirut, 1977.

Salv. *De gub.*
Salvien de Marseille: Oeuvres. Edited by G. Lagarrique. Vol. 2, *Du gouvernement de Dieu.* Sources chrétiennes, no. 220. Paris: Editions du Cerf, 1975.

Sebeos. *Sebeos: Histoire d'Héraclius.* Translated by F. Macler. Paris, 1904. Also translated by Robert Bedrosian as *Sebeos' History.* New York: Sources of the Armenian Tradition, 1985.

SEG
Supplementum epigraphicum graecum. Alphen aan den Rijn (etc.): Sijthoff and Noordhoff (etc.), 1923–.

Sidon, *Carm.*
Sidoine Apollinaire: Poèmes. Edited by A. Loyen. Paris: Belles Lettres, 1960.

Socrates
Socrates Scholasticus. *Historia ecclesiastica. PG* 67:33–841.

Sozomen
Sozomenus Kirchengeschichte. Edited by J. Bidez and G. C. Hansen. *GCS* 50 (1960).

*Le Synekdémos d'hiéroklès et l'Opuscule géographi-
que de Georges de Chypre.* Translated and
edited by E. Honigmann. Corpus Bruxellense
Historiae Byzantinae, Forma Imperii Byzan-
tini, no. 1. Brussels, 1939.

Ṭabarī, *Annales,*
or al-Ṭabarī
al-Ṭabarī, Abū Jaʿfar Muhammad b. Jarīr. *Taʾrīkh al-
rusul waʾl-mulūk.*
(a) Edited by M. J. de Goeje et al. 15 vols. Leiden:
E. J. Brill, 1879–1901.
(b) Edited by M. A. F. Ibrāhīm. 10 vols. Cairo: Dār
al-Maʿārif, 1960–69.
(c) Translated as *The History of al-Tabari,* under the
general editorship of Ehsan Yar-Shater. 38
vols. projected. Albany, N.Y.: State University of New York Press, 1985–.

TAPA
*Transactions and Proceedings of the American Philo-
logical Association.* Hartford (etc.), 1869–.

Theodoret of Cyrrhus
*Questions on
Genesis* or *Qu.
in Gen.*
*Theodoreti episcopi cyrensis Quaestiones in Gene-
sin.* Edited by J. P. Migne. *PG* 80:77–226.

Theoph. *Chron.*
Theophanis chronographia. Edited by C. de Boor.
2 vols. Leipzig: B. G. Teubner, 1883–85.
An earlier standard edition of this chronicle
appeared in the Bonn Corpus (*CSHB* 40–41
[1839–41]).

TL
*Theodosiani libri cum constitutionibus sirmondianis
et leges novellae ad theodosianum pertinentes.*
Edited by Theodor Mommsen et al. 2 vols. 3d
ed. Reprint. Berlin: Weidmann, 1962.

Vegetius *Epitome rei
militaris*
Flavi Vegeti Renati Epitoma rei militaris. Edited by
C. Lang. 2d ed. Leipzig: B. G. Teubner,
1885. Reprint. Stuttgart: Teubner, 1967.

Vict. Vit. *HP*
*Victoris vitensis Historia persecutionis africanae
provinciae sub Geiserico et Hunirico regibus
Wandalorum.* Edited by C. Halm. *MGH:AA*
3, pt. 1 (1879): 1–58.

Vie de Théodore de Sykéôn. Translated and edited by
A.-J. Festugière. Subsididia Hagiographica,
no. 48. Brussels, 1970.

Vitae sophistarum
Philostratus and Eunapius: The Lives of the Sophists.
Translated by Wilmer C. Wright. Loeb Classical Library. Cambridge, Mass.: Harvard University Press, 1968.

al-Yaʿqūbī, *Taʾrīkh*
al-Yaʿqūbī, Aḥmad b. Abī Yaʿqūb b. Wāḍiḥ. *al-
Taʾrīkh.* Edited by M. T. Houtsma as *Ibn*

	Wadhih qui dicitur al-Ja'qubi Historiae. 2 vols. Leiden: E. J. Brill, 1883. Reprint. 1969.
Yāqūt, *Mu'jam*	Yāqūt b. 'Abdallāh al-Ḥamawī. *Mu'jam al-buldān.* (*a*) Edited by F. Wüstenfeld as *Jacut's Geographisches Wörterbuch.* 6 vols. Leipzig: F. A. Brockhaus for the Deutsche Morgenländische Gesellschaft, 1866–73. (*b*) 5 vols. Beirut: Dār Ṣādir, 1955–57.
ZfdA	*Zeitschrift für deutsches Altertum und deutsche Literatur.* Wiesbaden (etc.), 1841–.
Zosimus *Hist.* or *Historia nova*	(*a*) *Zosimi comitis et exadvocati fisci Historia nova.* Edited by L. Mendelssohn. Leipzig: B. G. Teubner, 1887. (*b*) *Zosime: Histoire nouvelle.* Edited and translated by François Paschoud. Volumes in progress. Paris: Belles Lettres, 1971–.

B. MODERN SCHOLARSHIP

'Abd Dixon, 'Abd al Ameer. *The Umayyad Caliphate, 65–86/684–705.* London: Luzac, 1971.

Abel, F. *Histoire de la Palestine.* 2 vols. Paris: J. Gabalda, 1952.

Åberg, Nils Fritjof. *Die Goten und Langobarden in Italien.* Uppsala: Almqvist & Wiksell, 1923.

Abu-Lughod, Janet L. *Cairo: 1001 Years of the City Victorious.* Princeton, N.J.: Princeton University Press, 1971.

Adams, J. P. "The Logistics of the Roman Imperial Army: Major Campaigns on the Eastern Front in the First Three Centuries A.D." Ph.D. diss., Yale University, 1976.

Adcock, F. E., and D. J. Mosley. *Diplomacy in Ancient Greece.* London: Thames and Hudson, 1975.

Aĝa-Oĝlu, Mehmet. "Remarks on the Character of Islamic Art." *Art Bulletin* 36 (1954): 175–202.

Albertini, E. "Quelques inscriptions de Madaure." *Bulletin archéologique du Comité des travaux historiques et scientifiques,* 1930–31, pp. 247–55.

Alexander, J. J. G. "The Illustrated Manuscripts of the *Notitia Dignitatum.*" In *Aspects of the Notitia Dignitatum,* edited by Roger Goodburn and Philip Bartholomew, 11–50. British Archaeological Reports, Supplementary Series, no. 15. Oxford: British Archaeological Reports, 1976.

Alexander, Paul J. *The Byzantine Apocalyptic Tradition.* Edited by Dorothy de Ferrante Abrahamse. Berkeley and Los Angeles: University of California Press, 1985.

Allen, Terry. *A Classical Revival in Islamic Architecture.* Wiesbaden: Ludwig Reichert, 1986.

Audollent, Auguste. *Carthage romaine, 146 avant Jésus-Christ–698 après Jésus-Christ.* Bibliothèque des écoles françaises d'Athènes et de Rome, fasc. 84. Paris: A. Fontemoing, 1901.

Aymard, André. *Etudes d'historie ancienne.* Paris: Presses Universitaires de France, 1967.

Aymard, André. "Les ôtages barbares au début de l'empire." *Journal of Roman Studies* 51 (1961): 136–42.

Aymard, André. "Les ôtages carthaginois à la fin de la deuxième guerre punique." *Pallas* 1 (1953): 44–66.

Azizi, M. *La domination arabe et l'épanouissment du sentiment national en Iran.* Paris: Les Presses Modernes, 1938.

Badewien, J. *Geschichtstheologie und Sozialkritik im Werk Salvians von Marseille.* Göttingen: Vandenhoeck and Ruprecht, 1980.

Bagnall, Roger S., and K. A. Worp. *The Chronological Systems of Byzantine Egypt.* Zutphen: Terra Publishing Co., 1978.

Bagnall, Roger S., and K. A. Worp. *Regnal Formulas in Byzantine Egypt.* Bulletin of the American Society of Papyrologists, suppl. 2. Missoula, Mont.: Scholars Press, 1979.

Baillet, J. "Constantin et le dadouque d'Eleusis." *Comptes rendus de l'Académie des inscriptions et belles-lettres,* 1922, pp. 282–96.

Baker, Philip, and Chris Corne. *Isle de France Creole: Affinities and Origins.* Ann Arbor, Mich.: Karoma, 1982.

Baratte, François, and Noël Duval. *Catalogue des mosaïques romaines et paléochrétiennes du Musée du Louvre.* Paris: Editions de la Réunion des Musées Nationaux, 1978.

Barnes, Timothy D. *Constantine and Eusebius.* Cambridge, Mass.: Harvard University Press, 1981.

Barnes, Timothy D. *The New Empire of Diocletian and Constantine.* Cambridge, Mass.: Harvard University Press, 1982.

Barral i Altet, Xavier. *La circulation des monnaies suèves et visigotiques.* Beihefte der Francia, vol. 4. Zurich and Munich: Artemis Verlag, 1976.

Barth, Frederik. *Nomads of South Persia.* New York: Humanities Press, 1961.

Baye, J. "Bijoux vandales des environs de Bône." *Mémoires de la Société nationale des antiquaires de France* 48 (1887): 179–92.

Bayet, Jean. "L'*omen* du cheval à Carthage: Timée, Virgile et le monnayage punique." In *Mélanges de littérature latine,* edited by J. Bayet, 255–80. Rome: Edizioni di Storia e Letteratura, 1967.

Baynes, Norman H. *Byzantine Studies and Other Essays.* London: Athlone Press, 1955.

Baynes, Norman H., and H. St. L. B. Moss. *Byzantium: An Introduction to East Roman Civilization.* Oxford: Clarendon Press, 1948.

Becker, Carl H. *Beiträge zur Geschichte Ägyptens unter dem Islam.* 2 vols. Strassbourg: K. J. Trübner, 1902–3.

Becker, Carl H. "The Expansion of the Saracens." Chaps. 11–12 in *The Cambridge Medieval History,* edited by H. M. Gwatkin et al., vol. 2. Cambridge: Cambridge University Press, 1913.

Bellinger, Alfred R., Philip Grierson, et al. *Catalogue of the Byzantine Coins in the Dumbarton Oaks Collection and in the Whittemore Collection.* Volumes in progress. Washington, D.C.: Dumbarton Oaks Center for Byzantine Studies, 1966-.

Beltrán, Antonio, and Antonio Tovar. *Contrebia Belaisca (Botorrita, Zaragoza).* Vol. 1, *El bronce con alfabeto "iberico" de Botorrita.* Zaragoza: Universidad de Zaragoza, 1982.

Bengtson, Hermann. *Griechische Geschichte von den Anfängen bis in die römische Kaiserzeit.* 4th ed. Handbuch der Altertumswissenschaft, Abteilung 3, Teil 4. Munich: C. H. Beck, 1969.

Berchem, D. van. "L'annone militaire dans l'empire romain au III ᵉ siècle." *Mémoires de la Société nationale des antiquaires de France,* 8th ser., 10 (1937): 117–202.

———. "L'annone militaire est-elle un mythe?" In *Armée et fiscalité dans le monde antique.* Colloques Nationaux du Centre National de la Recherche Scientifique, no. 936. Paris: Editions du Centre National de la Recherche Scientifique, 1977.

Berchem, Max van, Josef Strzygowski, and Gertrude Bell. *Amida.* Heidelberg: C. Winter, 1910.

Berger, Pamela C. *The Insignia of the Notitia Dignitatum.* New York and London: Garland Publishing, 1981.

Bickerton, Derek. *Roots of Language.* Ann Arbor, Mich.: Karoma, 1981.

Bickerton, Derek, and Aquilas Escalante. "Palenquero: A Spanish-based Creole of Northern Columbia." *Lingua* 24 (1970): 254–67.

Biondi, B. *Il diritto romano cristiano.* 3 vols. Milan: Giuffrè, 1952–54.

Bischoff, B., and W. Koehler. "Un'edizione illustrata degli Annali ravennati del Basso Impero." *Studĭ romagnoli* 3 (1952): 1–17.

Bishop, M. C., ed. *The Production and Distribution of Roman Military Equipment.* Oxford: British Archaeological Reports, 1985.

Blass, F. W., and A. Debrunner. *A Greek Grammar of the New Testament and Other Early Christian Literature.* Translated by R. Funk. 9–10th ed. Chicago: University of Chicago Press, 1961.

Bleicken, J. *Verfassungs- und Sozialgeschichte des römischen Kaiserreiches.* 2 vols. Paderborn: F. Schöningh, 1978.

Blockley, R. C. *The Fragmentary Classicising Historians of the Later Roman Empire.* 2 vols. Liverpool: F. Cairns, 1981–83.

Boissier, Gaston. *La fin du paganisme, étude sur les dernières luttes religieuses en Occident au IV ᵉ siècle.* Paris: Hachette, 1891.

Bonfante, Giuliano, and Larissa Bonfante. *The Etruscan Language: An Introduction.* New York: New York University Press, 1983.

Bonnal, J. P., and Paul-Albert. Février. "Ostraka de la région de Bir Trouch." *Bulletin d'archéologie algérienne* 2 (1966–67): 239–49.

Bosl, K. *Frühformen der Gesellschaft im mittelalterlichen Europa: Ausgewählte Beiträge zu einer Strukturanalyse der mittelalterlichen Welt.* Munich: R. Oldenbourg, 1964.

Bowersock, G. W. *Roman Arabia.* Cambridge, Mass.: Harvard University Press, 1983.

Boyce. Aline Abaecherli. *Festal and Dated Coins of the Roman Empire: Four Papers.* Numismatic Notes and Monographs, no. 153. New York: American Numismatic Society, 1965.

Braunert, H. *Politik, Recht und Gesellschaft in der griechisch-römischen Antike.* Kieler historische Studien, vol. 26. Stuttgart: Klett-Kotta, 1980.

Broad, Charlie Dunbar. *Induction, Probability, and Causation.* Dordrecht: D. Reidel, 1968.

Brock, Sebastian. "Syriac Views of Emergent Islam." In *Studies on the First Century of Islamic Society,* edited by G. H. A. Juynboll, 9–22. Carbondale: Southern Illinois University Press, 1982.

Brown, Peter. *Religion and Society in the Age of Saint Augustine.* New York: Harper, 1972.

Brown, Peter. "Sexuality and Society in the Fifth Century A.D.: Augustine and Julian of Eclanum." In *Tria cordia: Scritti in onore di Arnaldo Momigliano,* edited by E. Gabba. Como: Edizioni New Press, 1983.

Brown, Peter. *The World of Late Antiquity.* New York: Harcourt Brace Jovanovich, 1971.

Brown, T. S. *Gentlemen and Officers: Imperial Administration and Aristocratic Power in Byzantine Italy A.D. 554–800.* London: British School at Rome, 1984.

Browning, Robert. *Byzantium and Bulgaria: A Comparative Study across the Early Medieval Frontier.* Berkeley and Los Angeles: University of California Press, 1975.

Bruckner, Wilhelm. *Die sprache der Langobarden.* Quellen and Forschungen zur Sprach- und Culturgeschichte der germanischen Völker, no. 75. Strasbourg: K. J. Trübner, 1895. Reprint. Berlin: de Gruyter, 1969.

Brunner, O., W. Conze, and R. Koselleck. *Geschichtliche Grundbegriffe: Historiches Lexikon zur politisch-sozialen Sprache in Deutschland.* 5 vols. thus far. Stuttgart: E. Klett, 1972–84.

Burian, J. "Zur historischen Glaubwürdigkeit der Gordiani tres in der Historia Augusta." In *Atti del colloquio patavino sulla Historia Augusta.* Rome: Bretschneider, 1963.

Bussière, J. "Note sur la datation d'une lampe à tête de cheval trouvée à Renault (Oranie)." *Antiquités africaines* 3 (1969): 237–42.

Buttrey, T. V. "The Coins." In *Excavations at Carthage, 1975, Conducted by the University of Michigan,* edited by J. H. Humphrey, vol. 1, 157–97. Tunis: Cérès Productions, 1976.

Cahen, Claude. "Points de vue sur la révolution Abbāside." *Revue historique* 230 (1963): 295–338.

Cahen, Claude. "The Turkish Invasions: The Selchükids." In *A History of the Crusades,* edited by Kenneth M. Setton et al., 1:135–76. Madison: University of Wisconsin Press, 1969.

Calderini, Aristide. *Aquileia romana: Ricerche di stoira e di epigrafia.* Milan: Vita e Pensiero, 1930.

Cameron, Alan. "The Date and Owners of the Esquiline Treasure." *American Journal of Archaeology* 89 (1985): 135–45.

Cameron, Averil. "Byzantine Africa: The Literary Evidence." In *Excavations at Carthage, 1978, Conducted by the University of Michigan,* edited by J. H. Humphrey, 7:29–62. Ann Arbor, Mich.: Kelsey Museum, 1982.

Cameron, Averil. "Corippus' *Iohannis:* Epic of Byzantine Africa." *Papers of the Liverpool Latin Seminar* 4 (1983): 167–80.

Cameron, Averil. *Procopius and the Sixth Century.* London: Duckworth, 1985.

Carandini, A. "Pottery and the African Economy." In *Trade in the Ancient Economy,* edited by P. Garnsey, K. Hopkins, and C. R. Whittaker, 145–62. London: Chatto and Windus, 1983.

Carcopino, Jérôme. *Le Maroc antique*. 13th ed. Paris: Gallimard, 1948.

Carrié, Jean-Michel. "L'Esercito, trasformazioni funzionali ed economie locali." In *Società romana e impero tardoantico*, vol. 1, *Istituzioni, ceti, economie*, edited by Andrea Giardina, 454–56. Rome and Bari: Editori Laterza, 1986.

Casson, Lionel. "Rome's Trade with the East: The Sea Voyage to Africa and India." *Transactions of the American Philological Association* 110 (1980): 21–36.

Castile, George P., and Gilbert Kushner, eds. *Persistent Peoples: Cultural Enclaves in Perspective*. Tucson: University of Arizona Press, 1981.

Cerati, André. *Caractère annonaire et assiette de l'impôt foncier au Bas-Empire*. Paris: Librairie Générale de Droit et de Jurisprudence, 1975.

Cesa, M. "La politica di Giustiniano verso l'occidente nel giudizio di Procopio." *Athenaeum*, n.s. 59 (1981): 389–409.

Chadwick, H., et al. *The Role of the Christian Bishop in Ancient Society*. Protocol of the 35th Colloquy, Center for Hermeneutical Studies. Berkeley, Calif.: The Center, 1980.

Chalon, Michel, et al. "Memorabile factum: Une célébration de l'évergétisme des rois vandales dans l'Anthologie latine." *Antiquités africaines* 21 (1985): 207–62.

Champetier, P. "Les conciles africaines durant la période byzantine." *Revue africaine* 95 (1951): 103–19.

Chapot, V. *La frontière de l'Euphrate de Pompée à la conquête arabe*. Paris: A. Fontemoing, 1907.

Charles, Henri C. *Tribus moutonnières du Moyen-Euphrats*. Damascus: Institut Français d'Etudes Arabes, n.d. (ca. 1937).

Chastagnol, André. "L'évolution de l'ordre sénatorial aux III e et IV e siècles de notre ère." *Revue historique* 244 (1970): 305–14.

Chastagnol, André, and Noël Duval. "Les survivances du culte impérial dans l'Afrique du Nord à l'époque vandale." In *Mélanges d'histoire ancienne offerts à William Seston*, 87–118. Paris: de Boccard, 1974.

Chavannes, ed. "Les pays d'occident d'après les Heou Han Chou." *Archives de l'Asie orientale* 8 (1907).

Chiabò, M. *Index verborum Ammiani Marcellini*. 2 vols. Hildesheim: G. Olms, 1983.

Christensen, A. *L'Iran sous les Sassanides*. 2d ed. Copenhagen: Munksgaard, 1944.

Cintas, J., and Noël Duval. "L 'église du prêtre Felix (région de Kélibia)." *Karthago* 9 (1958): 155–265.

Claude, D. *Die byzantinische Stadt im 6. Jahrhundert*. Byzantinisches Archiv, no. 13. Munich: C. H. Beck, 1969.

Clover, Frank M. "Carthage and the Vandals." In *Excavations at Carthage, 1978, Conducted by the University of Michigan*, edited by J. H. Humphrey, 7:1–22. Ann Arbor, Mich.: Kelsey Museum, 1982.

Clover, Frank M. "The Pseudo-Boniface and the *Historia Augusta*." In *Bonner Historia-Augusta-Colloquium 1977/78*, 73–95. Bonn: Rudolf Habelt, 1980.

Colt Archaeological Expedition: Excavations at Nessana. Princeton, N.J.: Princeton University Press, 1950–.

Courcelle, Pierre. *Histoire littéraire des grandes invasions germaniques*. 3d ed. Paris: Etudes Augustiniennes, 1964.

Courtney, E. "Observations on the Latin Anthology." *Hermathena* 129 (1980): 37–50.

Courtois, Christian. "Les monnaies de Gildo." *Revue numismatique,* 5th ser., 16 (1954): 71–77.

Courtois, Christian. *Les Vandales et l'Afrique.* Paris: Arts et Métiers Graphiques, 1955. Reprint. Aalen: Scientia Verlag, 1964.

Courtois, Christian, et al., eds. *Tablettes Albertini: Actes privès de l'époque vandale.* Paris: Arts et Métiers Graphiques, 1952.

Creswell, K. A. C. *Early Muslim Architecture.* 2 vols. 1932–40. Rev. ed. Oxford: Clarendon Press, 1969.

Creswell, K. A. C. *The Muslim Architecture of Egypt.* Oxford: Oxford University Press, 1952. Reprint. 1978.

Crone, Patricia, and Michael Cook. *Hagarism: The Making of the Islamic World.* Cambridge: Cambridge University Press, 1977.

Crone, Patricia, and Martin Hinds. *God's Caliph: Religious Authority in the First Centuries of Islam.* Cambridge: Cambridge University Press, 1986.

Cunliffe, Barry. *The Celtic World.* New York: McGraw-Hill, 1979.

Cuoq, J. *L' église d'Afrique du Nord du IIe au IXe siècle.* Paris: Le Centurion, 1984.

Dagron, Gilbert. *Naissance d'un capitale: Constantinople et ses institutions de 330 à 451.* Bibliothèque byzantine: Etudes, no. 7. Paris: Presses Universitaires de France, 1974.

Daniel, Elton. *The Political and Social History of Khurasan under Abbasid Rule, 747–820.* Minneapolis: Bibliotheca Islamica, 1979.

Deichmann, Friedrich Wilhelm. *Ravenna: Haupstadt des spätantiken Abendlandes.* 3 vols. 2d ed. of vol. 3. Wiesbaden: Franz Steiner Verlag, 1969–76.

Delbrueck, R. *Die Consulardiptychen und verwandte Denkmäler.* Berlin: de Gruyter, 1929.

Delbrueck, R. "Zwei christliche Elfenbeine des 5. Jahrhunderts." In *Spätantike und Byzanz: Neue Beiträge zur Kunstgeschichte des 1. Jahrtausends,* vol. 1. Forschungen zur Kunstgeschichte und christliche Archäologie, vol. 1. Baden-Baden: Verlag für Kunst und Wissenschaft, 1952.

Delehaye, H., ed. "Saints de Thrace et de Mésie." *Analecta Bollandiana* 31 (1912): 161–300.

Dennett, D. "Marwān b. Muḥammad and the Passing of the Umayyad Caliphate." Ph.D. diss., Harvard University, 1939.

Dennis, H. V. M. "Another Note on the Vandal Occupation of Hippo Regius." *Journal of Roman Studies* 15 (1925): 263–68.

Dentzer, J.-M. *Le motif du banquet couché dans le Proche-Orient et le monde grec du VIIe au IVe siècle avant J.-C.* Bibliothèque des écoles françaises d'Athènes et de Rome, no. 246. Paris: de Boccard, 1982.

De Ste. Croix, G. E. M. *The Class Struggle in the Ancient Greek World.* London: Duckworth, 1981.

Diehl, Charles. *L'Afrique byzantine.* Paris: E. Leroux, 1896.

Diesner, Hans-Joachim. *Das Vandalenreich: Aufstieg und Untergang.* Urban-Bücher, no. 95. Stuttgart: Kohlhammer, 1966.

Diesner, Hans-Joachim. "Zur Erforschung der langobardischen Gesellschaft." *Jahrbuch für internationale Germanistik* 10, no. 2 (1978): 63–76.

Dihle, A. "The Conception of India in Hellenistic and Roman Literature." *Proceedings of the Cambridge Philological Society,* n.s. 10 (1964): 15–23.

Dihle, A. "Indische Philosophen bei Clemens Alexandrinus." In *Mullus: Festschrift für Theodor Klauser,* 60–70. Münster: Aschendorff, 1964.

Dihle, A. "Die Sending des Inders Theophilus." *Politeia und Res Publica: Palingenesia* 4 (1969): 330–36.

Dihle, A. *Umstrittene Daten.* Cologne: Westdeutscher Verlag, 1965.

Dill, S. *Roman Society in the Last Century of the Western Empire.* 2d ed. London: Macmillan, 1933.

Dilleman, L. *Haute Mésopotamie orientale et pays adjacents.* Institut français d'archéologie de Beyrouth, no. 72. Paris: Geuthner, 1962.

Dimand, Maurice. "Studies in Islamic Ornament, II. The Origin of the Second Style of Samarra Decoration." In *Archaeologica Orientalia in Memoriam Ernst Herzfeld,* edited by George C. Miles, 62–68. Locust Valley, N.Y.: J. J. Augustin, 1952.

Donner, Fred M. *The Early Islamic Conquests.* Princeton, N.J.: Princeton University Press, 1981.

Dorian, Nancy C. "Gender in a Terminal Gaelic Dialect." *Scottish Gaelic Studies* 12 (1976a), 279–82.

Dorian, Nancy C. "Grammatical Change in a Dying Dialect." *Language* 49 (1973): 414–38.

Dorian, Nancy C. "A Hierarchy of Morphophonemic Decay in Scottish Gaelic Language Death: The Differential Failure of Lenition." *Celtic Linguistics—1976.* Published in *Word* 28 (1976b): 96–109.

Dorian, Nancy C. "The Problem of the Semi-Speaker in Language Death." *International Journal of the Sociology of Language* 12 (1977): 23–32.

Dreisch, Hans Adolf Eduard. *The Science and Philosophy of the Organism.* 2 vols. London: A. C. Black, 1908.

Dressler, Wolfgang U. "Wortbildung bei Sprachverfall." Manuscript, University of Vienna, n.d.

Dubois, L. J. J. *Description des objets d'arts qui composent le cabinet de feu M. le Baron V. Denon.* Vol. 2, *Monuments antiques, historiques, modernes; ouvrages orientaux, etc.* Paris, 1826.

Dunabin, Katherine M. D. *The Mosaics of Roman North Africa: Studies in Iconography and Patronage.* Oxford: Clarendon Press, 1978.

Dunabin, Katherine M. D. "A Mosaic Workshop in Carthage around A.D. 400." In *New Light of Ancient Carthage,* edited by J. G. Pedley, 73–83. Ann Arbor: University of Michigan Press, 1980.

Dunabin, Katherine M. D. "The Victorious Charioteer on Mosaics and Related Monuments." *American Journal of Archaeology* 86 (1982): 65–89.

Durliat, Jean. *Les dédicaces d'ouvrage de défense dans l'Afrique byzantine.* Collection de l'Ecole française de Rome, no. 49. Rome: Ecole Française de Rome, 1981.

Durliat, Jean. "La lettre L dans les inscriptions byzantines d'Afrique." *Byzantion* 49 (1979): 156–74.

Durry, Marcel. *Les cohortes prétoriennes.* Paris: de Boccard, 1938.

Duval, Amaury. *Monuments des arts du dessin chez les peuples tant anciens que modernes, recueilles par le Baron Vivant Denon.* . . . 4 vols. Paris, 1829.

Duval, Noël. "Comment distinguer les inscriptions byzantines d'Afrique?" *Byzantion* 51 (1981): 511–32.

Duval, Noël. "Les églises d'Haïdra, III: L'église de la citadelle et l'architecture byzantine en Afrique." *Comptes rendus de l'Académie des inscriptions et belles-lettres,* 1971, pp. 136–66.

Duval, Noël. "Etudes d'architecture chrétienne nord-africaine." *Mélanges de l'Ecole française de Rome* 84 (1972): 1071–72.

Duval, Noël. "Observations sur l'urbanisme tardif de Sufetula (Tunisie)." *Cahiers de Tunisie* 12 (1964): 87–106.

Duval, Noël. "Recherches sur la datation des inscriptions chrétiennes d'Afrique en dehors de la Maurétanie." In *Atti del tezzo congresso internazionale di epigrafia greca e latina (Roma. 4–8 settembre 1957),* 245–62. Rome: Bretschneider, 1959.

Duval. Noël. "Trois notes sur les antiquités chrétiennes d'Haïdra, l'ancienne Ammaedara (Tunisie)." *Bulletin de la Société nationale des antiquaires de France,* 1963, pp. 44–68.

Duval, Noël, and François Baratte. *Les ruines de Sufetula: Sbeitla.* Tunis: Société Tunisienne de Diffusion, 1973.

Duval, Yvette. *Loca Sanctorum Africae: Le culte des martyres en Afrique du IVe au VIIe siècle.* 2 vols. Collection de l'Ecole française de Rome, no. 58. Rome: Ecole Française de Rome, 1982.

Ellis, S. P. "Excavations in the Canadian Sector (2CC9)." *CEDAC Carthage* 5 (1985): 21–22.

Ennabli, Abdelmajid. *Lampes chrétiennes de Tunisie.* Paris: Editions du Centre National de la Recherche Scientifique, 1976.

Erdmann, Kurt. "Die Kapitelle am Taq i Bostan." *Mitteilungen der Deutschen Orient-Gesellschaft,* no. 80 (1943): 1–24.

Ess, Josef van. "Les Qadarites et la Gailānīya de Yazīd III." *Studia Islamica* 31 (1970): 269–86.

Ettinghausen, Richard. "The 'Beveled Style' in the Post-Samarra Period." In *Archaeologica Orientalia in Memoriam Ernst Herzfeld,* edited by George C. Miles, 72–83. Locust Valley, N.Y.: J. J. Augustin, 1952.

Ettinghausen, Richard. "The Character of Islamic Art." In *The Arab Heritage,* edited by N. A. Faris, 251–67. Princeton, N.J.: Princeton University Press, 1944.

Ettinghausen, Richard. "Interaction and Integration in Islamic Art." In *Unity and Variety in Muslim Civilization,* edited by Gustave E. von Grunebaum, 107–31. Chicago: University of Chicago Press, 1955.

Ettinghausen, Richard. "Medieval Islamic Metal Objects of Unusual Shapes and Decorations in the Metropolitan Museum of Art." *Islamic Archaeological Studies* (Cairo) 1 (1978 [1982]): 27–77.

Fage, J. D., and R. Oliver, eds. *The Cambridge History of Africa.* 8 vols. Cambridge: Cambridge University Press, 1975–86.

Feld, Otto. "Bericht über eine Reise durch Kilikien." *Istanbuler Mitteilungen* 13–14 (1963–64): 88–107.

Feld, Otto. "Zu den Kapitellen des Tekfur Saray in Istanbul." *Istanbuler Mitteilungen* 19–20 (1969–70): 360–67.

Ferron, J. "Le caractère solaire du dieu de Carthage." *Africa* 1 (1966): 41–63.

Février, Paul-Albert. "Inscriptions chrétiennes de Djemila (Cuicul)." *Bulletin d'ar-chéologie algérienne* 1 (1962–65): 207–26.

Flury, Samuel. "Samarra und die Ornamentik der Moschee des Ibn Tūlūn." *Der Islam* 4 (1913): 421–32.

Fiebiger, Otto. *Inschriftensammlung zur Geschichte der Ostgermanen.* Denkschriften der Akademie der Wissenschaften in Wien, Philologisch-histische Klasse, Band 70, Abteilung 3. Vienna: Die Akademie der Wissenschaften, 1939.

Förstemann, Ernst. *Altdeutsches Namenbuch.* 2 vols. 2d ed. Bonn: P. Hanstein's Verlag, 1900–16.

Foss, Clive. "Archaeology and the 'Twenty Cities' of Byzantine Asia." *Americal Journal of Archaeology* 81 (1977): 469–86.

Foss, Clive. "The Persians in Asia Minor and the End of Antiquity." *English Histori-cal Review* 90 (1975): 721–47.

Fraser, Peter M. *Ptolemic Alexandria.* 3 vols. Oxford: Clarendon Press, 1972. Reprint. Oxford: Clarendon Press, 1984.

Freeman, Philip, and David Kennedy, eds. *The Defence of the Roman and Byzantine East.* 2 vols. British Institute of Archaeology at Ankara, no. 8. British Archaeological Reports, International Series, no. 297. Oxford: British Archaeological Reports, 1986.

Frend, W. H. C. "The End of Byzantine Africa: Some Evidence of Transitions." *Bul-letin archéologique du Comité des travaux historiques et scientifiques,* n.s. 19B (1983 [1985]): 387–97.

Frend, W. H. C. "North Africa and Europe in the Early Middle Ages." *Transactions of the Royal Historical Society,* 5th ser., 5 (1955): 61–80.

Frend, W. H. C. "The North African Cult of Martyrs." In *Jenseitsvorstellungen in An-tike und Christentum: Gedenkschrift für Alfred Stuiber,* edited by E. Dassmann, 154–67. J. A. C. Egänzungsband, no. 9. Münster: Aschendorff, 1982.

Frend, W. H. C. Review of *Les Vandales et l'Afrique,* by Christian Courtois. *Journal of Roman Studies* 46 (1956): 161–66.

Friedländer, Julius. *Die Münzen der Vandalen.* Leipzig: Georg Wigand's Verlag, 1849.

Frye, Richard N. *The History of Ancient Iran.* Handbuch der Altertumswissenschaft, Abteilung 3, Teil 7. Munich: C. H. Beck, 1984.

Fuchs, Siegfried. "Bildnisse und Denkmäler aus der Ostgotenzeit." *Die Antike* 19 (1943): 109–53.

Fulford, M. G. "Carthage: Overseas Trade and the Political Economy, A.D. 400–700." *Reading Medieval Studies* 6 (1980): 66–80.

Gabrieli, Francesco. *Muhammad and the Conquests of Islam.* Translated by V. Luling and R. Linell. New York: McGraw-Hill, 1968.

Gagé, J. *Les classes sociales dans l'empire romain.* 2d ed. Paris: Payot, 1971.

Gall, Hubertus von. "Entwicklung und Gestalt des Thrones im vorislamischen Iran." *Archaeologische Mitteilungen aus Iran,* n.s. 4 (1971): 220–23.

Gamillscheg, Ernst. "Historica linguistica de los Visigodos." *Rivista de filologica es-pañola* 19 (1932): 117–50, 229–50.

Gamillscheg, Ernst. *Romania Germanica.* Grundriβ der germanischen Philologie, vol. 11, no. 2. Berlin: de Gruyter, 1935.

Ganz, Peter. "Langobardische Miszellen." *Zeitschrift für deutsches Altertum und deutsche Literatur* 87 (1957): 244–53.

Garnsey, P., K. Hopkins, and C. R. Whittaker, eds. *Trade in the Ancient Economy.* London: Chatto and Windus, 1983.

Garrigues, J. M. *Maxime le Confesseur.* Paris: Beauchesne, 1976.

Garrucci, Raffaele. *Storia dell'arte cristiana nei primi otto secoli della chiesa.* 6 vols. Prato: G. Guasti, 1873–81.

Garsoïan, Nina G., et al., eds. *East of Byzantium: Syria and Armenia in the Formative Period.* Washington, D.C.: Dumbarton Oaks, 1982.

Gauckler, Paul. "La personnification de Carthage: Mosaïque du Musée du Louvre." *Mémoires de la Société nationale des Antiquaires de France* 63 (1904): 165–78.

Gaudemet, J. "Les abus des 'potentes' au Bas Empire." *Irish Jurist* 1 (1966): 128ff.

Gautier, Emile Félix. *Genséric, roi des Vandales.* Paris: Payot, 1932.

Germanische Denkmäler der Völkerwanderungszeit. 7 vols. Berlin: de Gruyter, 1931–62.

Gibb, H. A. R. "The Fiscal Rescript of ʿUmār II." *Arabica* 2 (1955): 1–16.

Gibb, H. A. R. "Government and Islam under the Early Abbasids: The Political Collapse of Islam." In *L'élaboration de l'Islam,* 115–27. Paris: Presses Universitaires de France, 1961.

Gibbon, Edward. *The History of the Decline and Fall of the Roman Empire,* edited by J. B. Bury. 7 vols. London: Methuen, 1896–1913.

Gobineau, Arthur, comte de. *Essai sur l'inégalité des races humaines.* 4 vols. in 2. Paris: Firmin Didot, 1853–55.

Goldziher, Ignaz. "Historiography in Arabic Literature." In *Gesammelte Schriften.* 5 vols. Hildesheim: G. Olms, 1967–73.

Goldziher, Ignaz. "Muruwwa and Din." In *Muslim Studies,* translated by C. R. Barber and S. M. Stern, 1:11–136. London: Allen and Unwin, 1967.

Gonosová, Anna. "The Role of Ornament in Late Antique Interiors with Special Reference to Intermedia Borrowing of Patterns." Ph.D. diss., Harvard University, 1981.

Goodburn, Roger, and Philip Bartholomew, eds. *Aspects of the Notitia Dignitatum.* British Archaeological Reports, Supplementary Series, no. 15. Oxford: British Archaeological Reports, 1976.

Gothofredus, I. *Codex Theodosianus cum perpetuis commentariis.* 6 vols. Mantua, 1736–43. Reprint. Hildesheim: G. Olms, 1975.

Goubert, Paul. *Byzance avant l'Islam.* 2 vols. Paris: Picard, 1951–65.

Grabar, A. *Christian Iconography: A Study of Its Origins.* A. W. Mellon Lectures in the Fine Arts, vol. 10. Princeton, N.J.: Princeton University Press, 1968.

Grabar, Oleg. *The Formation of Islamic Art.* New Haven, Conn.: Yale University Press, 1973.

Graf, Georg. *Geschichte der christlichen arabischen Literatur.* 5 vols. Vatican City: Biblioteca Apostolica Vaticana, 1944–53.

Graindor, P. "Constantin et le dadouque Nicagoras." *Byzantion* 3 (1926): 209–14.

Gray, E. W. "The Roman Eastern Limes from Constantine to Justinian." *Proceedings of the African Classical Associations* 12 (1973): 24–40.

Gray, John. *A History of Jerusalem.* London: Robert Hale, 1969.

Grierson, Philip. "An Enigmatic Coin Legend: IMP XXXXII on *solidi* of Theodosius II." In *Studia numismatica labacensia Alexandro Jeločnik oblata,* edited by Željko Demo and Peter Kos. Situla 26. Ljubljana: Narodni Muzej, forthcoming.

Grierson, Philip. "The *Tablettes Albertini* and the Value of the *Solidus* in the Fifth and Sixth Centuries A.D." *Journal of Roman Studies* 49 (1959): 73–80.

Grierson, Philip, and Mark Blackburn. *Medieval European Coinage, with a Catalogue of the Coins in the Fitzwillian Museum, Cambridge.* Vol. 1, *The Early Middle Ages (5th–10th Centuries).* Cambridge: Cambridge University Press, 1986.

Grivaud de La Vincelle, Claude Madeleine. *Recueil de monumens antiques, la plupart inédits et découverts dans l'ancienne Gaule.* 2 vols. Paris, 1817.

Grønvik, Ottar. *Die dialektgeographische Stellung des Krimgotischen und die krimgotische cantilena.* Oslo: Universitetsforlaget, 1983.

Guéry, Roger. "Notes de céramique." *Bulletin d'archéologie algérienne* 3 (1968): 271–81.

Guéry, Roger, Cécile Morrisson, and H. Slim. *Recherches archéologiques franco-tunisiennes à Rougga.* Vol. 3, *Le trésor de monnaies d'or byzantines.* Rome: Ecole Française de Rome, 1982.

Guillou, André. *Culture et société en Italie byzantine (VIᵉ–XIᵉ s.).* London: Variorum Reprints, 1978.

Guillou, André. "La Sicile byzantine: Etat de recherches." *Byzantinische Forschungen* 5 (1977): 95–147.

Haag, H., ed. *Bibellexikon.* 2d ed. Zurich: Benziger, 1968.

Haldon, John. *Byzantine Praetorians.* Bonn: Rudolf Habelt, 1984.

Haldon, John. "Ideology and Social Change in the Seventh Century: Military Discontent as a Social Barometer." *Klio* 68 (1986): 139–90.

Haldon, John, and Hugh Kennedy. "The Arab-Byzantine Frontier in the Eighth and Ninth Centuries." *Zbornik Radova, Vizantoloshki Institut* (Belgrade) 19 (1980): 79–116.

Halkin, A. S. *Moslem Schisms and Sects.* Tel-Aviv: Palestine Publishing Co., 1935.

Hamerton-Kelly, Robert, and Robin Scroggs, eds. *Jews, Greeks and Christians: Religious Cultures in Late Antiquity—Essays in Honor of William David Davies.* Studies in Judaism in Late Antiquity, vol. 21. Leiden: E. J. Brill, 1976.

Hamilton, R. W. *The Structural History of the Aqsa Mosque: A Record of Archaeological Gleanings from the Repairs of 1938–1942.* London: Oxford University Press, 1949.

Hamilton, R. W. *Khirbat al-Mafjar: An Arabian Mansion in the Jordan Valley.* Oxford: Oxford University Press, 1959.

Hammond, Mason, and Lester J. Bartson. *The City in the Ancient World.* Cambridge, Mass.: Harvard University Press, 1972.

Harmand, L. *Libanius: Discours sur les patronages.* Paris: Presses Universitaires de France, 1955.

Helbling, Hanno. *Goten und Wandalen: Wandlung der historischen Realität.* Zurich: Fretz and Wasmuth, 1954.

Hellegouarc'h, J. *Le vocabulaire latin des relations et des parties politiques sous la république.* Paris: Belles Lettres, 1963.

Hendy, Michael. *Studies in the Byzantine Monetary Economy, c. 300–1450.* Cambridge: Cambridge University Press, 1985.

Herrin, Judith. "Aspects of the Process of Hellenization in the Early Middle Ages." *Annual of the British School of Athens* 68 (1973): 113–26.

Herzfeld, Ernst. "Damascus: Studies in Architecture." *Ars Islamica* 10 (1943): 13–70.

Herzfeld, Ernst. "Die Genesis der islamischen Kunst und das Mshatta-Problem." *Der Islam* 1 (1910): 27–63, 105–44.

Herzfeld, Ernst. "Mshattā, Ḥīra und Bādiya: Die Mittelländer des Islam und ihre Baukunst." *Jahrbuch der preuszischen Kunstsammlungen* 42 (1921): 104–46.

Herzfeld, Ernst. *Der Wandschmuck der Bauten von Samarra und seine Ornamentik.* Forschungen zur islamischen Kunst, edited by F. Sarre, vol. 1, ser. 2, Die Ausgrabungen von Samarra. Berlin: D. Reimer, 1923.

Herzfeld, Ernst. *Am Tor von Asien: Felsdenkmale aus Irans Heldenzeit.* Berlin: D. Reimer, 1920.

Hill, Jane H., and Kenneth C. Hill. "Language Death and Relexification in Tlaxcalan Nahuatl." *International Journal of the Sociology of Language* 12 (1977): 55–70.

Hinds, Martin. "The Ṣiffīn Arbitration Agreement." *Journal of Semitic Studies* 17 (1972): 93–129.

Hinks, R. P. *Catalogue of the Greek, Etruscan and Roman Paintings and Mosaics in the British Museum.* London: British Museum, 1933.

Hitchner, R. Bruce. "The Kasserine Archaeological Survey, 1982–1986." *Antiquités africaines* 24 (1988).

Hoddinott, Ralph F. *Bulgaria in Antiquity: An Archaeological Introduction.* London: Ernest Benn, 1975.

Hodges, R., and D. Whitehouse. *Mohammed, Charlemagne and the Origins of Europe.* London: Duckworth, 1983.

Hodgson, M. G. S. "How Did the Early Shīʿa Become Sectarian?" *Journal of the American Oriental Society* 75 (1955): 1–13.

Hodgson, M. G. S. *The Venture of Islam.* 3 vols. Chicago: University of Chicago Press, 1974.

Hoffmann, Dietrich. Review of *Scandinavia und Scandia: Lateinisch-nordische Namenstudien,* by J. G. A. Svennung. *Indogermanische Forschungen* 70, no. 2 (1965): 223–25.

Hoffmann, Dietrich. *Das spätrömische Bewegungsheer und die Notitia Dignitatum* 2 vols. Epigraphische Studien, vol. 7, nos. 1–2. Düsseldorf: Rheinland-Verlag, 1969–70.

Hoffman, Eva. "The Emergence of Illustration in Arabic Manuscripts: Classical Legacy and Islamic Transformation." Ph.D. diss., Harvard University, 1982.

Hoffmann, Georg. *Auszüge aus syrischen Akten persischer Märtyrer.* Abhandlungen für die Kunde des Morgenlandes, vol. 7, no. 3. Leipzig: Deutsche Morgenländische Gesellschaft, 1880.

Höfler, Otto. *Die hochdeutsche Lautverschiebung und ihre Gegenstücke bei Goten,*

Vandalen, Langobarden und Burgunder. Sonderabdruck aus dem Anzeiger der phil.-hist. Kl. der Oesterreichischen Akademie der Wissenschaften, Jahrgang 1956, no. 24, pp. 294–318. Vienna: Rohrer, 1957.

Honigmann, E. "La date de l'homélie du prêtre Pantaléon sur la fête de l'Exaltation de la Croix (VIIᵉ siècle) et l'origine des collections homiliaires." *Bulletin de la classe des lettres et des sciences morales et politiques, Académie royale de Belgique,* 5th ser., 36 (1950): 547–59.

Hornung, Maria. "Wer sind die Zimbern?" *Der Schlern* 10 (1977): 565–66.

Howard-Johnston, James. "Studies in the Organisation of the Byzantine Army in the Tenth and Eleventh Centuries." D.Phil. diss., Oxford, 1971.

Howard-Johnston, James. "Thema." In *Maistor,* 189–97. Canberra: Australian Association for Byzantine Studies, 1984.

Humphrey, John H. Review of *Excavations of Carthage: The British Mission,* by H. Hurst et al. *Journal of Roman Studies* 77 (1987): 230–36.

Hunt, E. D. *Holy Land Pilgrimage in the Later Roman Empire, A.D. 312–460.* Oxford: Clarendon Press, 1982.

Hurgronje, Christiaan Snouck. *Selected Works.* Edited by G.-H. Bousquet and J. Schacht. Leiden: E. J. Brill, 1957.

Hurst, H. "Excavations at Carthage 1975: Second Interim Report." *Antiquaries Journal* 56 (1976): 177–97.

Hurst, H., S. Roskams, et al., eds. *Excavations at Carthage: The British Mission.* Vol. 1, *The Avenue du Président Habib Bourguiba, Salammbo.* Pt. 1, *The Site and Finds Other than Pottery,* by Hurst and Roskams. Pt. 2, *The Pottery and Other Ceramic Objects from the Site,* by M. G. Fulford and D. P. S. Peacock. Sheffield: Department of Prehistory and Archaeology, University of Sheffield, 1984.

Huss, Werner. *Geschichte der Karthager.* Handbuch der Altertumswissenschaft, Abteilung 3, Teil 8. Munich: C. H. Beck, 1985.

Huxley, George. "Geography in the Acts of Thomas." *Greek, Roman and Byzantine Studies* 24 (1983): 71–80.

Instinsky, Hans Ulrich. *Alexander der Grosse am Hellespont.* Godesberg: H. Kupper, 1949.

Iordan, Iorgu, et al. *An Introduction to Romance Linguistics.* 2d ed. Oxford: Blackwell, 1970.

Jenkins, G. K., and R. B. Lewis. *Carthaginian Gold and Electrum Coins.* London: Royal Numismatic Society, 1963.

Jenkins, Romily J. H. *Byzantium: The Imperial Centuries, A.D. 610–1071.* London: Weidenfeld and Nicolson, 1966.

Jones, A. H. M. *The Later Roman Empire, 284–602: A Social, Economic and Administrative Survey.* 3 vols. Oxford: Blackwell, 1964.

Jones, A. H. M. *The Roman Economy: Studies in Ancient Economic and Administrative History.* Edited by P. A. Brunt. Oxford: Blackwell, 1974.

Jones, A. H. M., Michael Avi-Yonah, et al. *The Cities of the Eastern Roman Provinces,* 2d ed. Oxford: Clarendon Press, 1971.

Juynboll, G. H. A. *Muslim Tradition: Studies in Chronology, Provenance, and Authorship of Early Hadīth.* Cambridge: Cambridge University Press, 1983.

Kaegi, W. E. "The Annona Militaris in the Early Seventh Century." *Byzantina* 13 (1985): 591–96.

Kaegi, W. E. "Arianism and the Byzantine Army in Africa, 533–45," *Traditio* 21 (1965): 23–53.

Kaegi, W. E. *Army, Society and Religion in Byzantium.* London: Variorum Reprints, 1982.

Kaegi, W. E. *Byzantine Military Unrest 471–843: An Interpretation.* Amsterdam: A. M. Hakkert, 1981.

Kaegi, W. E. *Byzantium and the Decline of Rome.* Princeton, N.J.: Princeton University Press, 1968.

Kaegi, W. E. "The Frontier: Barrier or Bridge?" In *Major Papers, the 17th International Byzantine Congress,* 279–303. New Rochelle, N.Y.: A. D. Caratzas, 1986.

Kaegi, W. E. "Heraklios and the Arabs." *Greek Orthodox Theological Review* 27 (1982): 109–33.

Kaegi, W. E. "Initial Byzantine Reactions to the Arab Conquest." *Church History* 38 (1969): 139–49. Reprinted in *Army, Society and Religion in Byzantium.*

Kaegi, W. E. "Late Roman Continuity in the Financing of Heraclius' Army." *Kurzbeitraege Communications, 16e congrès international des études byzantines. Jahrbuch der österreichischen Byzantinistik,* 1982, pp. 53–61.

Kaegi, W. E. "Notes on Hagiographic Sources for Some Institutional Changes and Continuities in the Early Seventh Century." *Byzantina* 7 (1975): 59–70.

Kaegi, W. E. "Some Seventh-Century Sources on Caesarea." *Israel Exploration Journal* 28 (1978): 177–81. Reprinted in *Army, Society and Religion in Byzantium.*

Kaegi, W. E. "The Strategy of Heraclius." In *Proceedings of the Second Symposium on the History of Bilād al-Shām during the Early Islamic Period up to 40 A.H./640 A.D.; Fourth International Conference on the History of Bilād al-Shām (English and French Papers).* Vol. 1, edited by Muhammad Adnan Bakhit, 104–15. Amman, Jordan, 1987.

Kaegi, W. E. "Two Studies in the Continuity of Late Roman and Byzantine Military Institutions." *Byzantinische Forschungen* 8 (1982): 87–111.

Karayannopulos, J. *Das Finanzwesen des frühbyzantinischen Staates.* Munich: R. Oldenbourg, 1958.

Kaufmann, Henning. *Ernest Förstemann: Altdeutsches Namenbuch.* Vol. 1, *Personennamen, Ergänzungsband.* Munich: W. Fink Verlag; Hildesheim: G. Olms, 1968.

Kennedy, Hugh. *The Early Abbasid Caliphate.* London: Croom Helm, 1981.

Kennedy, Hugh. "From *Polis* to *Madina:* Urban Change in Late Antique and Early Islamic Syria." *Past & Present* 106 (1985): 3–27.

Kennedy, Hugh. "The Last Century of Byzantine Syria: A Reinterpretation." *Byzantinische Forschungen* 10 (1985): 141–85.

Kennedy, Hugh. "The Melkite Church from the Islamic Conquest to the Crusades: Continuity and Adaption in the Byzantine Legacy." In *Major Papers, the 17th International Byzantine Congress,* 325–43. New Rochelle, N.Y.: A. D. Caratzas, 1986.

Kessler, H. L. "Scenes From the Acts of the Apostles on Some Early Christian Ivories." *Gesta* 18 (1979): 109–19.

Khalidi, Tariff. *Islamic Historiography: The Histories of Mas'udi.* Albany, N.Y.: State University of New York Press, 1975.

Khalidi, T., ed. *Land Tenure and Social Transformation in the Middle East.* Beirut. American University of Beirut, 1984.

Kister, M. J. "The Battle of the Harra: Some Socio-Economic Aspects." In *Studies in Memory of Gaston Wiet,* edited by M. Rosen-Ayalon. Jerusalem: Institute of Asian and African Studies, Hebrew University of Jerusalem, 1977.

Kittel, G., and G. Friedrich, eds. *Theologisches Wörterbuch zum Neuen Testament.* 10 vols. Stuttgart: Kohlhammer, 1933–79.

Kitzinger, Ernst. "Stylistic Developments in Pavement Mosaics in the Greek East from the Age of Constantine to the Age of Justinian." In *La mosaïque gréco-romaine,* 341–52. Colloques Internationaux du Centre National de la Recherche Scientifique, 29 Aug.–3 Sept. 1963. Paris, 1965. Reprinted in *The Art of Byzantium and the Medieval West: Selected Studies by Ernst Kitzinger,* edited by W. Kleinbauer. Bloomington: Indiana University Press, 1976.

Ki-Zerbo, J., G. Mokhtar, et al., eds. *UNESCO General History of Africa.* 8 vols. London: Heinemann; Berkeley and Los Angeles: University of California Press, 1981–85.

Kleiss, Wolfram. "Die sasanidischen Kapitelle aus Venderni bei Kamyaran nördlich Kermanshah." *Archaeologische Mitteilungen aus Iran,* n.s. 1 (1968): 127–47.

Knopf, Rudolf, and Gustav Krüger. *Ausgewählte Martyrakten.* 4th ed. Tübingen: Mohr, 1965.

Kohlrausch, Robert. *Herrschaft und Untergang der Goten in Italien.* Jena: E. Diederichs, 1928.

Konowitz, E. "The Program of the Carrand Diptych." *Art Bulletin* 66 (1984): 484–88.

Kornemann, Ernst. *Gestalten und Reiche: Essays zur alten Geschichte.* Leipzig: Dieterich'sche Verlagsbuchhandlung, 1943.

Kranzmeyer, Eberhard. *Laut- und Flexionslehre der deutschen zimbrischen Mundart.* Edited by Maria Hornung. Beiträge zur Sprachinsel-forschung, vol. 1. Vienna: Verlag des Verbandes der Wissenschaftlichen Gesellschaften Österreichs, 1981.

Krautheimer, Richard. *Rome: Profile of a City, 312–1308.* Princeton, N.J.: Princeton University Press, 1980.

Krautheimer, Richard. *Three Christian Capitals: Topography and Politics.* Berkeley and Los Angeles: University of California Press, 1983.

Kremer, D. *Die germanischen Personennamen in Katalonien: Namensammlung und Etymologisches.* Barcelona: Institut d'Estudis Catalans, 1972.

Kühnel, Ernst. *Die Arabeske: Sinn und Wandlung eines Ornaments.* Wiesbaden: Dieterich'sche Verlagsbuchhandlung, 1949.

Kühnel, Ernst. "Arabesque." In the *Encyclopaedia of Islam,* 2d ed.

Lafaurie, Jean. "Trésor de monnaies de cuivre trouvé à Sidi Aïch (Tunisie)." *Revue numismatique,* 6th ser., 2 (1959–60): 113–30.

Lambton, A. K. S. *State and Government in Medieval Islam.* Oxford: Oxford University Press, 1981.

Lamm, Carl Johan. "The Spirit of Moslem Art." *Bulletin of the Faculty of Arts* (Cairo University) 3 (1935): 1–7.

Lassner, J. *Islamic Revolution and Historical Memory*. American Oriental Series, vol. 66. New Haven, Conn.: American Oriental Society, 1986.

Lassner, J. *The Shaping of ʿAbbāsid Rule*. Princeton, N.J.: Princeton University Press, 1980.

Lassner, J. *The Topography of Baghdad in the Early Middle Ages: Text and Studies*. Detroit: Wayne State University Press, 1970.

Latte, Kurt. *Römische Religionsgeschichte*. 2d ed. Handbuch der Altertumswissenschaft, Abteilung 5, Teil 4. Munich: C. H. Beck, 1967.

Lavin, Irving. "The Ceiling Frescoes in Trier and Illusionism in Constantinian Painting." *Dumbarton Oaks Papers* 21 (1967): 97–133.

Lavin, Irving. "The Hunting Mosaics of Antioch and Their Sources: A Study of Compositional Principles in the Development of Early Mediaeval Style." *Dumbarton Oaks Papers* 17 (1963): 179–286.

Lecomte, Gerard. *Ibn Qutayba: L'homme, son oeuvre, ses idées*. Damascus: Institut Français de Damas, 1965.

Lemerle, Paul. "Invasions et migrations dans les Balkans depuis la fin de l'époque romaine jusqu'au VIIIᵉ siècle." *Revue historique* 121 (1954): 267–308.

Lencek, Rado L. *Jan Baudouin de Courtenay on the Dialects Spoken in Venetian Slovenia and Rezija*. Documentation Series, no. 2. New York: Society for Slovene Studies Newsletter, 1977.

Lenormant, Charles, et al., eds. *Lettres du Baron Marchant sur la numismatique et l'histoire*. 2d ed. Paris: de Leleux, 1851.

Lepelley, C. *Les cités de l'Afrique romaine au Bas-Empire*. 2 vols. Paris: Etudes augustiniennes, 1979–81.

Lessing, C. *Scriptorum Historiae Augustae Lexicon*. 1901–06. Reprint. Hildesheim: G. Olms, 1964.

Le Strange, Guy. *Baghdad during the Abbasid Caliphate*. 2d ed. Oxford: Clarendon Press, 1924.

Lewis, B. "Islamic Concepts of Revolution." In *Revolution in the Middle East*, edited by P. J. Vatikiotis. London: Allen and Unwin, 1972.

Lewis, B. "On Revolutions in Early Islam." *Studia Islamica* 32 (1970): 215–31.

Lewis, B. "The Regnal Titles of the First ʿAbbāsid Caliphs." In *Dr. Zakir Husain Presentation Volume*. New Delhi, 1968.

Liebeschuetz, J. H. W. G. *Continuity and Change in Roman Religion*. Oxford: Clarendon Press, 1979.

Lilie, Ralph-Johannes. "Die zweihundertjährige Reform: Zu den Anfängen der Themenorganisation im 7. und 8. Jahrhundert." *Byzantinoslavica* 45 (1984): 27–39.

Löfstedt, Bengt. *Studien über die Sprache der langobardischen Gesetze: Beiträge zur mittelalterlichen Latinität*. Acta Universitatis Upsaliensis. Studia Philologiae Scandinavicae Upsaliensia, no. 9. Uppsala: Almqvist & Wiksell, 1961.

L'Orange, H. P. "Plotinus-Paul." *Byzantion* 25–27 (1955–57): 473–85.

Luschey, Heinz. "Zur Datierung der sasanidischen Kapitelle aus Bisutun und des

Monuments von Taq-i Bustan." *Archaeologische Mitteilungen aus Iran,* n.s. 1 (1968): 129–42.

McCormick, Michael. *Eternal Victory: Triumphal Rulership in Late Antiquity, Byzantium, and the Early Medieval West.* Cambridge: Cambridge University Press; Paris: Editions de la Maison des Sciences de l'Homme, 1986.

MacMullen, R. *Roman Government's Response to Crisis.* New Haven, Conn.: Yale University Press, 1976.

McNeill, William H. *Venice, the Hinge of Europe, 1081–1797.* Chicago: University of Chicago Press, 1974.

MacQueen, James G. *Babylon.* London: Robert Hale, 1964.

Maguire, Henry. "Adam and the Animals: Allegory and the Literal Sense in Early Christian Art." *Dumbarton Oaks Papers* 41 (1987): 363–74.

Maier, F. G. *Die Verwandlung der Mittelmeerwelt.* Fischer Weltgeschichte, vol. 9. Frankfurt am Main: Fischer Bücherei, 1968.

Mango, Cyril. "Byzantinism and Romantic Hellenism." *Journal of the Warburg and Courtauld Institutes* 28 (1965): 29–43.

Mango, Cyril. *Byzantium, the Empire of New Rome.* New York: Scribner, 1980.

Mango, Cyril. *Le développement urbain de Constantinople.* Travaux et mémoires du Centre d'histoire et civilisation de Byzance, Collège de France. Paris: de Boccard, 1985.

Mango, Marlia Mundell. "The Continuity of the Classical Tradition in the Art and Architecture of Northern Mesopotamia." In *East of Byzantium: Syria and Armenia in the Formative Period,* edited by Nina G. Garsoïan, Thomas F. Mathews, and Robert W. Thomson, 115–34. Washington, D.C.: Dumbarton Oaks Center for Byzantine Studies, 1982.

Marec, Erwan. "Epitaphe chrétienne d'époque byzantine trouvée aux environs d'Hippone." *Libyca: Archéologie-épigraphie* 3 (1955): 163–66.

Markey, Thomas L. "Diffusion, Fusion, and Creolization: A Field Guide to Developmental Linguistics." *Papiere zur Linguistik* 24 (1981): 3–37.

Markey, Thomas L. "Nordic *Níðhvísur:* An Instance of Ritual Inversion?" *Studies in Medieval Culture* 10 (1977): 75–85.

Markus, R. A. "Country Bishops in Byzantine Africa." *Studies in Church History* (Oxford) 16 (1979): 1–15.

Marriott, W. B. *The Testimony of the Catacombs and of Other Monuments of Christian Art.* London: Rivingtons, 1870.

Marriott, W. B. *Vestiarium Christianum.* London: Rivingtons, 1868.

Martinez, Francisco Javier. "Eastern Christian Apocalyptic in the Early Muslim Period." Ph.D. diss., Catholic University, 1985.

Marx, Emanuel. "The Ecology and Politics of Nomadic Pastoralists in the Middle East." In *The Nomadic Alternative,* edited by Wolfgang Weissleder, 41–74. The Hague: Mouton, 1976.

Maspero, J. *Organisation militaire de l'Egypte byzantine.* Paris: H. Champion, 1912.

Massé, Henri. "Reconstruction d'une aristocratie iranienne." *Cahiers d'histoire mondiale* 1, no. 4 (1954): 815–26.

Massmann, Hans Ferdinand. "Langobardisches Wörterbuch." *Zeitschrift für deutsches Altertum und deutsche Literatur* 1 (1841*a*): 548–62.

322   Works Cited

Massmann, Hans Ferdinand. "Gothica minora." *Zeitschrift für deutsches Altertum und deutsche Literatur* 1 (1841*b*): 294–393; 2 (1842): 199–204.

Mastrelli, Carlo Alberto. "Ancora dul nome dei Visigoti e una nota sui Visburghi." *Archivio glottologico italiano* 51 (1966): 26–40.

Matthews, J. F. "Gesandtschaft." *Reallexikon für Antike und Christentum* 10 (1977): 654–87.

Matthews, J. F. "Olympiodorus of Thebes and the History of the West." *Journal of Roman Studies* 60 (1970): 79–97.

Matthews, J. F. "The Tax Law of Palmyra: Evidence for Economic History in a City of the Roman East." *Journal of Roman Studies* 74 (1984): 157–80.

Mattingly, Garrett. *Renaissance Diplomacy*. Boston: Houghton Mifflin, 1955.

Mayer, R. "Zur Phonemik des Cimbro." *Linguistische Berichte* 11 (1971): 48–54.

Mayerthaler, Willi. *Ladinia non-submersa bzw. protoladinische Reste in Bairischen.* Oesterreichische Akademie der Wissenschaften. Forthcoming (*a*).

Mayerthaler, Willi. *Woher stammt der Name 'Baiern'?* Forthcoming (*b*).

Medawar, Peter Brian. *The Art of the Soluble*. London: Methuen, 1967.

Meid, Wolfgang, and Karin Heller. *Italienische Interferenzen in der lautlichen Struktur des Zimbrischen.* Oesterreichische Akademie der Wissenschaften, Philosophisch-historische Klasse, Sitzungsberichte, vol. 353. Vienna: Oesterreichische Akademie der Wissenschaften, 1979.

Meier, C. *Res Publica Amissa: Eine Studie zu Verfassung und Geschichte der späten römischen Republik.* Wiesbaden: Franz Steiner Verlag, 1966. Reprint. Frankfurt am Main: Suhrkamp, 1980.

Meile, Pierre. "Les Yavanas dans l'Inde tamoule." *Journal asiatique* 232 (1940–41): 85–123. (This issue of the journal published under the title *Mélanges Asiatiques*).

Meredith, David. "Annius Plocamus: Two Inscriptions from the Berenice Road." *Journal of Roman Studies* 43 (1953): 38–40.

Metcalf, William E. "The Coins—1978." *Excavations at Carthage, 1978, conducted by the University of Michigan*, edited by J. H. Humphrey, 7:63–168. Ann Arbor, Mich.: Kelsey Museum, 1982.

Meyer, C. *Sprache und Sprachdenkmäler der Langobarden: Quellen, Grammatik, Glossar.* Paderborn: F. Schöningh, 1877.

Millar, Fergus. *The Emperor in the Roman World, 31 B.C.–A.D. 337.* London: Duckworth, 1977.

Millar, Fergus. "Emperors, Frontiers and Foreign Relations, 31 B.C. to A.D. 378." *Britannia* 13 (1982): 1–23.

Millar, Fergus. "Paul of Samosata, Zenobia and Aurelian: The Church, Local Cultures and Political Allegiances in Third-Century Syria." *Journal of Roman Studies* 61 (1971): 1–17.

Millar, Fergus. "P. Herennius Dexippus: The Greek World and the Third Century Invasions." *Journal of Roman Studies* 59 (1969): 12–29.

Millar, Fergus, et al. *The Roman Empire and Its Neighbours.* 2d ed. London: Duckworth, 1981.

Miller, Wick. "The Death of a Language, or Serendipity among the Shoshoni." *Anthropological Linguistics* 13 (1971): 114–20.

Milne, J. G. "The Currency of Egypt in the Fifth Century." *Numismatic Chronicle,* 5th ser., 6 (1926): 43–92.

Mitteis, L. "Ueber dem Ausdruck 'Potentiores' in den Digesten." In *Mélanges Paul Frédéric Girard,* 2:225–35. Paris: Librairie Arthur Rousseau, 1912.

Mitzka, Walther. "Das langobardische und die althochdeutsche Dialektgeographie." *Zeitscrift für Mundartforschung* 20 (1951): 1–7.

Y. Modéran, "Corippe et l'occupation byzantine d'Afrique: Pour une nouvelle lecture de la *Johannide.*" *Antiquités africaines* 22 (1986): 195–212.

Mokhtar, G. See Ki-Zerbo, J.

Mommsen, Theodor. *Gesammelte Schriften.* 8 vols. 1905–13. Reprint. Berlin: Weidmann, 1965.

Mommsen, Theodor. "Stilicho und Alarich." *Hermes* 38 (1903): 101–15.

Monceaux, Paul. *Histoire littéraire de l'Afrique chrétienne depuis les origines jusqu'à l'invasion arabe.* 7 vols. Paris: E. Leroux, 1901–23. Reprint. Brussels: Culture et Civilization, 1966.

Montagne, Robert. *La civilisation du désert.* Paris: Hachette, 1947.

Moorhead, J. "Italian Loyalties during Justinian's Gothic War." *Byzantion* 53 (1983): 575–96.

Mor, Carlo Guido. "La stato longobardo nel VII secolo." *Settimane di studio del Centro italiano di studi sull'alto medioevo* 5 (1957): 271–306.

Morison, Stanley. *Selected Essays on the History of Letter-Forms in Manuscript and Print.* Edited by David McKitterick. 2 vols. Cambridge: Cambridge University Press, 1980–81.

Morony, Michael G. *Iraq after the Muslim Conquest.* Princeton, N.J.: Princeton University Press, 1984.

Morrisson, Cécile. *Catalogue des monnaies byzantines de la Bibliothèque nationale.* 2 vols. Paris: Bibliothèque Nationale, 1970.

Morrisson, Cécile. "Les origines du monnayage vandale." In *Actes du 8ème congrès international de numismatique, New York—Washington, September 1973,* 461–72. Paris and Basel, 1976.

Morrisson, Cécile. "Un trésor de solidi de Constantin IV de Carthage." *Revue numismatique,* 6th ser., 22 (1980): 155–60.

Morrisson, Cécile, and James H. Schwartz. "Vandal Silver Coinage in the Name of Honorius." *American Numismatic Society Museum Notes* 27 (1982): 149–79.

Morrisson, Cécile, and W. Seibt. "Sceaux de commerciaires byzantins du VIIᵉ siècle trouvés à Carthage." *Revue numismatique,* 6th ser., 24 (1982): 222–40.

Moscati, S. "Le massacre des Umayyades dans l'histoire et dans les fragments poétiques." *Archiv Orientální* 18 (1950): 88–115.

Muir, W. *The Caliphate.* London, 1898.

Mülhäusler, Peter. "Samoan Plantation Pidgin English and the Origin of New Guinea Pidgin." In *The Social Context of Creolization,* edited by Ellen Woolford and William Washabaugh, 28–76. Ann Arbor, Mich.: Karoma, 1983.

Musil, Alois. *The Manners and Customs of the Rwala Bedouins.* New York: American Geographical Society, 1928.

Musset, Lucien. *Les invasions.* Vol. 1, *Les vagues germaniques.* Vol. 2, *Le second assaut contre l'Europe chrétienne (VIIᵉ–XIᵉ siècles).* 2d ed. La nouvelle Clio:

324 Works Cited

L'histoire et ses problèmes, nos. 12, 12 *bis*. Paris: Presses Universitaires de France, 1969–71.

Nagel, Tilman. "Ein früher Bericht über den Aufstand des Muhammad b. ʿAbdallāh im Jahre 145 h." *Der Islam* 46 (1970): 227–62.

Nagel, Tilman. *Rechtleitung und Kalifat: Versuch über eine Grundfrage der islamischen Geschichte*. Vol. 2 of *Studien zum Minderheitenproblem im Islam*. Bonner orientalistische Studien, n.s. 27. Bonn: Seminar der Universität, 1975.

Nagel, Tilman. *Untersuchungen zur Entstehung des abbasidischen Kalifates*. Bonn: Selbstverlag des Orientalischen Seminars der Universität, 1972.

Neusner, Jacob. *Judaism in Society: The Evidence of the Yerushalmi: Toward the Natural History of a Religion*. Chicago: University of Chicago Press, 1983.

Nicolet, Claude. *Rome et la conquête du monde méditerranéen*. 2 vols. Paris: Presses Universitaires de France, 1977–78.

Nilsson, M. P. *Geschichte der griechischen Religion*. 3d ed. Handbuch der Altertumswissenschaft, Abteilung 5, Teil 2, Band 1. Munich: C. H. Beck, 1967.

Nodelman, S. A. "A Preliminary History of Characene." *Berytus* 13 (1960): 83–122.

Noth, Albrecht. "Der Charakter der ersten grossen Sammlungen von Nachrichten zur frühen Kalifenzeit." *Islam* 47 (1971): 168–99.

Noth, Albrecht. "Isfahan-Nihavand: Eine quellenkritische Studie zur frühislamischen Historiographie." *Zeitschrift der Deutschen Morgenländischen Gesellschaft* 118 (1968): 274–96.

Noth, Albrecht. "Die literarisch überlieferten Verträge der Eroberungszeit als historische Quellen für die Behandlung der unterworfenen Nicht-Muslims durch ihre neuen muslimischen Quellen." In *Studien zum Minderheitenproblem im Islam*, edited by Tilman Nagel, vol. 1. Bonner Orientalische Studien, n.s. 27. Bonn: Seminar der Universität, 1973.

Noth, Albrecht. *Quellenkritische Studien zu Themen, Formen, und Tendenzen in frühislamischen Geschichtsüberlieferung*. Bonn: Selbstverlag des Orientalischen Seminars der Universität, 1973.

Nöthlichs, Karl Leo. "Spätantike Wirtschaftspolitik und *Adaeratio*." *Historia* 34 (1985): 102–16.

Nowinski, J. *Baron Dominique Vivant Denon (1747–1825)*. Rutherford, N.J.: Fairleigh Dickinson University Press, 1970.

O'Donnell, James J. *Cassiodorus*. Berkeley and Los Angeles: University of California Press, 1979.

Ogilvie, R. M. *The Romans and Their Gods in the Age of Augustus*. London: Chatto and Windus, 1969.

Oikonomides, N. *Les listes de préséance byzantines des IXᵉ et Xᵉ siècles*. Paris: Editions du Centre National de la Recherche Scientifique, 1972.

Oikonomides, N. "Silk Trade and Production in Byzantium from the Sixth to the Ninth Century." *Dumbarton Oaks Papers* 40 (1986): 33–53.

Olster, David. "The Politics of Usurpation in the Seventh Century: The Reign of Phocas." Ph.D. diss., University of Chicago, 1986.

Omar, Farouk. *The ʿAbbāsid Caliphate 132/750–170/786*. Baghdad: National Print and Publishing Co., 1969.

Omar, Farouk. ʿAbbāsīyāt: Studies in the History of the Early ʿAbbāsids. Baghdad, 1976.

Omar, Farouk. Al-ʿAbbāsīyūn al-awāʾil. 2 vols. Beirut, 1970.

Omar, Farouk. "Al-Alwān wa dalālatuhā al-sīyasīyah fī al-ʿaṣr al-ʿAbbāsī al-awwal." Bulletin Faculty of the Arts (Baghdad University) 14 (1971): 827–36.

Ostrogorsky, Georg. Geschichte des byzantinischen Staates. 3d ed. Handbuch der Altertumswissenschaft, Abteilung 12, Teil 1, Band 2. Munich: C. H. Beck, 1963.

Paannanen, Uto. Sallust's Politico-Social Terminology: Its Use and Biographical Significance. Helsinki: Suomalainen Tideakatemie, 1972.

Palmer, L. R. The Latin Language. London: Faber and Faber, 1966.

Parker, S. Thomas. Romans and Saracens: A History of the Arabian Frontier. Dissertation series, no. 6. Winona Lake, Ind.: American Schools of Oriental Research, 1985.

Pedersen, Holger. The Discovery of Language. 1931. Reprint. Translated by John Webster Sprago. Bloomington: Indiana University Press, 1962.

Pedley, J. G., ed. New Light on Ancient Carthage: Papers of a Symposium Sponsored by the Kelsey Museum of Archaeology, The University of Michigan, and Marking the Fiftieth Anniversary. Ann Arbor: University of Michigan Press, 1980.

Pellat, Charles. "Le culte de Muʿawiya au IIIᵉ siècle de l'hégire." Studia Islamica 6 (1956): 53–66.

Pellat, Charles. The Life and Works of Jahiz. Translated by D. M. Hawke. Berkeley and Los Angeles: University of California Press, 1969.

Pératé, A. "La réorganization des musées florentins," Part 3, "Le musée national et la collection Carrand." Gazette des beaux arts, 3d ser., 8 (1892): 332–47.

Peters, F. E. "Byzantium and the Arabs of Syria." Annales archéologiques de Syrie 27–28 (1977–78): 97–107.

Petersen, E. L. "ʿAlī and Muʿāwiyah: The Rise of the Umayyad Caliphate, 656–661." Acta Orientalia 23 (1959): 157–96.

Petersen, E. L. ʿAlī and Muʿāwiya in Early Arabic Tradition: Studies on the Genesis and Growth of Islamic Historical Writing until the End of the Ninth Century. Copenhagen: Munksgaard, 1964.

Petersen, E. L. "Studies on the Historiography of the ʿAlī-Muʿāwiyah Conflict." Acta Orientalia 27 (1963): 83–118.

Petzold, K.-E. "Der politische Standort des Sallust." Chiron 1 (1971): 219–38.

Pewesin, W. Imperium, Ecclesia universalis, Rom: Der Kampf der afrikanischen Kirche um die Mitte des 6. Jahrhunderts. Stuttgart, 1937.

Philippson, Alfred. "Das byzantinische Reich als geographische Erscheinung." Geographische Zeitschrift 40 (1934): 441–55.

Pirenne, Henri. "Mahomet et Charlemagne." Revue belge de philologie et d'histoire 1 (1922): 77–86.

Planhol, Xavier de. "Charactères généraux de la vie montagnarde dans le Proche-Orient et dans l'Afrique du Nord." Annales de géographie 71 (1962): 113–30.

Poliak, A. N. "L'arabisation de l'Orient sémitique." Revue des études islamiques 12 (1938): 35–63.

Préaux, Claire. Le monde hellénistique: La Grèce et l'Orient (323–146 av. J.-C.). 2

vols. *La nouvelle Clio: L'histoire et ses problèmes,* nos. 6, 6 *bis.* Paris: Presses Universitaires de France, 1978.

Price, R. M. "The Role of Military Men in Syria and Egypt from Constantine to Theodosius II." D.Phil. diss., Oxford University, 1974.

Pringle, D. *The Defence of Byzantine Africa from Justinian to the Arab Conquest.* 2 vols. British Archaeological Reports, no. 99. Oxford: British Archaeological Reports, 1981.

Prokosch, Eduard. *A Comparative Germanic Grammar.* William Dwight Whitney Linguistics Series. Philadelphia: Linguistic Society of America, 1939.

Randall, John. *Aristotle.* New York: Columbia University Press, 1960.

Rapelli, Giovanni. "Bavareso in Val d'Illasi nell' xi secolo?" *Terra Cimbra* 11, no. 45 (1981): 17–24.

Rapelli, Giovanni. *I cognomi Cimbri.* Verona: Privately printed, 1980.

Rapelli, Giovanni. "L'onomastica personale e familiare nella Lessina Cimbra." In *Civiltà Cimbra,* edited by Giancarlo Volpato, 49–55. Verona: Bi & Ci, 1983*a.*

Rapelli, Giovanni. "Per una storia dei Cimbri Tredicicomunigiani." In *Civiltà Cimbra,* edited by Giancarlo Volpato, 75–83. Verona: Bi & Ci, 1983*b.*

Rapelli, Giovanni. "Il tauc di Giazza: Note di grammatica." In *Civiltà Cimbra,* edited by Giancarlo Volpato, 35–47. Verona: Bi & Ci, 1983*c.*

Rapelli, Giovanni. *Testi Cimbri: Gli scritti dei Cimbri dei Tredici Comuni Veronesi.* Verona: Editori Verona, 1983*d.*

Rawson, Elizabeth. *Intellectual Life in the Late Roman Republic.* Baltimore: Johns Hopkins University Press, 1985.

Reinicke, John E., Stanley M. Tsuzaki, David DeCamp, Ian F. Hancock, and Richard E. Wood. *A Bibliography of Pidgin and Creole Languages.* Oceanic Linguistics Publication no. 14. Honolulu: University Press of Hawaii, 1975.

Rhee, Florus van der. *Die germanische Wörter in den langobardischen Gesetzen.* Rotterdam: Drukkerij Bronder, 1970.

Rickman, Geoffrey. *Roman Granaries and Store Buildings.* Cambridge: Cambridge University Press, 1971.

Riegl, Alois. *Die ägyptischen Textilfunde im K. K. oesterreichischen Museum.* Vienna: R. von Waldheim, 1889.

Riegl, Alois. *Die spätrömische Kunst-Industrie nach den Funden in Österreich-Ungarn.* 2 vols. Vienna: K. K. Hof- und Staatsdruckerei, 1901–23.

Riegl, Alois. *Stilfragen.* Berlin: G. Siemens, 1893.

Robertson, Anne S. *Roman Imperial Coins in the Hunter Coin Cabinet, University of Glasgow.* 5 vols. Oxford: Oxford University Press, 1962–82.

Rosenblum, M. *Luxorius: A Latin Poet among the Vandals.* New York: Columbia University Press, 1961.

Rosenthal, Franz. "The Influence of the Biblical Tradition on Muslim Historiography." In *Historians of the Middle East,* edited by B. Lewis and P. M. Holt, 35–45. London: Oxford University Press, 1962.

Rosenthal, Franz. *The Return of the Caliphate to Baghdad. History of Al-Ṭabari.* Vol. 38. Albany, N.Y.: State University of New York Press, 1985.

Rossi, Lino. *Trajan's Column and the Dacian Wars.* Ithaca, N.Y.: Cornell University Press, 1971.

Rossi, U. "La collezione Carrand nel museo nazionale di Firenze." Parts 1, 2. *L'archivio storico dell'arte* 2 (1889): 10–228; 3 (1890): 24–34.

Rostovtzeff, M. *The Social and Economic History of the Roman Empire*. 2 vols. 2d ed. Oxford: Clarendon Press, 1957.

Rotter, Gernot. *Die Umayyaden und der zweite Bürgerkrieg (680–692)*. Wiesbaden: Franz Steiner Verlag, 1982.

Ruggini, Lellia Cracco. *Economia e società nell "Italia annonaria": Rapporti fra agricoltura e commercio dal IV al VI secolo d.c.* Milan: Giuffrè, 1961.

Ruggini, Lellia Cracco. "La Sicilia fra Roma e Bisanzio." In *Storia della Sicilia*, 3:1–96. Naples: Società Editrice Storia di Napoli e della Sicilia, 1980.

Russell, E. S. *The Directness of Organic Activities*. Cambridge: Cambridge University Press, 1945.

Sadighi, Gholam H. *Les mouvements religieux iraniens au IIe et au IIIe siècles de l'hégire*. Paris: Les Presses Modernes, 1938.

Salama, Pierre. "Bornes milliaires et problèmes stratégiques du Bas-Empire en Maurétanie." *Comptes rendus des séances de l'Académie des inscriptions et belles-lettres*, 1959, pp. 346–54.

Salama, Pierre. "Un *follis* d'Alexandre tyran conservé à Madrid." *Numario hispanico* 9 (1960): 171–77.

Salomonson, J. W. "Kunstgeschichtliche und ikonographische Untersuchungen zu einem Tonfragment der Sammlung Benaki in Athen." *Bulletin Antieke Beschaving* 48 (1973): 3–82.

Sammlung Consul Edward Friedrich Weber, Hamburg. 2 vols. Munich: J. Hirsch, 1908–9.

Sands, P. C. *The Client Princes of the Roman Empire under the Republic*. Cambridge: Cambridge University Press, 1908.

Sarre, Friedrich, and Ernst Herzfeld. *Archäologische Reise im Euphrat- und Tigris-Gebiet*. 4 vols. Berlin: D. Reimer, 1911–20.

Scardigli, Piergiuseppe. "Appunti Langobardi." In *Filologia e Critica, Studi in onore di Vittorio Santoli*, edited by P. Chiarini, 91–131. Rome: Bulzoni, 1976.

Scardigli, Piergiuseppe, ed. "Abhandlungen zum Rahmenthema XIII: Stand und Aufgaben der Langobardenforschung." *Jahrbuch für International Germanistik* 10, pt. 2 (1978): 56–86; 11, pt. 1 (1979): 58–110.

Schick, Robert. "The Fate of the Christians in Palestine during the Byzantine-Umayyad Transition, A.D. 600–750." Ph.D. diss., University of Chicago, 1987.

Schlumberger, Jörg A. *Die potentes in der Spätantike*. Historia Einzelschriften. Wiesbaden: Franz Steiner Verlag, forthcoming.

Schmidt, Ludwig. *Geschichte der Wandalen*. 2d ed. Munich: C. H. Beck, 1942. Reprint. Munich: C. H. Beck, 1969.

Schmidt, Ludwig. *Die Ostgermanen*. 2d ed. Munich: C. H. Beck, 1941. Reprint. Munich: C. H. Beck, 1969.

Schmitthenner, Walter, "Rome and India: Aspects of Universal History during the Principate." *Journal of Roman Studies* 69 (1979): 90–106.

Schmoll, Ulrich. *Die Sprachen der vorkeltischen Indogermanen Hispaniens und das Keltiberische*. Wiesbaden: Otto Harrassowitz, 1959.

Schröder, Edward. "Exkursus über die gotischen Adjektiva auf-*ahs.*" *Zeitschrift für deutsches Altertum und deutsche Literatur* 35 (1891): 376–79.

Schweizer, Bruno. *Zimbrische Sprachreste.* Halle: Niemeyer, 1939.

Seeck, Otto. *Geschichte des Untergangs der antiken Welt.* 6 vols. Stuttgart: J. B. Metzler, 1897–1921.

Seeck, O. *Regesten der Kaiser und Päpste.* Stuttgart: J. B. Metzler, 1919.

Segal, J. B. "Syriac Chronicles as Source Material for the History of Islamic Peoples." In *Historians of the Middle East,* edited by B. Lewis and P. M. Holt, 246–58. London: Oxford University Press, 1962.

Sellheim, Rudolph. "Der zweite Bürgerkrieg im Islam (680–692)." *Sitzungberichte der Wissenschaftliche Gesellschaft an der Johann Wolfgang Goethe-Universität Frankfurt/Main* 8, no. 4 (1969): 87–111.

Setton, Kenneth M., et al., eds. *A History of the Crusades.* 5 vols. Madison: University of Wisconsin Press, 1955–85.

Sezgin, Ursula. *Abū Miḥnaf: Ein Beitrag zur Historiographie der umaiyadischen Zeit.* Leiden: E. J. Brill, 1971.

Shaban, M. A. *The ʿAbbāsid Revolution.* Cambridge: Cambridge University Press, 1970.

Shahid, Irfan. *Byzantium and the Arabs in the Fourth Century.* Washington, D.C.: Dumbarton Oaks, 1984.

Shahid, Irfan. "Heraclius and the Theme System: New Light from the Arabic." *Byzantion* 57 (1987): 391–406.

Shahid, Irfan. *Rome and the Arabs.* Washington, D.C.: Dumbarton Oaks, 1984.

Sharf, Andrew. *Byzantine Jewry from Justinian to the Fourth Crusade.* New York: Schocken Books; London: Routledge and Kegan Paul, 1971.

Sharon, Moshe. "The ʿAbbāsid Daʿwa Re-examined on the Basis of the Discovery of a New Source." *Arabic and Islamic Studies* (Bar-Ilan University) 1 (1973).

Sharon, Moshe. "Alīyat ha-Abbāsīm la-sh-shilṭōn." Ph.D. diss., Hebrew University, 1970.

Sharon, Moshe. *Black Banners from the East.* Jerusalem: Magnes Press, 1983.

Shaw, Brent D. "'Eaters of Flesh, Drinkers of Milk': The Ancient Mediterranean Ideology of the Pastoral Nomad." *Ancient Society* 13/14 (1982–83): 5–31.

Shaw, Brent D. "Fear and Loathing: The Nomad Menace and Roman Africa." In *L'Afrique romaine/Roman Africa,* edited by Colin M. Wells, 29–50. Ottawa: University of Ottawa Press, 1982.

Shboul, Ahmed. *al-Masʿudi and His World.* London: Ithaca Press, 1979.

Shelton, Kathleen J. "The Consular Muse of Flavius Constantius." *Art Bulletin* 65 (1983): 7–23.

Shelton, Kathleen J. "The Diptych of the Young Office Holder." *Jahrbuch für Antike und Christentum* 25 (1982): 132–71.

Shelton, Kathleen J. *The Esquiline Treasure.* London: British Museum Publications, 1981.

Shelton, Kathleen J. "The Esquiline Treasure: The Nature of the Evidence." *American Journal of Archaeology* 89 (1985): 147–55.

Sherk, Robert K. "Roman Geographical Exploration and Military Maps." *Aufstieg und Niedergang der römischen Welt* 2, no. 1 (1974): 534–62.

Shoufani, Elias. *Al-Riddah and the Muslim Conquest of Arabia*. Toronto: University of Toronto Press, 1973.

Slicher van Bath, B. H. *Agrarian History of Western Europe, 500–1850*. London: E. Arnold, 1963.

Sodini, J.-P., G. Tate, B. Bavant, S. Bavant, J.-L. Biscop, and D. Orssaud. "Dénès: Campagnes I–III (1976–1978), recherches sur l'habitat rural." *Syria* 57 (1980): 1–304.

Solèr, Clau, and Theodor Ebneter. *Romanisch und Deutsch am Hinterrhein/GR, Hft. 1. Heinzenberg/Mantogna Romanisch*. Begleittexte zu den Sprechplatten des Phonogrammarchivs der Universität Zürich, no. 4. Zurich: Verlag des Phonogrammarchivs der Universität Zurich, 1983.

Sorabji, Richard. *Necessity, Cause, and Blame: Perspectives on Aristotle's Theory*. Ithaca, N.Y.: Cornell University Press, 1980.

Spuler, Bertold. "Iran: The Persistent Heritage." In *Unity and Variety in Muslim Civilization*, edited by G. von Grunebaum. Chicago: University of Chicago Press, 1955.

Spuler, Bertold. *The Mongols in History*. New York: Praeger Publishers, 1971.

Stein, Ernst. *Geschichte des spätrömischen Reiches*. Vol. 1, *Vom römischen zum byzantinischen Staate, 284–476 n. Chr.* Vienna: L. W. Seidel, 1928.

Stein, Ernst. *Histoire du Bas-Empire*. Edited by J.-R. Palanque. 2 vols. Paris: Desclée, De Brouwer, 1949–59. Reprint. Amsterdam: A. M. Hakkert, 1968.

Stein, Ernst. *Studien zur Geschichte des byzantinischen Reiches vornehmlich unter den Kaisern Justinus II. und Tiberius Constantinus*. Stuttgart: J. B. Metzler, 1919.

Stillwell, Richard. *The Excavations 1937–1939*. Vol. 3 of *Antioch-on-the-Orontes*. Princeton, N.J.: Department of Art and Archaeology, 1934–74.

Stratos, A. N. *Byzantium in the Seventh Century*. Vol. 1. Amsterdam: A. M. Hakkert, 1968.

Stratos, A. N. "La première campagne d'Héraclius contre les Perses." *Jahrbuch der österreischischen Byzantinistik* 28 (1979): 63–74. Reprinted in *Studies in Seventh-Century Byzantine Political History*.

Stratos, A. N. *Studies in Seventh-Century Byzantine Political History*. London: Variorum Reprints, 1983.

Streck, Maximilian. *Seleucia und Ktesiphon*. Der Alte Orient, vol. 16, pts. 3–4. Leipzig: J. C. Hinrichs, 1917.

Stroheker, K. F. *Germanentum und Spätantike*. Zurich and Munich: Artemis Verlag, 1965.

Suermann, Harald. *Die geschichtstheologische Reaktion auf die einfallenden Muslime in der edessenischen Apokalyptik des 7. Jahrhunderts*. Europäische Hochschulschriften, Reihe 23, Band 256. Frankfurt, Bern, and New York: Peter Lang, 1985.

Svennung, Josef G. A. *Jordanes und Scandia: Kritisch-exegetische Studien*. Skrifter utg. av K. humanistiska Vetenskaps-samfundet i Uppsala, vol. 44, no. 2a. Uppsala: Almqvist & Wiksell, 1967.

Svennung, Josef G. A. *Scandinavia und Scandia: Lateinisch-nordische Namenstudien*. Skrifter utg. av K. humanistika Vetenskaps-samfundet i Uppsala, vol. 44, no. 1. Uppsala: Almqvist & Wiksell, 1963.

Svennung, Josef G. A. *Skandinavien bei Plinius und Ptolemaios: Kritisch-exegetische Forschungen zu den ältesten nordischen Sprachdenkmälern.* Skrifter utg. av K. humanistika Vetenskaps-samfundet i Uppsala, vol. 45. Uppsala: Almqvist & Wiksell, 1974.

Syme, R. *Emperors and Biography: Studies in the Historia Augusta.* Oxford: Clarendon Press, 1971.

Szöverffy, J. *Weltliche Dichtungen des lateinischen Mittelalters.* Berlin: E. Schmidt, 1970.

Thompson, E. A. *The Early Germans.* Oxford: Clarendon Press, 1965.

Thompson, E. A. *The Goths in Spain.* Oxford: Clarendon Press, 1969.

Thompson, E. A. *Romans and Barbarians: The Decline of the Western Empire.* Madison: University of Wisconsin Press, 1982.

Thompson, E. A. "The Visigoths from Fritigern to Euric." *Historia* 12 (1963): 105–28. Reprinted in *Romans and Barbarians.*

Thompson, E. A. *The Visigoths in the Time of Ulfila.* Oxford: Clarendon Press, 1966.

Thomsen, Christian Jurgensen. *Catalogue de la collection de monnaies de feu Christian Jürgensen Thomsen.* 7 vols. Copenhagen: Muhle, 1866–76.

Thouvenot, R. "Lampes en bronze." *Publications du Service des antiquités du Maroc* 10 (1954): 217–26.

Tinnefeld, F. *Die frühbyzantinische Gesellschaft: Struktur-Gegensatz-Spannungen.* Munich: W. Fink Verlag, 1977.

Toumanoff, C. *Studies in Christian Caucasian History.* Washington, D.C.: Georgetown University Press, 1963.

Trell, Bluma L. "Phoenician Greek Imperial Coins." *Israel Numismatic Journal* 6–7 (1982–83): 128–41.

Troussel, M. "Les monnaies vandales d'Afrique: Découvertes de Bou-Lilate et du Hamma." *Recueil des notices et mémoires de la Société archéologique, historique et géographique de Département de Constantine* 67 (1950–51): 147–92.

Tucker, W. F. "'Abd Allāh ibn Muʿāwiya and the Janāḥiyya: Rebels and Ideologues of the Late Umayyad Period." *Studia Islamica* 51 (1980): 39–57.

Turcan, Robert. "Trésors monétaires trouvés à Tipasa: La circulation du bronze en Afrique romaine et vandale aux Vᵉ et VIᵉ siècles ap. J.-C." *Libyca: Archéologie-épigraphie* 9 (1961): 201–57.

Ulrich, Theodor. *Pietas (pius) als politischer Begriff im römischen Staate bis zum Tode des Kaisers Commodus.* Historische Untersuchungen, no. 6. Breslau: M. and H. Marcus, 1930.

Vloten, G. van. *De Opkomst der Abbasiden in Chorasan.* Leiden: E. J. Brill, 1890.

Vloten, G. van. *Recherches sur la domination arabe, le chiitisme et les croyances messianiques, sous le khalifat des Omayades.* Amsterdam: J. Müller, 1894.

Vasmer, Max. "Ein vandalischer Name der Goten." *Studia Neophilologica* 15 (1942): 132–34.

Vineis, Edoardo. *Le lingue indoeuropee di frammentaria attestazione/Die indogermanischen Restsprachen.* Atti della Società italiana di glottologia, no. 4. Pisa: Giardini Editori, 1983.

Vitelli, G. *Islamic Carthage: The Archaeological, Historical and Ceramic Evidence.* Tunis, 1981.

Volbach, W. F. *Elfenbeinarbeiten der Spätantike und des frühen Mittelalters.* 1952. Rev. ed. Mainz: Von Zabern, 1976.

Vryonis, Speros, ed. *Islam and Cultural Change in the Middle Ages.* Wiesbaden: Otto Harrassowitz, 1975.

Wacke, A. "Die 'potentiores' in den Rechtsquellen: Einfluβ und Abwehr gesellschaftlicher Übermacht in der Rechtspflege der Römer." *Aufstieg und Niedergang der römischen Welt,* no. 2, pt. 13 (1980): 562–607.

Waetzoldt, S. *Die Kopien des 17. Jahrhunderts nach Mosaiken und Wandmalereien in Rom.* Römische Forschungen der Biblioteca Hertziana, no. 18. Vienna and Munich: Schroll, 1964.

Walbank, F. W. "The Geography of Polybius." *Classica et Medievalia* 9 (1948): 155–82.

Walbank, F. W. *A Historical Commentary on Polybius.* 3 vols. Oxford: Clarendon Press, 1957–79.

Walbank, F. W. *Polybius.* Sather Lectures, vol. 42. Berkeley and Los Angeles: University of California Press, 1972.

Wallace-Hadrill, D. S. *Eusebius of Caesarea.* Westminster, Md.: Canterbury Press, 1961.

Wallace-Hadrill, J. M. *Early Germanic Kingship in England and on the Continent.* Oxford: Clarendon Press, 1971.

Walters, H. B. *Catalogue of the Greek and Roman Lamps in the British Museum.* London: Trustees of the British Museum, 1914.

Wansbrough, John. *The Sectarian Milieu: Content and Composition of Islamic Salvation History.* Oxford: Oxford University Press, 1978.

Ward-Perkins, J. B. *From Classical Antiquity to the Middle Ages: Public Building in Northern and Central Italy A.D. 300–850.* Oxford: Oxford University Press, 1984.

Ward Perkins, J. B. "Nicomedia and the Marble Trade." *Papers of the British School in Rome* 48 (1980): 23–69.

Warmington, E. H. *The Commerce between the Roman Empire and India.* 2d ed. London: Curzon Press, 1974.

Watt, W. M. *The Formative Period of Islamic Thought.* Edinburgh: Edinburgh University Press, 1973.

Watt, W. M. "God's Caliph." In *Iran and Islam,* edited by C. E. Bosworth, 565–71. Edinburgh: Edinburgh University Press, 1971.

Weiss, Helen. *Kausalität und Zufall in der Philosophie des Aristotles.* Basel: Verlag Haus zum Falken, 1942.

Weitzmann, Kurt, ed. *Age of Spirituality: Late Antique and Early Christian Art, Third to Seventh Century: Catalogue of the Exhibition at The Metropolitan Museum of Art, November 19, 1977, through February 12, 1978.* New York: Metropolitan Museum of Art, distributed by Princeton University Press, 1979.

Wellhausen, Julius. *Das arabische Reich und sein Sturz.* Berlin: G. Reimer, 1902. Translated by M. G. Weir, as *The Arab Kingdom and Its Fall.* Calcutta: University of Calcutta, 1927.

Wellhausen, Julius. *Prolegomena zur ältesten Geschichte des Islams.* Vol. 6 of *Skizzen und Vorarbeiten.* Berlin: G. Reimer, 1899.

Wellhausen, Julius. "Die religios-politischen Oppositionsparteien in alten Islam." In *Abhandlungen der Königlichen Gesellschaft der Wissenschaften zu Göttingen*, Philologisch-historische Klasse, n.s. 5, no. 2 (Göttingen, 1901). Translated by R. C. Ostle and S. M. Walzer as *The Religio-Political Factions in Early Islam*. Amsterdam: North Holland Publishing Co., 1975.

Wells, C. M. "Carthage 1976: La muraille théodosienne." *Echos du monde classique* 21 (1977): 15–23.

Wells, C. M., and E. M. Wightman. "Canadian Excavations at Carthage 1976 and 1978: The Theodosian Wall, Northern Sector." *Journal of Field Archaeology* 7 (1980): 43–63.

Wells, C. M. and E. Wightman. "Carthage 1978: La muraille théodosienne." *Échos du monde classique* 23 (1979): 15–18.

Wensinck, A. J. *The Muslim Creed: Its Genesis and Historical Development*. Cambridge: Cambridge University Press, 1932.

Wes, M. A. *Das Ende des Kaisertums in Westen des römischen Reichs*. Translated by K. E. Mittring. Archeologische studien van het Nederlands historische instituut te Rome, no. 2. The Hague: Stattsdrukerei, 1967.

Westwood, J. O. *A Descriptive Catalogue of the Fictile Ivories in the South Kensington Museum*. London, 1876.

Wheeler, Mortimer. *Rome beyond the Imperial Frontiers*. London: Bell, 1954.

Whittaker, C. R. "Late Roman Trade and Traders." In *Trade in the Ancient Economy*, edited by P. Garnsey, K. Hopkins, and C. R. Whittaker, 163–80. London: Chatto and Windus, 1983.

Wickham, Chris. *Early Medieval Italy*. London: Macmillan, 1981.

Wightman, E. M. "Geological Research and Excavation in the Northern Sector of Carthage, June–July 1983." *CEDAC Carthage* 5 (1985): 18–20.

Wilkinson, J., trans. *Egeria's Travels*. London: Society for Promoting Christian Knowledge, 1971.

Wolf, Karl. *Studien zur Sprache des Malalas*. 2 vols. Munich: Akademische Buchdruckerei, 1911–12.

Wolfram, Herwig. *Geschichte der Goten: Von den Anfängen bis zur Mitte des sechsten Jahrhunderts: Entwurf einer historischen Ethnographie*. 1979. 2d ed. Munich: C. H. Beck, 1980.

Wolfram, Herwig, et al. *Intitulatio*. 2 vols. Mitteilungen des Instituts für Oesterreichische Geschichtsforschung, Ergänzungsbände 21, 24. Vienna, Cologne and Graz: Hermann Böhlaus Nachfölger, 1967–73.

Wrede, Ferdinand. *Über die Sprache der Ostgoten in Italien*. Quellen und Forschungen zur Kulturgeschichte der germanischen Völker, no. 68. Strasbourg: K. J. Trübner, 1891.

Wrede, Ferdinand. *Über die Sprache der Wandalen: Ein Beitrag zur germanischen Namen- und Dialektforschung*. Quellen und Forschungen zur Kulturgeschichte der germanischen Völker, no. 52. Strasbourg: K. J. Trübner, 1886.

Wroth, Warwick. See List A, under the abbreviation *BMC Vand*.

Wulzinger, Karl, and Carl Watzinger. *Damaskus*. 2 vols. Berlin: de Gruyter, 1921–24.

Zacos, G., and A. Veglery. *Byzantine Lead Seals*. 2 vols. Basel, 1972–85.

Zeiss, Hans. *Die Grabfünde aus dem spanischen Westgotenreich.* Berlin: de Gruyter, 1934.

Zevi, F., and A. Techernia. "Amphores de Byzacène au Bas-Empire." *Antiquités africaines* 3 (1969): 173–214.

Ziegler, Karl-Heinz. *Die Beziehungen zwischen Rom und dem Partherreich: Ein Beitrag zur Geschichte des Völkerrechts.* Wiesbaden: Franz Steiner Verlag, 1964.

Index

References to Map 1 or Map 2 are set in parentheses and italics. Citations include the map number and the appropriate upper- and lower-case coordinates established by the Cartographic Laboratory of the University of Wisconsin-Madison.

WISCONSIN STUDIES IN CLASSICS

General Editors
Barbara Hughes Fowler and Warren G. Moon

E. A. Thompson
Romans and Barbarians: The Decline of the Western Empire

Jennifer Tolbert Roberts
Accountability in Athenian Government

H. I. Marrou
A History of Education in Antiquity
Histoire de l'Education dans l'Antiquité, Translated by George Lamb
(originally published in English by Sheed and Ward, 1956)

Erika Simon
Festivals of Attica: An Archaeological Commentary

G. Michael Woloch
Roman Cities: Les villes romaines by Pierre Grimal, Translated and Edited
by G. Michael Woloch, together with A Descriptive Catalogue of Roman
Cities by G. Michael Woloch

Warren G. Moon, *editor*
Ancient Greek Art and Iconography

Katherine Dohan Morrow
Greek Footwear and the Dating of Sculpture

John Kevin Newman
The Classical Epic Tradition

Jeanny Vorys Canby, Edith Porada, Brunilde Sismondo Ridgway, and
Tamara Stech, *editors*
Ancient Anatolia: Aspects of Change and Cultural Development

Wendy J. Raschke, *editor*
The Archaeology of the Olympics: The Olympics and Other Festivals
in Antiquity

WISCONSIN STUDIES IN CLASSICS

Ann Norris Michelini
Euripides and the Tragic Tradition

Paul Plass
Wit and the Writing of History: The Rhetoric of Historiography in Imperial Rome

Barbara Hughes Fowler
The Hellenistic Aesthetic

F. M. Clover and R. S. Humphreys, *editors*
Tradition and Innovation in Late Antiquity

Brunilde Sismondo Ridgway
Hellenistic Sculpture I: The Styles of ca. 331–200 B.C.